Land Back

*Relational Landscapes of
Indigenous Resistance across the Americas*

Dumbarton Oaks Colloquium on the History of Landscape Architecture XLV

Land Back

*Relational Landscapes of
Indigenous Resistance across the Americas*

Heather Dorries and Michelle Daigle
Editors

DUMBARTON OAKS, TRUSTEES FOR HARVARD UNIVERSITY   WASHINGTON, D.C.

© 2024 Dumbarton Oaks
Trustees for Harvard University, Washington, D.C.
All rights reserved.
Printed in the United States of America by Sheridan Books, Inc.

LIBRARY OF CONGRESS CATALOGING-IN-PUBLICATION DATA

NAMES: Dumbarton Oaks Colloquium on the History of Landscape Architecture (45th : 2021 : Online), creator. | Dorries, Heather, editor. | Daigle, Michelle, editor. | Dumbarton Oaks, host institution, issuing body.
TITLE: Land back : relational landscapes of Indigenous resistance across the Americas / Heather Dorries and Michelle Daigle, editors.
OTHER TITLES: Relational landscapes of Indigenous resistance across the Americas
DESCRIPTION: Washington, D.C. : Dumbarton Oaks, Trustees for Harvard University, [2024] | Includes bibliographical references and index. | Summary: "Relationships with land are fundamental components of Indigenous worldviews, politics, and identity. The disruption of land relations is a defining feature of colonialism; colonial governments and capitalist industries have violently dispossessed Indigenous lands, and have undermined Indigenous political authority through the production of racialized and gendered hierarchies of difference. Consequently, Indigenous resistance and visions for justice and liberation are bound up with land and land-body relationships that challenge colonial power. "Land Back" has become a slogan for Indigenous land protectors across the Americas, reflecting how relations to land are foundational to calls for decolonization and liberation. *Land Back: Relational Landscapes of Indigenous Resistance across the Americas* highlights the ways Indigenous peoples and anti-colonial co-resistors understand land relations for political resurgence and freedom across the Americas. Contributors place Indigenous practices of freedom within the particularities of Indigenous place-based laws, cosmologies, and diplomacies, while also demonstrating how Indigeneity is shaped across colonial borders. Collectively, they examine the relationship between language, Indigenous ontologies, and land reclamation; Indigenous ecology and restoration; the interconnectivity of environmental exploitation and racial, class, and gender exploitation; Indigenous diasporic movement; community urban planning; transnational organizing and relational anti-racist placemaking; and the role of storytelling and children in movements for liberation"—Provided by publisher.
IDENTIFIERS: LCCN 2023041722 | ISBN 9780884025016 (hardback)
SUBJECTS: LCSH: Indigenous peoples—Land tenure—America—Congresses. | Human ecology—America—Congresses. | Indigenous peoples—America—Politics and government—Congresses. | Indigenous peoples—Legal status, laws, etc.—America—Congresses.
CLASSIFICATION: LCC GN449.3 .D86 2024 | DDC 333.2—dc23/eng/20231220
LC record available at https://lccn.loc.gov/2023041722

Volume based on papers presented at the symposium "Land Back: Indigenous Landscapes of Resurgence and Freedom," organized by Dumbarton Oaks, Washington, D.C., and held virtually from April 29 to June 10, 2021.

GENERAL EDITOR: Thaïsa Way
ART DIRECTOR: Kathleen Sparkes
DESIGN AND COMPOSITION: Melissa Tandysh
MANAGING EDITOR: Sara Taylor

COVER ILLUSTRATION: The "Indian Land" sculpture by artist Nicholas Galanin (Yéil Ya-Tseen) is titled *Never Forget* and was part of the Coachella Valley 2021 Desert X free art exhibition in Palm Springs, California. Photograph by Lance Gerber / Nuvue Interactive LLC.

FRONTISPIECE ILLUSTRATION: A father and son set sail in a Rimajol-style *proa* (outrigger canoe), Honolulu, Hawaiʻi. Photograph by Kilipohe.

www.doaks.org/publications

Programs in urban landscape studies at Dumbarton Oaks
are supported by a grant from the Andrew W. Mellon Foundation
through their initiative in Architecture, Urbanism, and the Humanities.

~

ARTIST STATEMENT

In *Never Forget*, I address the historical misrepresentation of Indigenous people as "Indian" by colonial entities, the U.S. Constitution, and the current U.S. government. This term denies our sovereignty and erases the diversity of over five hundred distinct Indigenous nations. Despite over five hundred years of occupation, Indigenous land and communities remain resilient and beautiful.

This project challenges settler occupation and calls for collective action. It invites landowners to seek Indigenous leadership, center Indigenous knowledge for sustainability, support rent initiatives, and transfer land titles to Indigenous nations. Land acknowledgments often lack meaningful action, as less than 3 percent of U.S. land belongs to Indigenous people. The Land Back movement seeks recognition, respect, and the return of violently occupied land to protect ecosystems and ensure sustainable governance. We have a responsibility to care for the land for future generations. *Never Forget* marks our past and guides our future.

—*Artist Nicholas Galanin, October 2023*

CONTENTS

Foreword ... ix

Introduction ... 1
MICHELLE DAIGLE AND HEATHER DORRIES

I POLITICS OF RESISTANCE WITHIN AND BEYOND COLONIAL BORDERS

1 **A Hemispheric Approach to Relational and Embodied Anti-racist Placemaking** ... 21
SOFIA ZARAGOCIN

2 **Landscapes of Struggle**
Katarista Perspectives on the Environment in Bolivia, 1960–1990 ... 39
OLIVIA ARIGHO-STILES

3 **Anti-colonial Landscapes**
Land and the Emergence of Miskitu People's Territorial Resistance in the Moskitia ... 61
RUTH H. MATAMOROS MERCADO

4 **Placemaking as Indigenous Resurgence in the Oceanic Diaspora** ... 81
JAMES MILLER

5 **Theory through Hide Tanning**
Resurgence and Indigenous Mobility ... 105
MANDEE MCDONALD

II LANDSCAPES OF RELATIONALITY
Ecology, Restoration, and Indigenous Futures

6 **The Munsee Three Sisters Medicinal Farm**
A Ground for Cultural Restoration ... 123
CHIEF VINCENT MANN AND ANITA BAKSHI

7 **Ottawa Governance through Anishinaabe Ecological Restoration**
Nmé, Ethnobotany, and Memory   153
NATASHA MYHAL

8 **Language, Territory, and Law**
Mapuzugun as the Basis for Mapuche Spatial Planning
and Territorial Reconstruction   171
MIGUEL MELIN AND MAGDALENA UGARTE

9 **Moving with Land**
BlackIndigenous Stories of Place   191
NNENNA ODIM AND PAVITHRA VASUDEVAN

Contributors   217

Index   221

FOREWORD

At no moment has it been more important to collectively acknowledge that the scholarship and learning that comprises this volume is generated, created, and sustained with and within the lands of the Indigenous communities who have stewarded this land for thousands of years and remain as essential stewards of place. In Washington, D.C., where Dumbarton Oaks is located, we sit on the ancestral lands of the Nacotchtank and contemporary Piscataway communities. In this work, as with our contributors to this volume, we seek to build and sustain relationships between people and places, culture and landscape. At Dumbarton Oaks, as scholars of land and landscape histories, we have the honor and responsibility to contribute to more fully understanding and supporting Indigenous struggles for sovereignty and place and to find ways to reimagine how we can help in healing the violence of dispossession of landscape, past and present and future. This volume is a contribution to that ongoing effort.

In summer 2019, the Garden and Landscape Studies program at Dumbarton Oaks launched the initiative "Democracy and the Urban Landscape," supported by the Mellon Foundation. The purpose of the initiative remains to catalyze, sustain, and share scholarship that both expands and challenges narratives of landscape history by deeply inquiring into the legacies and practices of race, identity, and difference. We are interested in how these legacies shape democracy and sovereignty as community practices and as place-making projects. In this work, we believe that a landscape framework offers the opportunity to more fully understand and engage with the ways communities live in place and with land. We have in the years since hosted symposia, colloquia, and workshops that sought to tackle relevant questions and approaches, building a people's history of landscape and place through scholarship, teaching, and discourse.

This is not simply a matter of expanding the breadth of our scholarship in landscape history. The symposium "Land Back: Indigenous Landscapes of Resurgence and Freedom," upon which this volume is based, actively challenges core conceptions of landscape history in ways that are essential to our efforts to rethink and reimagine what narratives complex histories of place might offer. Led by colloquiarchs Michelle Daigle and Heather Dorries (both of the University of Toronto), this symposium tackled the foundations of landscape history through its interrogation of the very meaning of land and human relationships to land and the more-than-human world. By engaging in relationality as a methodology, the contributors sought to identify both resonances and incommensurabilities in a spirit of exploration and curiosity. This work led to ways of thinking intended to disrupt "totalizing tendencies and narratives" (9) of landscape histories. It is in this context that Daigle and Dorries led this significant project to bring scholarship, practice, and thinking to Dumbarton Oaks that had not been previously explored as deeply as is called for and desired. Further, this symposium was originally intended to be in person but due to COVID-19 was transformed into a series of four gatherings, each led by Daigle and Dorries alongside a remarkable community of authors, discussants, and participants. This has been important and groundbreaking work, and its legacy will likely be traced for decades to come.

When we launched the Mellon Democracy and Landscape Initiative, we sought to support the scholarship, thinking, and practices of scholars in Indigenous studies, for it is on the land on which they have lived and thought and continue to do so that we are seeking also to live and think. In many ways, it is building on Indigenous ways of thinking about place and land that we have come to consider the significance of histories grounded in place, on and with land and the more-than-human. In this work, we have sought to critique how we think about, define, and describe land and landscape. Land is place with which we are in relation. It is the ground upon which we collectively live and make community. In its physicality and geography, landscape describes the land that we, human communities, shape, cultivate, and engage with as a community, while in its use as an abstraction, it signifies the natural and built systems that comprise the environment in which and with which culture exists. Land is place through the relationships with humans and the more-than-human. This work expands the capacity of a landscape framework to identify the place of history, the sites on which history happens, offering a critical thread woven through not only these collected essays but also the ongoing discourses on place and landscape histories in the Dumbarton Oaks community.

Dumbarton Oaks has long held a reputation for scholarly excellence, and the Garden and Landscape Studies program has been a leader in supporting scholarship and teaching in landscape history. The Mellon Initiative has brought new scholars and audiences to our collective efforts while broadening attention to the humanities as a means of understanding the cultural constructs of our built environments. This volume builds on efforts to understand how spatial analysis and the study of landscapes are essential to reading spaces of placemaking through questions of sovereignty, community, politics, and social movements. The papers, first shared via the symposium and now comprising this collection, seek to challenge traditional historiographies of place to encompass emerging scholarship and thinking on the ideas and practices of Land Back as a way of being in the world and in community. This volume demonstrates the critical contributions of landscape history to this dialogue while suggesting directions for further research, discussion, and placemaking.

None of this could be accomplished without community. We thank the leaders of Dumbarton Oaks for supporting this important work as well as those at the Mellon Foundation who have made this possible. Leadership matters when one is trying to make real and enduring change, and the support of director Tom Cummins at Dumbarton Oaks and program director Dianne Harris, followed by Justin Garrett Moore, at the Mellon

Foundation was essential. We acknowledge the critical work of the Mellon Advisory Board and the Garden and Landscape Studies senior fellows. And as we all know, the publications staff are essential, including director of publications Kathy Sparkes, managing editor Sara Taylor, and our program staff Jane Padelford and Caroline Miller. We thank the discussants and our anonymous reviewers. Finally, we thank our brilliant editors and contributors who have generously shared their thinking with us in the form of essays intended to contribute to a deep and broad discussion of place, land, and life, past, present, and future.

        Thaïsa Way
        Director, Garden and Landscape Studies
        Dumbarton Oaks

Introduction

MICHELLE DAIGLE AND HEATHER DORRIES

"Land Back" is the demand to rightfully return colonized land—like that in so-called Canada—to Indigenous Peoples. But when we say "Land Back" we aren't asking for just the ground, or for a piece of paper that allows us to tear up and pollute the earth. We want the system that is land to be alive so that it can perpetuate itself, and perpetuate us as an extension of itself. That's what we want back: our place in keeping land alive and spiritually connected.[1]

We are on the verge of what could be a revolutionary moment.... As systems of colonization, oppression and white supremacy start to become dismantled, getting Indigenous lands back into Indigenous hands is necessary. Truth is, that all systems and institutions of oppression that uphold white supremacy were built on top of stolen land by stolen people; so to truly achieve racial justice and move into a revolutionary moment, we have to talk about how racial injustice on this continent began with settler colonialism, the theft of Indigenous lands, and the genocide of Indigenous people.[2]

In our world-views, we are beings who come from the Earth, from the water, and from corn. The Lenca people are ancestral guardians of the rivers, in turn protected by the spirits of young girls, who teach us that giving our lives in various ways for the protection of the rivers is giving our lives for the well-being of humanity and of this planet.[3]

Relationships with land are a fundamental component of Indigenous[4] worldviews, politics, and identity. The violent disruption of these land relations is a defining feature of colonialism and imperialism; colonial governments and capitalist industries have violently dispossessed Indigenous lands and bodies and undermined Indigenous political authority through the production of racialized and gendered hierarchies of difference. Consequently, Indigenous resistance and visions for liberation are bound up with land and land/body relations that challenge colonial power and violence. Land relations provide "ethical frameworks" that enable "process-centered modes of living that generate profoundly different conceptualizations of nationhood and governmentality—ones that aren't based on enclosure, authoritarian power, and hierarchy."[5] For Indigenous peoples, the concept of land encompasses multiple meanings and relations. Far beyond simply serving as the basis for territory or home, land is understood as a living relation and teacher, encompassing a set of ethical responsibilities.[6]

Recently, "Land Back"[7] has become a slogan for Indigenous land protectors across the Americas, reflecting how relations to land are foundational to calls for decolonization and liberation. While this slogan has increasingly circulated through social media, graffiti, and academic spaces, it encompasses a long history of Indigenous governance and care work, as well as confrontations and resistance against colonial governments and capitalist industries. As Jeff Corntassel (Cherokee Nation) writes:

> Broadly speaking, we can think of land back as the regeneration of Indigenous laws on Indigenous lands and waters. It is a call to liberate stolen lands and waters from current colonial encroachments and legal fictions. There is an urgency here as the health of Indigenous lands and waters is intrinsically linked to the health of Indigenous bodies and communities. According to a "LANDBACK Manifesto" based on the return of the Black Hills to Lakota peoples, "It is our belonging to the land—because—we are the land." Land is the lifework of Indigenous peoples. From this perspective, land back can be viewed as Indigenous-led reclamations grounded in "consent-based jurisdiction." The land back movement signals a reassertion of relational responsibilities around place-based values, intimacies, protocols, stories and governance.[8]

As Corntassel reflects, Land Back movements are shaped by complex conceptualizations of kinship responsibilities that require a reimagining of the world beyond private property regimes and colonial capitalist extractivism. Along these lines, calls for Land Back are embedded in the urgency to respond to detrimental impacts of climate change and biodiversity loss and to regenerate Indigenous and anti-colonial forms of land stewardship and protection. The above epigraph from the Canada-based Land Back Editorial Collective—just one of countless Indigenous collectivities across the Americas advocating for land justice—emphasizes how Land Back must be understood as an entire system: a way of (re)making the world through multiple forms of labor that protect and care for a web of human and nonhuman relations and that socially reproduce Indigenous life.[9] Similarly, Jacinta Ruru (Maori) writes, "The restitution of *whenua* (land), to me, means honouring the intent of, and responsibilities to, my ancestors and descendants, including those personified in the lands and waters around us; *Papatūānuku* [Mother Earth].... [T]he return [of land] enables the possibility of the return [of] humanness."[10]

The essays in this collection were first delivered for the symposium "Land Back: Indigenous Landscapes of Resurgence and Freedom" that took place in the spring of 2021. The symposium was hosted by Dumbarton Oaks, a Harvard University research institute located on the ancestral lands of the Nacotchtank and contemporary Piscataway tribes in Washington, D.C.[11] The symposium was originally planned as an in-person event that would bring together scholars and community leaders from Canada, the United States, Ecuador, Chile, and Honduras. However, it was reorganized as a virtual symposium due to the COVID-19 pandemic and held over four separate dates. Nevertheless, these discussions built a hemispheric dialogue on land-based movements and highlighted the scholarship of emerging anti-colonial scholars. The presentations were augmented through critical and generous feedback from four discussants who are leading scholars in Indigenous theory, political ecology, and critical feminist and race studies in the Americas: Isabel Altamirano-Jiménez (Zapotec), Clint Carroll (Cherokee), Dian Million (Athabascan), and Sharlene Mollett.

The essays in this collection highlight the many ways Indigenous peoples and anti-colonial co-resisters understand and practice land relations for political resurgence and freedom across the Americas. The authors place Indigenous practices of freedom within the particularities of Indigenous place-based laws, cosmologies, and diplomacies, while also demonstrating how Indigeneity is shaped across colonial borders. Collectively, the essays examine the relationship between language, Indigenous ontologies, and land reclamation; Indigenous ecology and restoration; the interconnectivity of environmental exploitation and racial, class, and gender exploitation; Indigenous diasporic movement; community urban planning; transnational organizing and relational anti-racist placemaking; and the role of storytelling and children in movements for liberation.

In the remainder of the introduction, we situate the volume with a brief historical overview of Land Back movements in the Americas, while also reflecting on the global context of Indigenous movements for decolonization in the twentieth and twenty-first centuries. We then unpack the ways Indigenous scholars have conceptualized land and the non-human world as relations with agency and the multiple forms of relational accountability that shape Indigenous Land Back movements. Building on this expansive understanding of land, we address how engaging Indigenous conceptualizations of relationality and the movements these conceptualizations engender inform the methodological approach of the volume. Finally, we delineate a brief overview of the volume by highlighting key contributions and concluding remarks on the dialogues and political engagements we hope the book will cultivate.

History of Land Back across the Americas

On July 3, 2020, land defenders from the NDN Collective blocked the road to Mount Rushmore in Ȟesápa, the Black Hills on the Sioux nation's ancestral lands, to protest against President Trump's Fourth of July event. As the President and CEO of the NDN Collective, Nick Tilsen asserts, "Mount Rushmore is an international symbol of white supremacy, and as people across America rightfully pull down statues of white supremacy, we have to look long and hard at how this national monument in the Black Hills upholds and maintains white supremacy on Indigenous lands."[12] Tilsen continues by explaining how the resistance embodied by Indigenous land defenders at Mount Rushmore was not solely a stand against Trump's racist rhetoric and actions, but a demand that all public lands in the Black Hills be returned to Indigenous peoples. A few months later, in October 2020, the NDN Collective launched the LANDBACK campaign on Indigenous Peoples' Day. As they explain, the Land Back movement has a long legacy of Indigenous resistance and expands from north to south across Turtle Island.[13] They view their campaign as part of a longer genealogy and broader relational landscape of Indigenous land struggles, as well as "mechanism to connect, amplify and resource the LANDBACK movement and the communities that have been fighting to reclaim stewardship of the land . . . to envision a world where Black, Indigenous and POC liberation co-exists."[14]

The work of the NDN Collective in the Black Hills is just one example of how Indigenous peoples have mobilized land-based rhetoric and practice in struggles for decolonization. Although it is deceptively simple as a rallying cry, Indigenous organizers and allies acknowledge how "Land Back is an incredibly complex call to action"[15] that is shaped by issues related to Indigenous law and political authority, land and colonial property making, state surveillance, bodily and sexual sovereignty, the restoration of ecological relations, Black and Indigenous solidarities, and the (re)building of Indigenous kinship and internationalism. While Land Back may have recently gained popularity, appearing on banners at solidarity actions around the globe and circulated through memes on social media, it must be understood in the context of longer histories of Indigenous anti-colonial resistance.

Mike Gouldhawke (Métis and Cree) traces Indigenous land struggles across Turtle Island through a hundred-year history from 1921 to 2020, expanding from Coast Salish to Mi'kmaq territories, chronicling a history of Land Back that demonstrates how resistance movements have been a feature of Indigenous life since the arrival of European colonizers. He provides an extensive overview of the various forms of labor that shape Indigenous struggles for land, including breakfast programs, teach-ins, access to housing, cultural-revitalization programs, reading groups, and community patrols. Additionally, he elaborates on the matrilineal roots of Land Back. In particular, he highlights how Indigenous women founded the Native Alliance for Red Power (NARP) in Vancouver in 1967 and the American Indian Movement (AIM) in Minneapolis in 1968; they later started the annual Women's Memorial March in Vancouver's Downtown Eastside in 1992 that, in part, led to the National Inquiry into Missing and Murdered Indigenous Women and Girls in Canada and community-led initiatives such as the Red Women Rising report in 2019.

Gouldhawke's examination of Land Back largely focuses on Canada and the United States, but he makes several connections to Indigenous resistance across the Americas. For example, the timeline draws connections between the defense actions at Oka led by the Mohawk community of Kanehsatà:ke and a nationwide Indigenous uprising in Ecuador during the same year.[16] A few years later, the Zapatista uprising started on January 1, 1994, following the passing of the North American Free Trade Agreement that terminated agrarian reform in Mexico and privatized collective *ejido* land tenures. As María Elena García and José Antonio Lucero write, "[T]he Zapatista Army of National Liberation (EZLN, in Spanish) became arguably the best-known Indigenous social movement in the Americas," an uprising that was inspired not only by historical activism in Chiapas but also by Indigenous resistance at Oka, as Gouldhawke highlights.[17]

Gouldhawke demonstrates that these events did not just coincide but offered opportunities for expressions of solidarity and support through community delegations. For example, land defenders from the Six Nations of the Grand River traveled to Oaxaca during the 2006–2007 popular uprising to build relationships between Indigenous communities based on a shared connection to land.[18] Indeed, Gouldhawke's brief timeline provides an entry point for more in-depth engagements with Indigenous historians who have written extensive analyses of the legal and extralegal confrontations that have galvanized Land Back movements in the twentieth and twenty-first centuries.[19] As Lower Brule Sioux historian Nick Estes illustrates, each iteration of Indigenous activism "adopt[s] essential features of previous traditions of Indigenous resistance."[20] In reflecting on the Red Power movement of the 1960s, Estes writes: "Red Power was not just an abstract theory or an intellectual exercise. It was a practice of everyday Native people taking charge of their lives and their communities. It was a movement, a revolution. Education, paternalism, police violence and incarceration, and the false promise of citizenship all had to be challenged, if not entirely undone. Red Power, built upon centuries-old traditions of Indigenous resistance, sprang into action in rural reservations and urban centers alike."[21]

Indigenous studies scholars in the North American context have also made important contributions to historicizing Indigenous struggles for land and liberation within the global scope of Indigenous social movements. In *The Fourth World: An Indian Reality*, Yellowknives Dene scholar Glen Sean Coulthard examines how the Red Power movement was inspired by decolonization movements around the globe. He attends to these global connections with particular attention to Secwépemc activist George Manuel's activism in the 1960s and 1970s. As Coulthard details, Manuel's thinking of the fourth world, which he frames as "a process or movement of decolonization grounded in the purposeful revitalization of those relational, land-informed Indigenous practices and modes of life that settler-colonization sought to destroy in its drive to transform Indigenous peoples' lands into the settler-state and capital,"[22] was largely inspired by international advocacy work he experienced as the chief of the National Indian Brotherhood.

Manuel's political consciousness was informed by his participation in delegations that brought him into dialogue with Indigenous and Black organizers from Aotearoa, Australia, Tanzania, and Sweden, as well as regional connections forged between NARP organizers in Vancouver and Black Panther organizers in Seattle. As Coulthard asserts, the "political cross-fertilizations"[23] between Black and Indigenous liberation movements was reflected through NARP's "eight-point program" adapted from the Black Panthers' "ten-point program," with both containing demands to end white supremacy and the exploitation of lands and people.[24] Situating this historical period of Indigenous activism in a global context illuminates how Indigenous political consciousness and activism have been historically inspired by Black and anti-colonial thought and political organizing.

In this context, we also begin to see how Indigenous rights-based frameworks and national and international legislation have historically culminated from the labor and organizing of Indigenous movements.[25] A pivotal moment of Indigenous land struggles and internationalism in the 1960s and 1970s occurred in 1975, during the first meeting of the World Council of Indigenous Peoples (WCIP) in Port Alberni, British Columbia, the first transnational conference on Indigenous peoples' rights that paved the way for the United Nations Working Group on Indigenous Populations in 1982 and the United Nations Declaration on the Rights of Indigenous Peoples in 2007. As García and Lucero write, Aymara activist Constantino Lima attended the 1975 WCIP meeting and, upon returning, stopped on the Kuna Island of Ustupa in Panama "where Kuna *saylas* told him that against efforts to put the label 'America' on these lands, the Kuna had a different term: Abya Yala, literally the 'land of life-blood,' or 'land in full splendor.'"[26] Lima committed to circulating knowledge on Abya Yala through his encounters, as Indigenous movements "were embraced as part of a new *pachakutik*, a Quechua and Aymara concept for renewal and transformation, or more precisely a return (*kutik*) to another time/place or world (*pacha*)."[27]

A global examination of Indigenous liberation helps us understand how localized and national movements such as Red Power have grown from sites of grassroots organizing to ones of international governing spaces such as the United Nations by building connections with Third World decolonization movements. In addition, applying a global lens to Indigenous resistance unravels the ways that genocide is intimately entangled with global processes of imperialism, anti-Blackness, neoliberal processes of privatization, colonial domestic policies and administration, and state surveillance of Indigenous, Black, and Brown bodies.

Indigenous Land/Body Relationalities

Indigenous social movements and everyday practices of land reclamation are historically premised on an ethic of care for a web of relations, including relationships between humans as well as relationships between humans, nonhumans (including land and water relations), and the cosmos. Drawing on Anishinaabe and Mohawk thought, Vanessa Watts argues that ecosystems are conceived as societies with ethical structures, interspecies treaties, and diplomatic agreements, where nonhumans are active members of society. Land and the nonhuman world, Watts argues, are animate; the animacy embodied by nonhuman actors does not merely equate to being alive, but to being "full of thought, desire, contemplation and will."[28] The sophistication of Indigenous governance systems, Watts writes, "is directly related to not only the animals' ability to communicate with us, but their *willingness* to communicate with us,"[29] thus stressing nonhuman political agency within Indigenous onto-epistemologies, rather than merely focusing on an animacy that is void of will and desire. As Watts and many other Indigenous scholars highlight, Indigenous onto-epistemologies of the nonhuman world are, in part, embedded and transmitted through origin stories, stories in which humans are the last ones to arrive on Earth, necessitating diplomatic agreements with animal and plant nations.[30] In other words, Indigenous life relies on the intelligence of nonhuman life and the maintenance of good relations between the human and nonhuman world.[31] As many of the essays in this collection will demonstrate, relations to land are embodied in Indigenous languages, legal orders, food systems, community planning, and knowledge systems that provide the material basis for Indigenous life.

This land/body relationality upon which Indigenous life relies underscores how land dispossession cannot happen without violence on Indigenous peoples' bodies. Colonial dispossession destroys the relations with land that are at the core of Indigenous governance structures, knowledge, and languages. Human and nonhuman relations are altered through the violent impacts of environmental contamination, pollution, and culminating impacts of climate change.[32] Meanwhile, the gendered politics of colonization have targeted the bodies of Indigenous women and queer and Two-Spirit people. Kinship relations have been severed through the imposition of heteropatriarchal governance structures such as the band council system in Canada or the tribal government system in the United States, undermining the sociopolitical roles of multiple actors or nodes of Indigenous relational networks.[33] Yet Indigenous peoples continuously (re)make these relations *through* an ethic of care that exceeds and refuses colonial forms of political recognition and spatial boundaries.

Land Back movements encompass multi-scalar practices that challenge colonial geopolitical orders as well as the ways colonial violence impacts how land relations are embodied. A land/body interrelation is mobilized by Indigenous women and Two-Spirit and queer organizers in Land Back movements to speak to how the restoration of the well-being of Indigenous peoples is directly connected to the well-being of Indigenous lands. In their report/toolkit *Violence on the Land, Violence on Our Bodies: Building an Indigenous Response to Environmental Violence*, the Native Youth Sexual Health Network and Women's Earth Alliance emphasize that Indigenous resistance to land dispossession and environmental violence must uphold all Indigenous peoples' self-determination over their bodies by supporting the leadership of women, youth, and Two-Spirit peoples in Indigenous communities and by understanding that violence results not only from colonial states and industry but also from "the role cis-supremacy and patriarchy play in both environmental destruction and environmental justice movements."[34] The report shows how women's bodies are crucial sites of knowledge that embody experiences of structural violence and resistance and how "Indigenous women's resistance—rooted in community, future generations, and ancestral struggles for land and livelihood—is a feminist resistance, but it is also fundamentally anti-capitalist and anti-imperial, demanding respect and protection not only of women's bodies, but also of land, water, mother earth, culture, and community."[35]

A land/body interrelation has also been foundational to Indigenous women's resistance in Abya Yala. Lorena Cabnal, an Indigenous Maya-Xinka thinker and member of the Association of Indigenous Women of Santa María Xalapán, Jalapa (AMISMAXAJ) in Guatemala, mobilizes the concept of *cuerpo-territorio* (body-territory) that emerges from dialogues occurring among Indigenous communitarian feminist groups across

Latin America. According to Cabnal, the land/body interrelation is vital to Indigenous struggles, as it illuminates the interconnections between colonial capitalist extraction on Indigenous lands and gendered and sexualized violence embodied by Indigenous women and girls across multiple generations.[36] As such, Cabnal is committed to recuperating the importance of Indigenous women's bodies by understanding how they are sites of memory, struggle, and healing that disrupt gendered and sexualized processes of colonization. She explains, "historical and oppressive violences exist both for my first territory, my body, as well as for my historic territory, the land. In that sense, all the forms of violence against women are attacks against that existence that should be whole and full."[37]

Sofia Zaragocin, a contributor to this volume, has also extensively engaged with the interrelationship of land and bodies through her analyses of the gendered geographies of elimination in Latin America and decolonial feminist praxis.[38] As she articulates with Martina Angela Caretta, *cuerpo-territorio* is "the inseparable ontological relationship between body and territory."[39] Her essay in this volume illustrates how conceptions of *cuerpo-territorio* are shaped by the embodied knowledge of Black, Indigenous, Latinx, and Latin American activists in Abya Yala, who are simultaneously inspired by the thought and political practices of anti-colonial feminists across the hemisphere. Thus, Zaragocin shows how *cuerpo-territorio* not only holds potential to build solidarities across Indigenous feminist movements throughout the Americas but is already an outcome of political solidarities that echo Third World/women of color feminist traditions.[40]

Indigenous feminist scholarship that takes up land/body relations provides renewed ways of understanding transnationality and resistance across the Americas. As Melanie Yazzie (Diné) writes, "Indigenous internationalist feminism provides a framework for transnational Indigenous practices that seek to build counterhegemonic power with other anti-colonial, anti-imperial, and anti-capitalist liberation struggles, both within and outside of the United States. At the center of these practices is an ethics of relationality between humans, and also between humans and our other-than-human kin."[41] Indigenous feminist and queer activism have always made the connections between theft of land and the direct attack on Indigenous peoples' bodily sovereignty, Indigenous kinship structures, gender and sexual diversity, and Indigenous intimacies.[42] In other words, they are committed to building intellectual frameworks and political projects that are committed to the rematriation of *all* Indigenous relationships.[43]

Relationality as a Methodology

The same ethic of relationality that informs Indigenous epistemologies of resistance also informs the contributions we have brought together. In our efforts, we have been inspired by an approach that is place-based, specific, and relational. In contrast to a comparative approach, a relational approach to studying relations to land across the Americas looks for both resonances and incommensurabilities without enshrining difference as the basis for analysis. Tiffany Lethabo King uses the geological metaphor of the shoal—a space of transition from deeper ocean to the shore characterized by the unpredictable drifting of granular material—to describe this method. She explains that "[b]y assembling, shoaling, and rubbing disparate texts against one another, unexpected openings emerge where different voices are brought into relationship. As new relationships among texts and voices are made, new and 'transgressive ground[s] of understanding' emerge...."[44] This relational approach also constitutes an ethical approach that is key to decolonial projects, as it "recognizes what is distinct, what is sovereign for project(s) of decolonization."[45] This is an approach that acknowledges that not all aspects of all projects can speak to each other. As Eve Tuck and K. Wayne Yang explain, "opportunities for solidarity lie in what is incommensurable,"[46] as such moments provide for momentary solidarities in their capacity to destabilize and unsettle assumptions. In other words, a relational approach becomes the basis for disrupting totalizing tendencies and narratives.

Resistance movements orient us toward relations shared by Indigenous peoples and toward the importance of solidarity at the hemispheric scale. However, with critical exceptions,[47] scholarship in the field of Indigenous studies has not always prioritized these common struggles; North-South dialogue has been all too rare in studies of imperialism and colonialism in the Americas.[48] The field of Indigenous studies has often privileged peoples and scholars of the Global North.[49] As Zaragocin details in her essay, there are numerous practical difficulties and ethical challenges of hemispheric-level political organizing and conceptual analyses that hinder North-South dialogue. As a result of the primacy of English, the unreciprocated expectation that scholars in Latin America will translate their work into English at their own cost has led to the marginalization of many South and Central American scholars and the exclusion of their intellectual contributions from important debates. Consequently, discussions of imperialism and colonialism in anglophone academia have often privileged concepts such as settler colonialism. We believe hemispheric discussions are long overdue. Relationality serves as a basis from which to challenge many of the key concepts that have been used to describe the colonial conditions that impact Indigenous life in the Americas and that might stand in the way of hemispheric dialogue. In particular, the terms "settler colonialism" and "Indigeneity" are often mobilized in ways that might hamper North-South dialogue. Although colonial projects across the Americas have many commonalities, much is lost in analyses that seek to apply a singular explanation or focus on comparison. A relational approach diverts us from colonial spatialities and provides alternatives that emphasize decolonial solidarity.

Within the field of Native American and Indigenous studies, settler colonialism has become a key framework for analyzing the violent ways that imperialism dominates Indigenous life globally. While settler colonialism can be useful for understanding the economic and political processes that restructure Indigenous relations to land through ongoing processes of elimination and dispossession, theorizations of settler colonialism contain several shortcomings. For instance, this framing of colonial processes relies on the ontological separation of land, labor, and ultimately life, a conceptualization that is challenged by Indigenous epistemologies.[50] While the contributions in this volume acknowledge the immense power of settler colonialism to disrupt and extinguish Indigenous life, several contributions, including those by Zaragocin, Nnenna Odim and Pavithra Vasudevan, James Miller, and Mandee McDonald, think beyond nationhood to foreground Indigenous resistance and relations to land and that place shared struggles and solidarity at the center of their analysis.

In addition to minimizing Indigenous epistemologies, settler colonialism occludes differences in the ways colonialism has articulated across the Americas. Chickasaw scholar Shannon Speed observes that "theorizations of the settler state (largely elaborated in the north) have not grappled fully enough with neoliberal capitalism, and theories of the neoliberal state (a primary focus in the south) fail to recognize the significance of settler logics that structure the conditions of state formation."[51] Similarly, Aníbal Quijano draws an ideological distinction between the settler colonialism perpetrated in North America and the processes that characterized Iberian imperial projects. Latin American states that were the products of Iberian colonialism "epitomized the coloniality of power"[52] even as the colonizer departed and new nations were founded. While still defined by the violent dispossession and elimination of Indigenous peoples, Iberian colonialism requires the incorporation of Indigenous peoples into the dominant body politic.[53] Thus, the contributions in this collection are often positioned in the context of specific national histories and political conditions. However, by foregrounding the multivalent ways Indigenous peoples practice relations to land, they also challenge the "methodological nationalism" that uncritically accepts the nation-state as its unit of analysis and naturalizes colonial territories.[54] These contributions challenge colonial conceptualizations of the state, pointing toward the ways that colonization has violated Indigenous conceptualizations of territory while also showing how Indigenous relations to territory persist despite ongoing colonialism.

Relationality also enables a reconsideration of the ways Indigeneity has often been understood and in particular challenges formulations of colonialism and Indigeneity that exclude Black life.[55] Supporters of Land Back recognize that the struggles of Indigenous peoples are "interconnected with the struggles of all oppressed Peoples" and that the liberation of Black people and people of color are also at the core of Indigenous liberation.[56] However, the settler-colonial framework relies on a native/settler/slave triad that erases Black Indigeneity in the Americas and makes too strong a distinction between transatlantic slavery and settler colonialism as processes that fundamentally shaped the Americas. Consequently, Indigeneity and Blackness have often been treated as distinct and unrelated racial categories.[57] Similarly, "singular narratives of Latin American and Caribbean identity also render Blackness invisible."[58] In this context, the term "Indigenous" itself is somewhat fraught. "Indigenous" came into common usage following the founding of the United Nations Special Forum on the Rights of Indigenous Peoples.[59] The term has some usefulness for describing people with a common struggle against colonialism and for self-determination. However, as an identity rather than the signifier of a political relation, this term can renormalize "taken-for-granted facets of Indigenous identity, as the de facto center against which other people(s) or forms of (collective) self-expression appear as aberrant or inauthentic."[60] In the context of settler-colonial studies, this has often meant a disavowal of both colonialism in Africa and the Indigeneity of Black peoples around the globe. Thus, following Maile Arvin, we suggest that "Indigenous" be understood as an analytic, rather than a category of identity. As an analytic, it "allows us to deeply engage the various power relations that continue to write Indigenous peoples as always vanishing"[61] and recognize how Indigenous peoples configure Indigenous life. As an analytic category, "Indigeniety" can also be understood as expansive and encompassing Black and African-descended peoples, a view that is taken up in depth in the essay by Odim and Vasudevan. This expansive framing of Indigeneity as one analytic of colonial power is key to taking a hemispheric approach and to identifying opportunities for relationality and decolonial solidarity.

Overview of *Land Back: Relational Landscapes of Indigenous Resistance across the Americas*

This volume is thematically organized into two sections: politics of resistance within and beyond colonial borders; and landscapes of relationality: ecology, restoration, and Indigenous futures.[62] Yet each essay brings together these overarching themes and challenges rigid colonial categorizations. As Clint Carroll aptly observed during the second session of the symposium, it is difficult to neatly categorize the themes weaved through each contribution to this collection, as Indigenous land struggles are founded on complex relations and circumstances that shape both colonial conquest as well as Indigenous and anti-colonial resistance and practices of liberation. Carroll's remarks align with recent collected editions in Indigenous studies that do not strictly adhere to conventional thematic categorizations that shape knowledge production in the academy, and thus we find it necessary to highlight the challenges of neatly organizing a set of essays that engage with a set of themes related to Indigenous land struggles, resistance, and liberation.[63]

The first set of essays addresses the ways that Indigenous peoples mobilize relations to land in practices of resistance to defy colonial territorialities. The book opens with an essay that addresses the complexity of calling for a hemispheric approach to Land Back movements. In "A Hemispheric Approach to Relational and Embodied Anti-racist Placemaking," Sofia Zaragocin examines *cuerpo-territorio* methodologies developed by feminist geography and anti-racist collectives in Latin America to understand how relational race relations have shaped collective organizing. In doing so, she focuses on how a *cuerpo-territorio* analytic and politic refuses colonial categorizations and borders, particularly as racial categorizations do not fully account for how Indigeneity and Blackness, for example, are embodied by one individual, and how these embodied realities generate distinct knowledge that complicates the concept of decolonial geographies.

The next two essays explore Indigenous ecological identities and their role in resistance. Olivia Arigho-Stiles offers a detailed genealogy of Indigenous discourses of nature in the context of Bolivia within the period of 1960–1990. In "Landscapes of Struggle: *Katarista* Perspectives on the Environment in Bolivia, 1960–1990," she explores how the *katarista* movement—groups and organizations committed to decolonial struggle by invoking the eighteenth-century Andean activist Tupaj Katari—took up concerns over ecology, resource exploitation, and class to position understandings of Indigeneity and in so doing repurposed the environment as a sphere of political contention. In "Anti-colonial Landscapes: Land and the Emergence of Miskitu People's Territorial Resistance in the Moskitia," Ruth H. Matamoros Mercado (Miskitu) focuses on Indigenous land ontologies within the context of legal struggles in the regions of Honduras and Nicaragua.

She examines how the Moskitia concept of *Klauna Laka* represents not only a way of understanding the ethos that underlies communal land ownership and relations to land but also shapes Indigenous resistance to colonial domination. Both essays demonstrate how Indigenous conceptions of land and natural resources resist the colonial state and legal frameworks that shape Indigenous land rights.

The final two essays in this section draw our attention to how movement is integral to Indigenous relationalities. James Miller (Kanaka Maoli) offers key insights into the interrelation between Indigenous movement and kinship by examining Indigenous grounded normativity within the context of the Marshallese climate diasporic movement. In "Placemaking as Indigenous Resurgence in the Oceanic Diaspora," he examines how Indigenous knowledge is transported, or travels, through spatial relations as they migrate to urban centers in the continental United States. He is particularly interested in how Marshallese grounded normativity comes into ethical relation with Indigenous hosts as they collaborate on community planning through Indigenous spatial knowledge, deep time, and *Vā Moana* (a theory that represents the expansive, relational, and generative nature of Indigenous spatial practice).

In "Theory through Hide Tanning: Resurgence and Indigenous Mobility," Mandee McDonald (Maskikow) complicates Indigenous land-based practices, political resurgence, and notions of homelands by providing an Indigenous feminist analysis of the hide-tanning movement. She centers Indigenous bodies as sites of knowledge production and mobility that transcend colonial containment and focuses on hide-tanning camps as sites of transnational praxis and relationship building. Crucially, McDonald's thinking offers provoking insights that complicate articulations of Indigenous political resurgence that center narratives of Indigenous homelands that risk excluding Indigenous peoples who are grounded in a myriad of histories that have compromised or severed ties to land.

The second set of essays directs our attention toward the knowledge and political possibilities recovered through restoring relations with the nonhuman world through practices of ecological restoration, language revitalization, and storytelling. In "The Munsee Three Sisters Medicinal Farm: A Ground for Cultural Restoration," Chief Vincent Mann (Ramapough Lunaape) and Anita Bakshi examine the Ramapough Lunaape's experiences of contamination and environmental degradation in the 1960s and 1970s. Through a community-based history, the authors examine how the community has responded to the impacts of toxicity through cultural-restoration programs such as the Munsee Three Sisters Medicinal Farm to renew Indigenous land-based knowledge and create new spaces of learning and community engagement. In "Ottawa Governance through Anishinaabe Ecological Restoration: Nmé, Ethnobotany, and Memory," Natasha Myhal (Sault Ste. Marie Anishinaabe and Ukrainian) examines how nmé (sturgeon) generate place-based knowledge as they navigate land and water fraught with colonial jurisdiction yet remain deeply embedded in Anishinaabe sociopolitical systems. Her research offers a crucial reframing of ethnobotany to account for the role of animals and how Indigenous conceptions of ecology and restoration are learned from elder brothers, or animal relatives, whose survival depends on the well-being of plant relations. These two essays turn our attention away from a human-centered approach to conceptions of Land Back by directing our attention toward the intelligence and resistance embodied through animal and plant relations.

The next essay focuses our attention on the role of language in maintaining relations to land and argues that language revitalization must be understood as a form of spatial planning. In "Language, Territory, and Law: Mapuzugun as the Basis for Mapuche Spatial Planning and Territorial Reconstruction," Miguel Melin (Mapuche Territorial Alliance) and Magdalena Ugarte examine how language revitalization is intimately entangled with struggles for land reclamation in what is now Chile. By examining how Indigenous resistance to land dispossession and territorial fragmentation is deeply interconnected with struggles for language revitalization, they give visibility to practices not always understood as a form of territorial resistance.

The concluding essay of the collection builds on insights of Black, Indigenous, and anti-colonial relations by attending to the scale of family, the lived experiences of children, and the liberatory potential of storytelling. In "Moving with Land: BlackIndigenous Stories of Place," Nnenna Odim and Pavithra Vasudevan examine how BlackIndigenous place-based knowledge of land and water is creatively remembered and passed on through migratory pathways and across colonial borders. They consider how the children's storybook *Auntie Luce's Talking Paintings* acts as a guide to BlackIndigenous collective memory and ancestral liberatory practices that nurture alternative futures for young children as descendants and ancestors in their everyday lives.

Together, the authors of this volume offer unique approaches to understanding Land Back movements by offering critical insights on the sociopolitical practices that regenerate Indigenous and anti-colonial forms of land stewardship and protection and that actively seek to (re)create the world in ways that refuse white masculinist heteropatriarchal supremacy. In bringing scholars and organizers from multiple places and backgrounds into dialogue with one another, we hope to make a modest contribution to historical and contemporary conceptualizations of Land Back movements and to cultivate ongoing dialogues among land protectors across the Americas.

While we seek to contribute to academic debates across a variety of fields, we feel it is important not to lose sight of the fact that Indigenous land struggles are a matter of life and death. In her 2018 report to the United Nations Human Rights Council, Special Rapporteur Victoria Tauli-Corpuz documents how Indigenous land protectors are surveilled, criminalized, and subjected to physical violence by colonial state authorities and private security firms hired by the extractive industry.[64] In engaging with the report, the Indigenous Environmental Network notes that the worst human rights violations Tauli-Corpuz highlights is the violation of Indigenous peoples' right to life, reflected in the murder of 312 land defenders in twenty-seven countries in 2017.[65] Attacks are especially apparent in Latin America, where one Indigenous land defender is assassinated every two days in the Amazon Basin of Bolivia, Brazil, Colombia, and Peru.[66] The Global Witness reports that "[b]etween 2015 and 2019 over a third of all fatal attacks have targeted indigenous people—even though indigenous communities make up only 5% of the world's population."[67]

Perhaps the most well-known of these assassinations is the targeted killing of Lenca activist Berta Cáceres in Honduras in March 2016. Cáceres was the cofounder of the

Council of Popular and Indigenous Organizations of Honduras (COPINH), an organization dedicated to defending the territorial, cultural, and spiritual rights of Lenca people as well as the Lenca lands, rivers, and the cultural and spiritual rights that adhere to these environments. She was also a supporter of Indigenous and intersectional feminist movements across the Americas, which she saw as deeply tied to decolonial struggle.[68] As she once told *Al Jazeera*, "I take lots of care but in the end, in this country where there is total impunity I am vulnerable. . . . [W]hen they want to kill me, they will do it."[69] Yet she remained wholly committed to the anti-colonial struggle. In her acceptance of the Goldman Environmental Prize, she reiterated the importance of resisting colonialism and environmental degradation for both Lenca people and the survival of the planet: "COPINH, walking alongside people struggling for their emancipation, validates this commitment to continue protecting our waters, the rivers, our shared resources and nature in general, as well as our rights as a people. Let us wake up! Let us wake up, humankind! We're out of time. We must shake our conscience free of the rapacious capitalism, racism, and patriarchy that will only assure our own self-destruction. The Gualcarque River has called upon us, as have other gravely threatened rivers. We must answer their call."[70]

NOTES

1. Nickita Longman, Emily Riddle, Alex Wilson, and Saima Desai, "'Land Back' Is More Than the Sum of Its Parts: Letter from the Land Back Editorial Collective," *Briarpatch*, September 10, 2020, https://briarpatchmagazine.com/articles/view/land-back-is-more-than-the-sum-of-its-parts.
2. NDN Collective, "NDN Collective LANDBACK Campaign Launching on Indigenous Peoples' Day 2020," October 9, 2020, https://ndncollective.org/ndn-collective-landback-campaign-launching-on-indigenous-peoples-day-2020/.
3. Goldman Environmental Prize, "Berta Cáceres Acceptance Speech, 2015 Goldman Prize Ceremony," YouTube video, 3:19, 2015, https://www.youtube.com/watch?v=AR1kwx8b0ms.
4. We use the term "Indigenous" to refer to the original sovereign peoples who have inhabited the Americas prior to colonial occupation and who have been adversely affected by colonial occupation, settlement, and displacement. The term can also be used to apply to other peoples around the globe who have been subject to processes of racialization that serve colonialism and imperialism, such as in Africa and Asia. We explain the complex meanings that might be given to this term later in the introduction.
5. Leanne Betasamosake Simpson, *As We Have Always Done: Indigenous Freedom through Radical Resistance* (Minneapolis: University of Minnesota Press, 2017), 22.
6. Mishuana Goeman, "Land as Life: Unsettling the Logics of Containment," in *Native Studies Keywords*, ed. Stephanie Nohelani Teves, Andrea Smith, and Michelle H. Raheja (Tucson: University of Arizona Press, 2015), 72.
7. As a slogan rather than a singular movement, "Land Back" has been stylized in multiple ways, including Landback and #landback. We capitalize "Land Back" to mark the term as designating a related set of social movements and events that share the common goal of dismantling colonial structures. At the same time, we recognize that "Land Back" also designates a diversity of actions led by diverse Indigenous peoples.
8. Jeff Corntassel, "Indigenous Laws on Indigenous Lands: Land Back as Community Resurgence," *Rooted* 1, no. 2 (Summer 2021): 16.
9. In this introduction, we use the term "nonhuman" to refer to nonhierarchical conceptions of animal relations, plant relations, cosmological relations, and spiritual relations that shape Indigenous societies and ontological conceptions of reality. We recognize that scholars theorizing at the intersections of Indigenous studies and other fields such as geography and anthropology use various terms such as "other-than-human" and "more-than-human" in rethinking a multispecies world.
10. Jacinta Ruru, "'We Love Her': The Lands of Aotearoa," *Rooted* 1, no. 2 (Summer 2021): 33.
11. We would like to thank Gabrielle A. Tayac, a member of the Piscataway tribe, for sharing her knowledge of Washington, D.C. As Tayac shared through email communication, Nacotchtank/Anacostans are the ancestral caretakers of this place. The Anacostia River and D.C. neighborhood are named after this Indigenous nation. The Nacotchtank people are part of the Piscataway chiefdom, and these groups merged by the early eighteenth century. As Tayac indicates, the 1666 Treaty between the Piscataway chiefdom and the English colony of Maryland provides insight into the relationship that existed between Piscataway and Nacotchtank peoples. Today's Piscataway people are descendants of the merged chiefdom that also includes the children of enslaved African peoples. According to Tayac, there were approximately a dozen tribal groups affiliated with Piscataway people that ranged from Great Falls to Point Lookout, and the Potomac to the Patuxent River in Maryland. The Piscataway were located at Moyaone, which is known as Accokeek today. As Tayac explains, there was a great deal of movement and intermarriage in this region, and neighboring nations included the Doeg/Tauxenent on the Potomac River, near the region of Mason Neck and Northern Virginia, and the Patawomeck near Stafford. Today, the city of Washington, D.C., is shaped by many intertribal and diasporic peoples.
12. NDN Collective, "NDN Collective LANDBACK Campaign Launching on Indigenous Peoples' Day 2020."
13. The term "Turtle Island" originates from the creation stories of the Anishinaabe and Haudenosaunee and is often used to describe the continent of North America. For some, it is preferable to "North America," which is rooted in colonial histories and relationalities. For the same reasons, some Indigenous peoples have adopted the Kuna term "Abya Yala" to refer to the continent of South America.
14. NDN Collective, "LANDBACK Updates: From Launch to Looking Forward," October 28, 2020, https://ndncollective.org/landback-updates-from-launch-to-looking-forward/.
15. Longman, Riddle, Wilson, and Desai, "'Land Back' Is More Than the Sum of Its Parts."

16 Mike Gouldhawke, "100 Years of Land Struggle," *Briarpatch*, September 10, 2020, https://briarpatchmagazine.com/articles/view/100-years-of-land-struggle.

17 María Elena García and José Antonio Lucero, "Resurgence and Resistance in Abya Yala: Indigenous Politics from Latin America," in *The World of Indigenous North America*, ed. Robert Warrior (New York: Routledge, 2015), 434. García and Lucero detail how Andean and Amazonian Indigenous organizing, which started in the 1960s, culminated in June 1990, as the Confederation of Indigenous Nationalities of Ecuador (CONAIE) mobilized a peaceful nationwide Indigenous uprising, demanding that the colonial government negotiate with Indigenous peoples on issues related to land conflict, education, and rural livelihoods.

18 Audrey Huntley, "A Warrior Woman's Journey: From Six Nations to Oaxaca," YouTube video, 29:37, May 11, 2013, https://www.youtube.com/watch?v=HwLDDKeKLWI. Huntley details how in 2006, Indigenous uprisings were taking shape in Oaxaca, Mexico, and in the Mohawk community of the Six Nations to resist a housing development. Doreen Silversmith (Cayuga), a land defender from the Six Nations who contributed to the Oka Peace Camp in 1990 and land defense in the Six Nations in 2006, traveled to Oaxaca during the 2006–2007 popular uprising.

19 Vine Deloria Jr., *Behind the Trail of Broken Treaties: An Indian Declaration of Independence* (New York: Delacorte Press, 1974).

20 Nick Estes, *Our History Is the Future: Standing Rock versus the Dakota Access Pipeline, and the Long Tradition of Indigenous Resistance* (London: Verso, 2019), 131.

21 Estes, *Our History Is the Future*, 178.

22 Glen Sean Coulthard, introduction to *The Fourth World: An Indian Reality*, by George Manuel and Michael Posluns (Minneapolis: University of Minnesota Press, 2019), xi.

23 Coulthard, introduction to *The Fourth World*, xxx.

24 Coulthard, introduction to *The Fourth World*, xxii–xxiii.

25 Coulthard, introduction to *The Fourth World*; and García and Lucero, "Resurgence and Resistance in Abya Yala."

26 García and Lucero, "Resurgence and Resistance in Abya Yala," 429.

27 García and Lucero, "Resurgence and Resistance in Abya Yala," 429.

28 Vanessa Watts, "Indigenous Place-Thought and Agency amongst Humans and Non-Humans (First Woman and Sky Woman Go on a European World Tour!)," *Decolonization: Indigeneity, Education & Society* 2, no. 1 (2013): 23.

29 Watts, "Indigenous Place-Thought amongst Humans and Non-Humans," 30.

30 See also Heidi Kiiwetinepinesiik Stark, "Respect, Responsibility, and Renewal: The Foundations of Anishinaabe Treaty Making with the United States and Canada," *American Indian Culture and Research Journal* 34, no. 2 (2010): 145–64; and Leanne Simpson, *Dancing on Our Turtle's Back: Stories of Nishnaabeg Re-creation, Resurgence and a New Emergence* (Winnipeg: Arbeiter Ring Publishing, 2011).

31 Robin Kimmerer, "Restoration and Reciprocity: The Contributions of Traditional Ecological Knowledge," in *Human Dimensions of Ecological Restoration: Integrating Science, Nature, and Culture*, ed. Dave Egan, Evan E. Hjerpe, and Jesse Abrams (Washington, D.C.: Island Press, 2011), 257; and Clint Carroll, "Fauna and Flux on the Plains' Edge: Animal Kinship, Place Making, and Cherokee Relational Continuity," in *The Greater Plains: Rethinking a Region's Environmental Histories*, ed. Brian Frehner and Kathleen A. Brosnan (Lincoln: University of Nebraska Press, 2021), 114–37.

32 Macarena Gómez-Barris, *The Extractive Zone: Social Ecologies and Decolonial Perspectives* (Durham, N.C.: Duke University Press, 2017); Kyle Whyte, "Indigenous Climate Change Studies: Indigenizing Futures, Decolonizing the Anthropocene" *English Language Notes* 55, nos. 1–2 (Spring/Fall 2017): 153–62; Erin Marie Konsmo and Karyn Recollet, "Afterword: Meeting the Land(s) Where They Are At: A Conversation between Erin Marie Monsmo (Métis) and Karyn Recollet (Urban Cree)," in *Indigenous and Decolonizing Studies in Education: Mapping the Long View*, ed. Linda Tuhiwai Smith, Eve Tuck, and K. Wayne Yang (New York: Routledge, 2019), 238–51; and Winona LaDuke and Deborah Cowen, "Beyond Wiindigo Infrastructure," *The South Atlantic Quarterly* 119, no. 2 (April 2020): 243–68.

33 Simpson, *As We Have Always Done*, 117.

34 Women's Earth Alliance and Native Youth Sexual Health Network, *Violence on the Land, Violence on Our Bodies: Building an Indigenous Response to Environmental Violence*, 2016, 6, http://landbodydefense.org/uploads/files/VLVBReportToolkit2016.pdf.

35 Heather Gies, "Facing Violence, Resistance Is Survival for Indigenous Women," *teleSUR*, March 7, 2015, https://www.telesurenglish.net/analysis/Facing-Violence-Resistance-Is-Survival-for-Indigenous-Women-20150307-0018.html.

36 Isabel Altamirano-Jiménez, "Indigenous Women Refusing the Violence of Resource Extraction in Oaxaca," *AlterNative: An International Journal of Indigenous Peoples* 17, no. 2 (June 2021): 215–23.

37 Lorena Cabnal, "On Constructing a Proposal of Communitarian Feminist Indigenous Women's Epistemic Thought in Abya Yala," trans. Elizabeth Mason-Deese (unpublished translation), 10, of Lorena Cabnal, "Acercamiento a la construcción de la propuesta de pensamiento epistémico de las mujeres indígenas feministas comunitarias de Abya Yala," in *Feminismos diversos: El feminismo comunitario* (Madrid: ACSUR-Las Segovias, 2010), 11–25.

38 Sofia Zaragocin, "Gendered Geographies of Elimination: Decolonial Feminist Geographies in Latin American Settler Contexts," *Antipode* 51, no. 1 (2019): 373–92.

39 Sofia Zaragocin and Martina Angela Caretta, "*Cuerpo-territorio*: A Decolonial Feminist Geographical Method for the Study of Embodiment," *Annals of the American Association of Geographers* 111, no. 5 (2021): 1504.

40 Cherríe Moraga and Gloria Anzaldúa, eds., *This Bridge Called My Back: Writings by Radical Women of Color*, 4th ed. (Albany: State University of New York Press, 2015).

41 Melanie K. Yazzie, "US Imperialism and the Problem of 'Culture' in Indigenous Politics: Towards Indigenous Internationalist Feminism," *American Indian Culture and Research Journal* 43, no. 3 (2019): 98.

42 Dian Million, *Therapeutic Nations: Healing in an Age of Indigenous Human Rights* (Tucson: University of Arizona Press, 2013); Audra Simpson, *Mohawk Interruptus: Political Life Across the Borders of Settler States* (Durham, N.C.: Duke University Press, 2014); Cabnal, "On Constructing a Proposal of Communitarian Feminist Indigenous Women's Epistemic Thought in Abya Yala"; and Jodi A. Byrd, "What's Normative Got to Do with It? Toward Indigenous Queer Relationality," *Social Text* 38, no. 4 (December 2020): 105–23.

43 Melanie K. Yazzie and Cutcha Risling Baldy, introduction to "Indigenous Peoples and the Politics of Water," ed. Cutcha Risling Baldy and Melanie K. Yazzie, special issue, *Decolonization: Indigeneity, Education & Society* 7, no. 1 (2018): 2.

44 Tiffany Lethabo King, *The Black Shoals: Offshore Formations of Black and Native Studies* (Durham, N.C.: Duke University Press, 2019), 30.

45 Eve Tuck and K. Wayne Yang, "Decolonization Is Not a Metaphor," *Decolonization: Indigeneity, Education & Society* 1, no. 1 (2012): 28.

46 Tuck and Yang, "Decolonization Is Not a Metaphor," 28.

47 Jack D. Forbes, "The Use of Racial and Ethnic Terms in America: Management by Manipulation," *Wicazo Sa Review* 11, no. 2 (Autumn 1995): 53–65; Estes, *Our History Is the Future*; and Sharlene Mollett, "Hemispheric, Relational, and Intersectional Political Ecologies of Race: Centring Land-Body Entanglements in the Americas," *Antipode* 53, no. 3 (2021): 810–30.

48 M. Bianet Castellanos, "Introduction: Settler Colonialism in Latin America," *American Quarterly* 69, no. 4 (December 2017): 777.

49 Castellanos, "Introduction: Settler Colonialism in Latin America."

50 See Bennett Brazelton, "On the Erasure of Black Indigeneity," *Review of Education, Pedagogy, and Cultural Studies* 43, no. 5 (2021): 379–97; Tiffany Lethabo King, "New World Grammars: The 'Unthought' Black Discourses of Conquest," in "On Colonial Unknowing," ed. Alyosha Goldstein, Juliana Hu Pegues, and Manu Vimalassery, special issue, *Theory & Event* 19, no. 4 (2016); King, introduction to *The Black Shoals*; and Jared Sexton, "The *Vel* of Slavery: Tracking the Figure of the Unsovereign," *Critical Sociology* 42, nos. 4–5 (July 2016): 583–97.

51 Shannon Speed, "Structures of Settler Capitalism in Abya Yala," *American Quarterly* 69, no. 4 (December 2017): 784.

52 Aníbal Quijano, "The Challenge of the 'Indigenous Movement' in Latin America," *Socialism and Democracy* 19, no. 3 (2005): 60.

53 Christopher A. Loperena, "Settler Violence? Race and Emergent Frontiers of Progress in Honduras," *American Quarterly* 69, no. 4 (December 2017): 801.

54 David Hugill, "Comparative Settler Colonial Urbanisms: Racism and the Making of Inner-City Winnipeg and Minneapolis, 1940–1975," in *Settler City Limits: Indigenous Resurgence and Colonial Violence*

in the Urban Prairie West, ed. Heather Dorries, Robert Henry, David Hugill, Tyler McCreary, and Julie Tomiak (Winnipeg: University of Manitoba, 2019), 72.

55. King, *The Black Shoals*.
56. "LandBack Manifesto," n.d., https://landback.org/manifesto/.
57. Paul Joseph López Oro, "A Love Letter to Indigenous Blackness: Garifuna Women in New York City Working to Preserve Life, Culture, and History across Borders and Generations Are Part of a Powerful Lineage of Resistance to Anti-Blackness," *NACLA Report on the Americas* 53, no. 3 (2021): 249.
58. Oro, "A Love Letter to Indigenous Blackness," 249.
59. Maile Arvin, "Analytics of Indigeneity," in *Native Studies Keywords*, ed. Stephanie Nohelani Teves, Andrea Smith, and Michelle H. Raheja (Tucson: University of Arizona Press, 2015), 119–29.
60. Mark Rifkin, "Indigenous Is to Queer as . . . : Queer Questions for Indigenous Studies," in *Sources and Methods in Indigenous Studies*, ed. Chris Andersen and Jean M. O'Brien (Abingdon: Routledge, 2017), 207.
61. Arvin, "Analytics of Indigeneity," 126.
62. We originally categorized the four sessions for the Dumbarton Oaks symposium along the following themes: landscapes of resistance; nature/ecology; caring for place; and movement/thinking across borders. In designating these categorizations, we encountered challenges, as many contributions to this collection provide important insights into each theme.
63. Linda Tuhiwai Smith, Eve Tuck, and K. Wayne Yang, eds., *Indigenous and Decolonizing Studies in Education: Mapping the Long View* (New York: Routledge, 2019); and Joanne Barker, ed., *Critically Sovereign: Indigenous Gender, Sexuality, and Feminist Studies* (Durham, N.C.: Duke University Press, 2017).
64. United Nations Human Rights Council, "Report of the Special Rapporteur on the Rights of Indigenous Peoples," August 10, 2018, https://documents-dds-ny.un.org/doc/UNDOC/GEN/G18/246/34/PDF/G1824634.pdf?OpenElement.
65. Indigenous Environmental Network, *Indigenous Resistance against Carbon* (Washington, D.C.: Oil Change International, 2021), 5.
66. Indigenous Environmental Network, *Indigenous Resistance against Carbon*, 5.
67. Global Witness, *Defending Tomorrow: The Climate Crisis and Threats against Land and Environmental Defenders* (London: Global Witness, 2020), 10.
68. María José Méndez, "'The River Told Me': Rethinking Intersectionality from the World of Berta Cáceres," *Capitalism Nature Socialism* 29, no. 1 (2018): 7–24.
69. Nina Lakhani, "Honduras Dam Project Shadowed by Violence," *Al Jazeera*, December 24, 2013.
70. Goldman Environmental Prize, "Berta Cáceres Acceptance Speech, 2015 Goldman Prize Ceremony."

1

Politics of Resistance
Within and Beyond Colonial Borders

1

A Hemispheric Approach to Relational and Embodied Anti-racist Placemaking

SOFIA ZARAGOCIN

Across the Americas, there are common narratives and praxis on decolonial placemaking that stem from similar questions regarding the coloniality of place. This is occurring at the hemispheric level.[1] The hemispheric offers an alternative geographical spatial imaginary where different forms of resistance to colonial spatial formations are possible. Nevertheless, arguments in favor for the hemispheric have tended to be concentrated in the Global North. I argue that the hemispheric needs to dialogue with Latin American embodied and racialized geographies to fully foster its political potential. Otherwise, this liberatory scale is truncated by only focusing on Anglophone literature and analysis stemming from North America. In doing so, this essay also speaks to the complexity of promoting a hemispheric approach to issues related to the Land Back movement in the United States from diverse theoretical and practical activist work of Indigenous, Black, Latinx, and Latin American scholars and activists working across the expanse of the Americas. Drawing on the experience of the Reexistencias Cimarrunas Collective, an autonomous transnational group of activists and researchers based in Ecuador that advocates for a hemispheric approach to anti-racism, I demonstrate how there are collective actions in favor of this imaginary scale, thus hoping to bridge this gap between the Americas. The hemispheric understood in this way can further the geographical reach of the Land Back movement to a global scale. Moreover, there are clear links that tie the hemispheric with embodied notions of territory such as the relationship between land-body and *cuerpo-territorio* (body-territory) epistemologies and methods.[2] Embodiment of territory is in direct dialogue with anti-racist praxis and thought propagated by Indigenous collectives as well as Black, Latinx, and Latin American scholars and activists in North, Central, and South America. In what follows,

I first discuss the hemispheric scale as a decolonial spatial imaginary, then draw out the connections between land-body and *cuerpo-territorio* decolonial feminist epistemologies. I conclude with an anti-racist approach to *cuerpo-territorio* resulting from relational anti-racist placemaking at a hemispheric scale that—as I will make the case for—ultimately benefits the Land Back movement.

The Hemispheric as a Decolonial Spatial Imaginary for the Americas

The geographies of the hemispheric are vast and plural. For certain scholars, the hemispheric includes the coasts of West Africa,[3] for others all the Americas,[4] and for some specific places within the Americas.[5] The hemispheric also acts as a platform for conceptual discussions to take place on race and anti-racist understandings and efforts. One of the first scholars to position debates on self-determination and the right to name land from Indigenous worldviews at the hemispheric scale was Indigenous scholar, activist, and creative writer Jack D. Forbes.[6] Forbes's critique of racial management from relational perspectives primarily concerning Indigenous and Black peoples demonstrates the connections between land, territory, and colonial racialization in the Americas. For Juliet Hooker, the hemispheric implies comprehending how scientific racism formed nationalist ideas of *mestizaje* in South America while simultaneously promoting white supremacy in North America.[7] Racialized politics across the Americas, for Hooker, are embedded in a state-sponsored neoliberal multiculturalism that, in turn, demonstrates how anti-racist praxis is confronting racialized capitalism.[8] Adam Bledsoe shows how marronage formed Black territorial formations of Black liberation—such as *quilombos*—in Brazil and the United States in similar but often ignored ways.[9] Following Bledsoe, Eloisa Berman-Arévalo situates her work on Afro-Latin American and Colombian Black geographies within a larger theoretical and political project of Black geographies at the hemispheric scale.[10] Tiffany Lethabo King highlights how Black liberation has been tied to water and Indigenous struggles to land, as she prompts the geographical space of the shoals where both Black and Indigenous peoples can coexist.[11] Meanwhile, Sharlene Mollett advocates for a hemispheric, relational, and intersectional focus to bring together racialized geographies of political ecology where one of the central components of political ecologies of race is that they are relational in the Americas.[12] In this way, there is a clear link made between the Americas and the hemispheric from activists and scholars working on Indigenous, feminist, Black, and anti-racist perspectives. Other scholars, though not explicitly engaged with the hemispheric, have brought together common historical connections across the Americas, noting similar struggles caused by colonialism. Mishuana Goeman points to the possibility of (re)mapping the territory of the Americas as Indigenous land.[13] My own work has focused on the hemispheric as an alternative to transnational analysis to decenter the colonial nation-state[14] and honor other spatial formations beyond methodological nationalisms to engage with a plurality of decolonial feminisms.[15] The hemispheric brings together distinct discussions on anti-racist placemaking while making historical connections between different racialized geographies and territories. As is evident, a hemispheric approach also allows for pending conversations and encounters, such as those proposed by discomfort feminisms within critical anglophone feminist geography that aim to bridge distinct feminist discussions across messy geographies.[16] Discomfort feminisms, from decolonial and anti-racist feminist geography perspectives, question the predominance of neoliberal feminist agendas found in "lean in" and "feel-good" feminisms and promote the need for discomfort, particularly within feminist discussions that deal with nationalism, capitalism, and imperialism.[17] One example of an encounter of discomfort feminism at the hemispheric scale is that between Latinx geographies and Latin American critical geography, where difficult questions about the relationship between these two strands of critical geography are developed.[18] The connections between Latinx and Latin American geographies are fraught with uncomfortable inquiries as to the lack of engagement with one another despite common struggles across the Americas. Often, encounters leading up to these discussions are the hardest part. In the case of bridging Latinx and Latin American feminist geographies, those of us who partook in this incipient conversation initially shared the different forms of rejection that we encountered in proposing creating these links. Both Latinx and Latin American feminist geographies are tightly woven spaces where the inclusion of the other is not prioritized. Those willing to have these conversations have experienced the need for them. Discomfort feminisms prioritized in feminist geography necessarily require alternative and imaginative geographies, such as the hemispheric scale, to carry out these encounters. Alternative imaginative geographies offer a place to connect the dots between racialized communities from a space outside colonial nation-state formations. Another example is illustrated by Madelaine Cahua's contributions to Latinx decolonial feminist geographies, which offer alternative geographies from the political and spatial experiences of Latinx peoples in Canada such as El Mundo Zurdo.[19] Cahuas has also mentioned that there would be no Latinx geographies without Black geographies, and the hemispheric is one more example of furthering the epistemic potential of relational anti-racist geographical thought and praxis.[20] Margaret Ramírez has also pointed to the potential of King's work for seeking other geographical imaginations that can make room for relational placemaking between Indigenous and Black struggles in the Americas.[21] In creating other geographical imaginations for relational anti-racist placemaking, such as the hemispheric, engagements between different racialized geographies occur. For example, Ramírez's reading of King's work highlights how King's theorizing of Blackness and Indigeneity speaks hemispherically, unsettling Latinx geographies in the process.[22] Relational anti-racist placemaking at the hemispheric scale prompts continuous interconnections between racialized geographies. Forbes mentions that throughout all the Americas, the right to name land from Indigenous languages and understandings of body-land connections was denied by colonial forms of modern governmentality.[23] The Land Back movement's emphasis on reparations of land and embodied understandings of land as forms of Indigenous self-determination could benefit from the strong links between racialized spaces at the hemispheric scale. My contribution to these discussions is the inclusion of Latin American decolonial feminist geographies to relational anti-racist placemaking that United States/Canada-based Black, Indigenous, and Latinx populations are already doing. Without the incorporation of discussion(s) outside the Global North and anglophone audiences, the hemispheric scale is severely hampered. The liberatory potentials of the hemispheric are only possible when dialogue and praxis occur *across all the Americas*. Incipient discussions between Latinx and Latin American decolonial feminist geographers can pave the way for what this looks like. When in relation to one another, Latinx and Latin American struggles have the ability to question the North-South binary across the Americas and advocate for a hemispheric approach. Critical geographical conversations between feminist, Black, Indigenous, Latinx, and Latin American geographies are possible and desired at the hemispheric scale.

As a scholar-activist writing and positioned in the Global South, I must flag that the hemispheric is not widely used as a politicized term within feminist, decolonial, and anti-racist academic and political praxis *in* Latin America. Other geographical imaginations are used to imply common struggles and praxis along all the Americas, such as Abya Yala, an alternative term to identify contemporary Latin America.[24] Abya Yala is a term used by the Kuna people in Panama and has been taken on by Latin American social movements as a decolonial alternative term to Latin America. In particular, Indigenous, decolonial, and communitarian feminisms have found a political and conceptual home in Abya Yala, where it has been defined as a utopian territory, a land in full maturity,[25] a counter geography,[26] and the geopolitical place for decolonial feminism stemming from Latin America.[27] However, we cannot assume that Abya Yala is equivalent to a hemispheric approach. The decolonial imaginary of Abya Yala, for example, as utilized by activist and research groups does not always include North America. Abya Yala has also been critiqued for not including a more explicit link with anti-racist placemaking, such as Lélia Gonzalez's term of Améfrica Ladina, which places Black struggle and territories at the heart of geographical understandings of Latin America.[28] There are important discrepancies as to what territories are included in Abya Yala. For some activist-scholars, Abya Yala includes all the Americas, and for others only Central and South America. I mention the existing tensions within decolonial geographical scholarship in the Americas because part of decolonizing geographical-knowledge construction is being transparent about the reach of its conceptual and political desires. This is also the case with respect to other concepts usually used in like-minded discussions, such as settler colonialism, which is interpreted differently across the hemisphere, as I explain below. Each context in the Americas prioritizes a particular way of understanding coloniality and spatial coloniality. In Latin America, the MCD (modernity, coloniality, and decoloniality) school of thought is still the most visible and prevalent colonial analytic. Settler colonialism is rarely used within Latin American activist research circles, in part because it is seen as a Northern colonial framework that can strengthen a North American gaze even when in dialogue with Indigenous and Black scholarship because it is written in English and mainly for Northern-based audiences. This is in line with how Indigenous and Black scholars in the North have also provided strong critiques of settler-colonial theory and how it reinforces the white gaze.[29] This is an important limitation for a hemispheric approach, in that different forms of understanding coloniality in place have direct consequences for underway decolonial praxis and relational anti-racist placemaking. And while I have made the case for settler colonialism along Latin American borderlands,[30] as well as applied the hemispheric perspective to decolonial embodiments of aquatic space (in a text written in

Spanish),[31] the continual use of certain decolonial terms must be decided by those who *live this space*.

In November 2021, I was invited along with other Latin American decolonial anti-racist feminist scholars such as Mara Viveros, Sayak Valencia, and Karina Ochoa to the University of Granada to dialogue with Spanish scholars around contemporary issues of gender and development in Latin America and Spain. None of the Latin American scholars presented on issues of development, as that term no longer represents a topic of importance for Latin American feminisms and because of the contemporary colonial implications of the term. Mara Viveros presented on the connections between United States, Brazilian, and Colombian Black feminisms; Karina Ochoa talked about the consequences of simultaneously being a Latin American decolonial feminist and a *mestiza* woman; and Sayak Valencia presented on the contemporary issues of femicide and decriminalization of abortion in Latin America. I presented part of my reflections on the hemispheric approach drawn out in this essay, as well as the relationship between Latinx and Latin American decolonial geographies with respect to the feminist debates of territory across the Americas. Europe was very much left out of these reflections, and as I gave the talk, I began to wonder how the hemispheric translates to Spain and other colonial powers. Many Global South scholars often must do translation (cultural and linguistic) when reentering global centers of knowledge production for our work to make sense in these contexts. We already do the work of translating theory produced in the Global North, and having our work make sense outside the Global South is deemed common practice. However, in this specific example, I didn't feel the all-too-common urge to figure out how to make the hemispheric approach sensible to my Spanish counterparts. They could figure out how to make sense of our discussions and what would be deemed relevant to them. Nevertheless, and to my surprise, there were many reactions to the hemispheric. The concluding remarks made by Spanish feminist scholars included the recognition of the need to move beyond the North-South binary and that the hemispheric approach aided in conceptual and methodological praxis for Latin diasporic dynamics in Europe, meaning that there is something to understanding difficult, uncomfortable relations across this geographical imaginary.

Despite not having common terminology across the Americas (and including Western Europe) on the hemispheric, what *is* apparent is the political praxis that is uniting common reflections on coloniality, anti-racisms, and intersectional feminisms. And one such space where this has become apparent is Reexistencias Cimarrunas, an Ecuador-based collective that came about in 2018 to bring together hemispheric reflections across the Americas concerning racism. It is one of the few collective spaces in Latin America that positions itself directly from a hemispheric scale. This collective unites Black and Indigenous struggles while developing relational understandings of racism. It is made up of Indigenous, Black, and *mestizo* scholar-activists pertaining to Black Lives Matter in the United States and Ecuadorian-based social movements such as Runa Feminista and the Critical Geography Collective of Ecuador. Members are from the United States, Brazil, Spain, Ecuador, and Colombia and came together given the dearth of collective reflections on racism in Ecuador. Explicit anti-racist praxis has been absent from social movements, and we sought to fill that gap while also providing grounded reflections on racism in Ecuador. Indigenous and ecological struggles have focused on limiting or doing away with extractive industry, while Indigenous struggles have centered on obtaining collective, political, and cultural rights. Reflections on ethnic tensions have been addressed through Indigenous and Black struggles for recognition under the Ecuadorian Constitution and local governmental structures. Anti-racist efforts and the questioning of structural forms of racism, such as environmental and racialized capitalism, are very recent affairs for Ecuadorian social movements that previously focused on capitalist and patriarchal frameworks sustained by the state.

In Ecuador, as in other parts of Latin America, interculturality—not multiculturalism—has been the framework for state-sponsored cultural coexistence. For the Reexistencias Cimarrunas Collective, relational understandings of racism and racist territorial formations have been key to making sense of interculturality. The main difference is that whereas multiculturalism depends on vertical understandings of majority and minority race relations, interculturality prompts horizontal relations where there is neither a majority nor a minority.[32] Multicultural neoliberalism in Ecuador is seen as relatively tolerant and participatory in the recognition of Indigenous peoples but not redistributive or implementing structural changes.[33] And while in actuality multicultural neoliberalism has defined how cultural coexistence really occurs in everyday life,[34] interculturality still is the political goal of interracial relations in Ecuador. It is embedded in the Ecuadorian Constitution and has been a hallmark of Indigenous struggles, particularly with respect to *buen vivir* and ethno-educational models.[35] Interculturality has had a direct effect on the type of critical race reflections the collective has prompted. The collective would meet twice a month and put together a reading list of texts in Spanish, English, and French from all over the Americas. The plan was to read, reflect, and then impact Ecuadorian society through visual, artistic, and cartographic material. We started off with readings and discussions on white privilege in the United States. The *mestizo* members of the collective wanted to provoke a discussion on *mestizo* privilege, like that of white privilege in the United States. The idea was to enumerate *mestizo* privileges, make a provocative poster, and place these all around the capital city of Quito. This idea was not accepted by the Black and Indigenous members of the collective, who wanted reflections stemming from relational race relations, meaning that the interconnections between relational race decolonial placemaking in Ecuador stems from understanding how racism occurs not in multicultural forms of cultural coexistence but from interculturality.[36] The co-construction of racialized geographies is understood not from hierarchical majority-minority race relations but from specific territorialized race relations. Territorialized race relations for the collective mean understanding that historical constructions of race are heavily influenced by place and complex social dynamics determined by capitalism and patriarchy. Drawing on the previous discussion on settler colonialism in Latin America in this essay, the type of coloniality in place addressed in specific territories is, in turn, crucial for understanding decolonial praxis. White and *mestizo* logics dominate public space and national territorial formations implicit in racialized capitalism and environmental racism. However, binary ideas of racism are sidelined, and relational race relations are embraced to understand how racism takes form from entangled histories of oppression.

One of the main objectives of the Reexistencias Cimarrunas Collective has been to translate both culturally and linguistically critical race theory at the hemispheric scale. We have chosen to use the term "hemispheric" because we can draw out the connections between different schools of coloniality and critical race theories across all the Americas. This is not necessarily possible with terms such as Abya Yala that denote a particular form of coloniality and specific geographies and are not necessarily tied directly to anti-racist thought and praxis. In line with wanting to honor the use of language and terminology by those who live colonized spaces, we have chosen the term "hemispheric" because we want to draw out the connections between places that have seemed separate. Being able to connect the dots between the coloniality of place and the construction of racism at the hemispheric scale for anti-racist praxis employed by the Reexistencias Cimarrunas Collective is key. Themes such as structural racism, racialized capitalism, and environmental racism are written in English and concerned with the American context a great deal. Martin Müller has recently written on linguistic privilege implicit in the dominance of English in geographical production where language is an important category of difference that sustains uneven epistemic landscapes.[37] Paradoxically, most of the critical race literature concerning the Americas or from a hemispheric scale is published and produced in the English language. In places like Ecuador, much of the literature in Spanish on Indigeneity has been written by *mestizo* scholars from disciplines such as anthropology, sociology, and ethnic studies. Meanwhile, Indigenous and Black scholars are largely absent from Ecuadorian universities. In this context, Indigenous feminist and Black feminist perspectives are taking a more central role in academic-activist *collective* spaces, such as the Reexistencias Cimarrunas Collective and others. Translocation, a feminist theory of translation across the Americas,[38] can be used to understand the processes of interpreting critical race theory across the Americas. In a recent investigation carried out by the Reexistencias Cimarrunas Collective and the Critical Geography Collective of Ecuador on the relationship between structural racism and COVID-19, we made use of the concepts of racialized capitalism and environmental racism. For our theoretical framework, there was no way around citing mostly English written texts. Hence, the process of translocation of critical race theory from the United States was paramount for our collective decolonial praxis.

~

Collective discussions, authorship, and reflections are key in assuring the decolonization of geographical-knowledge construction. Collectives across Latin America are autonomous political groups focused on a range of social issues and often engage activist research praxis. We decided to curate an anthology as a collective response and praxis to the dearth of literature in Spanish. Given the absence of theoretical anti-racist work and praxis in Ecuador, one of our first agreements was that this process be done in a collective manner. Under no circumstance would one person write about structural racism from an individual perspective or authorship. There is a clear link between the collective approach to decolonial anti-racist activism and knowledge construction and the territorialized race relations desired. Relational decolonial reflections on racism must be had among many racialized voices from a plurality of geographies and territories. In this way, the Reexistencias Cimarrunas Collective is unique. It is one of the few collectives in Latin America to position itself at the hemispheric scale and not solely from South and Central America or Abya Yala. Many collectives in Latin America wish to distance themselves from North American counterparts and the English language given the coloniality of power present in contemporary anglophone academia.[39] The transnational makeup of the collective prompts a different discussion from a particular place—the hemispheric. As a collective, we did not follow the path of our Latin American counterparts and distance ourselves from English but rather decided to do the complete opposite and directly engaged with Black feminist literature from North America. Positioned in the Global South, we recognized the absence of literature on racism within Ecuador and the inequalities that result in transcultural spaces of power for people who do not speak English.[40] To contribute to the absence of literature on the topic and to bridge the conceptual and linguistic gap between North and South, as a collective we published the first anthology on racism in Ecuador, written in Spanish. The anthology includes all forms of written and non-written text from individuals, communities, and collectives. As a collective, we asked Mara Viveros, an Afro-Colombian anthropologist and a leading voice on Black feminism in Latin America, to comment on the book in late 2021. She applauded our effort to publish from Black feminist thought and praxis but questioned our lack of engagement with the Colombian Pacific. In other words, she was asking us why we didn't look to our Latin American neighbors to further discuss Black feminist activism and instead dialogued with United States–based Black feminism. Following Viveros's comments, as a collective we have also questioned why our first engagement was with the work of Angela Davis and not Brazilian Black feminist scholars such as Lélia Gonzalez, Sueli Carneiro, Luiza Bairros, and Beatriz Nascimento, among others. In this sense, the hemispheric does not necessarily do away with structural inequalities and internal colonialisms but rather exposes them in proximity to one another. There is no right or wrong way to go about the hemispheric. Rather, we must be attentive to the flow of knowledge and praxis at this scale.

Aside from the collective's monthly meetings, we have held film forums and a reading group on the work of Angela Davis. One of the most prominent frameworks present in our publication is that of intersectionality and Black feminisms from the scale of the body, stemming from reflections made from our book club on the work of Angela Davis in Spanish.[41] Neighboring countries such as Colombia and Brazil have undergone similar pedagogical exercises in reading and inviting Angela Davis to their countries. During the COVID-19 pandemic, we also held several webinars on the intersections of anti-racism and intersectional feminism. One of the webinars focused on the relationship between *cuerpo-territorio* and racism with insights from Indigenous, Latinx, Latin-American, and Black activists, which I will draw from next.

Feminist Decolonization from Bodies, Land, and Territory

Decolonizing space demands a very particular relationship between bodies, land, and territory at the hemispheric scale. The work of various Indigenous, Black, Latinx, and

Latin American scholars in and around critical geography in the Americas is necessary to further make this point. Mishuana Goeman is key to understanding how across the Americas spatial decolonization directly involves embodied understandings of the land.[42] Meanwhile, the work of Guatemalan Indigenous feminist Lorena Cabnal on *cuerpo-territorio* brings forth an ontological understanding of bodies and territories focused on healing the colonial past in spatial terms.[43] Both proposals stem from Indigenous feminist interventions on colonial space from different places in the Americas. Though not in direct dialogue with one another, Goeman and Cabnal question colonial spatial formations from the scale of the body and an intimate relationship with territory (in the case of Latin America) and land (in the case of North America). By reading, citing, and thinking through these two proposals together, we can highlight the epistemic potentials of a hemispheric approach. These two Indigenous women illustrate the parallel calls for embodiment of territory and land across the Americas. The translation of land and territory across the Americas has been taken on by Brazilian critical geographer Rogerio Haesbaert, who has noted that land is to anglophone geography what territory is to Latin American critical geography.[44] Nevertheless, as Latinx and Black scholars have mentioned, Indigenous geographies and Black geographies cannot exist without one another.[45] The latter in particular further nuances our understanding of the connections between land and territory where anti-racist placemaking is at the center. In this vein, the work of Black scholars who engage with the hemispheric scale, such as Sharlene Mollett, is crucial to further relational anti-racist discussions and praxis.

Mollett's work further highlights the link between the struggles that Indigenous and Black communities face regarding land and territorial control in the Americas. For Mollett, political ecologies of race are hemispheric, relational, and intersectional. Moreover, race and coloniality relationally condition Indigenous and Black peoples' lives, and land control embodies intersectional forms of power.[46] This essay dialogues directly with Mollett's call for a hemispherical, relational, and intersectional understanding of race and coloniality in political ecology by making the link across the Americas on embodied territory. Until now, Indigenous feminist conceptions of the body, territory, community, and socionatures have been fundamental to contemporary discussions in Latin American political ecology.[47] However, other discussions, such as the link between Latin American Black feminism and political ecology, have been sidelined. This is one more example of how the hemispheric scale can connect parallel discussions and promote links that have yet to materialize.

The gendered violence inflicted on racialized colonial geographies includes Indigenous, Black, Latinx, and Latin American spaces. Creating decolonial hemispheric territorialities that question the colonial state implies engaging with new territorial concepts and ways of doing space. Bodies and embodiment are vehicles of plausible resistance and liberation. This follows Goeman's call for (re)mapping land where the body is at the center.[48] Leanne Betasamosake Simpson has powerfully stated that embodied knowledge systems exist in similar ways across Indigenous landscapes.[49] Sarah Hunt and Cindy Holmes have suggested we embody decolonial politics and practice these in our everyday lives as part of a decolonial queer praxis,[50] while Adam Barker and Jenny Pickerill have recently suggested that furthering decolonizing geography means placing emphasis on *doing* geography from the body. Doing as a praxis demonstrates how emotions, feelings, and intuition come into being with regards to land and sea.[51] *Doing from the body with other bodies, places, and objects, including the nonhuman,* is where *cuerpo-territorio* as decolonial feminist geographical method and concept stemming from Latin American debates on territory can be fruitful. *Cuerpo-territorio* is a distinct geographical and decolonial feminist method grounded in the ontological unity between bodies and territories.[52] *Cuerpo-territorio* is a central discussion in contemporary Latin American feminist political-ecology frameworks in which Indigenous feminist epistemologies are positioning the nonhuman in all the social sciences,[53] as well as promoting ideas on the sustainability of life from feminist and women's collectives in Abya Yala,[54] in relation to the reproduction of life and vital cycles.[55] *Cuerpo-territorio* has also been discussed within other spatial identities such as aquatic space, in particular the sea and rivers, resulting in ideas concerning water-body-territories.[56] Along with Martina Caretta, I have made the case of *cuerpo-territorio* as concept and method that can decolonize anglocentric feminist geographies.[57] As a method, territory is drawn on the body in individual and collective representations, reversing social-cartography methods that have tended to draw bodies on territories. *Cuerpo-territorio* method puts territory (including aquatic spaces) onto bodies, most often with regard to emotions. Emotions are what make territory on bodies palpable, and the *cuerpo-territorio* method illustrates this.[58] The body becomes the canvas that never parted from territory or land. In this way, *cuerpo-territorio* highlights the intimate relationship between territories in the Latin American context or land in the United States to racialized bodies through emotions. In this essay, I wish to take the *cuerpo-territorio* method and concept and highlight its potential to *do* decolonizing geographical-knowledge construction *in all the Americas*, particularly through land-based epistemologies. In a recent research report written with Lisset Coba, Mónica Maher, and Ivette Vallejo on the links between feminist political ecology with feminist geography, feminist theology, and feminist anthropology within the work of South American scholars and activists, one of our collective findings was the lack of a discussion with anti-racist efforts, meaning that Latin American ecofeminisms and political ecology seldom dialogue with Black feminism and anti-racist literature and praxis.[59] The hemispheric can shed light on Black scholars who are making these connections across the Americas, such as the work of Mollett.

Critical geography in the Americas has split racialized geographies into various subcategories (Black geographies, Indigenous geographies, Latinx geographies, and Latin American geographies). This explains in part why critical-geography praxis and reflection has fallen within the North-South divide and why Latinx and Latin American geographies seldom engage with one another. Moreover, when we situate our work within one racialized geography, the geographical reach of that body of work is not clear-cut. For example, unless we make it evident that we are speaking from a hemispheric scale, then most often our work will fall within the geographical space of the language we are writing from or where we are situated at that specific place and time. Our relationship to our work is then limited to static notions of where we are from, truncating the possibilities of mobile populations that belong to more than one racialized geography.[60] The hemispheric in this case allows for a multiplicity of connections across the Americas from decolonial geographies. This text is in line with Michelle Daigle and Margaret Ramírez's understanding that decolonial geographies are "a diverse and interconnected landscape grounded in the particularities of each place, starting with the Indigenous lands/waters/peoples from which a geography emerges, and the ways these places are simultaneously sculpted by radical traditions of resistance and liberation embodied by Black, Latinx, Asian and other racialised communities."[61] But what happens when one belongs (conceptually, linguistically, politically) to more than one racialized geography across the Americas? How are the intersections between racialized geographies developing from embodied positionalities? And what can we learn from prompting messy interactions among us as relational race relations would have us do? "[D]ecolonial geographies as constellations of co-resistance and liberation" powerfully define the possibilities of hemispheric relationship building through different processes of embodied knowledge.[62] Ramírez and Daigle build on Simpson's concepts of constellations of co-resistance that were, in turn, based on the work of Jarrett Martineau, Stefano Harney, and Fred Moten.[63] With foundational grounding in the work of Indigenous scholars, artists, and activists, we can turn to the constellations of the hemispheric as the conceptual doorway for understanding ourselves in relation to one another on an international scale. Simpson has theorized the internationalization of Indigenous notions of the nation to include the nonhuman (plant, animal, and spiritual) evident in Indigenous ethics that have always existed in Indigenous intellectual practices. Like the link between the hemispheric and the Americas, we can extend the hemispheric to Indigenous internationalism. Simpson further highlights how, despite being rooted in place, Indigenous existence has always been international and networked even with external beings and territories. Constellations are based on relationships and networks and not individual praxis or thought processes.[64] The relationship between *cuerpo-territorio* in the South and land-based epistemologies in the North is an example of constellations in formation as forms of Indigenous embodied knowledge.[65] The use of *cuerpo-territorio* by other racialized geographies seeking territorial forms of *reexistencia* has been highlighted by Latin American–based geographers and collectives.[66] Furthermore, geographers such as myself who belong to both Latinx and Latin American feminist geographies can move concepts such as *cuerpo-territorio* along the hemispheric from the scale of the body and link it to land-based epistemologies in the North. If there are to be conceptual and political advantages to human mobility across the Americas, then may it be to aid in the movement of politicized concepts and methods. This has already been occurring from different feminist collective spaces and geographers across the Americas. Most recently, reflections on *cuerpo-territorio* in Latin America have gone beyond a focus on gendered violence to include discussions of systemic and environmental racisms from North America.

The Hemispheric as a Constellation of Co-resistance and Liberation in Relational Anti-racist Placemaking

The Reexistencia Cimarrunas Collective held a series of webinars on structural racism during 2020 to promote multiple conversations on anti-racist praxis and thought from hemispheric perspectives. Black, Indigenous, and *mestizo* scholars and activists from Abya Yala participated in three online conversations on the following topics: (1) state-sponsored racism and genocidal politics; (2) *cuerpx-territorx* and racism in the Americas; and (3) whiteness and racism in Latin America. The first webinar on state-sponsored racism and genocidal politics focused on transnational reflections of the killing of George Floyd and Tony McDade by the Minneapolis and Tallahassee police, respectively. Links were made with the disproportionate representation of Afro-Ecuadorians in Ecuadorian prisons as well as the increase in criminalization against Black populations in Brazil during the COVID-19 pandemic. White supremacy was discussed as a common culprit and used not only for the United States context but also for the Latin American context. The latter is novel because *mestizaje* instead of white supremacy tends to dominate these discussions, and the discussions between white supremacy and *mestizaje* are often fraught with tensions. There are pending questions on how to think of whiteness in Latin America and, in particular, with regards to racialized territories.[67] Tensions arise because white supremacy and questions of whiteness are seen to be a Northern issue despite significant literature from Latin American decolonial feminist and Black scholars on the topic.[68] Finally, the webinar on *cuerpo-territorio* and anti-racism brought together two Indigenous feminist scholar-activists from Ecuador, an Afro-Latina activist from Peru and a Black trans activist from Ecuador. The use of *cuerpo-territorio* was highlighted by all the participants as a conceptual framework from which to honor their lived experiences as racialized, gendered bodies in racist geographies. The connection between *cuerpo-territorio* and environmental racisms and racial capitalism has so far been limited in Latin America.[69] Connecting embodied landscapes, territorial struggles, and anti-racist efforts is paramount for multiple reasons. First, *cuerpo-territorio* is directly related to autonomy. Autonomy of the state and state regulations and processes of recognition are akin to the conceptualizations of refusal of the colonial nation-state and its recognition policies in Northern contexts.[70] Creating, fostering, and prioritizing the relationship between body and territory is fundamental to feminist ideas and politics of autonomy that have long been important in Latin American decolonial feminisms.[71] Furthering this point, *cuerpo-territorio* strengthens self-determination and corporeal sovereignty in gendered and racialized ways. *Cuerpo-territorio* allows for racialized, gendered bodies to define themselves in relation to their territory or land and in their own terms. This is crucial for racialized bodies across all the Americas that have experienced common forms of territorialized colonial violence, particularly with regard to extractive industry. Prioritizing the body through its relationship to territory lets us decide who we are and how we want to create space in our territories and land. This is a decolonial praxis in geographical-knowledge construction. It is a way toward attaining Goeman's call for spatial justice[72] through the embodiment of land and Cabnal's praxis of the healing of territory through the healing of our bodies.

Conclusions

Who seeks the hemispheric? What becomes possible by linking embodied territories and anti-racist efforts from this scale? And finally, what can the Land Back movement gain from a hemispheric perspective? The reflections in this essay have attempted to respond to these questions for scholars and activists across the Americas. This implies that I am speaking simultaneously to both Northern and Southern scholars and activists, and particularly to those who are seeking the links in-between and attempting to connect the dots. The hemispheric scale has been used mainly by Black, Indigenous, and Latinx scholars in the North, with much more limited engagement in the South.[73] By bringing the example and reflections stemming from the Reexistencia Cimarrunas Collective, a transnational anti-racist collective that speaks from the hemispheric scale, I have longed to bridge this gap in the Americas. In doing so, I hope to not have idealized, sustained, and constant relationships across the Americas, for I and others believe the hemispheric allows for a place to have difficult conversations, such as those between Latinx and Latin American geographies within discomfort feminisms.[74]

Relational anti-racist placemaking at the hemispheric scale needs continuous interconnections between racialized geographies. The constellations of co-resistance[75] and Indigenous internationalism[76] already in place in the Northern hemisphere are highlighting our interconnectedness. The similarities found in the embodiment of territory in the North and South become important for human and nonhuman connections that are nomadic or constantly on the move. *Cuerpo-territorio* as a concept and method, for example, is starting to be used in many places outside the Global South and in relation to environmental racism and racialized capitalism. Nevertheless, important questions remain, such as how do we explain a more overt interest from North America toward South and Central America in developing the hemispheric and not the other way around? One of the motivating forces to develop this essay has been to unsettle the Northern gaze on the hemispheric scale by showing that collective activist actions in the South are developing embodied anti-racist critiques alongside and connected to the North. Meanwhile, my interest is also in disrupting collective action and thought in Latin America that tend to reside in essentialist understandings of the North, often ignoring the Latinx diaspora and any connection with anti-racist efforts beyond Latin America. In sum, there are important limitations in collective thinking and praxis in Latin America that would highly benefit from a hemispheric approach, while the North simply cannot position the hemispheric without asking itself if the hemisphere is used in the South. Mutual curiosity across space is a necessity in this process and for sustaining this decolonial imaginary.

The hemipheric scale can give the Land Back movement a global place from which to further the liberation of Black, Indigenous, and other racialized communities. The connections between racialized peoples from this proposed place put emphasis on the multiplicity of relationships between body, land, and territory that already exist between Turtle Island and Abya Yala. The hemispheric scale is not completely novel to Indigenous futurity, as the key work of Jack Forbes and others has shown; what is apparent is a recent move toward putting the relationships between land-body-territory at the center of this proposed scale. The connection between land-body-territory from anti-racist, feminist, and decolonial geographies puts the embodiment of space at the core and in that way furthers Indigenous epistemological and political collective liberation.

NOTES

1 Juliet Hooker, *Theorizing Race in the Americas: Douglass, Sarmiento, Du Bois, and Vasconcelos* (New York: Oxford University Press, 2017), 1–15; Adam Bledsoe, "Marronage as a Past and Present Geography in the Americas," *Southeastern Geographer* 57, no. 1 (2017): 30–50; Tiffany Lethabo King, *The Black Shoals: Offshore Formations of Black and Native Studies* (Durham, N.C.: Duke University Press, 2019), 25–35; Sharlene Mollett, "Hemispheric, Relational, and Intersectional Political Ecologies of Race: Centring Land-Body Entanglements in the Americas," *Antipode* 53, no. 3 (2021): 810–30; Margaret Marietta Ramírez, review of *The Black Shoals: Offshore Formations of Black and Natives Studies*, by Tiffany Lethabo King, *Society & Space*, https://www.societyandspace.org/articles/a-review-of-the-black-shoals-offshore-formations-of-black-and-native-studies-by-tiffany-lethabo-king-2; Sofia Zaragocin, "Espacios acuáticos desde una descolonialidad hemisférica feminista," *Mulier sapiens* 10 (2018): 6–19; Sofia Zaragocin, "Decolonial Feminist Geography," *Geopauta* 4, no. 4 (2020): 18–30; Eloisa Berman-Arévalo, "Geografías Negras del arroz en el Caribe Colombiano: *Tongueo* y cuerpo territorio 'en las grietas' de la modernización agrícola," *Latin American and Caribbean Ethnic Studies* 18, no. 3 (2023): 437–55; and Ana Laura Zavala Guillen, "Afro-Latin American Geographies of In-betweeness: Colonial Marronage in Colombia," *Journal of Historical Geography* 72 (2021): 13–22.

2 Lorena Cabnal, "Acercamiento a la construcción de la propuesta de pensamiento epistémico de las mujeres indígenas feministas comunitarias de Abya Yala," in *Feminismos diversos: El feminismo comunitario*, ed. ACSUR (Las Segovias: ACSUR, 2010), 11–25, and Lorena Cabnal, "Tzk'at, red de sanadoras ancestrales del feminismo comunitario desde Iximulew-Guatemala," *Ecología política*, no. 54 (2017): 98–102.

3 King, *The Black Shoals*, 25–35.

4 Jack D. Forbes, "The Use of Racial and Ethnic Terms in America: Management by Manipulation," *Wicazo Sa Review* 11, no. 2 (1995): 53–65; and Mishuana Goeman, *Mark My Words: Native Women Mapping Our Nations* (Minneapolis: University of Minnesota Press, 2013), 45–56.

5 Bledsoe, "Marronage as a Past and Present Geography in the Americas." While Bledsoe focuses on maroon communities in all the Americas and at a hemispheric scale, he specifically analyzes Brazil and the United States.

6 Forbes, "The Use of Racial and Ethnic Terms in America."

7 Hooker, *Theorizing Race in the Americas*, 1–20.

8 Juliet Hooker, introduction to *Black and Indigenous Resistance in the Americas: From Multiculturalism to Racist Backlash; A Project of the Antiracist Research and Action Network (RAIAR)*, ed. Juliet Hooker, trans. Giorleny Altamirano Rayo, Aileen Ford, and Steven Lownes (Lanham, Md.: Lexington Books, 2020), 1–20.

9 Bledsoe, "Marronage as a Past and Present Geography in the Americas."

10 Berman-Arévalo, "Geografías Negras del arroz en el Caribe Colombiano."

11 King, *The Black Shoals*, 1–20.

12 Mollett, "Hemispheric, Relational, and Intersectional Political Ecologies of Race."

13 Goeman, *Mark My Words*, 25–35.

14 This is very much a context-specific debate. Key reflections on the different scales of the transnational (global) and intersectional (domestic) have been developed by women of color in the United States and beyond; see Sylvanna M. Falcón and Jennifer C. Nash, "Shifting Analytics and Linking Theories: A Conversation about the 'Meaning-Making' of Intersectionality and Transnational Feminism," *Women's Studies International Forum* 50 (2015): 1–10.

15 Zaragocin, "Decolonial Feminist Geography."

16 Banu Gökarıskel, Michael Hawkins, Christopher Neubert, and Sara Smith, introduction to *Feminist Geography Unbound: Discomfort, Bodies, and Prefigured Futures*, ed. Banu Gökarıskel, Michael Hawkins, Christopher Neubert, and Sara Smith (Morgantown: West Virginia University Press, 2021), 1–24.

17 Gökariskel, Hawkins, Neubert, and Smith, introduction to *Feminist Geography Unbound*.

18 Ramírez, review of *The Black Shoals*; and Sofia Zaragocin, "Challenging Anglocentric Feminist Geography from Latin American Feminist Debates on Territoriality," in *Feminist Geography Unbound: Discomfort, Bodies, and Prefigured Futures*, ed. Banu Gkarıskel, Michael Hawkins, Christopher Neubert, and Sara Smith (Morgantown: West Virginia University Press, 2021), 235–52.

19 Madelaine C. Cahuas, "Reaching for El Mundo Zurdo: Imagining-Creating-Living Latinx Decolonial Feminist Geographies in Toronto," *Gender, Place & Culture* 28, no. 9 (2021): 1213–33.

20 Madelaine C. Cahuas, "Interrogating Absences in Latinx Theory and Placing Blackness in Latinx Geographical Thought: A Critical Reflection," *Society & Space*, 2019, www.societyandspace.org/articles/interrogating-absences-in-latinx-theory-and-placing-blackness-in-latinx-geographical-thought-a-critical-reflection.
21 Sofía Zaragocin, Margaret Marietta Ramírez, Maria Alexandra García, and Yolanda González Mendoza, "LatinX and Latin American Geographies: A Dialogue / Diálogo entre las geografías LatinX y latinoamericanas," *Antipode Online*, https://antipodeonline.org/2022/08/08/latinx-and-latin-american-geographies/.
22 Ramírez, review of *The Black Shoals*.
23 Forbes, "The Use of Racial and Ethnic Terms in America."
24 Elsa Ivette Jiménez Valdez, "Disputa por los cuerpos territorios en Abya Yala: De zonas de sacrificio a espacios de sanación," *Geopauta* 4, no. 4 (2020): 68–92, and Márcia Maria Tait Lima and Renata Moreno, "Emergencias ecofeministas en la praxis latinoamericanas," *Ecología política*, no. 61 (2021): 16–20.
25 Almudena Cabezas González, "Mujeres Indígenas constructoras de región: Desde América Latina hasta Abya Yala," *Scientific Journal of Humanistic Studies* 4, no. 6 (2012): 12–34.
26 Paola Castaño, "América Latina y la producción transnacional de sus imágenes y representaciones: Algunas perspectivas preliminares," in *Cultura y transformaciones sociales en tiempos de globalización: Perspectivas latinoamericanas*, ed. Daniel Mato and Alejandro Maldonado Fermín (Buenos Aires: CLACSO, 2007), 231–32.
27 Yuderkys Espinosa Miñoso, Diana Gómez Correal, and Karina Ochoa Muñoz, eds., introduction to *Tejiendo de otro modo: Feminismo, epistemología y apuestas descoloniales en Abya Yala* (Popayán: Editorial Universidad del Cauca, 2014), 18–31.
28 Diana Gómez Correal, "Améfrica Ladina, Abya Yala y Nuestra América: Tejiendo esperanzas realistas," *LASA Forum* 53, no. 3 (2019): 55–59.
29 King, *The Black Shoals*, 1–20.
30 Sofia Zaragocin, "Gendered Geographies of Elimination: Decolonial Feminist Geographies in Latin American Settler Contexts," *Antipode* 51, no. 1 (2019): 373–92.
31 Zaragocin, "Espacios acuáticos desde una descolonialidad hemisférica feminista," 6–19.
32 Catherine Walsh, *Interculturalidad, estado, sociedad: Luchas (de)coloniales de nuestra época* (Quito: Universidad Andina Simón Bolivar, 2009), 69–79.
33 Carmen Martínez Novo, "El desmantelamiento del estado multicultural en el Ecuador," *Ecuador debate* 98 (2016): 35–50.
34 Charles R. Hale, "Neoliberal Multiculturalism: The Remaking of Cultural Rights and Racial Dominance in Central America," *Political and Legal Anthropology Review* 28, no. 1 (May 2005): 10–28.
35 Catherine Walsh, "Etnoeducación e interculturalidad en perspectiva decolonial" (presentation, Cuarto Seminario Internacional Etnoeducación e Interculturalidad: Perspectivas Afrodescendientes, Lima, Peru, September 7, 2011), 1–14, https://yessicr.files.wordpress.com/2013/03/walsh-etnoed-e-interculturalidaddecolonial.pdf.
36 Rose Barboza and Sofia Zaragocin, eds., introduction to *Racismos en Ecuador: Reflexiones y experiencias interseccionales* (Quito: Friedrich-Ebert-Stiftung Ecuador, 2021), 1–18.
37 Martin Müller, "Worlding Geography: From Linguistic Privilege to Decolonial Anywheres," *Progress in Human Geography* 45, no. 6 (2021): 1440–66.
38 Sonia E. Alvarez, "Introduction to the Project and the Volume/Enacting a Translocal Feminist Politics of Translation," in *Translocalities/Translocalidades: Feminist Politics of Translation in the Latin/a Américas*, ed. Sonia E. Alvarez, Claudia de Lima Costa, Verónica Feliu, Rebecca Hester, Norma Klahn, and Millie Thayer (Durham, N.C.: Duke University Press, 2014), 1–18.
39 Aníbal Quijano, "Coloniality of Power, Eurocentrism, and Latin America," *Nepantla: Views from South* 1, no. 3 (2000): 533–80.
40 Sávio Siqueira, "Inglês como língua franca não é zona neutra, é zona transcultural de poder: Por uma descolonização de concepções, práticas e atitudes," *Línguas & letras* 19, no. 44 (2018): 93–113.
41 Rose Barboza, "Haciendo cuerpe en el problema: Testimonio colectivizado de una subjetivación negra en permanente desplazamiento," in *Racismos en Ecuador: Reflexiones y experiencias interseccionales*, ed. Rose Barboza and Sofia Zaragocin (Quito: Friedrich-Ebert-Stiftung Ecuador, 2021), 221–25.
42 Goeman, *Mark My Words*.

43 Cabnal, "Acercamiento a la construcción de la propuesta de pensamiento epistémico de las mujeres indígenas feministas comunitarias de Abya Yala," 11–25; and Cabnal, "Tzk'at," 98–102.

44 Rogerio Haesbaert, "Del cuerpo-territorio al territorio-cuerpo (de la Tierra): Contribuciones decoloniales," *Cultura y representaciones sociales* 15, no. 29 (2020): 267–301.

45 Cahuas, "Interrogating Absences in Latinx Theory and Placing Blackness in Latinx Geographical Thought," 1–7; and Ramírez, review of *The Black Shoals*.

46 Mollett, "Hemispheric, Relational, and Intersectional Political Ecologies of Race," 1–21.

47 Melissa Moreano and Diana Vela-Almeida, "El lugar de la ecología política dentro de la geografía latinoamericana: El caso de CLAG," *Journal of Latin American Geography* 19, no. 1 (January 2020): 74–83.

48 Goeman, *Mark My Words*, 25–35.

49 Leanne Betasamosake Simpson, *As We Have Always Done: Indigenous Freedom through Radical Resistance* (Minneapolis: University of Minnesota Press, 2017), 191–210.

50 Sarah Hunt and Cindy Holmes, "Everyday Decolonization: Living a Decolonizing Queer Politics," *Journal of Lesbian Studies* 19, no. 2 (2015): 154–72.

51 Adam J. Barker and Jenny Pickerill, "Doings with the Land and Sea: Decolonising Geographies, Indigeneity, and Enacting Place-Agency," *Progress in Human Geography* 44, no. 4 (2020): 640–62.

52 Geobrujas, "Subvertir la cartografía para la liberación," *Revista de la Universidad de México*, July 2018, https://www.revistadelauniversidad.mx/articles/21a6cb3c-d651-45cd-b8e6-49d3c46b2390/subvertir-la-cartografia-para-la-liberacion; Geobrujas, "Cuerpos, fronteras y resistencia: Mujeres conjurando geografía a través de experiencias desde el otro lado del muro," *Journal of Latin American Geography* 20, no. 2 (June 2021): 156–67; Sofia Zaragocin and Martina Angela Caretta, "*Cuerpo-territorio*: A Decolonial Feminist Geographical Method for the Study of Embodiment," *Annals of the American Association of Geographers* 111, no. 5 (2021): 1503–18; Haesbaert, "Del cuerpo-territorio al territorio-cuerpo," 267–301; Astrid Ulloa, "Repolitizar la vida, defender los cuerpos-territorios y colectivizar las acciones desde los feminismos indígenas," *Ecología política*, no. 61 (2021): 38–48; and Giulia Marchese, "Del cuerpo en el territorio al cuerpo-territorio: Elementos para una genealogía feminista Latinoamericana de la crítica a la violencia," *EntreDiversidades* 6, no. 2 (July–December 2019): 9–41.

53 Ulloa, "Repolitizar la vida," 38–48.

54 Tait Lima and Moreno, "Emergencias ecofeministas en la praxis latinoamericanas," 16–20.

55 Lidia Blásquez Martínez, "Ecofrontera: Análisis ecofeminista de los espacios intersticiales como cuerpos-territorios," *Ecología política*, no. 61 (2021): 22–29; and Marchese, "Del cuerpo en el territorio al cuerpo-territorio."

56 Fany Lobos Castro, "Agua-cuerpo-territorio: Las cicatrices y reexistencias de las mujeres rurales en el Maule Sur precordillerano de Chile," *Ecología política*, no. 61 (2021): 112–16; Paola Bolados García, Fabiola Henríquez Olguín, Cristian Ceruti Mahn, and Alejandra Sánchez Cuevas, "La eco-geo-política del agua: Una propuesta desde los territorios en las luchas por la recuperación del agua en la provincia de Petorca (Zona central de Chile)," *Revista rupturas* 8, no. 1 (January–June 2018): 167–99; and Zaragocin, "Espacios acuáticos desde una descolonialidad hemisférica feminista."

57 Zaragocin and Caretta, "*Cuerpo-territorio*."

58 Geobrujas, "Subvertir la cartografía para la liberación"; and Geobrujas, "Cuerpos, fronteras y resistencia."

59 Lisset Coba, Mónica Maher, Sofía Zaragocín, and Ivette Vallejo, "Indisciplinas e interdisciplinas: Diálogos cruzados sobre feminismos y ecologías desde una perspectiva descolonial y comunitaria," in *Feminismo y ambiente: Un campo emergente en los estudios feministas de América Latina y el Caribe*, ed. Karen Lorena Romero Leal et al. (Buenos Aires: CLACSO, 2021), 48–69.

60 Manuel Bayón Jiménez, Karolien Van Teijlingen, Soledad Álvarez Velasco, and Melissa Moreano Venegas, "Cuando los sujetos se mueven de su lugar: Una interrogación al extractivismo y la movilidad en la ecología política latinoamericana," *Revista de geografía Norte Grande* 80 (2021): 103–27.

61 Michelle Daigle and Margaret Marietta Ramírez, "Decolonial Geographies," in *Keywords in Radical Geography: Antipode at 50*, ed. Tariq Jazeel et al. (Hoboken, N.J.: Wiley Blackwell, 2019), 78.

62 Daigle and Ramírez, "Decolonial Geographies," 79.

63 Jarrett Martineau, "Creative Combat: Indigenous Art, Resurgence, and Decolonization" (PhD diss., University of Victoria, 2015); and Stefano Harney and Fred Moten, *The Undercommons: Fugitive Planning & Black Study* (Wivenhoe: Minor Compositions, 2013).

64 Simpson, *As We Have Always Done*, 211–32.

65 Daigle and Ramírez, "Decolonial Geographies," 81–82.
66 Barboza and Zaragocín, *Racismos en Ecuador*.
67 Barboza and Zaragocín, introduction to *Racismos en Ecuador*, 1–18.
68 María Teresa Garzón Martínez, "Oxímoron: Blanquitud y feminismo descolonial en Abya Yala," *Descentrada* 2, no. 2 (September 2018); Diogo Marçal Cirqueira, Geny Ferreira Guimarães, and Lorena Francisco de Souza, "Introdução do caderno temático 'Geografias Negras,'" in "Geografias Negras," ed. Diogo Marçal Cirqueira, Geny Ferreira Guimarães, and Lorena Francisco de Souza, special issue, *Revista da ABPN* 12 (April 2020): 3–11; and Mara Viveros Vigoya, "Género, raza y nación: Los réditos políticos de la masculinidad blanca en Colombia," *Maguaré* 27, no. 1 (January–June 2013): 71–104.
69 Berman-Arévalo, "Geografías Negras del arroz en el Caribe Colombiano."
70 Audra Simpson, *Mohawk Interruptus: Political Life Across the Borders of Settler States* (Durham, N.C.: Duke University Press, 2014).
71 Espinosa Miñoso, Gómez Correal, and Ochoa Muñoz, introduction to *Tejiendo de otro modo*.
72 Goeman, *Mark My Words*.
73 Exceptions include Berman-Arévalo, "Geografías Negras del arroz en el Caribe Colombiano," and Zaragocin, "Decolonial Feminist Geography."
74 Zaragocin, "Challenging Anglocentric Feminist Geography from Latin American Feminist Debates on Territoriality"; and Ramírez, review of *The Black Shoals*.
75 Daigle and Ramírez, "Decolonial Geographies"; and Simpson, *As We Have Always Done*, 55–70.
76 Simpson, *As We Have Always Done*, 55–70.

2

Landscapes of Struggle

Katarista Perspectives on the Environment in Bolivia, 1960–1990

OLIVIA ARIGHO-STILES

We the Aymara, Qhechwa, Camba, Chapaco, Chiquitano, Moxo, Tupiguarani and other *campesinos* are the rightful owners of this land. We are the seed from which Bolivia was born, and we are exiles in our own land. We want to regain our liberty of which we were deprived in 1492, to bring our culture back into favor and, with our own personality, be subjects and not objects of our history....[1]

Qhiparu nayraru uñtas sartañani
   (Looking back, we will move forward)

—Aymara proverb

The rise of Indigenous political movements in Latin America in the 1990s has been closely linked with an environmental agenda.[2] This is especially noticeable in Bolivia, where a strong connection between international stances on climate change and the highly successful "Indigenous politics" of former president Evo Morales clearly exists. In the Morales era, *buen vivir* (*suma qamaña* in Aymara), or living well in harmony with nature, became an abiding principle of the Bolivian state, at least at a discursive level.[3] While there has been great attention devoted to contemporary Indigenous struggles against ecological and social harms generated by extractive projects,[4] there is a dearth of works tracing back the genealogy of the twenty-first-century "Indigenous awakening" and its attendant environmentalist agenda beyond the 1990s. The existing scholarship on Bolivia fails to historicize the evolving purpose and importance of nature and environment in Indigenous and peasant social movements. Beyond Bolivia, however, exceptions to this exist. In the Brazilian case, environmental historian Oscar de la Torre offers a compelling study of the political subjectivities of Afro-Brazilian peasants in nineteenth-century Amazonia ("sons of the river") that formed in parallel with their ecological traditions.[5] Elsewhere, in the context of protests against the Dakota Access Pipeline (DAPL) in the United States in 2016, historian Nick Estes has documented the history of Indigenous resistance to environmental projects in the United States, framing the struggle within settler-colonial processes that have nefariously impacted both human and other-than-human ways of life over time.[6]

In this essay, I focus on the organized politics of the *katarista* movement in the period from 1960 to 1990, that is to say, the political groups and *campesino* (peasant) organizations of highland Bolivia that devoted themselves to decolonial struggle by invoking the memory of eighteenth-century Andean leader Tupaj Katari. Excavating the long history of land dispossession and Indigenous insurrection in the Andes, *kataristas* sought to recover histories and epistemologies that subvert the Bolivian nation-state.[7] In symbolic terms, this was reflected in the recovery of Tupaj Katari as an anti-colonial figurehead. When Tupaj Katari was executed by the Spanish on November 15, 1781, after leading a rebellion against Spanish rule, his body was dismembered into four parts and scattered. Oral tradition holds that Katari's dying words were, "'Nayawa jiwtxa, nayjarusti waranqa waranqaranakawa kutanïpxa—I die, but I shall return tomorrow as thousands and thousands.'"[8]

Katarismo was multifarious and far from monolithic. The label offers a capacious umbrella for syndicalist, ethno-nationalist, and autonomist currents broadly aimed at the revindication of the Indian and the end to class-based exploitation and racialized oppression. Although I focus on the political currents of the movement rooted in party politics, I include reference to the peasant union confederation, the Confederación Sindical Única de Trabajadores Campesinos de Bolivia (CSUTCB), as the syndical expression of *katarismo*. Anthropologist Xavier Albó argues that the *katarista* perspective can be captured in the theory of the *dos ojos* (two eyes), that is to say, a recognition of the dialectic of class exploitation as peasants, along with all the exploited classes, and as racially oppressed peoples, along with all the oppressed nations of the country.[9] The political currents of *katarismo* crystallized principally in two parties: the Movimiento Revolucionario Tupaj Katari (MRTK) and the Movimiento Indio Tupaj Katari (MITKA). In its political manifestations from the late 1970s, *katarismo* can be broadly characterized as having radical and moderate camps. These diverged in their willingness to operate in coalition with non-Indigenous leftist parties, as well as in their more fundamental understanding of the relationship between ethnicity and class in political struggle.[10]

I locate *katarismo* as a turning point in the new articulation of Indigenous ecological identities at the political level in twentieth-century Bolivia. I argue that in *katarista* discourse debates over natural resources reflected visions about how the economy and society should be arranged, which departed from the singular focus on resource nationalism of earlier decades. It is evident that *kataristas* were acutely aware of the ecological facets of imperialism and the environment's importance within Indigenous identities. It marked the first time that a self-consciously Indigenous vision of natural resources, and the natural world more broadly, was articulated at the political level. The findings in this essay hence provide an important and timely addition to scholarship on the varied ways Indigenous *campesino* peoples have mobilized around ecology and the natural world in twentieth-century decolonial struggles. I begin by setting out the methodological approach adopted in this essay. I then provide an overview of the literature surrounding this topic before presenting my main findings.

Defining Terms

It is important to be clear on how I deploy the terms "Indigenous" and "Indian" in this essay. Language within historic Latin American discourses on race and ethnicity is notoriously difficult to unpack given that racial categories such as Indian and Indigenous, as well as Black, have changed over time and have varied in meaning according to territorial and legal context. As I discuss later, these definitions are connected with the politics of Indigeneity that emerged in the twentieth century. *Indio*, or Indian, is the colonial term; *indígena* began to be used in Bolivia in Simon Bolívar's early nineteenth-century decrees.[11] In the 1881 La Paz census in Bolivia, occupations and geographical locality were indices of race. To be a rural laborer, for example, meant one was ipso facto an Indian.[12] A law was later passed in 1921 that defined an Indian as a person from the "aymara, quechua, or guarani race" who lived in the countryside or worked the land. However, the 1950 census in Bolivia took the speaking of Native languages as the indicator of Indianness.[13] In marked contrast, in the 2001 census, Indigeneity was recorded through self-definition alone, allowing participants to assert their own preferred identities. Laura Gotkowitz locates the 1940s as a turning point in how debates around who was an Indian and who could speak for Indians were articulated in Bolivia. In 1945, as the regime of Gualberto Villarroel tried to win favor with *campesinos*, the first Indigenous Congress took place in Bolivia following similar congresses held in Ecuador and Peru. Shortly after this, prominent Movimiento Nacionalista Revolucionario (MNR) politician Hernán Siles Zuazo proposed a measure by which to establish Indigenous juries to conduct oral trials in Native languages. Siles used the terms *indio* and *indígena* interchangeably in order to refer to "the man who works . . . and lives in the countryside."[14] However, the measure was ultimately unsuccessful because the political elites and the Indigenous movement itself could not decide for whom the measure was intended: "Indians? Peasants? Indigenous peasants? The indigenous race? Indian and mestizo peasants? A race, or a class? The National Congress could not agree on terms."[15]

Whereas the term "Indigenous" is now positively associated with an emancipatory human rights agenda, "Indian" is conversely burdened by tainted histories of exclusion and exploitation linked to colonial and neocolonial paradigms. As anthropologist Andrew Canessa observes, "*Indigenous* appears as a much more neutral descriptor and erases the power relations that are inescapable when talking about indians."[16] Indian is often used by historical protagonists—and indeed in contemporary Bolivia—as an evocative political term that conjures the centuries-long and ongoing struggle against colonial oppression. The pioneering *indianista* Fausto Reinaga defiantly used the term *indio* as part of an emancipatory vision of Indian struggle, proclaiming that "the Indian is not a social class, s/he is a race, a Nation, a history, a culture. The Indian is an oppressed and enslaved people. The Indian does not have to integrate or assimilate to anyone. The Indian has to free himself. And the liberation of the Indian will be the work of the Indian himself."[17]

Other terms still in use during the twentieth century include *indígena originario* and *indígena contribuyente*. These terms are important because they have both racial and fiscal implications, as historically only Indians contributed tribute (tax) to the state.[18] They also denote differences in land ownership; the term *originario* came to refer to Indigenous community members who possessed more sizable plots of land, for example.[19] By the twenty-first century, this distinction was largely nullified, and *pueblos originarios* is generally used interchangeably with *pueblos indígenas* in political discourse. In the 1970s, the *kataristas* and the *campesino* movement more commonly referred to themselves in parallel as *campesinos* and through the language of their nation (i.e., Aymaras, Quechuas, etc.), although the term *pueblos indígenas*, or Indigenous peoples, was widely used. It is for this reason I use both Indigenous and *campesino* interchangeably, in recognition of their use in the same way by historical actors. In the twenty-first century, *indígena originario campesino* (Indigenous-originary-peasant) was the tripartite term incorporating elements of class, race, history, and identity adopted by the state in the 2009 Plurinational Constitution.

Methods

The findings in this essay derive from an interdisciplinary doctoral project exploring the connections between radical Indigenous politics and the environment in twentieth-century Bolivia. As an intellectual movement that straddles rural and urban worlds, *katarismo* offers a rare lens through which historians can understand the unfolding politics of indigeneity in the Andes from the perspective of the Indigenous actors themselves. In this essay, I draw on *katarista* pamphlets, periodicals, and publications in the Spanish language, mainly *El katarismo, Boletín Chitakolla,* and *Collasuyo.* I also make extensive use of pamphlets, published interviews, and documents from the *katarista* movement throughout the 1970s and 1980s derived from archival research in the Archivo y Biblioteca Nacionales de Bolivia (ABNB) in Sucre as well as from public collections located in the Senate House Library, London, and the Bodleian Library, Oxford, in the United Kingdom. These include documents published by the CSUTCB, as well as nongovernmental organizations. For material relating to agrarian reform, I made use of papers in the Walter Guevara Arze archive at the ABNB as well as newspapers from the period. I also assess audio recordings of CSUTCB national and regional congresses between 1984 and 1989, housed in the Museo Nacional de Etnografía y Folklore (MUSEF) in La Paz, Bolivia.

Conceptual Framework

This essay draws on decolonial and post-development scholarship as a theoretical underpinning. Decolonial thinkers such as Aníbal Quijano have intimated that the question of Indigenous movements is tied up with the historical structuring of Latin American states along a racial axis of colonial origin.[20] As Latin America's postindependence states came into being in the early nineteenth century, their architects were confronted with the problem of Indigenous peoples who had been designated as "inferior races" under colonial

FIGURE 2.1 Family harvesting potatoes in west La Paz Department, ca. 1934–1969. American Geographical Society Library, University of Wisconsin, Milwaukee.

rule. Indigenous peoples could not be incorporated into the new states *as Indigenous peoples* because this category was antithetical to citizenship of new political systems still tied to this colonial matrix of power.[21] At the same time, post-development theorists have emphasized how the political struggles of peasant and Indigenous groups relate not only to rights of natural resources and territories but to ways of being and knowing,[22] echoing the Foucauldian theory of subjugated knowledges.[23] This literature points out that while colonial regimes in Latin America pursued the exploitative appropriation of nature, they also marginalized Indigenous knowledge systems in an intertwined process. Capitalism—and colonialism as its constitutive force—entails both epistemic and economic dimensions, as Boaventura de Sousa Santos elucidates in the "epistemologies of the south" concept,[24] requiring the suppression of non-Western understandings of relating to land and ways of living. The rapacious exploitation of nature in pursuit of market-driven economic growth is linked intimately with the separation of nature from human society embedded within Western paradigms. The ecological conflicts waged by Indigenous *campesino* movements therefore acquire an important epistemological dimension because they challenge the erasure of Indigenous knowledge systems from state discourses on the environment.[25]

This essay also draws on the extensive anthropological literature that documents human relations with the other-than-human in the Americas. A core component of this has been the problematization of the nature/culture antithesis.[26] The anthropological canon has long recorded the far-reaching relations with the natural world held by Indigenous peoples across the Americas.[27] For example, as José Teijeiro Villarroel argues, "For the Aymara, nature is part of themselves, that is, the communion between nature and man becomes the synthesis of life."[28] In her work with the Páez peoples of the Colombian Andes, historical anthropologist Joanne Rappaport deploys the concept of "sacred geographies" to describe how histories of struggle are encoded within the landscape of their territory.[29] Elsewhere, anthro-linguistic approaches to the Andes have pointed out that in Quechua and Aymara languages there exists no discrete term for the zoological category of "animal."[30] Clear-cut divides between humans and animals, or indeed other natural beings such as trees and plants, do not possess resonance in Andean cosmovisions. Nature instead, in these anthropological readings, is a site of multiple but connected communities comprising human and other-than-human. Ethnographic accounts of rituals practiced by Quechua-speaking peasants in Bolivia stress the relations of reciprocity and mutual dependence between peasants and their physical environment. Ethnomusicologist Henry Stobart describes how peasants in Macha, Northern Potosí, believe that their crops are sentient and will "weep" (*waqay* in Quechua) if not cared for properly.[31] Meanwhile, John McNeish observes how the physical environment acts as a repository of history for the highland Aymara community of Santuario de Quillacas, Oruro.[32] Mountains, hills, and even the weather and seasons are understood to be intimately connected with local people's daily life and to provide a tangible connection with ancestors. Agricultural rituals tied to the environment are integral to Aymara spirituality. Human relations with the other-than-human are inscribed through principles of reciprocity and care; the natural world must be protected and communicated with via *achachilas* (mountain spirits) and Pachamama if it is to bear life.[33]

In particular, I draw on Marisol de la Cadena's work on the other-than-human in the Peruvian Andes.[34] De la Cadena exposes how Indigenous struggles around "earth beings" can be understood as decolonial struggles because they call into question the epistemic division between humans and the natural world.[35] By understanding nonhuman entities as political actors, ecological struggles waged by Indigenous peoples hence have the potential to exceed "the notion of politics as usual."[36] De la Cadena explains: "In the story

I am telling, land was *"not only"* the agricultural ground from where peasants earned a living—it was also the place that tirakuna [people of the *ayllu*] with runakuna [nonhuman beings] were.... As the convergence of both, land was the term that allowed the alliance between radically different *and* partially connected worlds. The world inhabited by leftist politicians was public; the world of the ayllu, composed of humans and other-than-human beings, was not."[37] De la Cadena's approach thereby offers an analytical framework in which historians of Indigenous movements can interrogate nature's significance beyond the singular category of "natural resource" and attempt to make a place for "earth beings" as actors within historical processes. Deploying de la Cadena's approach, a central argument of this essay is that nature emerged in *katarista* mobilization both as a natural resource in the world of conventional resource politics and as an expression of Aymara and Indigenous-*campesino* epistemologies. As such, the concept of nature was understood across registers and encompassed multiple worldviews.

Literature

Scholarship on *katarismo* first appeared in the 1980s in works by groundbreaking sociologists Silvia Rivera Cusicanqui, Javier Hurtado, and Xavier Albó.[38] In recent decades, the election of Evo Morales and the Movimiento al Socialismo (MAS) in 2005, in tandem with cycles of Indigenous mobilization between 2000 and 2005, has compelled new scholarship and popular engagement with *katarismo* and its influences on contemporary politics, particularly in relation to state-led decolonization efforts. This developing historiography is reflected in works by Pedro Portugal Mollinedo, Carlos Macusaya Cruz, and Iván Apaza Calle, among others.[39] Many of these authors are active in current *katarista* projects such as Jichha and Periódico Pukara that provide a popular forum to discuss *katarista* histories and contemporary politics. Histories of *katarismo* therefore touch on debates around decolonization and the state that remain urgent in contemporary Bolivia.

In her work *"Oprimidos pero no vencidos": Luchas del campesinado aymara y qhechwa, 1900–1980*, Rivera unveils the notions of "long memory" and "short memory" as defining features of *katarismo*, drawing on French sociologist Maurice Halbwachs's earlier theory of social memory.[40] This was similarly taken up by Albó in his motif of a "great arc" stretching from Tupaj Katari in 1780 to the *kataristas* of 1980.[41] Rivera argues that *kataristas* were influenced by generational memories stretching back to colonial-era repression and resistance led by Tupaj Amaru and Tupaj Katari in the eighteenth century. This long memory was accompanied by the short memory of the Bolivian Revolution of 1952, which failed to fulfill the promises of meaningful social and economic transformation for Bolivia's Indigenous peoples. Portugal and Macusaya reject Rivera's notion of long memory specifically. They lament that "one of the most popularized and vulgarized ideas about the Indigenous movements of the Andes has its origin in that book [Rivera's *"Oprimidos pero no vencidos"*]: the idea of 'long memory,' which is very attractive for certain social strata distanced from the 'Indigenous.'"[42] They argue that notions of dormant memory are ahistorical and fail to account for the ways in which younger-generation *kataristas* actively constructed a memory and language of past oppression unassisted by older generations.

FIGURE 2.2 Farmer working field with ox-drawn plough in west La Paz Department, ca. 1934–1969. American Geographical Society Library, University of Wisconsin, Milwaukee.

Portugal and Macusaya also raise the question of the relationship between *indianismo* and *katarismo*, which are generally considered to be interrelated although operationally distinct movements. *Indianismo*, influenced by the works of Reinaga, places primary emphasis on the racial oppression experienced by Indians and asserts an essential difference between Indian and non-Indian subjects. Portugal and Macusaya conclude: "*Indianismo* was a movement and a discourse that centered its criticism and struggle on the racialized character of the social structure in Bolivia; meanwhile, *katarismo* was a movement that focused on the economic and cultural differences of the peasantry."[43] I build on this existing scholarship by using ecology as a lens by which to analyze *katarismo* and complicate historical interpretations of the *katarista* movement.

The Origins of *Katarismo*

Since the colonial era, land and resource use has been structured around race in Latin American societies.[44] Prior to the Spanish conquest in the sixteenth century, Bolivia was incorporated into the Inca Empire and known as Qullasuyu. Spanish colonization of Bolivia from the outset was bound up with a violent reordering and division of space and territory. This began with the issuing of property titles by the Spanish Crown, a process that initiated a catastrophic loss of land for Indigenous communities, as the Crown increasingly sold off land for *haciendas* (estates under the control of landlords).[45] Bolivia achieved independence from Spain in 1825 under the leadership of Spanish-descendant elites, and Indigenous peoples were still required to pay a tax known as the indigenous contribution. Later, the passage of the Ley de Exvinculación (Law of Disentailment) in 1874 precipitated the loss of extensive Indian lands by opening them up to privatization and sale; the law attempted to abolish forms of communal land tenure and initiate the individualization of land titling. Indeed, by the 1880s, one third of community lands were alienated, most of them in the department of La Paz.[46]

In the twentieth century, *katarismo* arose in the capital city of La Paz and El Alto among Aymara workers, organic intellectuals, and students, many of whom had emigrated from rural areas and felt the loss of their rural *campesino* origins with acuity. A major influence in *katarismo* were the ideas of Reinaga, who first formulated *indianista* thought in the 1960s. He developed a radical critique of Bolivian race relations, arguing that Bolivia was bifurcated into "Creole-European Bolivia" and an invisible "Indian Bolivia."[47] As with *indianismo*, *katarismo* must be understood in part as a response to disillusionment with the 1952 Bolivian revolution. Indeed, the abiding refrain of the *katarista* movement was, "Ya no somos los campesinos de 1952" (We are not the peasants of 1952), which underscores *katarismo*'s repudiation of what was perceived to be a profoundly incomplete revolution.[48] The revolution ushered in three transformations: the nationalization of the mining sector, the introduction of universal suffrage, and the expropriation of landed estates in the highlands through a process of reform initiated in 1953. The ideological driving force of the revolution was resource nationalism, which had acquired especial vigor in the 1950s as the MNR and a broad populist coalition rallied around a developmentalist agenda based on the exploitation of national resources on behalf of the Bolivian people, rather than foreign and domestic elites.[49]

However, it was agrarian reform that would have the most decisive impact for Bolivia's Indigenous *campesinos*. Prior to 1953, 4 percent of landowners possessed 82 percent of land.[50] The Indian population of the highlands was expected to fulfill labor obligations for large landowners in exchange for the right to cultivate a small parcel of land in a deeply exploitative practice known as *pongueaje*. Although the Indian communities of the highlands benefited from the redistribution of land through agrarian reform, the devaluation of the *ayllu* and the privileging of individual landownership (which eventually led to excessive smallholding) were perceived to be culturally and economically damaging by peasants. Publications and recordings from CSUTCB general meetings in the 1980s show that agrarian reform continued to be a problem for the peasantry due to its unequal application.[51] Its 1983 *Tesis sindical y política* states that agrarian reform "culminated a long process of fragmentation of our communitarian organizational forms. . . . [O]ur oppressors have advocated by various means a systematic dispossession of our historical identity. They tried to make us forget our true origins and reduce ourselves only to peasants without personality, without history, and without identity."[52]

Agrarian reform and the state's drive to transform rural space was also suffused with a racial logic. The term *campesino* was officially adopted by the architects of the 1952 revolution as part of a homogenizing vision of Bolivian society that sought to expunge the nation's Indian elements and assimilate Indigenous peoples into the body politic.[53] The terms *indígena* and *indio* were deemed feudal and pejorative, and thus were replaced in state and popular discourse with the ostensibly modern, race-blind label *campesino*. An article published under the alias "Huascar" on July 26, 1953, in the national newspaper *La Nación* declares that "agrarian reform is the policy of liquidating the indigenous as indigenous." Agrarian reform would "destroy and eliminate forever the condition of misery, hunger, and the condition of a colonial country." The article goes on to claim that it would boost productivity in the countryside, "elevating [the Indigenous] to the category of producer and consumer citizen."[54] Agrarian reform was thus part of a racial project that aimed to establish a system of agrarian capitalism and transform Indians into clients of the MNR regime.[55] This required a transformation of Indigenous relations to land and territory, not least because of the new processes of privatization it initiated. As Hurtado notes, after the agrarian reform, many *aynocas*—lands owned and controlled by the community but owned by a family—were parceled up and privatized on an individual basis, undermining the communitarian basis of highland land tenure.[56] This had the effect of disrupting the agrarian economy and, by extension, Indigenous ways of relating to land and landscape in the altiplano. In the 1960s, rural migration to La Paz swelled the city as processes generated by agrarian reform led to the increasing semi-proletarianization of the peasantry, with large numbers migrating to urban centers to supplement income from agriculture.[57] According to the 1976 census, 25 percent of the La Paz population was made up of Aymara migrants from the altiplano.[58] These migrant communities were radicalized by the social alienation and racial discrimination they experienced in the city.[59]

In 1964, General René Barrientos seized power in a military coup that overthrew the government of Víctor Paz Estenssoro and brought the postrevolutionary government of the MNR to an abrupt end. The Barrientos regime (1964–1969) introduced the Military-Peasant Pact, which bound the peasant leadership to the right-wing military government in exchange for a promise to not undo the 1953 Agrarian Reform Law. The government sought to prevent an alliance between workers, miners, and peasants and deployed clientelist practices to co-opt the peasantry and suppress struggles from organized workers and miners. State massacres of miners in 1965 and 1967 further crushed efforts to resist.[60]

By 1970, however, the Military-Peasant Pact was quickly breaking down following attempts by the Barrientos government to introduce a new rural-property tax that generated huge discontent from the peasantry.[61] At the same time, efforts were underway by *kataristas* at the provincial level to seize control of the peasant unions away from *dirigentes* co-opted by the state. In 1970, *katarista* Aymara leaders Jenaro Flores Santos and Macabeo Chila were elected to the senior positions in the peasant unions in La Paz and Oruro departments, respectively.[62] Their arrival heralded a rupture with the status quo characterized by state-controlled peasant unions. In symbolic terms, they added "TK" to the end of the union name in honor of Tupaj Katari.[63] In June 1979, the Central Obrera Boliviana (COB), the powerful national trade union federation, sponsored the First Congress for Peasant Unity in La Paz. The CSUTCB was founded during this congress as the culmination of efforts by *katarista* peasants to build an autonomous peasant movement. From its founding, it was headed by Secretary General Jenaro Flores, who came from Sica Sica, La Paz, the birthplace of Tupaj Katari two centuries earlier. In 1980, he also unsuccessfully ran for president with the MRTK party. When the COB leadership was murdered, in hiding, or imprisoned following the coup by Luis García Meza between July 17, 1980, and June 19, 1981, Flores became the de facto leader of the COB, the first time that an Indigenous peasant unionist had ascended to the leadership.[64] It cemented the link between the CSUTCB and the broader workers' movement. For example, in an interview conducted shortly after the coup in 1980, Flores declared: "[T]hey previously tried to alienate the workers from the peasants.... But now there is a close relationship between mining workers and peasants because ultimately they are also from peasant extraction."[65]

Accordingly, the MRTK under the leadership of Chila and Flores adopted a more pragmatic and conciliatory line when it came to partnerships with other political parties and the wider labor movement.[66] For example, in the 1978 elections, it united with the left coalition of Siles's Unidad Democrática Popular (UDP).[67] In an interview published in *Collasuyo*, a monthly *katarista* periodical, Chila states that "the MRTK understands that it must work in the aim of a firm alliance between both [peasant and worker] classes that definitively constitute the great motor of the National Revolution." He envisioned MRTK to be "the political instrument of the Bolivian peasantry" to win liberation from capitalist and imperialist exploitation.[68]

In contrast, radical *katarismo*, sometimes elided with *indianismo*, came to fruition under MITKA, which was founded on April 27, 1978, in Pacajes, La Paz.[69] It was rife with the internecine conflicts that are mentioned frequently in testimonies from protagonists of the era. MITKA repudiated alliances with other political parties, arguing that none adequately represented the interests of the peasantry, and was far more visceral in its condemnation of the creole Left or the *q'aras* (foreigners). Anthropologist José Antonio Rocha argues that for MITKA, in contrast to the MRTK, "the left is as bad as the right; both tendencies belong to the 'white' world. In its conception, Bolivian society is a world divided between whites and Indians, a society in which the white minority exploits and subjugates the majority of Indians."[70] Later, in 1985, another of the more moderate factions, the Movimiento Revolucionario Tupaj Katari de Liberación (MRTKL), formed as an offshoot of the MRTK.

FIGURE 2.3 Miners in elevator at tin mining facility in Oruro, Bolivia, ca. 1934–1969. American Geographical Society Library, University of Wisconsin, Milwaukee.

The *katarista* program was codified in the Tiahuanaco Manifesto. It was written in 1973 and symbolically unveiled at Tiahuanaco, the Pre-Columbian archaeological site near La Paz. The manifesto is a rallying cry on behalf of Bolivia's peasantry and a searing denunciation of the coloniality at the heart of the Bolivian nation-state. The document's signatories are grassroots organizations including the National Association of Peasant Teachers, the Peasant Students Association of Bolivia, the Túpac Katari Peasant Center, the Center for the Coordination and Promotion of the Peasantry (also known as MINK'A), and the

Puma Aymara Defense Union. A preoccupation with development is a defining feature of the manifesto and indeed the *katarista* movement more widely. The manifesto proclaims: "We peasants want economic development, but it must come from our own values. We do not want to give up our noble ancestral integrity in favor of pseudo-development. We believe that the false 'developmentalism' imported from abroad is not genuine and does not respect our deep values." The manifesto asserts the importance of Indigenous collectivist modes of production in the rural world, which it positions in polar opposition to Bolivia under colonial capitalist relations: "[T]he cooperative system is inherent in a people that created modes of production in mutual aid such as the *ayni*, the *mink'a, yanapacos, camayos*.... Private property, individualism, class differentiation, internal struggles came to us with colonialism and were accentuated by the Republican regimes. Agrarian reform is also conceived within this scheme."[71]

As the centrality of history within the manifesto attests, in *katarismo*, a politics of state transformation was fused with highland Aymara and Quechua culture and, particularly, an emphasis on recovering histories of Aymara struggle as part of future political visions. This manifested in the spread of cultural projects such as the Taller de Historia Oral Andina (THOA), which was founded in 1983 by a group of Aymara students under the direction of Silvia Rivera at the Universidad Mayor de San Andrés in La Paz. THOA produced books and radio programs on hitherto sidelined stories of Indigenous resistance in the altiplano. It was a radical activist-intellectual project aimed at recovering Native epistemologies and challenging the erasure of Indigenous peoples from the Bolivia national imaginary. In later years, the September 1985 issue of *Boletín Chitakolla* announced the creation of a cultural center in La Paz named Qullasuyu. Its general objectives include revitalizing Aymara-Quechua music and dance among young people and promoting the spread of cultural projects among Aymara-Quechua immigrants to urban centers.[72] Prior to this, in the late 1960s, a group of Aymara students formed a study group known as the Movimiento Noviembre 15, a reference to the date of Tupaj Katari's death, in which the ideas of Reinaga were debated. On May 27, 1969, Aymara residents in La Paz created MINK'A.[73] MINK'A promoted education and cultural activities for both rural and urban Indigenous peoples, as well as disseminated radio programs in the Aymara language.

To summarize, I have drawn here on the historiography of twentieth-century Bolivia to outline how several key developments in the post-1952 milieu are important in explaining the rise of *katarismo*. In particular, the grievances generated by the political limitations and cultural erasure of the 1952 revolution, combined with the decline of the Military-Peasant Pact, were crucial in the rise of a new autonomous political space for *katarista campesinos*. It was in this space, as I argue next, that new framings of the environment as a site of political potential emerged.

Environmental Politics and *Katarismo*

I will focus here on key elements of *katarista* discourse that elucidate their position on ecology and the environment. I argue that from the 1970s the environment and the natural world emerged as a new locus of thought and political action for Indigenous *campesino* political movements. It is evident that *kataristas* were acutely aware of both the ecological facets of imperialism and the environment's importance within Andean Indigenous identities. As Victor Flores, a *katarista* union leader from Aiquile, Cochabamba, puts it: "Throughout the last 500 years we peasants have been stepped on by the wealthy, the mestizos, and the Spaniards; the trees and animals similarly have been abused and are being extinguished, and thus we share much suffering along with the environment."[74] Invoking the exploitation of natural resources in the language of conventional politics on the one hand offered an easily digestible metaphor for Indian exploitation within *katarista* discourse, but the connection between human and environmental suffering also departed from the merely symbolic or rhetorical. Over the period from 1960 to 1990, *katarista* discourse shifted from a preoccupation with control of natural resources to one that additionally stressed spiritual and cosmological facets of the natural world as part of a program of decolonization.

This is reflected in the articles and excerpts appearing in the *katarista* press. The February 1986 issue of *Boletín Chitakolla* features an excerpt from a Peruvian work entitled *Indianidad y revolución: Raíz y vigencia de la indianidad* (*Indianness and Revolution: Origin and Validity of Indianness*) by Virgilio Roel, published in 1980: "That is why the stars, clouds, hills, seas, lagoons, rivers, valleys, trees, stones, condors, birds, butterflies, flowers, in short, everything which belongs to Pachamama, maintains a constant and mutual reciprocal influence." It goes on to offer an anti-imperialist reading of the ecological disasters that afflict the countryside: "As a counterpart to Western aggression, we Indians know that if we do not return what we have taken from the land, if we do not treat Pachamama with respect, that if we attack the beautiful animals that are also her beloved children, it will mean that in her anger, the farming areas will turn into deserts and the animals will disappear."[75] This depicts Pachamama, or the Andean holistic earth-mother concept, as a willful life force with agency.

The belief in human-nature reciprocity as an integral part of the peasant's social world is reflected in the spate of discussions around Pachamama that took place in the *campesino* movement at the behest of *kataristas* in the late 1980s. Proposals from the group Ofensiva Roja de Ayllus Tupakataristas (ORAT) to the Fourth Regular Congress of the CSUTCB in Tarija in September 1989 included a subsection entitled "*Pachamama o muerte*" ("Pachamama or death"). Led by veteran *guerrillero* Felipe "El Mallku" Quispe, ORAT was a more militant *katarista* group. ORAT's proposals state: "The reasons that compel us to present this document are to make it known to all the brothers and sisters of our race, who come from the brown Pachamama, that we cultivate and till our lands in the highlands, valleys, tropics and in the east from sun to sun, our foreheads dripping with sweat *for Mother Nature*. . . ."[76] The report goes on: "We cultivate with all our dedication and care [*esmero*] for Pachamama, from dawn until dusk to subsidize and maintain the production of our agricultural produce. . . ."[77] For ORAT, "these foreigners [*q'aras*] of different ideological currents inherited from European invaders, have only come to mutilate, trample, loot, and desecrate the riches of our beloved Pachamama."[78]

This colonial memory is further reflected when their proposals state: "Since before Christ, we worshiped the hills, *pukaras*, *wak'as*, stones, *apachites*, in ceremonial and cosmic places. We are older than Western Christianity. Like our grandparents both in the time of Tiwanakinses and in the Incanate, the sacrifices made with gold and silver, colored wool, coca, etc., every year to our Sun [*Tata Inti*], moon, stars, and the Pachamama endure from generation to generation to the present day."[79] Spirituality is inextricably tied to place, with the natural world representing the locus of precolonial spiritual practice. The hills and "cosmic places" form vessels of memory as a source of tangible continuity between colonial past and present.

Yet in a somewhat different realm, grievances at the volume of food imports in Bolivia emerge as an equally germane issue in the group's proposals. In emotive rhetoric, they lament: "Unfortunately it is terrible that instead of producing wheat, barley, quinoa, *kañawa,* beans, rice, maize, cassava, banana, potato, tubers, beans, etc., we are living off the foreigners and waiting for the *gringos* to send us their rotten leftovers from their rubbish dumps, [so] we are falling into food dependency."[80] The 1980s were a particularly fraught time for agricultural production in Bolivia. In 1983 and 1984, severe droughts in the highlands and flooding in the lowlands caused so much damage that agricultural output fell by 23 percent in 1983, meaning substantial amounts of food had to be imported for many years afterward.[81] These natural disasters are explained by ORAT as symptoms of Pachamama's willful anger and vengeance: "[T]he communities that we live in, 'MACH'AS' [a communal unit comprising several *ayllus*], no longer produce crops, the animals die, it no longer rains, and day by day we receive the punishments of our Mother Nature with hail, frost, and drought. The once fertile Pachamama becomes sterile and no longer gives her produce to us native children as before."[82] In this, we see how *katarista* invocations of the other-than-human make visible the agency of the natural world and seek to expand the parameters of what—and who—constitutes a political actor.

For both MITKA and the MRTK, the natural world is invoked as the carrier of Tupaj Katari's spirit. The social memory of past struggles finds form and significance in the natural surroundings of the Andes. In an article published on May 23, 1978, in the national daily newspaper *Presencia*, Isidoro Copa Cayo, a Quechua-speaker from Potosí and a MITKA electoral candidate, outlines the objectives of the party and advocates for "[l]ife in communion with nature as a mode of civilization and culture." He goes on: "[MITKA] emerges as a historical-political response, as the shout of a wounded social body, as a cry of an oppressed people, like a voice crying in the altiplano, valleys, and plains. . . ."[83]

The MRTK placed great emphasis on the *ayllu* as a political and economic model with links to past and present Andean society. A pamphlet from the MRTK declares, "The community practice, for example, subsists in numerous *aillus* [*ayllus*] of *Kollasuyo* (today Bolivia). Its persisting practice is the umbilical cord that connects us with our historical past."[84] *Ayllus* are not political assemblages along the lines of the nature-culture divide in the Western political tradition.[85] Simón Yampara instead points out, "To speak of 'economy,' in addition to being a borrowed and inappropriate concept practiced by other cultures . . . does not explain the communal sense and development of the *ayllu*."[86] *Ayllus* instead are structured in part around the environment and the spirits and life forces contained within nature, including humans. By invoking the *ayllu*, the MRTK was hence advocating a political structure that encompasses both humans and the natural world in reciprocity.

Javier Medina, an intellectual associated with the *katarista* movement and writing in the June 1985 issue of *Boletín Chitakolla*, argues that *katarismo* proposes "a rupture of the state and civilization, with the current modes of production and, looking toward the past, has endeavored to seek its own path towards a society that we will call ... communal (2) [*sic*]; in other words, toward a mode of production based on ecological balance."[87] He argues that the ideals of communism and socialism will only be viable in Bolivia when realized through the Andean *ayllu* or, in other words, through an Indigenous institutional formation. Medina goes on to argue that "[o]ur ancestors, with these communal technologies, knew how to create self-sufficient societies. This would be a sensible and possible goal: to return and fight for Bolivia to be a self-sufficient country in food."[88]

Meanwhile, the January 1986 issue of the MRTKL publication *El katarismo* featured an article on the concept of (gender) complementarity in the Andean world, using the case study of Marka Llica. The author Clara Flores notes that "each thing in nature is dual: interwoven coexistence of plants, land, mountains, *pujyus* (deep spring waters) that are the productive social well-being of the communities. Therefore, they are considered as human beings in nature because they coexist with us in us, giving us life." She goes on to argue that "[t]he constitution of our family is our physical-spiritual-communal constitution. And this is the product of our climate, geography, experience, which is life and communication with the hills, mountains, salt flats, and our arid but strong land."[89] By the 1980s, it is clear that arguments around Indigenous rights were tightly linked with planetary well-being in *katarista* discourse.

Consistent throughout *katarista* political discourse is resentment at the perceived absence of rural development rooted in the needs and wishes of the peasants themselves. The economic exploitation of the peasantry is tied up with the lack of control over natural resources and means of production in the rural setting. For example, at a CSUTCB congress, ORAT states, "We small farmers do not have any kind of economic aid, we are practically excluded from national life and seen as simple beasts of burden, treated as foreigners in our ancestral soil.... [W]e are unable to develop a coherent agricultural policy nor modernize or mechanize our fields...."[90] Macabeo Chila, a leader of the MRTK, believed that development policies did little to remedy the overarching problem of capitalist penetration in rural areas: "Backwardness and misery is another problem that cannot be overcome with the development policy of so-called denaturalized and fascistic nationalists; happiness and prosperity cannot be achieved through stopgap measures [*remiendos*], but through a total change of the system of capitalist exploitation by another system of community character."[91]

It is clear that the exploitation of Indian labor under capitalism for the MRTK is deeply connected with the exploitation of natural resources. In an interview published in June 1978 in *Collasuyo*, Chila explains: "Discrimination, either social or racial, exists, but it exists as a pejorative means of exploitation and pillaging of our natural wealth. Consequently, for the MRTK, there is no mere discrimination by discrimination, but as a phenomenon of humiliation wielded by the dominant circles of the financial oligarchy relative to the capitalist system of exploitation." He goes on to express frustration with the existing state of land ownership and the co-option of the peasantry, professing: "The problem is that land that was once communal, today, due to agrarian reform has passed into feudal ownership and has neutralized the combative spirit of the peasantry by turning them into private owners of pathetically small plots that are subjugated under the *minifundio* that is propped up by the legal system. . . ."[92] Even within MITKA, a more *indianista* and less class-struggle-driven organization, the issue of land distribution was profoundly salient. In 1986, one of its leaders, Luciano Tapia, was sixty-two years old, an ex-miner and ex-*colonizador* in the subtropical zones in Bolivia.[93] In an interview, Tapia explains: "The agrarian revolution is one of the main approaches of MITKA, but for us, agrarian revolution is not 'AGROPODER,'[94] it is not 're-distribution of agrarian reform.' For us, the agrarian revolution is a political project."[95]

Conclusion

I have argued that debates over natural resources in *katarista* discourse reflected broader visions about how the economy and society should be arranged. *Katarismo* represented a new articulation of natural resources, and the natural world more broadly, as a central political concern for the Indigenous *campesino* movement. In this way, *katarismo* represented a major shift from the ethno-assimilationist logics and resource nationalism of the MNR era in the 1950s. A close reading of *katarista* discourse reveals a sustained engagement with a politics of the environment that was used to bolster wider arguments addressing the coloniality at the heart of the Bolivian state. In contrast to the earlier focus on resource nationalism by the COB, the state, and assorted Left actors in mid-twentieth-century Bolivia, a more complicated vision of natural resources emerged in *katarista* perspectives on the environment by the 1980s. These heralded a new way of articulating an Indigenous vision of natural resources and the other-than-human by centering Indigenous concepts such as Pachamama, *achachilas*, *w'akas*, etc., within critiques of colonial capitalism. The ways in which their mobilization made visible the nonhuman presented an epistemological challenge to state agencies. The *katarista* currents explored in this essay straddle both rural and urban worlds, and their emphasis on the environment reflects how natural landscapes were encoded with memories of historic struggle over land rights and cultural practices in the twentieth century. Landscape, territory, and natural space emerge as a quite literal terrain connecting Indigenous struggles of the past and present and resonate far beyond the borders of Bolivia. The history of the *kataristas* in Bolivia is, therefore, deeply relevant for contextualizing ongoing struggles against land dispossession, exploitation, and racial oppression experienced by Indigenous peoples in Bolivia and the Americas.

NOTES

1. Confederación Sindical Única de Trabajadores Campesinos de Bolivia, *Tesis política*, 1979, 3, https://archive.org/details/tesis-politica-de-la-csutcb/mode/2up [translation my own].
2. Tania Murray Li, "Environment, Indigeneity and Transnationalism," in *Liberation Ecologies: Environment, Development, Social Movements*, ed. Richard Peet and Michael Watts, 2nd ed. (London: Routledge, 2004), 309–37.
3. Kepa Artaraz and Melania Calestani, "*Suma qamaña* in Bolivia: Indigenous Understandings of Well-Being and Their Contribution to a Post-neoliberal Paradigm," *Latin American Perspectives* 42, no. 5 (September 2015): 216–33.
4. See Eduardo Gudynas, "Estado compensador y nuevos extractivismos: Las ambivalencias del progresismo sudamericano," *Nueva sociedad*, no. 237 (January–February 2012): 128–46; and Maristella Svampa, *Neo-extractivism in Latin America: Socio-environmental Conflicts, the Territorial Turn, and New Political Narratives* (Cambridge: Cambridge University Press, 2019).
5. Oscar de la Torre, *The People of the River: Nature and Identity in Black Amazonia, 1835–1945* (Chapel Hill: University of North Carolina Press, 2018).
6. Nick Estes, *Our History Is the Future: Standing Rock versus the Dakota Access Pipeline, and the Long Tradition of Indigenous Resistance* (London: Verso, 2019).
7. Javier Sanjinés C., "*Mestizaje* Upside Down: Subaltern Knowledges and the Known," *Nepantla: Views from South* 3, no. 1 (2002): 39–60.
8. Andrew Canessa, "Contesting Hybridity: *Evangelistas* and *Kataristas* in Highland Bolivia," *Journal of Latin American Studies* 32, no. 1 (2000): 125.
9. Xavier Albó, "¿ . . . Y de Kataristas a MNRistas? La sorprendente y audaz alianza entre Aymaras y neoliberales en Bolivia," *Boletín de antropología americana*, no. 25 (July 1992): 54.
10. Sanjinés C., "*Mestizaje* Upside Down."
11. Rossana Barragán, "The Census and the Making of a Social 'Order' in Nineteenth-Century Bolivia," in *Histories of Race and Racism: The Andes and Mesoamerica from Colonial Times to the Present*, ed. Laura Gotkowitz (Durham, N.C.: Duke University Press, 2011), 130n1.
12. Barragán, "The Census and the Making of a Social 'Order' in Nineteenth-Century Bolivia," 125.
13. Mario C. Araoz, *Nuevo digesto de legislación boliviana*, 1:335, quoted in Laura Gotkowitz, *A Revolution for Our Rights: Indigenous Struggles for Land and Justice in Bolivia, 1880–1952* (Durham, N.C.: Duke University Press, 2007), 13.
14. República de Bolivia, *Redactor de la Convención Nacional de 1945* (La Paz: n.p., 1945), 2:737, quoted in Laura Gotkowitz, "'Under the Dominion of the Indian': Rural Mobilization, the Law, and Revolutionary Nationalism in Bolivia in the 1940s," in *Political Cultures in the Andes, 1750–1950*, ed. Nils Jacobsen and Cristóbal Aljovín de Losada (Durham, N.C.: Duke University Press, 2005), 156n2.
15. Gotkowitz, "'Under the Dominion of the Indian,'" 148.
16. Andrew Canessa, *Intimate Indigeneities: Race, Sex, and History in the Small Spaces of Andean Life* (Durham, N.C.: Duke University Press, 2012), 7.
17. Fausto Reinaga, *Tesis india*, 4th ed. (La Paz: MINKA, 2010), 75.
18. Erick D. Langer, "Bringing the Economic Back In: Andean Indians and the Construction of the Nation-State in Nineteenth-Century Bolivia," *Journal of Latin American Studies* 41, no. 3 (August 2009): 539. See also Tristan Platt, *Estado boliviano y ayllu andino: Tierra y tributo en el Norte de Potosí* (Lima: Instituto de Estudios Peruanos, 1982).
19. Government of Bolivia, "Disentailment and Its Discontents," trans. Alison Spedding, in *The Bolivia Reader: History, Culture, Politics*, ed. Sinclair Thomson, Rossana Barragán, Xavier Albó, Seemin Qayum, and Mark Goodale (Durham, N.C.: Duke University Press, 2018), 187n1.
20. Aníbal Quijano, "The Challenge of the 'Indigenous Movement' in Latin America," *Socialism and Democracy* 19, no. 3 (2005): 55–78.
21. Aníbal Quijano, "Coloniality of Power and Eurocentrism in Latin America," *International Sociology* 15, no. 2 (June 2000): 215–32.
22. Arturo Escobar, *Territories of Difference: Place, Movements, Life, Redes* (Durham, N.C.: Duke University Press, 2008).

23 Michel Foucault, *Power/Knowledge: Selected Interviews and Other Writings, 1972–1977*, ed. Colin Gordon, trans. Colin Gordon, Leo Marshall, John Mepham, and Kate Soper (New York: Pantheon Books, 1980), 81–83.

24 Boaventura de Sousa Santos, *Epistemologies of the South: Justice against Epistemicide* (Abingdon: Routledge, 2016).

25 Enrique Leff, *Epistemología ambiental* (São Paulo: Cortez, 2001); and Enrique Leff, "Pensamiento ambiental latinoamericano: Patrimonio de un saber para la sustentabilidad," supplement, *Environmental Ethics* 34 (Summer 2012): 97–112.

26 Philippe Descola, *Beyond Nature and Culture* (Chicago: University of Chicago Press, 2013); and Escobar, *Territories of Difference*.

27 Descola, *Beyond Nature and Culture*; and Marisol de la Cadena, *Earth Beings: Ecologies of Practice across Andean Worlds* (Durham, N.C.: Duke University Press, 2015).

28 José Teijeiro Villarroel, *La rebelión permanente: Crisis de identidad y persistencia étnico-cultural aymara en Bolivia* (La Paz: Programa de Investigación Estratégica en Bolivia, 2007), 121–22 [translation my own].

29 Joanne Rappaport, *The Politics of Memory: Native Historical Interpretation in the Colombian Andes* (Durham, N.C.: Duke University Press, 1998), 8.

30 Penelope Dransart, "Living Beings and Vital Powers: An Introduction," in *Living Beings: Perspectives on Interspecies Engagements*, ed. Penelope Dransart (London: Bloomsbury, 2013), 3.

31 Henry Stobart, *Music and the Poetics of Production in the Bolivian Andes* (Aldershot: Ashgate, 2006), 26.

32 John McNeish, "Globalization and the Reinvention of Andean Tradition: The Politics of Community and Ethnicity in Highland Bolivia," *The Journal of Peasant Studies* 29, nos. 3-4 (2002): 228–69.

33 Simón Yampara Huarachi, "'Economía' comunitaria andina," in *La cosmovisión aymara*, ed. Hans van den Berg and Norbert Schiffers (La Paz: UCB Hisbol, 1992), 156–58.

34 De la Cadena, *Earth Beings*.

35 De la Cadena, *Earth Beings*, 110–11.

36 Marisol de la Cadena, "Indigenous Cosmopolitics in the Andes: Conceptual Reflections Beyond 'Politics,'" *Cultural Anthropology* 25, no. 2 (May 2010): 364.

37 De la Cadena, *Earth Beings*, 110.

38 Silvia Rivera Cusicanqui, *"Oprimidos pero no vencidos": Luchas del campesinado aymara y qhechwa, 1900–1980* (La Paz: Hisbol–CSUTCB, 1984); Javier Hurtado, *El katarismo* (La Paz: Hisbol, 1986); and Xavier Albó, "From MNRistas to Kataristas to Katari," in *Resistance, Rebellion, and Consciousness in the Andean Peasant World, 18th to 20th Centuries*, ed. Steve J. Stern (Madison: The University of Wisconsin Press, 1987), 379–419.

39 Pedro Portugal Mollinedo and Carlos Macusaya Cruz, *El indianismo katarista: Un análisis crítico* (La Paz: Fundación Friedrich Ebert, 2016); and Iván Apaza Calle, *Contra el indianismo y el katarismo* (La Paz: Jichha, 2020).

40 Maurice Halbwachs, *The Collective Memory* (New York: Harper & Row, 1980).

41 Albó, "From MNRistas to Kataristas to Katari," 412.

42 Portugal Mollinedo and Macusaya Cruz, *El indianismo katarista*, 31–32 [translation my own].

43 Portugal Mollinedo and Macusaya Cruz, *El indianismo katarista*, 26 [translation my own].

44 Eduardo Galeano, *Open Veins of Latin America: Five Centuries of the Pillage of a Continent*, trans. Cedric Belfrage (New York: Monthly Review Press, 1997).

45 Rossana Barragán and Florencia Durán, "Tras las huellas de la historia," in *Collana: Conflicto por la tierra en el Altiplano*, ed. Fundación Tierra (La Paz: Fundación Tierra, 2003), 27–28.

46 Forrest Hylton and Sinclair Thomson, *Revolutionary Horizons: Past and Present in Bolivian Politics* (London: Verso, 2007), 52–53.

47 Esteban Ticona Alejo, *Saberes, conocimientos y prácticas anticoloniales del pueblo aymara-quechua en Bolivia* (La Paz: AGRUCO, 2010), 42.

48 Xavier Albó, "El retorno del indio," *Revista andina* 2, no. 9 (1991): 312.

49 Kevin A. Young, *Blood of the Earth: Resource Nationalism, Revolution, and Empire in Bolivia* (Austin: University of Texas Press, 2017), 16–19.

50 Susan Eckstein, "Transformation of a 'Revolution from Below'—Bolivia and International Capital," *Comparative Studies in Society and History* 25, no. 1 (January 1983): 108.

51 Willem Assies, "Land Tenure Legislation in a Pluri-cultural and Multi-ethnic Society: The Case of Bolivia," *The Journal of Peasant Studies* 33, no. 4 (2006): 569–611.
52 CSUTCB, *Tesis sindical y política* (La Paz: mimeo, 1983), 1, quoted in Victor Hugo Cárdenas, "La CSUTCB: Elementos para entender su crisis de crecimiento (1979–1987)," in *Crisis del sindicalismo en Bolivia*, ed. Carlos F. Toranzo Roca (La Paz: FLACSO; ILDIS, 1987), 226 [translation my own].
53 Rivera, *"Oprimidos pero no vencidos,"* 129.
54 Newspaper cutting of "Huascar" in *La Nación*, July 26, 1953, Walter Guevara Arze Collection, Archivo y Biblioteca Nacionales de Bolivia (*ABNB*), Sucre, Bolivia [translation my own].
55 Rivera, *"Oprimidos pero no vencidos,"* 129.
56 Hurtado, *El katarismo*, 19.
57 Uri Mendelberg, "The Impact of the Bolivian Agrarian Reform on Class Formation," *Latin American Perspectives* 12, no. 3 (Summer 1985): 45–58.
58 Silvia Rivera Cusicanqui, "Luchas campesinas contemporáneas en Bolivia: El movimiento 'katarista,' 1970–1980," in *Bolivia, hoy*, ed. René Zavaleta Mercado (Mexico: Siglo Veintiuno Editores, 1983), 139.
59 Albó, "From MNRistas to Kataristas to Katari," 391.
60 Rivera, *"Oprimidos pero no vencidos,"* 169.
61 Assies, "Land Tenure Legislation."
62 Rivera, *"Oprimidos pero no vencidos,"* 176.
63 Albó, "From MNRistas to Kataristas to Katari," 392.
64 Rivera, *"Oprimidos pero no vencidos,"* 208–9.
65 "Entrevista a Genaro Flores en el mes de septiembre" by CSUTCB, October 1980, year 1, no. 1, International Institute of Social History, Amsterdam, The Netherlands [translation my own].
66 Rivera, *"Oprimidos pero no vencidos,"* 136.
67 Albó, "From MNRistas to Kataristas to Katari," 402.
68 "Movimiento Revolucionario Tupaj Katari: Reportaje al dirigente Macabeo Chila P.," *Collasuyo* 1, no. 2 (1978): 4 [translation my own].
69 Jean-Pierre Lavaud, *Identité et politique: Le courant Tupac Katari en Bolivie* (Paris: CREDAL-ERSIPAL, 1982), 10 [translation my own].
70 José Antonio Rocha, "Apuntes en torno al planteamiento politico aymara," in van den Berg and Schiffers, *La cosmovisión aymara*, 260 [translation my own].
71 *Manifiesto de Tiahuanaco* (N.p.: mimeo, 1973) [translation my own].
72 *Boletín Chitakolla* 3, no. 24 (1985): 3.
73 Hurtado, *El katarismo*, 38.
74 Victor Flores, interview, March 30, 1991, quoted in Karl S. Zimmerer, "Soil Erosion and Social (Dis)courses in Cochabamba, Bolivia: Perceiving the Nature of Environmental Degradation," in "Environment and Development, Part 1," ed. Richard Peet and Michael Watts, special issue, *Economic Geography* 69, no. 3 (July 1993): 323.
75 *Indianidad y revolución: Raíz y vigencia de la indianidad* (Ottawa: Consejo Mundial de los Pueblos Indígenas, 1980), quoted in *Boletín Chitakolla* 29 (February 1986): 3 [translation my own].
76 "Propuesta de declaracion político-sindical al IV Congreso Ordinario de la CSUTCB: Ofensiva roja de ayllus tupakataristas," in *El desafío de mantener la unidad: IV Congreso Ordinario de la CSUTCB* (La Paz: CEDOIN, 1990), 29 [translation my own; emphasis added].
77 José Enrique Pinelo N., Miguel Urioste F. de C., and Ricardo Calla Ortega, *CSUTSB: Debate sobre documentos politicos y asamblea de nacionalidades*, http://cedla.org/publicaciones/diytf/csutsb-debate-sobre-documentos-politicos-y-asamblea-de-nacionalidades/.
78 "Propuesta de Declaración Político-Sindical: Ofensiva Roja de Ayllus Tupakataristas," in *El desafío de mantener la unidad* (La Paz: CEDOIN, 1990), 30 [translation my own].
79 "Propuesta de Declaración Político-Sindical: Ofensiva Roja de Ayllus Tupakataristas," 30 [translation my own].
80 "Propuesta de Declaración Político-Sindical: Ofensiva Roja de Ayllus Tupakataristas," 32 [translation my own].
81 Arthur Young, *Briefing Book: USAID/Bolivia* (Washington, D.C.: United States Agency for International Development [USAID], 1986), 6, https://pdf.usaid.gov/pdf_docs/PNABB819.pdf.

82 "Propuesta de Declaración Político-Sindical: Ofensiva Roja de Ayllus Tupakataristas," 32 [translation my own].
83 Isidoro Copa Cayo, "Expone: Movimiento indio Tupaj Katari-MITKA," *Jichha*, n.d., http://jichha.blogspot.com/2015/08/expone-movimiento-indio-tupaj-katari.html#google_vignette [translation my own].
84 Pamphlet "Los aymaras–quechuas oprimidos pero nunca vencidos," L320 PAM/JD/11/23. James Dunkerley Collection, Senate House Library, London, 1981.
85 Arturo Escobar, "Latin America at a Crossroads: Alternative Modernizations, Post-liberalism, or Post-development?," *Cultural Studies* 24, no. 1 (2010): 1–65.
86 Yampara, "'Economia' comunitaria aymara," 143 [translation my own].
87 Javier Medina, "Cobismo y katarismo: Algunas divagaciones para su meditación," *Boletín Chitakolla* 3, no. 22 (June 1985): 4 [translation my own].
88 *Boletín Chitakolla, No. 12, Year 3*, Simon Yampara, La complejidad de la problematica agraria 1-3 (1985) [translation my own].
89 Clara Flores, in *El katarismo* 2 (January–February 1987): 5 [translation my own].
90 CSUTCB, *Informe del Comite Ejecutivo saliente al IV Congreso Nacional Ordinario de la CSUTCB* (La Paz: CEDOIN, 1989), 32 [translation my own].
91 "Movimiento Revolucionario Tupaj Katari," 4 [translation my own].
92 "Movimiento Revolucionario Tupaj Katari," 4 [translation my own].
93 *Colonizadores* were Quechua and Aymara workers who migrated in the 1980s from mining centers in the highlands to "colonize" the lowland areas of Bolivia, often working in coca production.
94 *AGROPODER* was an MNR strategy to aid exports and agricultural development launched in 1985 and was concentrated in the Santa Cruz region.
95 "Entrevista (Luciano Tapia)," *Boletín Chitakolla*, no. 29 (1986): 3–4 [translation my own].

3

Anti-colonial Landscapes

Land and the Emergence of Miskitu People's Territorial Resistance in the Moskitia

RUTH H. MATAMOROS MERCADO

"We cannot share our land with the *colonos*. They do not see land the way we do." These are the words of a Miskitu elder, reflecting on the presence of settlers (*colonos*) from other parts of Nicaragua in his ancestral territories.[1] In 2003, the Nicaraguan legislature approved Law 445, which established five stages of land demarcation with significant repercussions for land governance for the Miskitu Indigenous and Afro-descendant peoples on the Caribbean Coast, historically known as the Moskitia.[2] Although the Nicaraguan state carried out the first four stages of the demarcation process and provided land titles to twenty-three Indigenous territories, it has failed to carry out the fifth stage, the *Saneamiento*, the title clearance that requires the removal of settlers living in Indigenous territories without a lease agreement with the communities.

Indigenous peoples have continued raising their voices and demanding respect for their lands and natural resources. Unable to solve the conflicts caused by the presence of settlers in Indigenous territories, the Nicaraguan state is trying to put forward a cohabitation project that, if approved, will allow settlers to legally occupy lands in Miskitu territories. Miskitu people have opposed this idea, arguing that settlers do not see and relate to land the way Indigenous peoples do. In contrast, settlers argue that those lands are national lands and should be occupied by whoever needs them. One of the proposed cohabitation strategies is to require settlers to pay a rental fee for the land they occupy and to maintain a peaceful coexistence with Indigenous peoples. However, the violence exerted by settlers on Indigenous peoples has shown that peaceful coexistence is unlikely.

Through this essay, the term "settler" is understood as individuals or collectives originating from divergent cultural and geographical backgrounds, mainly *mestizo* inhabitants from the Pacific side of Nicaragua, who migrated and established residency in territories historically inhabited by Indigenous peoples in the Moskitia. These settlers do not possess rights over these lands as per the Nicaraguan legal framework pertaining to Indigenous land rights. Locally, these settlers are referred to as *colonos*, a synonym for colonizer. Throughout this essay, "settler" and *colono* will be used interchangeably to denote the same group and dynamic of individual and collective power relations in and around the Moskitia.

According to recent reports presented by the Centro por la Justicia y el Derecho Internacional and The Oakland Institute, the arrival of settlers has dramatically increased since the approval of Law 445. As a result, Indigenous peoples are left vulnerable to armed settlers who migrate to these territories in search of gold, wood, and land. Settlers are not only occupying Indigenous communal property and destroying the ecosystems in these communities but also kidnapping, torturing, raping, and murdering Indigenous peoples of this region. This situation has forced Indigenous peoples to leave the only land they have known and inhabited and to search for refuge in other communities or urban areas.[3] Those who stay cannot access their land for farming, hunting, or fishing, which they have historically drawn on to sustain themselves and their families. Additionally, the discrepancy between settler and Indigenous ways of relating to land further challenges the cohabitation initiative, as land is viewed as property to be owned and controlled by settlers and a relative to be cared for and respected by Indigenous peoples.

This essay explores how colonialism puts the Miskitu people's survival at risk, placing this within a broader context of colonial subjugation of Indigenous peoples and lands. For Miskitu people, land is at the heart of their society's life cycle and sustenance. By violently disrupting this relationship, colonialism destroys the social and cultural relations that maintain survival and balance for the Miskitu and "commits environmental injustice through the violent disruption of human relationships to the environment."[4] Colonialism also violently disrupts *Klauna Laka*, an ancestral system of mutual collaboration and reciprocity that promotes survival, life, and self-determination in Miskitu communities. It represents the core of Miskitu people's eco-social traditions and includes practices of reciprocity and solidarity among members of a given community relying entirely on the subsistence resources obtained from the land.

In what follows, I offer a Miskitu conceptualization of *Klauna Laka*, its various forms of expressions, its social effects, and its connection to good living (*buen vivir*), then consider the interdependence of *Klauna Laka* and good living to Miskitu people's access to land and natural resources. I propose that the institutional policies of the Nicaraguan state endanger the *Klauna Laka* tradition and interrupt its connection to good living in two ways. First, state policies deny access to land as the material basis for the reproduction of sociocultural traditions by failing to remove non-Indigenous peoples illegally occupying land in Indigenous territories. Second, the interruption of Indigenous peoples' relations to land also interrupts the capacity for intergenerational transmission and reproduction of traditional knowledges. In turn, Miskitu people's identities, grounded in land-based practices for time immemorial, are at risk, as younger generations have limited knowledge of land relations or, in some cases, refuse to build and renew this knowledge.

My analysis draws upon traditional ecological knowledge (TEK)[5] theory as well as scholarship on Indigenous research methodologies and Indigenous epistemologies from Indigenous studies.[6] With regard to my analysis of colonial land dispossession and the cohabitation project, I am particularly interested in the way TEK literature underscores the epistemic differences between Indigenous and western knowledge systems, which can contribute to environmental and territorial conflicts.[7] Meanwhile, scholarship on Indigenous research methodologies and epistemologies advocates for Indigenous scholars to engage with their own forms of knowledge production by "reclaiming, reconnecting, and reordering those ways of knowing that were submerged, hidden, or driven underground."[8] Additionally, this scholarship urges us to "move beyond the human-centred approach to one of understanding, accepting, enacting, respecting, and honouring relationships with all of Creation."[9]

Drawing on Indigenous theory outside of Nicaragua, especially theory generated within the Canadian context, helps in foregrounding Miskitu perspectives. While Miskitu mobilization for land rights has been the subject of social-scientific research in Nicaragua, scholarship addressing Miskitu people's eco-social relations and notions of land is limited.[10] Some scholarship explores Miskitu people's construction of identity, pointing out how territorial identity is connected to a particular place that enables individuals to develop a sense of belonging.[11] Further, this scholarship suggests that identities connected to specific places result from a particular interpretation of socio-environmental meaning and that life experiences can reinforce a sense of territorial identity.[12] However, these studies have generally neglected the broader concerns of the colonial contexts in which the Miskitu people's land rights struggles are embedded. Thus, literature from other Indigenous theoretical traditions and colonial contexts can shed light on the Miskitu situation, considering that colonialism does not occur in isolation but circulates through a global imperial system. In this sense, *Klauna Laka* establishes a compelling link between grassroots politics of Miskitu communities struggling with land dispossession and ongoing debates in North American Indigenous studies, including calls for knowledge production grounded in Indigenous epistemologies.

Miskitu people's ecological knowledge systems are being actively endangered as part of colonization. The voices of Indigenous peoples have been excluded for centuries, yet their worlds have survived and adapted using different conceptions of nation, language, spirituality, laws, institutions, and values. Practicing *Klauna Laka* helps in reframing Indigenous peoples' knowledge in producing renewed political subjectivities and agendas that align with how Indigenous peoples conceive their territories and land relations.

I consider how restoring the *Klauna Laka* tradition assists Indigenous peoples' resistance and resurgence through contemporary Miskitu ecological knowledge, influenced by the interaction of precolonial knowledge systems and land ownership. These systems of knowledge are rooted in diverse local ecosystems and, therefore, are dependent on community experiences and geographical locations. These knowledge systems are epistemologically distinct from Western ecological knowledge. They encompass a relationship of reciprocity between humans, nonhumans, and supernatural entities directly associated with the care of land and natural resources, such as *Unta Dawanka* (the guardian

FIGURE 3.1 Wangki River. Photograph by Ruth H. Matamoros Mercado.

of the forest), *Liwa Mairin* (the guardian of the rivers/waters), *Prahaku* (the guardian of the winds), *Swinta* (the guardian of the plains), and *Uhra* (the guardian of the swamps).

Throughout this essay, I highlight the importance of placing concepts of land and natural resources at the center of Miskitu people's territorial struggles, going beyond the legal framework—specifically Law 28[13] and Law 44—often used to address Indigenous peoples' land rights in Nicaragua. From the many variations of Indigenous land-based practices, I chose to focus on *Klauna Laka* because, as stated by the elders I interviewed, it is at the core of Miskitu people's sociocultural traditions. Written knowledge about the *Klauna Laka* tradition is nonexistent; therefore, I rely on empirical research carried out as part of my doctoral dissertation, where I conducted a total of seventeen semi-structured interviews in Bilwi, the main city on the North Caribbean Coast of Nicaragua.[14] The interviews explore the cultural views of Miskitu people concerning land and natural resources and resistance struggles led by community leaders. The interviews reveal a broader understanding of Miskitu territorial resistance, relying on the collective memory of community land defenders. These interviews were crucial for understanding how issues of land and natural resources shape Miskitu people's resistance struggles. The interviews were complemented by observation and informal conversations with community members in Wasla, a Miskitu community located on the banks of the Wangki River on the North Caribbean Coast of Nicaragua (Figure 3.1). For a month, I observed the day-to-day lives of the community members to identify different forms of land use in subsistence activities such as farming, hunting, fishing, and sacred land use, as well as spiritual and healing practices, in order to gain a better understanding of the way they relate to land and natural resources.

Context

The Miskitu is the largest Indigenous group that inhabits the Moskitia. Today, the Moskitia has been reduced to a small portion of a vast territory that, during the fifteenth and sixteenth centuries, extended through the Caribbean Coast of Central America from Belize to Bocas del Toro in Panama (Figure 3.2).[15] The territory was first known as Tulu Walpa (Tulu meaning "oropendola," Walpa meaning "stone"), then deformed into Taguzgalpa.[16] Today, the name Moskitia represents an anti-colonial language intended to resist the names imposed by the Nicaraguan state: first, the Zelaya Department in reference to General José Santos Zelaya, then the Autonomous Regions, and today the Caribbean Coast.

Before Nicaragua officially annexed the Miskitu region in 1984, scholars generally agree that the development of the eastern coast and the Miskitu people was largely influenced by the economic activities and political influence of British officials, settlers, and traders.[17]

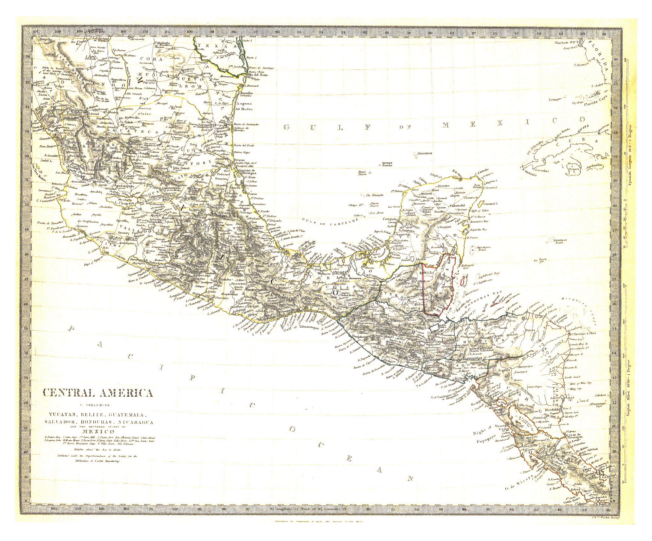

FIGURE 3.2 Central America, 1842, in *Maps of the Society for the Diffusion of Useful Knowledge (Great Britain)*, vol. 1 (London: Chapman and Hall, 1844).

The relationship between the Miskitu people and the British Empire represents a departure from conventional colonial paradigms. Rather than adhering to traditional models of colonialism, the British–Miskitu interaction is more aptly described as an instance of "trade colonialism" or "mercantile colonialism." In this form of colonial engagement, the colonial periphery serves as a supplier of raw materials to the metropole, which, in turn, produces manufactured goods such as firearms and textiles for distribution within its colonial territories. Notably, this model does not necessarily involve the permanent occupation or settlement of the colonized region.[18] This initial contact evolved into a broader political-military alliance that enabled the establishment of a Miskitu monarchy, although this was more symbolic than material. This alliance served as an anti-Spanish strategy that allowed the Miskitu people to resist the Spanish colonization and the forced assimilation that was taking place on the Pacific side of modern-day Nicaragua.[19] Through this alliance, the Miskitu people were able to maintain their identity as Indigenous peoples. The Miskitu monarchy ended in 1894 when the British withdrew from the region, and the emerging Nicaraguan state, politically and diplomatically aided by the United States, forced the incorporation of the Moskitia into the Nicaraguan domain.[20] Similar to the British Empire, the Nicaraguan state was also interested in the natural resources of the Moskitia, but above all, it had a political and cultural interest in the assimilation of Indigenous peoples. This perspective has been highlighted in the often overlooked racial dynamics of Miskitu–*colono* land disputes in Honduras.[21] These disputes, in essence, mirror a predicament, where Indigenous communities across the globe lack legally recognized claims to their territories.[22] This vacancy is perceived by settlers as an invitation to occupy these ostensibly vacant lands. Some of the most relevant aspects of these conflicts include cultural contrast in land utilization in such a way that the Miskito people's lifeways of hunting, fishing, and frequent movement within their territories present a stark contrast to the agricultural practices of the *colono*.[23] Additionally, Miskitu people's bond with their lands extends beyond mere material resources, incorporating significant cultural and spiritual elements.[24] These disparities are often leveraged to legitimize the invasion of Miskito territories, as both settlers and the state depict Miskito land usage as inefficient or unproductive. Furthermore, the intricacies of land ownership and agriculture are not simply connected to the livelihoods of the *colono* but are also deeply intertwined with their cultural identity and national sentiment. These settlers, identifying as the "authentic" farmers and citizens, often perceive their incursion onto Miskito territories as an affirmation of their identity.[25] Additionally, portrayals of Miskitu people as savages are commonly used by both the state and settlers to undermine their land-use practices. Such characterizations serve as justifications for the invasion of Miskitu territories and the imposition of settler land-use norms.

The perceived cultural superiority of the *mestizo* population has significantly influenced the region's social dynamics, leading to the social and economic marginalization of Indigenous communities in Moskitia. Currently, this perceived superiority exacerbates land disputes, as *mestizo* populations feel justified in encroaching upon Indigenous territories. This way, *colonos*' migration to Miskitu's territory, both in Nicaragua and Honduras, represents geographical interest that has also influenced and shaped the minds of Indigenous peoples with deep cultural and racial implications where the *mestizo* representatives of the Nicaraguan nation-state impose their language, practices, and beliefs upon the Miskitu population.

The assimilation project has seen many forms, from various methods of cultural oppression to centralized educational models. The most vivid example of the latter, as I will examine later on, was the Fundamental Education Project implemented throughout the 1960s. In essence, this project aimed to assimilate Indigenous peoples into Nicaragua's larger *mestizo* (Spanish-speaking) population by suppressing Indigenous peoples' beliefs, traditions, and languages.

Theoretical Framework

A growing number of academics and activists describe colonial domination as violent and disruptive. Although this violence is multifaceted and can take many forms, I direct attention to violence inflicted upon Indigenous peoples' ecological relations and the effects of this violence on their knowledge and cultural practices.[26] TEK scholarship provides an important framework for understanding the relational dimensions of colonial violence, as it illuminates the connections between the human and nonhuman world. As Kyle Whyte states, TEK is a "body of knowledge . . . embedded within multiple relationships among living beings, non-living things, and the environment."[27] This approach suggests that humans take from nature the resources needed for their subsistence and, in return, they provide nature the care and protection it needs to ensure its continuation for future generations. TEK is disrupted when violence occurs on the land through the exploitation of natural resources that, in turn, denies Indigenous peoples the primary sources of their life-making practices and knowledge systems. When land is violently commodified through colonialism, it becomes a source of profit rather than life. Accordingly, the resources that Indigenous peoples depend on to survive and to shape their identity are also destroyed, as ecological violence inflicted by colonialism interrupts the relationships of reciprocity between humans and nonhumans. Colonial ecological violence is also an attack on Indigenous epistemologies. Indigenous peoples' relations to land represent one of their primary sources of knowledge. Consequently, the "disruption of Indigenous relationships to land represents a profound epistemic, ontological, cosmological violence"[28] resulting in the destruction of their knowledge. Therefore, restoring Indigenous peoples' relation to land is crucial for their resistance and resurgence.

In her work with Josephine Mandamin and the Mother Earth Water Walk (MEWW), Deborah McGregor elaborates on this perspective by analyzing the "love, mutual respect, and responsibility towards the natural world, and water in particular."[29] Although McGregor refers explicitly to water, her work opens up the possibility of considering the broader networks of support and responsibilities that Indigenous peoples have with the land and its natural resources that ensure their survival and continuity. These responsibilities become severed through the workings of colonialism, as colonial ecological violence "disrupts Indigenous eco-social relations and generates specific risks and harms for Native peoples and communities."[30] Such violence led to the destruction of the *Klauna Laka* tradition, the epitome of Miskitu people's eco-social relations.

The concept of cultural categories, developed by Guillermo Bonfil, is helpful in understanding how Indigenous resistance to colonial violence is grounded in land relations.[31] This concept identifies four categories, depending on who owns the resources and who holds the decision-making capacity over those resources, including: (a) autonomous culture, which encompasses the resources that belong to a subordinated group and how the capacity to use those resources remains with that group; (b) appropriated culture, which includes the resources that belong to the subordinating group, but the subordinated group can still have access to them; (c) imposed culture, which refers to cases where neither the resources nor the decision-making capacity over them belongs to the subordinated group; and (d) alienated culture, which refers to the resources that belong to the subordinated group, but where they lack decision-making capacity over them. Cultural categories do not explicitly refer to colonial relationships of power. Nevertheless, they can be mobilized to describe the colonial power relations that continue to permeate access to land and natural resources in Moskitia and the colonial context in which Miskitu people's connections to land have been shaped and transformed over time.

Indigenous communities in Nicaragua and elsewhere around the globe continue to struggle to preserve and protect their sacred relationships with land and to restore alternative ways of relating with land that differ from the colonial narrative. The resilience of Indigenous peoples in contexts of colonial oppression is not always expressed through overt acts of resistance. The term "infrapolitics" refers to the political conflict in which the political expression of subordinated groups, for fear of expressing their opinion without any protection, gives rise to the development of a "hidden transcript."[32] Often, simple acts by Indigenous peoples, who incorporate social and political traditions into their daily lives, are enough to be considered effective resistance against the colonial structures of the state.[33] Collective continuance as a form of social resilience is a form of resistance to ecological violence and contributes to Indigenous resurgence amid conditions of colonial environmental injustice.[34] Resistance, in its various forms and through quotidian practices, provides a framework to examine transformation in conceptions of land and natural resources through the daily practices of those protecting their land against colonial incursions.

Klauna Laka: An Ancient System of Mutual Collaboration, Survival, and Self-Determination

Within this theoretical and historical context, I approach *Klauna Laka*, which, according to prominent Miskitu leaders, cultural specialists, and intellectuals, represents the core of Miskitu people's eco-social traditions and, until recently, represented an essential element of their identity and collective survival. *Klauna Laka* can be broadly translated as the practice of self-determination. Combining the opinion of different local experts, *Klauna Laka* could be defined as an eco-social tradition of Miskitu people consisting of practices of reciprocity and solidarity among members of a given community, regardless of family bonds and without the intervention of money. The tradition is based on the subsistence resources obtained from the land, and it is manifested through sharing labor, goods, and services in subsistence activities, community work, festivities, and emergencies, including sickness and death.

Klauna Laka emerged in the context of a subsistence economy prior to the incursion of Miskitu people into wage labor following the arrival of transnational companies in the late 1800s. Land was the essential feature that enabled the configuration of *Klauna Laka* as the core of Miskitu people's eco-social relations, but not the land as such or by itself. Instead, the form of land ownership—communal ownership, as opposed to individual property—made possible the social configuration and reproduction of the *Klauna Laka* tradition. When asked about the cohabitation project that the Nicaraguan state is trying to put forward, which will inevitably lead to land privatization, Miskitu spiritual leader William Webster strongly emphasized, "There is no individual property!"[35]

From the perspective of Miskitu people, land is conceived at three levels: communal land, areas of collective use, and areas of individual use. The communal land is conceived as a legacy from the ancestors and is collectively owned; it is then divided into different areas for subsistence activities depending on the resources they contain. These include areas for agriculture, hunting, forestry, fishing, and recreational use. These are also areas of collective use and ownership. The area for agriculture is further divided into individual parcels for each family. These parcels and the areas used for housing constitute the only areas for individual use. However, the mechanism through which they become areas of individual use does not involve legal formalities or paperwork. Instead, when a community member does agricultural work in the area designated for agricultural purposes or builds a house on an available piece of land, this community member becomes entitled to individually own that specific piece of land as the person who first invested work, time, and energy on that piece of land. In this sense, the only requirement to individually own a piece of land is to work or build on it (Figure 3.3). This way, the land belongs to whoever works for it, and work is the only condition that legitimizes individual ownership in a Miskitu community. From that moment on, the person can pass the land on to future generations without the intervention of written documents. This form of land ownership opposes how settlers occupy land in Indigenous communities, involving written and notarized documents. Further, while Miskitu communities mark their boundaries using natural elements such as sacred places or geographical locations like trees or rivers, settlers appropriate the land individually and fence what they consider to be their property within the communities.

The demarcation process resulting from Law 445 fragmented Indigenous territories into twenty-three smaller territories rather than preserving the land as conceived and used by Miskitu people for centuries as a communal space. These divisions also imposed boundaries between communities and territories, causing delimitation conflicts. Before Law 445, these conflicts did not occur, as people coexisted peacefully and commonly shared these lands based on the *Klauna Laka* principle of *pana pana lui laka*, which implies that people crossed the limits from one community to another in search of resources for their subsistence.

FIGURE 3.3
Design of a typical Miskitu house. Photograph by Ruth H. Matamoros Mercado.

Collective land ownership enables the configuration of particular social and cultural mechanisms such as *Klauna Laka*, which provides equal access to all the resources land offers to all community members. Consequently, community members experienced a deep sense of solidarity and reciprocity that enabled the conditions leading to the configuration of the *Klauna Laka* tradition. Reciprocity is a core value within *Klauna Laka* practices. It entails a sense of mutual responsibility for giving and receiving, not only among humans but also between humans and other living things.

Local experts identify eight reciprocation modalities manifested in different community activities. These modalities are *Pana-Pana*, *Tawi-Tawi*, *Yuwi-Yuwi*, *Pruwan Bikaia*, *Bakahnu Yuska*, *Latwan Laka Kum*, *Maihsa Wilkan Daknika*, and *Taika nani Daknika*. *Pana-Pana* can be broadly translated as "I give you and you give me" (in this case, a hand) and consists of community people voluntarily agreeing to help each other. This form of reciprocity was mainly practiced through all stages of agricultural activities, including harvesting and transporting harvested products to people's households. Broadly speaking, *Tawi-Tawi* evokes the idea of returning; in this case, it refers to returning a favor. It is another form of mutual collaboration mainly practiced for house- and canoe-construction activities. In this way, all members of the community help each other in those types of activities. In *Pana-Pana* and *Tawi-Tawi*, the recipient of solidarity does not provide monetary remuneration to the people who collaborate. Their only commitment is to provide food while they work. *Yuwi-Yuwi* can be translated as "distribution" and consists of sharing edible products obtained from harvesting, hunting, and fishing. Widows, single mothers, orphans, and people with disabilities are given priority in the distribution process. *Pruwan Bikaia* translates to "burying the dead" and refers to community members' support to a grieving person or family. While the mourning lasts, the entire community ceases all activities to support the grieving family in various ways, including coffin construction, the preparation of the burial site, the preparation of food for the funeral, and spiritual support through songs and prayers during the funeral and burial. *Bakahnu Yuska* represents one of the primary expressions of *Klauna Laka*. It translates as "to use collectively," referring to the goods for collective use within the community's land, and is directly linked to the communal ownership of the land. The goods for collective use include areas of abundant resources, such as fertile soils for agricultural purposes, water sources, fishing banks, forests, spiritual sites, and beautiful landscapes used for recreational purposes. These are areas of collective use and, therefore, are shared among all community members. The elders identify a variety of lower-ranking expressions of solidarity practiced in various areas beyond subsistence activities. These include *Latwan Laka Kum*, a love bond intended to aid widows, sick people, single mothers, and orphaned or helpless children. *Maihsa Wilkan Daknika* is a team that unifies efforts toward achieving a specific goal. *Taika nani Daknika* is similar to the previous one but includes only family members. These eight modalities of reciprocity are collectively conceived as *Klauna Laka*. It can be inferred then that *Klauna Laka* embodies Miskitu people's ability to autonomously assume the satisfaction of the economic, social, and cultural needs of community people as long as they have access to the material resources that land provides to sustain these needs.

When practiced, *Klauna Laka* generates strong tangible and intangible social effects. It ensures the conditions for food self-sufficiency. It strengthens social ties such as trust, mutual respect, solidarity, and unity. Practicing *Klauna Laka* also results in decreased rates of violence and criminality. It produces a collective climate of security, peacefulness, and freedom. These conditions contribute to constructing a sense of cultural identity built around the practice of *Klauna Laka* and good living (*buen vivir*).

Klauna Laka traditions began to deteriorate, though not as intensely, with the arrival of transnational (mainly U.S.) corporations. This scenario caused the incursion of Miskitu people into the market economy, as they engaged in wage labor in these companies.[36] This scenario marked the beginning of the deterioration and gradual abandonment of *Klauna Laka* by introducing money in exchange for products and services as opposed to the previous form of reciprocity without monetary remuneration. Additionally, these corporations continued the exploitation of natural resources for nearly a hundred years, causing the physical elimination of many thousands of trees, the massive contamination of water sources, the destruction of local ecosystems, and the extinction of wild species of birds, reptiles, and mammals. This irrational exploitation of natural resources denied Indigenous peoples the primary conditions for their survival due to the pressure on their lands and territories. Although there is no written account, local experts agree that *Klauna Laka* deteriorated drastically during the 1950s and 1960s. It is worth noticing a combination of factors during these decades that exacerbated the deterioration of *Klauna Laka*: first, the transformation from a subsistence economy to a market economy; and second, the educational institutions and land policies implemented by the Nicaraguan state through the Fundamental Education Project and the Instituto de Fomento Nacional (INFONAC), respectively.

Assimilationist Education

The Nicaraguan government implemented a vast education plan through the Fundamental Education Project to assimilate the Indigenous population into the larger non-Indigenous/Spanish-speaking Nicaraguan society. An elder described the project as "an instrument to twist the Indigenous mindset" by fostering an aversion to the values of Miskitu identity in children and youth and replacing these with a sense of Nicaraguan *mestizo* identity.[37]

Mestizo is the term widely used in Latin America for people with identities based on ethnic and cultural mixture that supposedly occurred in the distant past and then became nationalized as the dominant group in Nicaragua, among other places. The Fundamental Education Project sought to erase Miskitu as Indigenous peoples, instead pushing them to join "civilization" represented by the Nicaragua nation-state. In this context, erasure meant that their only chance of becoming part of the nation was to abandon their identity, language, ways of life, and, above all, their lands. One method used in this project was hiring and bringing to Miskitu communities only Spanish-speaking professors who lacked knowledge of the Miskitu language and culture. Required classes were delivered only in Spanish, and children were severely punished for speaking Miskitu in the classroom and during recess. In their interviews, the elders described different punishments for schoolchildren: being beaten with wooden rulers, chalkboard erasers, leather straps, and tree branches; being placed in the sun and holding heavy books in the air with arms fully extended for long periods; being forced to kneel over rocks or graters; having their ears and hair pulled; and being violently shaken and struck on the head. Attending school in these conditions was torturous and resulted in high dropout rates.

Fidel Wilson, an elder, notes: "The educational experience was one of suffering. A few endured the suffering and could continue, but most of us could not. When I started first grade, we were a group of around twenty children, and only five of us reached sixth grade because of the language barrier and punishments. Those who continued resorted to memorizing the class content without any deeper educational advancement."[38] Simultaneously, this project replaced the elders in their educational role by forcing children to attend school instead of receiving the knowledge passed on to them by the elders in their household. As a result, elders could no longer transmit traditional knowledge, including *Klauna Laka*, from one generation to another. Implementing an exogenous educational model had an alienating rather than beneficial effect. An elder recalls: "It was more important for children to take care of their food plantations than to go to school. I think seventy-five percent of the population felt that way because that was the only life we knew."[39] As noted by local experts, this project represents a tragic loss of Miskitu people's knowledge and eco-social traditions, since it did not include any of these topics in its educational curriculum.

Today's educational model may not be as abusive, but it remains alienated from Indigenous peoples' cultural perspectives and knowledge. As a result, children and young people are detached from their land, history, and social and cultural practices that form the foundation for constructing a Miskitu identity. Another elder, Naboth Zacarias, states: "If the educational system included teaching topics related to the *Klauna Laka* traditions,

Miskitu peoples' history, the Miskitu way of life, it would be very good. But their teaching is not like that. They teach only what the government cares about. In this way, education came to us, but when it comes to our practices, traditions, and our *Klauna Laka*, we are left behind. Our youth do not understand the problems of our communities. Only a few still preserve their sense of Miskitu identity after graduating."[40] Local experts unanimously agree that the capacity for intergenerational transmission of Miskitu knowledge and traditions is almost nonexistent.

Appropriation of Land and Resources

In 1953, the Nicaraguan legislature approved Law 11, creating INFONAC. This law enabled the Nicaraguan state to request that the administration of what they considered to be "national lands" and other forest resources be transferred to the institute. Through INFONAC, the Nicaraguan state exercised direct and absolute control over the land and natural resources in Indigenous territories, endangering Miskitu people's ways of life. Rufino Lucas, one of the elders interviewed, remembers the following:

> Many people were imprisoned on charges of setting the forest on fire, but that was not true. There was a contradiction [between the law imposed by the Nicaraguan state and Miskitu people's ways of life]. Miskitu people's subsistence depended partly on the consumption of *kakamuk* [a black, spiny-tailed iguana] and *siakwa* [plain turtle]. In January and February, when the *kakamuk* and *siakwa* are suitable for spawning and consumption, they use the plains and sandy terrains for spawning, so people would set part of the plains on fire, not on a whim, but to find and follow the footprints of these animals. The livelihoods of Miskitu communities also depend on hunting and fishing. When it comes to hunting deer, people would use fire as a way to attract deer that feed on the ashes and grass sprouts. Because of this, many people were imprisoned under INFONAC's policies.[41]

Additionally, INFONAC started to control access to other forest resources, mainly lumber, limiting Miskitu people's ability to obtain wood for the construction of houses and canoes. As a result, the nation-state was structured on the assumption that Indigenous lands were idle lands and had to be put to work through capitalist and extractive logics and practices; Indigenous people had to be civilized and incorporated into Nicaraguan society through education. In this way, the Nicaraguan state consolidated its territorial dominance to the complete detriment of Indigenous peoples.

This damage is not only physical but also political, social, economic, and cultural, as it resulted in the destruction of their ways of life and caused ongoing damage to their identity. That same logic is used for the current invasion of Indigenous people's lands. Those mechanisms were not dismantled; they continue to be reproduced today with the support and protection of new laws approved and enacted by the Nicaraguan state, such as the cohabitation project. These policies and laws express colonial violence to land and "profound epistemic, ontological, [and] cosmological violence."[42] The disruption of Miskitu people's relations to land and its resources, combined with the current lack of access to lands that settlers have occupied, makes it impossible to sustain and reproduce Miskitu people's eco-cultural traditions and their sense of cultural identity built around land-based practices. As has been accurately described, "colonial ecological violence" is a process of "[disrupting] Indigenous eco-social relations."[43]

Going back to the cultural categories detailed earlier, it can be seen that *Klauna Laka*'s practices remained strong when the Miskitu people related to land under the parameters of autochthonous culture, meaning that land and resources belonged to the community, and they had not yet lost their decision-making capacity over those resources. The practices of *Klauna Laka* started to decline with the British Empire's implementation of franchise colonialism, the arrival of American transnational companies, and the imposition of an exogenous educational model under the Nicaraguan nation-state. Finally, such practices sharply declined when Miskitu people were vilified as an alienated culture, which they continue to live through today. In this context, the Nicaraguan state exercises almost absolute control of the lands and natural resources of Moskitia, denying Indigenous peoples access to it. One elder notes: "The ability to transmit the *Klauna Laka* tradition is closely linked to the control of natural resources. Having ownership over resources gives great capacity and power to our communities. There are abundant resources on the ground and underground. But ownership of these resources is denied to our people."[44]

Land, *Klauna Laka*, and the Politics of Resistance and Resurgence

The accelerated decline of *Klauna Laka* in these decades also prompted Indigenous peoples to organize for the first time to defend their rights. This organizational effort led to the creation of the Alianza para el Progreso de Miskitus y Sumus (ALPROMISU), the first Indigenous organization that brought together the Miskitu and the Mayangna.[45] ALPROMISU was the first organization that emerged from within Indigenous communities to meet the needs of Indigenous peoples. It facilitated cultural synergy among the Miskitu and Mayangna communities and planted the seed of resistance. ALPROMISU later evolved and transformed into various Miskitu resistance movements leading to today's Yapti Tasba Masraka (Sons and Daughters of Mother Earth [YATAMA]). These organizations have been the voice of Indigenous peoples throughout the last seventy years, including during the armed conflict with the Sandinistas during the 1980s.[46]

This conflict ended when the government approved Law 28, which granted autonomous status to Indigenous territories. There are still sometimes controversies with different factions within and around these organizations in the political sphere, but the formation of Indigenous political movements has had a significant impact. As a result of these resistance movements, there have been some legal victories. In addition to Law 28 and Law 445, in 1987, the Nicaraguan Constitution was changed to recognize Nicaragua as a multicultural state and accepted and promoted the use of Indigenous languages. This scenario meant that, for the first time, Nicaragua acknowledged the existence of Indigenous peoples, marking a shift from assimilation to multiculturalism.

In 2002, in order to create the conditions for the approval of Law 445, the Nicaraguan Constitution was modified again to include communal property, granting it the same status as other forms of property recognized until then, such as private and public property. Communal property is directly related to the communal ownership of Indigenous territories, as opposed to the individual appropriation of lands in other parts of the country. Nicaragua has also ratified the ILO Convention 169 and the Escazú Agreement and adopted the United Nations Declaration on the Rights of Indigenous Peoples.

The Nicaraguan government takes pride in having one of the most comprehensive legal frameworks on the rights of Indigenous peoples throughout Latin America. However, this legal framework does not translate into improving the living conditions of Indigenous communities. When asked about the level of satisfaction about achieving these laws, most of the Miskitu people I interviewed said they were deeply unsatisfied because the results do not correspond to people's needs and demands. They describe the Autonomy Law and Law 445 as a failure and regret the decreased access to their traditional lands due to ongoing settlers' invasions, resulting in the erasure of their identity built around land-based practices. For example, Amalia Dixon says, "We began resistance movements for our land, which was our first right [the most important one], but we did it under the influence of external forces. We were disoriented, [our efforts] were not oriented correctly. Over time, we have lost [our path] to external forces, those that have come upon us. We did not know how to handle them, so we have fallen into acculturation [assimilation]. Yes, working the land is one of our rights, but we no longer know how to do that. Younger generations do not know how to work the land."[47]

We see, then, that colonial institutions and policies imposed by the Nicaraguan state over these territories have erased the social fabric of these peoples. There is no respect for Indigenous peoples' knowledge and ways of life. While this persists, it will be impossible for the laws themselves to contain this wave of violence, racism, and colonialism. This scenario is combined with the imposition of an external educational system that does not include teaching traditional practices, thus threatening to gradually exterminate Indigenous communities by depriving them of their livelihoods and suppressing their knowledge. As Teodoro Downs states: "Our identity trait that is still striving is our language, but as far as our land-based practices go, we are in terrible shape. Our language is only one aspect of our identity. The most crucial part is our relationship with the land, but we miss that part of our identity. Losing *Klauna Laka* is a tragedy. It is the main value of our identity. It is like being orphaned by the death of a mother."[48]

A strong theme that emerges from the interviews is that of younger generations falling into a state of self-denial. They express that the identity crisis is more common among young people who do not want or know how to relate to land because it is not being taught to them. As Alvaro Cirilo notes, education is an opportunity for our improvement, but at the same time, it is the cause of our regression:

> The education system has these two opposite effects. It means that education is very advanced today. But this same educational advance brings terrible consequences for us. We experience the erasure of our identity, which is a consequence of the

advancement of education. What happens is that our youth who study reject the use of our language and other traits that form part of our identity, like our food.[49]

This quote manifests the main characteristic of cultural oppression. When everything around you is intended to make you feel that your language, culture, appearance, and skin color are wrong, eventually, you will want to free yourself from that burden. You will seek to blend in with what you are taught is good—that is, the identity of the *mestizo*, the language of the *mestizo*.

Land, the resources it provides, and the collective ownership of both have played a vital role in the reproduction of *Klauna Laka* as the representation of Miskitu people's eco-social traditions. Therefore, practicing *Klauna Laka* represents a "hidden transcript" that embodies expressions of resistance against the colonial state.[50] *Klauna Laka* disrupts Nicaraguan colonial policies by opposing the legal processes used to address Indigenous peoples' struggles for land, absorbing their claims within the state's legal apparatuses linked to institutional processes. In this sense, I follow Black scholar Robin Kelley, who refers to being Black as "not just political struggle but the struggles of everyday life . . . : fighting, dancing, begging, cajoling, teaching, thinking, loving."[51] Miskitu people's relation to the land and their everyday practices manifested in *Klauna Laka* inform the basis of their resistance and ultimately provide insights into how the discourses and practices of resistance are embodied at multiple scales.

Klauna Laka, as a system of reciprocity between humans and nonhumans, also opposes notions of development and progress imposed by the Nicaraguan state from a capitalist standpoint. By collectively using the land and the resources it provides to attend to their material, social, spiritual, and cultural needs, Miskitu people make sure there are enough resources for everyone while at the same time protecting the environment by not taking more than they need. In this scenario, *Klauna Laka* serves as an authentic mechanism of self-determination in order to protect their ways of life and their natural resources. Therefore, it is essential to recover the ownership of these lands to facilitate the restoration of *Klauna Laka* practices, reaffirming the ancestral form of political agency for Miskitu people. The restoration of *Klauna Laka* can only be achieved by recovering the land and restructuring the educational model. This, in turn, will lead to the conditions that generate a sense of good living aligned with Miskitu people's worldview. Avelino Cox expresses this succinctly: "We cannot talk about good living from a Western perspective. Good living for us does not translate to having luxurious cars and houses; money in the bank is not that! For us, good living is having our Mother Land and sharing everything we have."[52]

The current struggle for land rights that Miskitu people are undergoing and their refusal to share the land with the settlers bring a ray of hope for reconfiguring their identity in a way that reclaims *Klauna Laka*. I suggest that Miskitu people's identity is not lost; instead, it is adapting to the new economic and social reality. If *Klauna Laka* served to shape Miskitu identity in a context of a subsistence economy before the introduction of capitalism as the dominant economic model, the current territorial resistance must lead to the construction of a new identity, keeping land at the center to enable the restoration of *Klauna Laka* practices.

NOTES

1. The Miskitu people are one of the largest Indigenous groups in the Moskitia, a region inhabited mainly by Indigenous and Afro-descendant peoples on the Caribbean Coast of Nicaragua and Honduras. My research focuses on the North Caribbean Coast of Nicaragua.
2. Law 445 is officially known as the Law of Communal Property Regime of the Indigenous Peoples and Ethnic Communities of the Autonomous Regions of the Atlantic Coast of Nicaragua and the Rivers Bocay, Coco, Indio, and Maíz.
3. Centro por la Justicia y el Derecho Internacional, *Resistencia Miskitu: Una lucha por el territorio y la vida*, July 2020, https://cejil.org/publicaciones/resistencia-miskitu-una-lucha-por-el-territorio-y-la-vida-actualizacion-a-julio-de-2020-2/; and The Oakland Institute, *Nicaragua's Failed Revolution: The Indigenous Struggle for Saneamiento*, 2020, https://www.oaklandinstitute.org/nicaragua-failed-revolution-indigenous-struggle-saneamiento.
4. Kyle Powys Whyte, "Settler Colonialism, Ecology, and Environmental Injustice," *Environment and Society* 9, no. 1 (2018): 125.
5. Nicholas James Reo and Kyle Powys Whyte, "Hunting and Morality as Elements of Traditional Ecological Knowledge," *Human Ecology: An Interdisciplinary Journal* 40, no. 1 (2012): 15–27.
6. Linda Tuhiwai Smith, *Decolonizing Methodologies: Research and Indigenous Peoples*, 2nd ed. (London: Zed Books Ltd., 2012); and Deborah McGregor, "Honouring Our Relations: An Anishnaabe Perspective on Environmental Justice," in *Speaking for Ourselves: Environmental Justice in Canada*, ed. Julian Agyeman, Peter Cole, Randolph Haluza-DeLay, and Pat O'Riley (Vancouver: University of British Columbia Press, 2009), 27–41.
7. Reo and Whyte, "Hunting and Morality as Elements of Traditional Ecological Knowledge"; Kyle Powys Whyte, "On the Role of Traditional Ecological Knowledge as a Collaborative Concept: A Philosophical Study," *Ecological Processes* 2, no. 1 (2013): 1–12; and Arturo Escobar, "*Sentipensar* con la tierra: Las luchas territoriales y la dimensión ontológica de las epistemologías del Sur," *Revista de antropología iberoamericana* 11, no. 1 (January–April 2016): 11–32.
8. Smith, *Decolonizing Methodologies*, 69.
9. McGregor, "Honouring Our Relations," 33.
10. Charles R. Hale, *Resistance and Contradiction: Miskitu Indians and the Nicaraguan State, 1894–1987* (Stanford, Calif.: Stanford University Press, 1994); Mary Finley-Brook and Karl Offen, "Bounding the Commons: Land Demarcation in Northeastern Nicaragua," *Bulletin of Latin American Research* 28, no. 3 (2009): 343–63; Charles R. Hale, "'Wan Tasbaya Dukiara': Contested Notions of Land Rights in Miskitu History," in *Remapping Memory: The Politics of TimeSpace*, ed. Jonathan Boyarin (Minneapolis: University of Minnesota Press, 1994), 67–98; Julie Cupples, "Wild Globalization: The Biopolitics of Climate Change and Global Capitalism on Nicaragua's Mosquito Coast," *Antipode* 44, no. 1 (2012): 10–30; Theodore McDonald, "The Moral Economy of the Miskito Indians: Local Roots of a Geopolitical Conflict," in *Ethnicities and Nations: Processes of Interethnic Relations in Latin America, Southeast Asia, and the Pacific*, ed. Remo Guidieri, Francesco Pellizzi, and Stanley J. Tambiah (Houston: Rothko Chapel, 1988), 107–53; and Bernard Nietschmann, *Between Land and Water: The Subsistence Ecology of the Miskito Indians, Eastern Nicaragua* (New York: Seminar Press, 1973).
11. Claudia García, "'Estar en casa': Identidad regional e identidad comunitaria de los Miskitu de Asang, río Coco," *Mesoamérica* 36 (December 1998): 517–37.
12. Karl Henry Offen, "The Miskitu Kingdom Landscape and the Emergence of a Miskitu Ethnic Identity, Northeastern Nicaragua and Honduras, 1600–1800" (PhD diss., University of Texas, Austin, 1999).
13. Autonomy Statute of the Regions of the Atlantic Coast of Nicaragua, Law 28, October 1987.
14. I conducted the interviews in Miskitu, then transcribed and translated them into Spanish and English. The first set of interviews was conducted with well-known Miskitu cultural specialists, thinkers, elders, and spiritual leaders.
15. Robert A. Naylor, *Penny Ante Imperialism: The Mosquito Shore and the Bay of Honduras, 1600–1914; A Case Study in British Informal Empire* (Rutherford, N.J.: Farleigh Dickinson University Press, 1989).
16. Karl H. Offen, "Narrating Place and Identity, or Mapping Miskitu Land Claims in Northeastern Nicaragua," *Human Organization* 62, no. 4 (2003): 389.

17 Karl H. Offen, "The Sambo and Tawira Miskitu: The Colonial Origins and Geography of Intra-Miskitu Differentiation in Eastern Nicaragua and Honduras," *Ethnohistory* 49, no. 2 (2002): 320.
18 Nancy Shoemaker, "A Typology of Colonialism," *Perspectives on History*, 2015, https://www.historians.org/research-and-publications/perspectives-on-history/october-2015/a-typology-of-colonialism.
19 Troy S. Floyd, *The Anglo-Spanish Struggle for Mosquitia* (Albuquerque: University of New Mexico Press, 1967).
20 Philip A. Dennis and Michael D. Olien, "Kingship among the Miskito," *American Ethnologist* 11, no. 4 (1984): 726.
21 Sharlene Mollett, "Racial Narratives: Miskito and 'Colono' Land Struggles in the Honduran Mosquitia," *Cultural Geographies* 18, no. 1 (2011): 43–62.
22 Mollett, "Racial Narratives," 1.
23 Mollett, "Racial Narratives," 6.
24 Mollett, "Racial Narratives," 9.
25 Mollett, "Racial Narratives," 12.
26 Eve Tuck and K. Wayne Yang, "Decolonization Is Not a Metaphor," *Decolonization: Indigeneity, Education & Society* 1, no. 1 (2012): 1–40; and Vanessa Watts, "Indigenous Place-Thought and Agency amongst Humans and Non-humans (First Woman and Sky Woman Go on a European World Tour!)," *Decolonization: Indigeneity, Education & Society* 2, no. 1 (2013): 20–34.
27 Whyte, "On the Role of Traditional Ecological Knowledge as a Collaborative Concept," 4.
28 Tuck and Yang, "Decolonization Is Not a Metaphor," 5.
29 Deborah McGregor, "Indigenous Women, Water Justice and *Zaagidowin* (Love)," *Canadian Woman Studies* 30, nos. 2–3 (2013): 71.
30 J. M. Bacon, "Settler Colonialism as Eco-social Structure and the Production of Colonial Ecological Violence," *Environmental Sociology* 5, no. 1 (2019): 59.
31 Guillermo Bonfil, "La teoría del control cultural en el estudio de procesos étnicos," *Estudios sobre las culturas contemporáneas* 4, no. 12 (1991): 165–204.
32 James C. Scott, *Domination and the Arts of Resistance: Hidden Transcripts* (New Haven: Yale University Press, 1990), 183–201.
33 Theresa McCarthy, *In Divided Unity: Haudenosaunee Reclamation at Grand River* (Tucson: University of Arizona Press, 2016).
34 Whyte, " Settler Colonialism, Ecology, and Environmental Injustice," 131.
35 William Webster (Miskitu elder and spiritual leader), interviewed by Jorge Matamoros, May 2019.
36 Mary W. Helms, "Miskito Slaving and Culture Contact: Ethnicity and Opportunity in an Expanding Population," *Journal of Anthropological Research* 39, no. 2 (Summer 1983): 179–97.
37 Naboth Zacarias (Miskitu elder and spiritual leader), interviewed by Jorge Matamoros, October 2020.
38 Fidel Wilson (Miskitu cultural specialist), interviewed by Jorge Matamoros, October 2020.
39 Amalia Dixon (Miskitu educator), interviewed by the author, October 2020.
40 Naboth Zacarias (Miskitu elder and spiritual leader), interviewed by Jorge Matamoros, October 2020.
41 Rufino Lucas (director of the National Commission of Territorial Demarcation [CONADETI]), interviewed by Jorge Matamoros, October 2020.
42 Tuck and Yang, "Decolonization Is Not a Metaphor," 5.
43 Bacon, "Settler Colonialism as Eco-social Structure and the Production of Colonial Ecological Violence," 59.
44 Yurintin Toledo (Miskitu elder and spiritual leader), interviewed by Jorge Matamoros, October 2020.
45 The Mayangna is the second-largest Indigenous group on the North Caribbean Coast of Nicaragua. Mayangnas gained national and international prestige in 2001 after winning a lawsuit against the government of Nicaragua before the Inter-American Court of Human Rights for a concession granted to the Soles del Caribe (SOLCARSA) company in Mayangna territory, specifically the community of Awas Tingni. Law 445 resulted from a long process accelerated by the court's judgment, which determined that the Nicaraguan government should include a law providing legal protection to Indigenous territories in its legal framework.
46 The Frente Sandinista de Liberación Nacional (FSLN) is a left-wing Nicaraguan political party that came to power in 1979 after overthrowing the dictator Anastasio Somoza. The Sandinistas were voted out of office in 1990 but came back in 2007 and have been in power since then, despite ongoing accusations of

human rights violations and being labeled as a dictatorship by the U.S. government and the international community.

47 Amalia Dixon (Miskitu educator), interviewed by the author, October 2020.
48 Teodoro Downs (Miskitu elder and spiritual leader), interviewed by Jorge Matamoros, October 2020.
49 Alvaro Cirilo (Miskitu elder), interviewed by Jorge Matamoros, October 2020.
50 Scott, *Domination and the Arts of Resistance*.
51 Robin Kelley, "On the Density of Black Being," in *Scratch*, ed. Christine Kim (New York: Studio Museum of Harlem, 2005), 10.
52 Avelino Cox (Miskitu elder and cultural specialist), interviewed by Jorge Matamoros, October 2020.

4

Placemaking as Indigenous Resurgence in the Oceanic Diaspora

JAMES MILLER

Roots *and* their identities and traditions are also *routed*, both metaphorically and literally.[1]

Mobility is an important and growing spatial practice of Indigenous communities. For Pacific Islanders, being rooted and routed is a common experience that lives within us through our genealogy and carries forward through our contemporary transnational experience. Vicente Diaz demonstrates that "native roots and routes are not mutually exclusive but mutually and powerfully constitutive and generative."[2] Roots refer to the ancestral homeland, the land in which Indigenous technical and ecological knowledge is developed, inclusive of the sea. Routes reflect the historical paths that our ancestors took across the ocean to new lands and the knowledge that was developed through voyaging practices; routes also refer to a continuation of these practices and processes. Roots and routes also include the notion of transplanting. Transplanting is a "relational construct" and "also marks the possibilities in taking root and growing in a different soil while continuing to maintain an originary location and emphasizing indigeneity as a central form of identification."[3] This essay explores notions of mobility shared across the Pacific diaspora and critically examines placemaking practices of these diasporic Indigenous communities to understand what it means to be in relation. Engaging with the discourse of *Vā Moana* (Pacific spaces of relationality), research conducted with Rimajol (Marshallese) communities in the United States highlights the importance of Native depth within their placemaking practices and reflects metaphysical connections to land within their negotiation of space across routes. Diaz defines Native depth as "deep Indigenous ancestral and ecological verticality."[4] The discourse of *Vā Moana*, as developed by Albert Refiti and

Anna-Christina Engels-Schwarzpaul, studies Pacific notions of space through Indigenous Pacific and Western thought.[5] To draw from Refiti and Engels-Schwarzpaul, "How do communities, professional artists, architects, scholars, and other contributors to diasporic identity and community formation engage with vā in local, regional and global constellations?"[6] *Vā Moana* provides an effective orientation for examining Indigenous planning as a placemaking practice, in particular exploring how Indigenous planning may provide new possibilities for Indigenous futures as Native-to-Native-to-Settler relations govern the creation of urban space.

In the examination of diasporic Indigenous placemaking, Land Back becomes multifaceted. It concerns the negotiation of spatial production through Indigenous-to-Indigenous relations governed by the specificities of the local, and it concerns the ability of diasporic communities to perpetuate their Indigenous identities. In the process of making, socio-spatial relations are redefined beyond the structure of settler colonialism, transforming settler-colonial spaces into Indigenous spaces. Within this process, the solidarity between marginalized communities in urban environments is examined to understand how Indigenous and diasporic Indigenous relationship building might be possible to create Indigenous futures. Relations and governance are significant in mediating the production of built environments.

The question of relationality has been raised among Indigenous and settler scholars to analyze what it means to be in good and generative relations with Indigenous communities as opposed to the settler-colonial state. Since placemaking is mediated within social fields, the meanings applied in the construction of space reflect negotiations between multiple actors: culture, place-specific practices, power, etc.[7] For placemaking practices to demonstrate Indigenous resurgence, they need to uphold Indigenous presence and knowledge; through this process, these practices destabilize settler colonialism. The work of Diaz with Micronesian and Dakota communities in Mní Sóta Makhóčhe provides guidance on how these forms of placemaking practices take place. Diaz opens the possibilities in "Native-to-Native-to-Settler relations" within community-based and engaged work through which diasporic Indigenous "are able to learn the 'seas' of their homeland and their new homes, and all the prerequisite ecological and cultural knowledge necessary to locate—to emplace—oneself properly in time/space in indigenous terms."[8] Diaz employs the analytical framework of transindigeniety to "imagine new ways of being indigenous but that also describes deep aboriginal cultural belongings to specific places while also permitting wide lateral reach across time and space, albeit in ways that do not lose familiar and signature indigenous belongings and accountabilities to place, to site, and cultural specificity."[9] These relationships, grounded in decolonial praxis, demonstrate radical Indigenous relationalities. Through the sites of engagement discussed in this essay, the Native-to-Native-to-Settler relations are explored within placemaking practices of Rimajol communities. How might we establish more pathways toward decolonial futures that build upon frameworks of transindigeneity as seen in the production of built environments? Might Native-to-Native practices in the coproduction of Indigenous futures provide multiple potentialities for Land Back?

The essay explores "arriving in relation" as an essential component of routes in the Pacific diaspora, drawing from Diaz and J. Kēhaulani Kauanui's framing of roots and routes,[10] Emalani Case's use of "routed" in the theorization of *Kahiki*,[11] and Diaz's development of Native depth and Native reach.[12] I develop the concept of routed normativity as a corresponding concept to Glen Coulthard and Leanne Betasamosake Simpson's grounded normativity for diasporic Pacific Islanders. Grounded normativity "refers to the ethical frameworks provided by these Indigenous place-based practices and associated forms of knowledge."[13] Routed normativity reflects the deep Indigenous ancestral and ecological knowledge that allowed for routes to form across Oceania and establish Native-to-Native relations. Routed normativity takes into consideration the multifaceted relationships in mediating placemaking practices explained previously, while taking into consideration the critical relations between Indigenous and diasporic Indigenous communities; these relations complicate and challenge the structure of settler colonialism, building toward Indigenous resurgence.[14] This essay explores the potential of grounded normativity reflected in routes as diasporic Oceanic communities arrive in relation to new places, constructing space to support their community and create a sense of place. Through the analysis of Rimajol (Marshallese) and Kanaka Maoli (Native Hawaiian) placemaking practices, I aim to demonstrate that diasporic Indigenous placemaking is a process that challenges settler colonialism as Indigenous communities co-construct Indigenous futures grounded in place-based ethics. The concept of deep time is used to challenge settler control of urban spatial production and work with Rimajol communities in Hawai'i, Oregon, and Arkansas and provides empirical examples of "new islands" through transnational spatial relationships.

I locate myself within the work through a positionality statement, then introduce key terms through a literature review. The essay then explores deep time as a method for dissolving settler layers of spatial production to uncover Indigenous pasts, presents, and futures as an approach to understanding the place-based genealogies of knowledge within grounded normativity. Weaving Kanaka Maoli and *Vā Moana* theories in the analysis of Rimajol grounded and routed normativity, the essay explores Rimajol placemaking and spatial relations within the diaspora. Finally, exploring three specific examples of diasporic Indigenous placemaking practices, I theorize routed normativity in coproduction of relational space.

To make a few points on terminology, I use the terms *Moana*, Pacific, and Oceania somewhat interchangeably. Each term has its own meaning within different contexts, and their use is not intended to highlight some groups within the Pacific Ocean while excluding others. As Tēvita O. Ka'ili states, *Moana* provides a term for Indigenous Pacific scholars to talk back to Western knowledge production.[15] My use of terms draws on the reframing of *Moana* by scholars within the Vā Moana research cluster at Auckland University of Technology. I acknowledge *Moana* privileges a "Polynesian" framing of Oceania, a term most notably established in Epeli Hau'ofa's essay "Our Sea of Islands," that is more broadly accepted among my colleagues and friends in Aelon Kein Ad (our sea and sky of islands, the Marshallese term for the territory referred to as the Republic of the Marshall Islands).[16] The term "Pacific" is used for its broader use in knowledge production on and within the Pacific Ocean. Lastly, the terms *vā* and *wā* are used interchangeably as cognates from different parts of Polynesian Oceania; *vā* (Samoa) refers to space and *wā* (Hawai'i) refers to space-time.

Positionality: Diasporas and Fields of Research

Settler colonialism is an experience shared among displaced and dispossessed Indigenous communities. While the specifics of each experience are different, there are overarching patterns across time and space; it is in these patterns of everyday life that solidarity is built to decolonize the settler structure. Within Indigenous research, it is particularly important to analyze our positionalities as they influence our relations within communities and our interpretations of the field of study. To locate myself within this work, in relationships to people and place, my positionality influences understandings of key concepts discussed: Land Back, diaspora, and space-time.

I am hapa, Kanaka Maoli, Japanese, Hungarian, diasporic Indigenous, and a third-generation immigrant, born and raised within the Pacific diaspora as an uninvited guest on Potawatomi, Peoria, Miami, and Kaskaskia lands. My position as an uninvited guest on Indigenous lands has continued throughout my life, yet I have been unable to return to Hawai'i for a viable career due to the same settler-colonial apparatus that led my father away from the islands in the first place. These diasporic experiences are complexly intertwined with implications often dictated by the settler structure that negatively impacts Indigenous hosts and diasporic Indigenous.

While I am not a member of the Marshallese communities discussed in this essay, I was a member of the broader Pacific Islander community in Oregon in addition to sharing experiences and ancestry with members from these communities that inform relationship building and the research collaborations that have emerged from this context. In the context of Ho'oulu 'Āina in Hawai'i, I am genealogically connected to both the place and community. The shared experiences of diaspora, placemaking, relationship building, and identity are what draw me to this work. Raised within the diaspora, I was not embedded in ancestral land relations, but I had the privilege of understanding the value of place through visits with my extended family.[17] Diasporic experiences—whether they are shaped by a rural-urban divide or by oceans such as the Pacific diaspora—are shaped by a sense of placelessness, or living between two worlds where one does not fully belong. Through dispossession, Indigenous peoples are removed from their land relations, which has bearing on one's identity formed through land relations and their ability to become grounded. Diaz's work with Micronesians in Minnesota speaks to the importance of forming land identity through radical Native-to-Native relations. What I hope to accomplish in this essay is to show how Indigenous peoples reclaim land relations while living in diasporic conditions with attention to the material and grounded identity of this land reclamation.

In this essay, I conceive of Land Back as a process of resisting systems of oppression that create asymmetrical power dynamics in our relationships with human and nonhuman worlds. Land Back is a set of practices that are grounded in Indigenous relationality, even for those living away from their ancestral lands. Land Back entails a recognition and acknowledgment of the histories that have led Indigenous peoples to various places around the globe and an understanding of how colonial legacies (and continuities) have forcefully relocated Indigenous peoples from their ancestral lands and waters. Today, I reside on lands of the Coast Salish people, in particular the Lummi and Nooksack. As a guest here, it is their governance systems that I must be in relation with—not those of the settler. Building this relationship between guest and host is a first step toward delinking from colonial relations. The next step is developing relationships built on reciprocity.

Routed Normativity

Diasporic Pacific Islander communities hold a spatial practice influenced by mobility, moving between roots in ancestral homelands and routes along the diaspora, which includes communities forming across different geographies. For communities like the Marshallese that face the detrimental impacts of militarization and climate change, mobility can become empowering. Leanne Betasamosake Simpson expresses mobility as an important Indigenous practice of resurgence in response to settler colonialism. Routed normativity demonstrates the practice of mobility within the Oceanic experience of routes:

> Mobility shatters and refuses the containment of settler colonialism and inserts Indigenous presence . . . mobility within grounded normativity as an embedded Indigenous practice, mobility as a response to colonialism as resistance, mobility as a deliberate and strategic resurgence, and mobility as direct or indirect forced expulsion, relocation, and displacement and the creation of Indigenous diaspora. . . . I see this as us using our mobility as a flight path out of settler colonialism and into Indigeneity. I see mobility imbued with agency as resurgence.[18]

Routed normativity builds on Simpson's placement of "mobility within grounded normativity as an embedded Indigenous practice" and expands upon concepts of roots and routes developed by Diaz, Kauanui, and Case.[19] As Case explores through *Kahiki*, routed normativity is anchored through place-based practices that are rooted. We carry knowledges that come from land and sea with us; in transplanting these systems within our routes, we continue the practice of these knowledges. These deeply place-based systems connected to our roots help to ground us in Indigeneity. A sovereignty of consciousness helps to maintain embodied practices of land within our memory, as we look forward to the past to guide us into the future.

In the production of place, grounded normativity creates spaces grounded in Indigenous place-based understandings of relationality. Leon Noʻeau Peralto defines *Aloha ʻĀina* as Kanaka Maoli grounded normativity, rooted in everyday place-based Indigenous processes.[20] Expanding on Indigenous practices of mobility and *Aloha ʻĀina* normativity, I argue that routed normativity provides a basis for diasporic Indigenous members to enter into solidarity with their Indigenous hosts through shared ethical frameworks;

those relationships are built on mutual understanding, respect, and reciprocity. Through *moʻokuʻauhau* (genealogy), we bring our responsibility to land and people with us.[21]

I locate routed normativity within an Oceanic framing of spatial relations to develop the relational aspects of diasporic Indigenous placemaking that are explored through the analysis of placemaking projects among Rimajol communities. In "Our Sea of Islands," Hauʻofa expresses the fluid state of *Moana* as the metaphysical and material space that connects us, providing interstitial spaces for relationality between land, water, and each other.[22] Diaz challenges the temptation by scholars to privilege the expansive and fluidic notion of *Moana* at the loss of Native depth.[23] Diaz emphasizes the distinct knowledges formed within relations of land and sea that guide us along routes and help distinguish transitions into the lands of others. Contributing to the development of *Vā Moana* theory, routed normativity helps to encompass the relational aspects of diasporic Indigenous placemaking while maintaining the specificity of Indigenous knowledge and roots that provide laws and ethics for mobility.

Vā, simply translated as "space," expresses the "ever-moving present," or the "Space-Between-All-Things that defines us and makes us part of the Unity-that-is-all."[24] *Moana* is the ocean, and together *Vā Moana* defines relational spaces of connectivity. *Vā Moana* represents the relationships formed across space and time; it establishes land as an embodied, ethereal location built into our consciousness. At once it is memory, place, home, mother, relation, family, *mana*, movement, and self.[25] Oceanic scholars Hūfanga ʻOkusitino Mahina, Refiti, and Kaʻili, among others, have developed the concept of *Vā Moana* to explore socio-spatial relations within Oceanic experiences, in particular within diasporic communities.[26] Similar to *Vā Moana*, *Kahiki* recalls the responsibility to our larger Oceanic family and locates us as arrivals in relation.[27] We are connected through our kinship, through ancestral lines that dart back and forth in time and across the great expanses of *Moana*, following us into expansions of relationality within diasporic realities. Yet we are called back to our ancestral lands and carry them with us through our genealogical connection to our *ʻiwi kapuna* (bones of our ancestors). Land: the place from which our way of knowing and being in this world was born, a concept of human and nonhuman relationships that reminds us we are all one. Unfortunately, these pathways and lines of relationality have been fractured and constricted by colonization, acts that attempt to deracinate, delegitimize, and alienate our worlds. Diasporic Indigenous placemaking challenges settler colonialism as a practice of Indigenous resurgence guided by routed normativity.

To better understand the transportation of knowledge systems that are brought with diasporic communities in routed normativity, the concept of deep time is helpful. Routes are not contemporary phenomena but have been an integral component of the Oceania way of life, placing mobility as a central component to knowledge systems as emphasized in Oceanic wayfinding or the utilization of routed networks to provide safe havens following tsunamis and typhoons. Within *Vā Moana*, time is not linear. Rather, the present is surrounded by that which is beyond—past and future (see Figure 4.1). In ʻŌlelo ʻŌiwi, *I ka wā ma mua, ka wā ma hope* means to stand firmly in the present with our backs to the future, while looking to our ancestors to bring us the knowledge we need to move forward.[28]

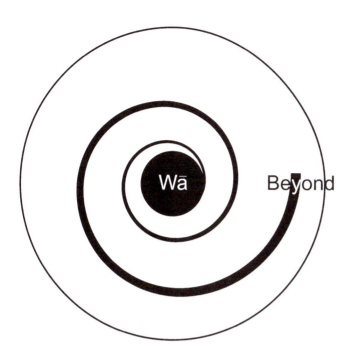

FIGURE 4.1
The diagram on the left conveys the concept that *wā* (space) reflects the present moment, surrounded by the past and future, representing that which is beyond. This understanding of space and time is connected to the concept of the *piko* (located on the right), which connects one to the ancestors through the umbilical cord, to the future through the genitals, and to the heavens through the head. Illustration by James Miller.

These understandings of space and time mediate our relationships with the fields around us, contributing to the notions of reciprocity, respect, and trust. This way of thinking produces reciprocal rather than extractive relationships between humans and nonhumans.

Deep time is a method for understanding the relationship between culture and the environment, helping to examine aspects of Indigenous knowledge that are applicable to urban planning and architecture. It is a method of understanding that binds us genealogically and temporally, locating us in conversation with ancestors and future ancestors. Deep time helps to conceptualize and investigate the significance of the culture-environment relationships and the systems of knowledge that have been developed and maintained throughout our genealogical lines to support us.[29] It is walking forward into the past.[30] When located in a specific place, deep time represents the intensities—the assemblage of time, space, and the cosmos; it is the sense of place as defined by its overlapping histories and stories. In ʻŌlelo Hawaiʻi, *ʻike honua* reflects the sense of place, demonstrating the knowledge gained through land. This knowledge of place is representative of its *moʻokuʻauhau*, the genealogical memory of place that encompasses the intersection of human and nonhuman histories. *Moʻokuʻauhau* expresses the woven fabrics of history, chants, stories, and songs passed from generation to generation. Deep time becomes an analytical tool for understanding Native depth.

Routed normativity provides a place-based ethical framework for Indigenous communities that are both rooted and routed. Deep time becomes a concept that helps examine genealogical place-based practices despite the overlays of settler spatial production. The next section explores the intersection of settler colonialism and routes to understand the ways in which settler colonialism influences spatial organization in the diaspora and relations. An example of deep-time analysis in Honolulu will be used to demonstrate the method prior to delving into the analysis of Rimajol placemaking. Framing these processes within settler cities helps us to challenge the structure of settler colonialism and reframe Indigenous spatial relations.

Settler Planning and Urbanization

Settler colonialism commodifies land, dispossesses Indigenous peoples, and reproduces sociopolitical systems based on colonial norms, values, and knowledge. To borrow from Aníbal Quijano's coloniality of power, these systems control the economy, authority, gender, sexuality, subjectivity, and Western knowledge.[31] Planning and architecture become tools of settler colonialism to reproduce structures of power within urbanization. Through a methodical process of land appropriation, water divergence, resource extraction, and the manipulation of the landscape, the settler city is a place created to dispossess Indigenous peoples and locate them in gray spaces—spaces in which marginalized people struggle to exist.[32] The city as we know it is a colonial structure designed to erase the Native, exploit the land and people for global capitalism, uphold settler-colonial hegemony, and normalize society within the economic force of capitalism.[33]

The built environment and its allied disciplines of architecture and planning provide apparatuses of the settler-colonial structure. Eric Nay has developed a central thesis in his work that the Western canon of architecture reproduces colonialism; thus, practitioners become complicit in perpetuating coloniality.[34] Settler architectures lay the groundwork for settler colonialism to subjugate Indigenous peoples. Lorenzo Veracini links the ideology of Manifest Destiny within the settler-ontological and material construction of the suburbs to demonstrate the continued erasure of Indigenous identities to place through the transformation of land relations supportive of grounded normativity to a foreign landscape of concrete, steel, and ticky-tacky homes.[35] While Veracini does not provide a distinction between Indigenous, settler, and arrivant in his theoretical development of settler urbanization, there is a multiplicity of experiences among urban dwellers based on their intersectional identities.

Architecture and planning produce both a desired aesthetic of "good taste" and structures to assimilate the working class. Housing developments are illustrative of coloniality's goals for the built environment. Injecting Western systems of standardization in spatial design and construction methods subscripts economically disenfranchised Black, Indigenous, and people of color (BIPOC) dwellers into a colonial machine for living. Housing as a tool of settler colonialism limits or excludes the participation of the user. This process is evident in the work of Le Corbusier's Algiers project and the Canadian housing program for Northern communities during the 1960s that came with a handbook, *Living in the New Houses*.[36] As an icon of Western modernization, Le Corbusier's project demonstrates a regularization of everyday habitation as an "expression of the French 'colonial consensus.'"[37] *Living in the New Houses* provided a manual to assimilate First Nations and Inuit communities into the domestic norms of Canadian society, not taking into account the cultural specificity of dwelling in the North. These projects reflect the colonial systems of codes, laws, design, and land use implemented to control and dispossess the Native "other." These structures reflected in land-use laws and building regulations continue to perpetuate exclusionary policies embedded in the development of the built environment.

While the agency of users in the city is active in processes of placemaking and adaptation, it is particularly strenuous for BIPOC communities. The argument that adaptation to these environments allows for cultural patterns to persist may be valid, but a common pattern is the assimilation into settler patterns of urbanization, such as real estate speculation. What I would like to bring forward in this essay is the need to unsettle a system that perpetuates the injustice of settler-colonial spaces through land-based practices of Indigenous routed normativity. How do planners, architects, and designers participate in dismantling the hidden agendas of contemporary city building in order to weave back the *moʻokuʻauhau* of place that has been buried by settler colonialism? Sacred sites, everyday sacred places, and traditional hunting and gathering spaces, to name a few, are continually shaped through Indigenous spatial practices that are often obscured by settler urban architecture. Urban Indigenous have reclaimed urban spaces through community building practices, such as urban *marae* identified by Serge Marek in Aotearoa and Native hubs on Turtle Island by Renya Ramirez.[38] Ramirez describes Native hubs as multimodal networks that provide a compelling case for the co-reclamation of urban space through Indigenous and diasporic Indigenous relations.[39]

Within the settler-colonial context of North America, cities have always been sites of contestation between Indigenous caretakers of those places and Eurocentric settlers. Tensions are created through colonial housing policies, building and land-use regulations, and code enforcement. In places like Hawaiʻi, these policies become weapons of the settler state to place Kanaka Maoli and diasporic Oceania communities on the margins of existence. Because Hawaiian homelands are restricted by racist blood quantum laws, Kanaka Maoli families are left to compete with settlers in one of the most expensive housing markets in the United States due to militourism,[40] as well as the Compact of Free Association (COFA) communities vying for limited public housing, resulting in houselessness or in the departure from their ancestral lands.[41] These pressures are further exacerbated by land-use codes and city ordinances, such as those that reinforce the nuclear family in residency requirements. Such restrictions have implications on the cultural norms of communities that rely on many living under one roof for sociocultural support systems, such as those apparent in multigenerational housing. Land-use codes, particularly single-family zoning, restrict housing typologies that may support such collective living arrangements. Other various forms of cultural practices shared by Oceanic communities, such as outdoor kitchens and earth ovens, are restricted by land-use codes and building regulations.

Honolulu provides a useful example to express the implications of settler colonialism on the urban environment, which is representative of Western values and American futures rather than Indigenous values and Indigenous futures.[42] Urban development in Honolulu works to erase the memory of the Hawaiian Kingdom as various periods of urban renewal claim Kanaka spaces. In Kapālama, Kanaka Maoli families were displaced by urban-renewal projects following statehood to make way for the development of highway infrastructure, increased airport capacity for tourism, industrial development, and the development of government public housing such as Mayor Wright Homes. These spaces of continental urban program regimes would become the gray spaces that hosted diasporic *Moana* communities competing with Kanaka Maoli families, leading to daily conflict, as I observed in Mayor Wright Homes. Yet by utilizing deep time to uncover that which is below the surface, we see the reclamation of spaces. As the *moʻokuʻauhau* of the Kalihi *ahupuaʻa* is analyzed, an unraveling of histories brings to life the palimpsest of the Hawaiian Kingdom. Beneath the industrialized urban landscape are the outlines of significant Kanaka spaces, such as the Muʻolaulani, the home of Queen Liliʻuokalani.[43] Today we work to reclaim these spaces as evident in the work of Hōkūlani K. Aikau and Vernadette Vicuña Gonzalez's *Detours: A Decolonial Guide to Hawaiʻi*.[44]

Honolulu represents the dispossession of Kanaka Maoli with a long history of pulling human labor from across the Pacific Ocean into the plantations and hotels of Oʻahu. In addition, Honolulu becomes the stopping point for former Trust Territory communities crossing the Pacific into the continental United States as part of the education, labor, and medical migrations supported through COFA. Through the intersections of U.S. imperialism and settler colonialism within Hawaiʻi, Honolulu has become a bastion of diversity. This particular feature of settler urbanism in Honolulu has led to a complicated reality of everyday racism among Oceanic communities, such as in Mayor Wright Homes. Several authors, such as Kuʻualoha Hoʻomanawanui, have spoken on racial conflict and competition driven by settler colonialism, while many others like Emalani Case recognize it in theorizing futures in relation to our Oceanic family.[45] Honolulu is a space of Rimajol placemaking as will be explored through the *ʻāina* organization Hoʻoulu ʻĀina, which represents a center of Indigeneity that challenges the narrative of racism and disrupts settler colonialism. Uncovering the truths of shared histories among *Moana* and Oceania alike, Indigenous resurgence is growing in Honolulu.

The migration of people to urban centers accelerates due to environmental, social, and economic injustice, which raises the question: How do we create more just cities? How do we ensure that a pluriverse—to borrow from Arturo Escobar[46]—of worldviews shares the right to the city, the right to the environment, the right to abundance, the right to social equity, and the right to autonomy? The structure of settler colonialism locates diasporic Indigenous communities within settler structures of spatial relations rather than Indigenous frameworks of spatial relations. As transnational movements increase, routed normativity demonstrates the strength of Indigenous knowledge within immigrant communities and provides a method for subverting Western spatial ontologies. The project of decolonization is apparent as diasporic Indigenous peoples work together with their Indigenous hosts to build Indigenous futures.

Assessing Diasporic Realities through Deep Time

To apply the theoretical frameworks shaping the first half of this essay, I now turn toward Rimajol placemaking to understand how routed normativity influences diasporic Indigenous placemaking. The framework of deep time is used to analyze the knowledge systems that allowed for the continuity of Marshallese spaces in the Republic of the Marshall Islands (RMI). These systems of Indigenous design knowledge prevailed despite colonization and militarization, often (re)creating a sense of wholeness within Marshallese habitation. As Rimajol reframe relations to Aelon Kein Ad to be inclusive of diasporic communities, Indigenous practices of mobility connect the past, present, and future within an expansion of Rimajol relationality. Routed normativity becomes a counter to the damage-centered narrative of forced migration, empowering communities to maintain Indigenous practices. Within the expansion of Rimajol relationality through their routes, we see the transportation of Indigenous placemaking patterns across space and time in the formation of "new islands" across Aelon Kein Ad.[47] As the establishment of diasporic communities, the transplantation of lifeways demonstrates a placemaking practice. As stated previously, placemaking is mediated within the social field, constructed through cultural, social, and political factors; it is a practice that negotiates between culture and place-specific social practice. Thus, diasporic Indigenous placemaking negotiates between Native-to-Native-to-Settler practices while being governed by the specific laws of the local Indigenous. While routed normativity can demonstrate a way in which land and seas and the knowledge born of those human-environment relations can transcend geographic place through transported landscapes of diasporic placemaking, it must not be at the expense of Indigenous sovereignty nor replicate settler colonialism.

In the next section, emphasis is placed on the "new islands" of Arkansas and Oregon, reflecting the extension of Aelon Kein Ad into diasporic placemaking.[48] In addition to the placemaking practices of Rimajol communities, Hoʻoulu ʻĀina is explored to demonstrate the nurturing relationships that are supported as Oceanic arrivants follow the protocol and worldviews of the Kanaka ʻŌiwi host rather than the settler. The approach to the relationship between arrivant and host, embedded in Indigenous practices of reciprocity, is significant as it transforms binaries of visitor/host, immigrant/national, and settler/Native, among others.

Aelon Kein Ad: The Marshall Islands

There are many examples of how diasporic Indigenous communities engage in resurgence and practices of reclaiming land and identity. Looking to stories from Oceania highlights how Indigenous communities undertake placemaking practices within their routes to maintain the deep connections to their land and seas. One story that has been making headlines in recent news concerns the "sinking islands" of Aelon Kein Ad. This small atoll nation in the middle of the Pacific Ocean, halfway between Hawaiʻi and Australia, that spans from five degrees north of the equator to twelve degrees north is an array of thirty-two atolls in a vast area of ocean. As a low-lying atoll nation, the RMI is receiving the brunt of climate change and sea-level rise. It is at the center of the debate on the international status of climate refugees along with Tuvalu and Kiribati. My research became focused on the RMI after mentioning to my uncle that I wanted to conduct research for my PhD on slow-onset disasters. He told me to go to the RMI, stating, "In Oceania, we see each other as cousins"; from this conversation, I felt a sense of responsibility to respect our genealogical connection.

FIGURE 4.2
A father and son set sail in a Rimajol-style *proa* (outrigger canoe), Honolulu, Hawaiʻi. Photograph by Kilipohe.

To introduce the research, I want to begin with a conversation with a collaborator, Dial Keju. Dial Keju is a Rimajol urban planner working in the United States with an urban and regional planning degree from the University of Hawaiʻi at Mānoa. Dial believes that our ancestors crossed paths in canoes long ago; his ancestors helped mine and now, many generations later, my family is returning that favor. Could this relationship be bound by DNA memories tying Dial and myself through space and time, asking for balance to be restored within the relationship? I like to imagine that these canoes represent a *piko* (umbilical cord, connecting us to our kinship and genealogy) within *Moana* that allows for the collapse of space and time and the intersection of the cosmos, pulling us together through forces beyond our spatiotemporal understandings. The *wāʻa* (outrigger canoe) becomes the object that moves us across space and time, across *Moana*, and connects us to our ancestors

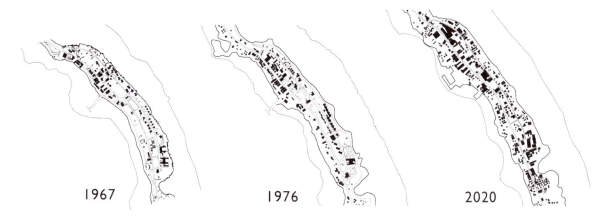

FIGURE 4.3 Maps demonstrating the morphology of the built environment over time from the period of the Trust Territory headquarters from 1967 to 1976, when lands began to be returned to ancestral keepers, and to 2017, when the population increased. Maps by James Miller.

through reciprocal relationships—past and present. I believe Dial is right—our ancestral lines have been reconnected through *Vā Moana*. Figure 4.2 depicts a *proa* (Marshallese-style outrigger canoe) that reflects these relationships; the *proa* was created by a Kanaka Maoli educator inspired by Marshallese and Pingelapese friends who are fellow canoe builders and wayfinders. Through the *wāʻa*, relations are shared and continued across *Moana*.

Like many nations in the Pacific, the RMI was colonized by European nations, Japan, and the United States. Within the colonized built environment, the traditional form of the built environment was entirely replaced. In construction practices, Rimajol became reliant on imported materials, technology, and methods. Not unlike other places across the Global South, the Western concrete building is seen as the only safe structure to weather a typhoon or mitigate sea inundation.[49] The Rimajol built environment was further affected by the impacts of the U.S. nuclear program, most notably the Bravo Shot—a sixty-megaton hydrogen bomb that eradicated life on Bikini Atoll, along with the ancestral homes of an entire population.[50] More recent typhoons further replaced the vernacular architecture of remote atolls with USDA rural housing and disaster-relief housing. Figure 4.3 shows the change over time of three islets on Majuro Atoll, Delap-Uliga-Djarrit. These three islets were occupied by the United States administrative headquarters for the United Nations Trust Territory of the Pacific in the Marshall Islands. Following the removal of the Trust Territory headquarters, the lands were returned to their ancestral keepers.

On the surface, it might appear as though the Marshallese identity and relationship with the land was forever changed through the forces of colonization. It is easy to forget that the influence of colonization is only two hundred years deep, and Rimajol have survived on their atolls for millennia. In studying the persistence of Indigenous knowledge within the Rimajol production and adaptation of the built environment, I gained understanding of six important components of the Rimajol way of life. The six components provide generative mechanisms that shape space, place, and the environment in a manner that maintains the Rimajol way of life—even if expressed within a modern aesthetic. These are

Placemaking as Indigenous Resurgence in the Oceanic Diaspora

(1) land as abundance; (2) land as identity, both of which are embedded within the *wato*, which represents the Indigenous resource-management and land-tenure system through matrilineal inheritance of the Marshallese; (3) *ippan doon* (togetherness), which manifests in the clustering of housing; (4) *juon kijeek* (one fire, one family), which represents the interconnection of family through the sharing of resources and stories; (5) *emlapwoj*, which represents the multigenerational family living arrangement; and (6) *jemjem meil* (sharpening the stones together), which represents the collective nature of constructing buildings. "Indigenous Placemaking in the Climate Diaspora: Rimajol Resettlement in the U.S." explores the application of these patterns within the development of community foundations in *aelona kaal* (new land).[51] These generative patterns become important in mediating diasporic placemaking.

These patterns represent Rimajol grounded normativity and the genealogical knowledge that is attached to place; they help communities mediate the social fields to engage with placemaking practices. Grounded normativity produces Indigenous space that enacts spaces of solidarity through our relationship to the land. Even through the impact of colonization and the Japanese and U.S. occupations, Rimajol families were able to continue their spatial practices within Rimajol urbanism. From this conceptual understanding, it is possible to see the everyday actions in Oceanic diasporas that represent the transportation of Indigenous placemaking practices.

Patterns of Resurgence

In his work on Tongan diasporas in Hawai'i and beyond, Ka'ili demonstrates the importance of these spatial relationships that keep community connected while maintaining *Moana* worldviews.[52] Applying Ka'ili's work on spatial relationships within diasporas helps us better understand the intentionality of social ties across space and time. Placemaking practices, such as the *kava* ceremony, create spatial opportunities for these communities to come to wholeness—relinking to genealogy and land.[53]

In the Rimajol diaspora in the U.S. mainland and Hawai'i, communities are not only defined by geographical locations; they are also created through kinship-based social networks identifiable through family names. As families migrate to the United States, they may spread across multiple states and cities, or across one city (see Figure 4.4). What is noticeable is that their spatial location within the city does not represent a typical enclave settlement pattern; rather, their sense of community is often defined by their kinship networks. These networks represent the extension of land-based genealogies that locate Rimajol families in their ancestral land while simultaneously helping them navigate their new contexts. These relationships represent the expansion of Rimajol relationality beyond the bounds of Aelon Kein Ad.

Moana migrations can be seen as a positive extension of kinship lines, unlike the literature that speaks mainly to the damage. Speaking to both Rimajol and my Hawaiian experience, I frame forced migration and resettlement not from a place of damage, but from one of positive expansion of Pacific Islanders.[54] Rimajol communities are building new foundations within the diaspora, utilizing the same concept for forming communities

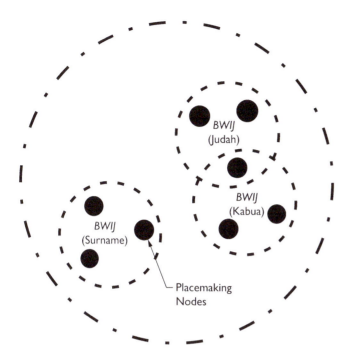

FIGURE 4.4
Diagram depicting the relationships of Marshallese networks in the United States. The outer circle represents the Marshallese continuum inclusive of Aelon Kein Ad and the diaspora. Each inner circle represents a clan sharing a surname that links the clan directly to an atoll in Aelon Kein Ad. Each solid circle is a node in the diaspora that connects the clan to a place in the United States, such as Oregon or Arkansas. Illustration by James Miller.

FIGURE 4.5 A map at the RMI Consulate in Springdale, Arkansas, that locates Marshallese communities across the United States, each being represented by a thumbtack. Photograph by James Miller.

Placemaking as Indigenous Resurgence in the Oceanic Diaspora

in Aelon Kein Ad—*pedped ijin, pedped ijon* (a concept shared by Kanaka Maoli too).[55] Colleagues from Namdrik and Majuro have referred to the formation of outer-atoll communities in the capital, Majuro, as Muon (name of atoll). Research participants from the Marshallese community in Salem, Oregon, identified this process occurring in the U.S. mainland where Marshallese communities are formed as transplanted villages, reflective of their worldviews (see Figure 4.5). While the transplanting of atoll communities onto Turtle Island provides a continuity of Marshallese practices of mobility (routes), the significance of specific local knowledges (roots) needs to be considered in combination with the prioritization of the Indigenous host communities to prevent the reproduction of settler colonialism.

Springdale, Arkansas

Springdale has been referred as "our new island" by the Rimajol community in Arkansas and has been recognized by the larger Rimajol community in the United States as an extension of Aelon Kein Ad. The largest population of Rimajol outside of the RMI resides in Northwest Arkansas, and the RMI consulate is in Springdale, Arkansas. While the Marshallese community and broader Micronesian community are one of the larger minority populations in the city, they are still small compared to the even larger Latine community. Migration to this area began roughly forty years ago, initiated by higher-education programs developed under the Trust Territory and grown through labor migrations under COFA after the RMI became independent. Rimajol population growth has accelerated in Northwest Arkansas over the past decade, becoming one of the most populated "atolls" in Aelon Kein Ad with growing support through nongovernmental organizations and representation from the RMI government.[56]

The Marshallese Education Initiative (MEI) is a nonprofit Marshallese organization that was originally formed by Dr. Jessica Schwartz and Dr. April Brown, who are non-Marshallese advocates, along with Tina Stege and others from the broader Marshallese transnational community. MEI started with a small grant received by Brown to conduct an oral history project with elders of the Rimajol community in Springdale and has grown from there to be a major advocate for Marshallese participation in policy decisions revolving around Marshallese education and culture. Their mission states: "Through educational programming, MEI promotes the cultural, intellectual, and historical awareness of the Marshallese people and facilitates intercultural dialogue to foster positive social change."[57]

MEI has grown to be a significant resource for the Rimajol community in Springdale, supporting their ability to create a sense of place and advocating for the community's access to education and the local economy. Through their advocacy and community work and supported by the integrative design approach taken by the Jones Center, MEI has been working with the Jones Trust as part of a committee of minority representation in Springdale to transform part of the Jones Center into a culturally responsive and supportive community center. The community center has been used by the Marshallese community for over a decade, and now they have a seat at the planning and decision table. In this renovation and expansion project, representatives of the Marshallese community are working with the Jones Trust along with representatives from other equity-seeking communities to provide a spatial design supportive of their cultural activities and needs. Representatives from MEI spoke to the particular needs of their elder community and spaces for them to support everyday activities, such as *bwebwenato* (storytelling as oral history) and teaching youth crafts. These spaces would support the practice of knowledge dissemination between elders and youth, reflective of the *emlapwoj*.

Where the Marshallese community in Arkansas demonstrates the continuity of *ippan doon, juon kijeek*, and collective action, this project will bring a visible identity of Marshallese practices to Springdale. Additionally, MEI has supported the Arkansas community with the pre-planning for the Alele Cultural Center, a project that I hope to support through design work and grant writing in collaboration with MEI and hopefully the Fay Jones School of Architecture and Design. Through collaborative partnerships with nonprofit advocates, the Marshallese community is demonstrating a resurgence in their way of life through patterns such as *ippan dron* (togetherness), *kumit* (helping each other in a collective manner, such as in building a house), and *jake jebol eo* (sharing resources with one another). While the ongoing placemaking practices of the Marshallese community in Arkansas create supportive spaces, the presence of Native-to-Native relationality has not been identified.

Oregon

There are two predominant Marshallese communities in Oregon: La Grande and Salem. These communities have historically formed around colleges (Western Oregon University, University of Oregon, Oregon State University, and Eastern Oregon University) and the canning industries. Today we see a community that is active in the transformation of legislation and policy to support COFA communities and the broader Pacific Islander community. Migration from the RMI to the United States has increased steadily since COFA was signed between the two countries following the departure of the United Nations Trust Territory of the Pacific in 1986, which renews every twenty years. Currently the RMI and the United States are under negotiation for the next twenty years. COFA provides financial assistance through the Joint Economic Management and Financial Accountability Committee, as well as allows for Rimajol to freely migrate to the United States without visa requirements. For the purpose of this essay, I want to highlight two particular placemaking projects in Portland, Oregon.

In 2015, the Portland State University Native American Student and Community Center (NASCC) collaborated with Living Islands and other campus clubs to support a traditional Marshallese canoe build. Living Islands, a Marshallese nonprofit, sponsored master carver and builder Tiem Clement to share with students and the broader community Rimajol *manit* (culture). Through a partnership with the Grande Ronde tribe, a redwood was sourced for the outrigger projects. Events held at the end of the build brought together members of the Grande Ronde, the NASCC, and the Pacific Island community in Oregon (Figure 4.6). This project brought together Native Americans and Pacific Islanders through the shared practice of canoe building, opening relational spaces through protocol and shared place-based practices. In the production of Indigenous space, knowledge practices strengthen relationships built on respect and reciprocity

FIGURE 4.6 The events surrounding the Outrigger Canoe Build in Oregon. Photographs by Jesper Angelo.

to each other and the land. The creation of these relational spaces is demonstrative of routed normativity.

The future vision of a Pacific Islander cultural center represents another space where co-creation of space is based on Indigenous concepts of relationships, including those between human and nonhuman actors. Led by the vision of Living Islands director Kianna Angelo Judah, members of the Micronesian and Polynesian communities in Portland came together to study the feasibility of a Pacific Islander space along the Columbia River at Hayden Island. As a former member of this community, I collaborated with Living Islands, Metaamo Studio, and Matt Bunza (principal of Metaamo), among others, to support a terminal studio taught at the University of Oregon. Matt Bunza developed the studio to engage students with critical topics, such as climate change migration and social justice, while working on behalf of the Pacific Islander community in Portland to support Living Islands' vision. With a focus on process and collaboration, the studio envisions the possibilities of a cultural and community center that would be a meeting space, inclusive of Rimajol, other Oceanic communities, and Native American communities in Portland. The shared connection to the water and canoe culture is a driving force. Figure 4.7 illustrates a student's design vision for this space. Like the example from

FIGURE 4.7 Martin Hilden's design for the Pacific Islander Cultural Center at Hayden Island Project as part of the Fluid States Studio at the University of Oregon, directed by Matthew Bunza. Illustrations by Martin Hilden.

Arkansas, this project will be an opportunity to put everyday Rimajol practices of placemaking into a co-productive space with other Indigenous peoples, supporting Native-to-Native-to-Settler relations in the creation of decolonial futures.

Hoʻoulu ʻĀina

At the end of Kalihi Street in the *ahupuaʻa* of Kalihi on the *moku* of Oʻahu is Hoʻoulu ʻĀina, where one can find a nature preserve built on Hawaiian principles of relationality with the *ʻāina*. This space represents intensive properties weaving *moʻolelo* (storytelling as oral history), *moʻokuʻauhau*, and *mana*; this place demonstrates the importance of Kanaka Maoli space opening up relational spaces for all. As we enter onto Hoʻoulu ʻĀina, we respect the practices of our hosts, Kanaka Maoli; through protocol, we enter an Indigenous space, leaving the structures of the settler city. Hoʻoulu ʻĀina is a center, a spatial node that creates a gravitational pull to those who have experienced its spirit, not unlike the story that Dial and I share. Families visiting from afar, such as myself, come to Hoʻoulu ʻĀina and join through a resurgence of relationality.

Hoʻoulu ʻĀina is also an important space because it brings together other Pacific Islanders through shared land-based practices in abundance, emphasizing a Native-to-Native-to-Settler relation.[58] Hoʻoulu ʻĀina opens and closes in protocol every day, inviting arrivals to enter a decolonial space of Indigenous relationality and leave behind the settler city. Here Micronesians participate within Hawaiian spatial practices and share their

Placemaking as Indigenous Resurgence in the Oceanic Diaspora

knowledge of carving and canoe building, as well as tell stories of voyaging and learn the importance of food production and nutrition. Within the settler city of Honolulu, the racialization of Oceanic peoples is a common struggle as coloniality pits minority groups against each other. Hoʻoulu ʻĀina provides a stark contrast from Mayor Wright Homes just a couple of miles down Kalihi Street; in Hoʻoulu ʻĀina, we are reminded that we are family, a space where *Kahiki* is ever present. It becomes a space for repair among not only diasporic Kanaka like me, but also a space for the repair of relationships across *Moana*, across Oceania. Hoʻoulu ʻĀina is a truly special space at the heart of Indigenous resurgence. As Mary Barker conveys in her work with Hoʻoulu ʻĀina, the place represents Hawaiian futures of abundance.[59]

Moʻokuʻauhau resurges at Hoʻoulu ʻĀina. Through intentional practices grounded in *ahupuaʻa* resource management, the settler urbanization of Honolulu is countered and Indigenous futures are reclaimed. Through this process of reclaiming spaces through both a material connection to land and a consciousness of routed normativity, Land Back is present for both Kanaka Maoli and diasporic Oceania diasporas. *Moʻokuʻauhau* urbanism builds upon Sean Connelly's work on *ahupuaʻa* urbanism to demonstrate the significance of Indigenous knowledge systems resurfacing through the psychogeographies of place.[60] This perspective of design within architecture, urban design, and planning generates spaces that unsettle settler spaces. Indigenous design knowledge maintains wholeness, spaces that are nurturing and beautiful, informed through grounded normativity.

Conclusion

In "Is Urban a Person or a Place?," Susan Lobo argues that urban Indigenous culture and community are based on nodes of networks and relationships.[61] The Oceanic diaspora is emblematic of these relationships as described in the Rimajol continuum. Networks and nodes direct placemaking across geographies. Questions unanswered here are: How does the expansiveness of contemporary Indigenous migrations relate to fundamental principles in land-based practices? Do pluralities of grounded normativities or routed normativities form within these Indigenous spaces? In the study of Rimajol placemaking in Springdale, the application of ethical frameworks of relationality are less apparent. What needs to happen in this space to transform settler spaces?

The sites of placemaking described here by diasporic Indigenous represent the desire to maintain Native depth (roots) while learning to mediate across social fields, from the everyday sharing of food cooked over one fire to larger cultural celebrations. This interpretation of placemaking as Indigenous resurgence begins to challenge the settler-colonial production of the built environment, bringing into question contemporary social constructions of land and the expansiveness of Indigenous relationships. As Diaz reminds us, geographic expansion (Native reach) does not exist without the Native depth that provided the Indigenous ingenuity to expand, and the mobility reflected in Native reach must not reproduce settler colonialism.[62] The idea of routed normativity provides a useful analytic for understanding how Pacific Islanders maintain Native-to-Native relations that cultivate Indigenous principles and values. Renya Ramirez illustrates this expansiveness as the spiral, incorporating the past into both the present and the future; universal relationships are expressed as a circle of interdependency involving all the elements of existence.[63] Routed normativity might provide us a way to think through practices of Indigenous mobility within the decolonial project of transforming settler cities into Indigenous futures.

In our routes, as we awaken from the fog that colonialism has created, we might find that our ancestors are with us; together, the ancestors and the land remind us of our place-based ethical frameworks within our routes. As we become reconnected with diaspora as a generative structure of our Kanaka ʻŌiwi (Indigenous identity), our focus on assimilated identities dissipates. We are reminded of our responsibility to each other as family along our routes. Within this shift of consciousness, a consciousness of sovereignty informed by routed normativity, we are empowered to practice the land-water relationality of our ancestors in the present and mediate spatial relationships between our ancestors and our future relations. These routes we find ourselves on are rooted in place-based systems where our *iwi* (bones) lie. Our ancestors live with us. As we reawaken to our future, we begin anew. This process is the extension of *Vā Moana*, of *Aloha ʻĀina*. Placemaking as Indigenous resurgence represents the reattachment of our minds, bodies, and spirits to the network of relationships and ethical place-based practices that generate routed normativity.

NOTES

1. Vicente M. Diaz and J. Kēhaulani Kauanui, "Native Pacific Cultural Studies on the Edge," *The Contemporary Pacific* 13, no. 2 (Fall 2001): 319.
2. Vicente M. Diaz, "Oceania in the Plains: The Politics and Analytics of Transindigenous Resurgence in Chuukese Voyaging of Dakota Lands, Waters, and Skies in Miní Sóta Makhóčhe," *Pacific Studies* 42, nos. 1–2 (2019): 33.
3. Diaz and Kauanui, "Native Pacific Cultural Studies on the Edge," 320.
4. Native depth expresses the depth of knowledge that comes from the human-environment relation across deep time and space; see Diaz, "Oceania in the Plains," 33.
5. "About Vā Moana Pacific Spaces," Vā Moana Pacific Spaces, www.vamoana.org/about.
6. "Call for Papers: 'Vā Moana: Space and Relationality in Pacific Thought and Identity' Conference," Vā Moana Pacific Spaces, https://www.vamoana.org/news/call-for-papers-va-moana-space-and-relationality-in-pacific-thought-and-identity-conference.
7. James Miller, "Indigenous Placemaking in the Climate Diaspora: Rimajol Resettlement in the U.S.," *Traditional Dwellings and Settlements Review* 32, no. 2 (2021): 39–52.
8. Diaz, "Oceania in the Plains," 28.
9. Diaz, "Oceania in the Plains," 2.
10. Diaz and Kauanui, "Native Pacific Cultural Studies on the Edge."
11. Emalani Case, *Everything Ancient Was Once New: Indigenous Persistence from Hawaiʻi to Kahiki* (Honolulu: University of Hawaiʻi Press, 2021).
12. Diaz, "Oceania in the Plains."
13. Glen Coulthard and Leanne Betasamosake Simpson, "Grounded Normativity / Place-Based Solidarity," *American Quarterly* 68, no. 2 (June 2016): 254.
14. Tēvita Kaʻili, Albert Refiti, Kēhaulani Kauanui, Emalani Case, Daniel Hernandez, Vince Diaz, and many others have made contributions to an ongoing dialogue on diasporic Indigenous identities, transnationalism, and relations that are in conversation with the work presented here.
15. Tēvita O. Kaʻili, *Marking Indigeneity: The Tongan Art of Sociospatial Relations* (Tucson: The University of Arizona Press, 2017), 23–24.
16. Epeli Hauʻofa, "Our Sea of Islands," *The Contemporary Pacific* 6, no. 1 (Spring 1994): 148–61.
17. I actively challenge Akhil Gupta and James Ferguson's theory of assimilation in Akhil Gupta and James Ferguson, eds., *Culture, Power, Place: Explorations in Critical Anthropology* (Durham, N.C.: Duke University Press, 1997).
18. Leanne Betasamosake Simpson, *As We Have Always Done: Indigenous Freedom through Radical Resistance* (Minneapolis: University of Minnesota Press, 2017), 196–97.
19. Diaz and Kauanui, "Native Pacific Cultural Studies on the Edge"; and Case, *Everything Ancient Was Once New*.
20. Leon Noʻeau Peralto, "Kokolo Mai Ka Mole Uaua O ʻĪ: The Resilience & Resurgence of Aloha ʻĀina in Hāmākua Hikina, Hawaiʻi" (PhD diss., University of Hawaiʻi at Mānoa, 2018), 108.
21. Vicente M. Diaz, "No Island Is an Island," in *Native Studies Keywords*, ed. Stephanie Nohelani Teves, Andrea Smith, and Michelle H. Raheja (Tucson: The University of Arizona Press, 2015), 90–108.
22. Hauʻofa, "Our Sea of Islands."
23. Diaz, "Oceania in the Plains."
24. Albert Wendt, "Pacific Maps and Fiction(s): A Personal Journey," in *Asian and Pacific Inscriptions: Identities, Ethnicities, Nationalities*, ed. Suvendrini Perera (Bundoora: Meridian, 1995), 15.
25. *Mana* translates to power, spirit, and authority in ʻŌlelo Hawaiʻi (Hawaiian language).
26. Hūfanga ʻOkusitino Māhina, "*Tā*, *Vā*, and Moana: Temporality, Spatiality, and Indigeneity," *Pacific Studies* 33, nos. 2–3 (2010): 168–202; Albert L. Refiti, "Mavae and Tofiga: Spatial Exposition of the Samoan Cosmogony and Architecture" (PhD diss., Auckland University of Technology, 2014); and Kaʻili, *Marking Indigeneity*.
27. See Case, *Everything Ancient Was Once New*, for an exploration of the concept of *Kahiki* within Kanaka Maoli philosophy.
28. Lilikalā Kameʻeleihiwa, *Native Land and Foreign Desires: Pehea Lā E Pono Ai?* (Honolulu: Bishop Museum Press, 1992).

29   James Miller, "The Continuity of Deep Cultural Patterns: A Case Study of Three Marshallese Communities" (PhD diss., University of Oregon, 2018).

30   Manulani Aluli Meyer, "Our Own Liberation: Reflections on Hawaiian Epistemology," *The Contemporary Pacific* 13, no. 1 (Spring 2001): 124–48.

31   Aníbal Quijano, "Coloniality of Power, Eurocentrism and Latin America," *Nepantla: Views from South* 1, no. 3 (2000): 533–80.

32   Oren Yiftachel, "Critical Theory and 'Gray Space': Mobilization of the Colonized," in *Cities for People, Not for Profit: Critical Urban Theory and the Right to the City* (London: Routledge, 2012), 150–70.

33   Lorenzo Veracini, "Decolonizing Settler Colonialism: Kill the Settler in Him and Save the Man," *American Indian Culture and Research Journal* 41, no. 1 (2017): 1–18; and James Belich, *Replenishing the Earth: The Settler Revolution and the Rise of the Anglo-World, 1783–1939* (Oxford: Oxford University Press, 2009).

34   Eric Nay, "Canonizing Le Corbusier: The Making of an Architectural Icon as Colonial Hegemony" (PhD diss., University of Toronto, 2018).

35   Lorenzo Veracini, "Suburbia, Settler Colonialism, and the World Turned Inside Out," *Housing, Theory and Society* 29, no. 4 (2012): 339–57.

36   G. H. Needham, *Living in the New Houses*, trans. Harriet Ruston and Joanasie Salomonie (Ottawa: Education Branch, Northern Administration Branch, Department of Indian Affairs and Northern Development, 1968), https://publications.gc.ca/site/eng/9.839771/publication.html.

37   Zeynep Çelik, "Le Corbusier, Orientalism, Colonialism," *Assemblage*, no. 17 (April 1992): 74.

38   Serge A. Marek, "Indigenous Urban Geographies of Empowerment: Māori Urban Geographies of *Whakamanatanga*," *Espace populations sociétés*, nos. 1–2 (2020), https://journals.openedition.org/eps/10001; and Renya K. Ramirez, *Native Hubs: Culture, Community, and Belonging in Silicon Valley and Beyond* (Durham, N.C.: Duke University Press, 2007).

39   Ramirez, *Native Hubs*, 11–24.

40   "Militourism" is a term Sean Connelly has used to describe the intersecting systems of tourism and military to dispossess Kanaka Maoli of their land (Sean Connelly, "Our City as Ahupuaʻa: For Justice-Advancing Futures," in *The Value of Hawaiʻi 3: Hulihia, the Turning*, ed. Noelani Goodyear-Kaʻōpua, Craig Howes, Jonathan Kay Kamakawiwoʻole Osorio, and Aiko Yamashiro [Honolulu: University of Hawaiʻi Press, 2020], 231–36).

41   The Compact of Free Association Act of 1985 (Public Law 99-239) is a joint resolution between the United States of America, the Republic of the Marshall Islands (RMI), and the Federated States of Micronesia (FSM). COFA terminated the U.S. trusteeship over the former Trust Territories of the Pacific Islands. Through negotiations between the U.S. and the RMI and FSM, citizens of the RMI and FSM are allowed to freely enter the U.S. to work, gain education, and receive medical care.

42   Kara Puketapu-Dentice, Sean Connelly, and Michelle Thompson-Fawcett, "Towards Integrating Indigenous Culture in Urban Form," *Justice Spatiale/Spatial Justice*, no. 11 (2017): 11.

43   Ralph Thomas Kam, "Remembering the Royal Residences of Kapālama: The Homes of Princess Ruth Keʻelikōlani and Queen Liliʻuokalani," *The Hawaiian Journal of History* 47 (2013): 147–77.

44   Hōkūlani K. Aikau and Vernadette Vicuña Gonzalez, eds., *Detours: A Decolonial Guide to Hawaiʻi* (Durham, N.C.: Duke University Press, 2019).

45   Kuʻualoha Hoʻomanawanui, "'This Land Is Your Land, This Land Was My Land': Kanaka Maoli versus Settler Representations of ʻĀina in Contemporary Literature of Hawaiʻi," in *Asian Settler Colonialism: From Local Governance to the Habits of Everyday Life in Hawaiʻi*, ed. Candace Fujikane and Jonathan Y. Okamura (Honolulu: University of Hawaiʻi Press, 2008), 116–54. Emalani Case explores *Kahiki* as a relational space that demonstrates our responsibility to our broader Oceanic family through our shared ancestors in *Everything Ancient Was Once New*.

46   Arturo Escobar, *Designs for the Pluriverse: Radical Interdependence, Autonomy, and the Making of Worlds* (Durham, N.C.: Duke University Press, 2018).

47   The colonial apparatus of the United States present in the RMI includes COFA and the United States Army Garrison on Kwajalein Atoll. While COFA imparts U.S. influence on Rimajol identities, I argue that Rimajol families and individuals co-opt the colonial apparatus within their own resurgent practices in the face of dispossession and climate change vulnerabilities. See Greg Dvorak, *Coral and Concrete: Remembering Kwajalein Atoll between Japan, America, and the Marshall Islands* (Honolulu: University of

Hawai'i Press, 2018); and Lauren Hirshberg, *Suburban Empire: Cold War Militarization in the US Pacific* (Oakland: University of California Press, 2022).

48 James Miller, "Aelon Kein Ad: A Case Study of Rimajol Place Identity in the United States," in *Pacific Spaces: Translations and Transmutations*, ed. Anna-Christina Engels-Schwarzpaul, Lana Lopesi, and Albert L. Refiti (New York: Berghahn Books, 2022), 129–47.

49 Miller, "Continuity of Deep Cultural Patterns"; James Miller, "The Evolution of the Marshallese Vernacular House," *Fabrications* 30, no. 1 (2020): 110–36; and James Miller, "Climate Change Adaptation, Displacement and the Vernacular Architecture of the Marshallese," in *Vernacular Environments, Culture and Global Change in Australasia and Oceania*, ed. Paul Memmott, John Ting, and Tim O'Rourke (London: Bloomsbury Publishing, forthcoming).

50 To learn more about the nuclear legacy of the RMI, refer to the work of Lauren Hirshberg, Jessica Schwartz, and in particular Barbara Rose Johnston and Holly M. Barker, *Consequential Damages of Nuclear War: The Rongelap Report* (Walnut Creek, Calif.: Left Coast Press, 2008).

51 Miller, "Indigenous Placemaking in the Climate Diaspora."

52 Tēvita O. Ka'ili, "Tauhi vā: Nurturing Tongan Sociospatial Ties in Maui and Beyond," *The Contemporary Pacific* 17, no. 1 (Spring 2005): 83–114.

53 Daniel Hernandez, "Rootz Vaka Transits: Traversing Seas of Urban Diasporic Indigeneity by Collapsing Time and Space with the Songs and Stories of the Kava Canoe" (PhD diss., University of Auckland, 2019).

54 Seeing forced migration as a positive process of expansion is influenced by Eve Tuck's work countering the narrative of damage-centered research (Eve Tuck, "Suspending Damage: A Letter to Communities," *Harvard Educational Review* 79, no. 3 [Fall 2009]: 409–27).

55 *Pedped ijin, pedped ijon* reflects the reef flat that extends out in the intertidal zone. It translates to building foundations and metaphorically translates to protecting the land from the destructive forces of the ocean. This concept is shared by Kanaka Maoli decolonial educators, such as in Brian Martin, Georgina Stewart, Bruce Ka'imi Watson, Ola Keola Silva, Jeanne Teisina, Jacoba Matapo, and Carl Mika, "Situating Decolonization: An Indigenous Dilemma," *Educational Philosophy and Theory* 52, no. 3 (2020): 312–21.

56 During the 2014 election year, representatives came to Springdale to campaign. Legislation was introduced in 2016 to eliminate absentee voting through postal ballots; the bill was officially denied in 2019.

57 "Meet Team MEI," Marshallese Educational Initiative, https://www.mei.ngo/about.

58 For discussion on abundance and Ho'oulu 'Āina, see Mary Tuti Baker, "Waiwai (Abundance) and Indigenous Futures," in *Routledge Handbook of Postcolonial Politics*, ed. Olivia U. Rutazibwa and Robbie Shilliam (London: Routledge, 2018), 22–31.

59 Baker, "Waiwai (Abundance) and Indigenous Futures."

60 Sean Connelly, "Urbanism as Island Living," in *The Value of Hawai'i 2: Ancestral Roots, Oceanic Visions*, ed. Aiko Yamashiro and Noelani Goodyear-Ka'ōpua (Honolulu: University of Hawai'i Press, 2014), 88–99.

61 Susan Lobo, "Is Urban a Person or a Place? Characteristics of Urban Indian Country," *American Indian Culture and Research Journal* 22, no. 4 (1998): 89–102.

62 Diaz, "Oceania in the Plains."

63 Ramirez, *Native Hubs*.

5

Theory through Hide Tanning

Resurgence and Indigenous Mobility

MANDEE MCDONALD

Since 2011, the year I started learning to tan hides, I've witnessed an explosion of passion and interest in hide tanning as well as an increased motivation in individuals and communities to organize their own camps and hide-tanning initiatives. I've been working in the field of Indigenous land-based programming in Denendeh since 2013. I'm a Maskîgow iskwew and a member of York Factory First Nation originally from Churchill, Manitoba, and I spent most of my life living in Sǫ̀mbak'è (Yellowknife, Northwest Territories), the traditional territories of the Yellowknives Dene First Nation. I've tanned moose or caribou hides on the lands of the Yellowknives Dene First Nation, Łútsęlk'é First Nation, and the Tłı̨chǫ, Dehcho, Cowichan, Gwich'in, Stoney Nakoda, Blackfoot Confederacy, Dene Tsuut'ina, and Maskîgow peoples, usually as a facilitator working with elders, and I've turned down invitations to attend hide camps in different territories when I was too burned out or tired to travel. I'm not sharing this to position myself as an expert hide tanner, because I am certainly not, but to demonstrate the growing desire among different Indigenous peoples to learn hide tanning today. For the purposes of this essay, I refer to the massive and recent uptake of hide tanning as the hide-tanning movement. This essay is an Indigenous feminist analysis of this movement, which is composed of many different Indigenous-led hide-tanning initiatives, but the thoughts presented here are informed by the camps I've (co-)organized or attended and the theory that's being generated by the work in which I'm directly involved, including my own felt knowledge generated through my engagement with hide tanning, teaching hide tanning, and doing the administrative labor of building and delivering hide-tanning programs with friends and collaborators. I acknowledge there are many hide-tanning initiatives to which I have no direct connection, and I can't speak to them.

Hide-tanning theory is the knowledge generated in hide-tanning camps and by the relationships they animate. When I speak of hide tanning, I am referring to the multiplicity of practices, entities, and relationships involved in the preparation of a hide. Hide-tanning praxis, which is theory, action, and self-reflection in relation to hide tanning, has the potential to shift the predominant idea that Indigeneity must be tethered to a specific, bounded homeland or traditional territory because it demonstrates the ways in which Indigenous knowledges are generated through movement over lands and through engagement with different peoples in different places. This is but one of many interventions that an analysis of the hide-tanning movement yields. An Indigenous feminist analysis of the hide-tanning movement also reveals the ways in which it is informed by experiential knowledge of joy, desire, and violence (physical, lateral, and gendered marginalization). This analysis reveals the ways in which the movement is transcending colonial containment and the exclusionary logic of some articulations of resurgence by creating models of inclusive resurgent action and organizing that facilitate spaces for Indigenous peoples to connect to land and community from their own positionalities, whatever they may be.

In terms of the theme of this collection, Land Back, the hide-tanning movement is regenerating Indigenous thought systems that are informed by a relationship to land. This type of work is reflected by the editors of the Land Back issue of *Briarpatch*: "We want the system that is land to be alive so that it can perpetuate itself, and perpetuate us as an extension of itself. That's what we want back: our place in keeping land alive and spiritually connected."[1] Drawing from Glen Coulthard's (Yellowknives Dene) articulation of Indigenous anti-colonial theory, the hide-tanning movement is part of "a struggle primarily inspired by and oriented around *the question of land*—a struggle not only *for* land in the material sense, but also deeply *informed* by what the land *as system of reciprocal relations and obligations* can teach us about living our lives in relation to one another and the natural world in nondominating and nonexploitative terms."[2] The hide-tanning movement is regenerating Indigenous thought systems by relationally reorienting people to land.[3] These land-based systems of thinking and being ("the system that is land" and "the land *as a system of reciprocal relations*") are central to the movement for Indigenous self-determination, of which Land Back is a recent iteration. Experiential/embodied/felt knowledge is an important element of reproducing and regenerating these systems, which an analysis of the hide-tanning movement brings clearly into view.

The concept of felt knowledge is an Indigenous feminist contribution to the field of Indigenous studies and Indigenous-centered academia more broadly. The Indigenous body is a producer of valuable felt knowledge. Dian Million's (Tanana Athabascan) work on felt theory centers the body, particularly the body in pain, as a producer of knowledge about colonization.[4] Million emphasizes the importance of felt experience as community knowledge that informs our positions as Indigenous scholars, particularly as Indigenous women scholars.[5] An analysis of the hide-tanning movement demonstrates that felt knowledge can be experienced as many different feelings and emotions, including pain, joy, and desire. The felt knowledge produced by my own body from tanning hides with my friends, organizing camps, and connecting with all the new and old relations animated in a camp informs my position as a Maskîgow iskwew thinker, writer, junior scholar, and program administrator. Felt knowledge determines action, and so it must be considered within theorizations of Indigenous governance and political movements.

Felt knowledge is marginalized by Western thought and the academy. Western thought and Enlightenment rationalism have discursively separated the mind from the body and the human from nature. It is this colonially imposed thought system that many Indigenous peoples are trying to unlearn via the implementation of land-based programming. For the Māori, for example, "the physical realm was not divorced from other realms, such as the mind (*hinengaro*) or spirituality (*mauri/wairua*)."[6] Indigenous epistemologies challenged, and continue to challenge, the principles of Enlightenment rationalism that assume the existence of objective truth and that the world is inherently knowable. This assumption is premised on the separation of the mind from the body and the human from the rest of nature. These principles have many implications: rationality and reason are situated as human, masculine, and of the mind, while emotions are situated as irrational, feminine, and of the body; humans are situated as superior to nature and animals;[7] and Indigenous epistemologies that challenge these principles are unintelligible to Western thought.[8] Brendan Hokowhitu (Ngāti Pūkenga) writes:

> In the condition of postcoloniality it is difficult to disengage with a mind/body duality, and it is at this fundamental level that theorizing toward epistemological transformation must begin: with the thinking body, the conceptualization of the body as a material producer of thought, the body as a holistic notion in which physiology and the interplay between history, present, and future interact to produce social meaning, which may be freeing and/or disciplinary.[9]

He calls for Indigenous studies scholars to pay attention to the everyday, the immediacy of the here and now, and body logic, which is what culture "feels like" as opposed to the production of culture to be viewed or preserved.[10] Considering the body logic and felt knowledge of Indigenous peoples who are participating in the hide-tanning movement demonstrates how Indigenous peoples have meaningful and deeply transformative experiences in relation to a multitude of lands and peoples rather than (only or primarily) with a narrowly defined geographical territory and/or group of peoples.

Hide Camps

Hide-tanning camps, resourced and designed with intention, are beautiful examples of Indigenous aesthetics and the role of aesthetics in transmitting knowledge about governance and law.[11] Hide-camp aesthetics refer to the full-body, sensory experiences of a hide camp, including emotional, physical, visual, tactile, auditory, etc. The hide camps I help to organize are at least two weeks long. This is a good length because it's enough time to almost completely finish a hide if the weather is conducive. Two weeks is long enough to experience most of the steps of tanning a hide without feeling too rushed. It's also a good amount of time for people to get to know each other and the land. We hire elders and local knowledge holders to help run and maintain the camp, and all the participants usually sleep at the camp each night in tents or cabins. Three meals a day and snacks are typically provided, but participants eat whenever they're hungry. Sometimes we eat together, or sometimes we eat quickly in between tasks. Every day we work on hides or harvest materials like spruce boughs or wood that we need for the hides. We eat fish and drink water from the lakes or rivers. Everything smells like smoke—fire smoke, smoked hides, smoked fish, and/or smoked dried meat. Every day sounds like fire crackling, water splashing, hides scraping, food cooking, wind gusting, boat motors, generators, and singing and laughing.

Hide Tanning, Governance, and Resurgence

Hide tanning is a relational land-based practice with important implications for Indigenous governance because it transmits knowledge of Indigenous governance while also facilitating a process of knowledge embodiment.[12] The hide-tanning movement reflects the relational paradigmatic approach described by Gina Starblanket (Cree/Saulteaux) and Heidi Kiiwetinepinesiik Stark (Turtle Mountain Ojibwe), who argue that a shift toward a relational paradigm can "dissolve the boundaries imposed by Western discursive, social, and political orders" that ultimately undermine and bind the generative potential of Indigenous thought.[13] Contemporary hide-tanning practices such as hide-tanning camps are understood through a relational paradigm, a lens of ethical love and Indigenous relational aesthetics.[14] Drawing from bell hooks (African American) and Leanne Betasamosake Simpson (Michi Saagiig Nishnaabeg), Jas Morgan (Cree-Métis-Saulteaux) writes: "Ethical love is a pedagogy of relationality taught to Indigenous peoples by their kin—siblings, aunties, grandparents, and other individuals of influence—and activated, its animated self, through attentiveness to kinship responsibilities. Ethical love, being in a good way with all Creation, is something that is learned by feeling, doing, being, building, and even destroying—by enacting relations with one's self and the surrounding world."[15]

Morgan also writes that Indigenous relational aesthetics describe the relational ways of making art encoded within Indigenous epistemologies, which aligns with hide tanning because the practice is encoded with many teachings, values, relationships, and stories. These teachings, values, relationships, and stories are also encoded into every other element of a hide-tanning camp, such as the food that is prepared, how waste is disposed, where we sleep, what and how we harvest, and how we care for each other. Emotional embodied knowledge like ethical love drives hide-tanning praxis.

Bringing emotion, embodied connection, and relationality back into theories of governance is a crucial element of Indigenous resurgence. Simpson writes: "[R]esurgence must be concerned with the reattachment of our minds, bodies. [sic] and spirits to the network of relationships and ethical practices that generates grounded normativity. It means the reattachment of our bodies to our lands, regardless of whether those lands are rural, reserves, or urban."[16] Grounded normativity means that the values and practices informed by generations-long relationships to land also inform how we engage with the rest of the world, including, I add, our relationships to ourselves and our own bodies. It is "the modalities of Indigenous land-connected practices and longstanding experiential knowledge that inform and structure our ethical engagements with the world and our relationships with human and nonhuman others over time."[17] These modalities of practices that inform engagements and relationships should also inform governance in theory and practice. Indigenous resurgence is political because the purpose of it is to facilitate radical transformation.[18] Kiera Ladner writes that, within Indigenous intellectual systems, "governance is 'the way in which a people lives best together' or the way a people has structured their society in relationship to the natural world."[19] Similarly, Simpson explains: "Governance was *made* every day. Leadership was embodied and acted out every day. Grounded normativity isn't a thing; it is generated structure born and maintained from deep engagement with Indigenous processes that are inherently physical, emotional, intellectual, and spiritual. Processes were created and practiced."[20] The ethic of everyday governance is informed by felt knowledge because the things we choose to do every day are driven by feelings of desire, longing, satisfaction, care for self and others, discipline, or responsibility. Hide tanning is very much a political and governance-oriented practice, and many Indigenous governance principles are activated and redefined in a hide camp. The embodied experience of hide tanning, connecting to the land and people in camp while engaging with each other to share information and make plans, is a type of political mobilization commonly enacted by Indigenous women around kitchen tables or other informal venues.[21]

The hide-tanning movement also has lessons to share about the resurgence of Indigenous economies, or making a living in relation to land, which is another aspect of governance. Hide tanning is a relational economic practice that embodies the Nêhiyawak concept of *pimâcihowin*.[22] To explain the dynamic nature of Nêhiyawak society, Shalene Jobin (Métis/Red Pheasant Cree First Nation) shares this quote from Liam Haggarty: "'[N]êhiyawak [Cree] culture is not easily analysed or summarised. As a fluid, ever-changing and evolving set of interconnected relationships and meanings, it cannot be succinctly described or condensed. Even if this were possible, the result would not represent the experiences of all nêhiyawak peoples at any given time, much less through time.'"[23] *Pimâcihowin* connotes both a connection to land and an ability to make a living or have a good life in relation to land.[24] Jobin's articulation of a livelihood economy and *pimâcihowin* reflects the hide-tanning movement today because hide tanning contributes to Indigenous economies in several important ways. Hide-tanning camps are spaces that animate Indigenous economic principles like sharing and respect. We also fundraise money to deliver camps, and by doing so we are able to compensate knowledge holders and helpers for their time and expertise with money. Tanned hides are used to create artwork and garments for friends and family, and these items are often gifted, traded, or sold. As an economic practice, hide tanning strengthens and generates relational webs, as opposed to extractive economic practices that exploit the labor of bodies and compromise the integrity of lands.

Hide-tanning camps are spaces that facilitate the kinds of relationships that promote the value of self-determination as defined by Rauna Kuokkanen (Finnish Saami), who argues that "Indigenous self-determination is a foundational value that fosters the norm of integrity manifested in two central forms, integrity of the land and individual integrity, including freedom from bodily harm and violence."[25] Indigenous self-determination "cannot materialize or be exercised without restructuring *all* relations of domination."[26] Indigenous self-determination requires a relational reorientation to land that explicitly addresses violence against the land and Indigenous peoples' bodies. She argues that Indigenous feminist examinations of self-determination call for transformation centered on reorientation to the land, not simply adding women's perspectives to mainstream discourse on self-determination.[27]

Hide-tanning camps are Indigenous feminist praxis: Indigenous women attempting to relationally reorient themselves and their communities to the land. The theoretical work of considering what kinds of relations promote the value of self-determination—combined with the work of creating and implementing opportunities where these relations can be fostered and the critical self-reflection required to negotiate for power, spaces, and resources to do this work—is the contribution of the hide-tanning movement to Indigenous self-determination, resurgence, and governance theory today. Even though the camps may not explicitly address physical violence against Indigenous women, they are intended to support the capacity of participants to be self-determining and to live freely in relation to all of creation,[28] and so hide-tanning camps are considered a type of harm prevention. Camps are designed to be free of violence, including lateral violence, and such violence is addressed if it is noticed in the camp, requiring significant emotional labor from camp organizers and participants. Camps are harm prevention because they facilitate the development of support networks and friendships; they empower camp participants to (re)learn their culture and language and to (re)connect to land and community. Elders, teachers, and camp staff also model self-determination because they embody it. They either do so unprompted, or they are encouraged to via a camp orientation or throughout the planning process. In so doing, people in camp demonstrate and promote an ethic of care and nonviolence. Situating the hide-tanning movement as Indigenous feminist praxis means understanding how hide tanning, by promoting joy and relationality, is also informed by a deep understanding of structural violence against Indigenous women.

A shared felt understanding of structural violence against Indigenous women is usually apparent among people at a hide camp. This becomes apparent in a camp simply because people talk to each other about their lives, sometimes pretty openly, especially after a few days together on the land. One of many policies that contribute to structural violence against Indigenous women is the Indian Act. Many Indigenous women, through many mediums and in many spaces, have shared felt knowledge about the Indian Act. Countless writers have addressed the Indian Act and the impacts it continues to have on Indigenous women and their children.[29] Million writes: "An intimate realignment of Indian social relationships through the Indian Act was at the core of what colonization meant in practice. The strongly gendered training in residential schools coupled with the 1876 Indian Act radically reorganized Indigenous familial relations to conform to a uniform patriarchal order."[30] Jobin writes that the "Indian Act system has crushed complex kinship and wahkohtowin norms."[31] Beverly Jacobs (Mohawk) writes:

> Since the inception of the Indian Act, there have been missing Indigenous women who were forcefully displaced from their traditional territories for "marrying out."

This was the beginning of missing Indigenous women. The genocidal policies of the Indian Act also had an impact on Indigenous governance systems where the women's decision-making qualities were silenced and no longer part of the balance of these systems.[32]

The loss of status for Indigenous women meant the loss of material resources like treaty monies, educational funding, childcare funding, health benefits, and tax benefits, which contributed to the economic marginalization and isolation of Indigenous women that makes them especially vulnerable to violence.[33] The descendants of these women continue to experience the loss of community belonging, which impacts identity and the ability to learn and practice the knowledge systems of their peoples, nations, and ancestors.

Homeland Narratives

An Indigenous feminist analysis of the hide-tanning movement offers an intervention into a confusing dissonance within resurgent theorizing: the often stated or implied requirement for Indigenous peoples to connect or go to their own homelands, which contradicts broader conceptions of relationality and mobility in Indigenous epistemologies. Even though relationality is central to Indigenous epistemologies, some iterations of Indigenous resurgence reflect assumptions about land ownership and a relation to homeland that have problematic implications that actually undermine relationality. Hide-tanning praxis can not only contribute to interrogating these implications, but also to identifying less clearly marked resurgent pathways, thus transcending some of the exclusionary principles implied by some resurgent rhetoric.

Many Indigenous writers use the language of "our" land as opposed to "the" land to assert claims over land against settlers. However, the implications of the use of "our" over "the" in many cases seems to impose a proprietary relation.[34] This language conflates Indigenous homeland with a Western capitalist ideal of land ownership, imposing a discursive boundary around land that over-determines how Indigenous peoples can relate to specific lands based on who owns it. The discursive boundary around land is the imposition of a colonial proprietary relationship. From a Western perspective, ownership determines rights and responsibilities. Therefore, I have no rights or responsibilities to land that's not mine/my homelands. Thus, my ability or allowability to develop a relationship to said land is limited, or at least predefined, by virtue of it not being mine. This propriety relation, or lack thereof, is also something that is visceral and felt, and it's an example of ontological containment resulting from the establishment of spatial boundaries meant to contain Indigenous peoples physically.

An example of this is how some urban Indigenous students, or relocatees,[35] find it challenging to see their place or locate themselves within the canon of Indigenous resurgence literature or within spaces of resurgent action (Indigenous community organizing and land-based learning) because they've been living in someone else's homelands their entire lives. While affirming the reality and importance of Indigenous territoriality—that Indigenous nations have rights and responsibilities to their homelands and traditional territories—it's also important to note how colonial containment has influenced Indigenous claims to particular lands that actually remove, erase, and/or undermine other Indigenous peoples' responsibilities to those same lands. For example, modern land-claims processes do not acknowledge shared authority over land, sometimes resulting in conflicts between neighboring nations.[36] The hide-tanning movement transcends these boundaries because many camps are actually organized by Indigenous women and/or Two-Spirit people who have been marginalized from their homelands, sometimes over multiple generations, whether that marginalization is a result of losing status for marrying out, transphobia, homophobia, or lateral and/or physical violence. The discursive boundaries around homelands undermine the relational paradigm described by Starblanket and Stark.[37]

A relational paradigm centers the interconnectedness of all things, which is a defining feature of Indigenous epistemologies.[38] Relationality is a key analytic and normative principle articulated by many Indigenous scholars,[39] especially resurgence theorists. Starblanket and Stark challenge Indigenous studies scholars and resurgence theorists to think about the ways in which relationality can either advance or inhibit Indigenous political movements and also how it can be invoked, both positively and negatively, in the context of individual and collective well-being.[40] Their discussion on relationality, land, and boundaries is particularly interesting. They write: "In our efforts to assert our political authority in the face of state assertions of title over our territories, we ask how we have foreclosed alternative forms of resistance by centring our attentions on articulations of land that risk reifying statist notions of bounded space."[41] They question how tethering Indigeneity to land, or to a specific bounded geographical area, limits Indigenous knowledge production. Similarly, Hokowhitu argues that the "glue of Indigenous identity markers such as land, language, and performance of culture has, as a consequence, bounded Indigenous resistance movements."[42] Drawing from Foucault's work on biopower, Hokowhitu argues some Indigenous subjectivities are marked for life and some for death. The ones marked for life have acquired authority, and this functions to allow alternative subjectivities to die. Markers of Indigenous authenticity definitionally exclude those who do not reflect those markers, and so they are marked for death.[43] Those markers today include language, performance of culture, resistance, and land, with an emphasis on homeland or a connection or relationship to a defined traditional or ancestral territory. Indigenous peoples who don't reflect those markers are deemed inauthentic or incomplete.

In using the language of my land/your land or homeland, many Indigenous writers expressly encourage Indigenous peoples to return to, or go for the first time to, some specific homelands. For example, Simpson, one of the most prolific resurgence writers today, writes that "any Indigenous person with motivation to learn to think inside the land should be interacting with their own Elders and experts in their own homelands instead of reading me."[44] What I think Simpson means is that anyone with the motivation to think inside the land should actually be doing work on the land with knowledge holders rather than just reading about resurgence. Still, this statement, and ones like it, reproduces a narrative that centers a particular relation to a homeland. The homeland narrative implies that

Indigenous peoples are not whole until they return to their homelands, despite whatever forces influenced them to leave in the first place. I draw out this quote from Simpson here for its concision and because of the sheer reach of her work, though she does provide a generous and nuanced account of Indigenous mobility later in *As We Have Always Done*. The quote is from Simpson's 2014 article "Land as Pedagogy: Nishnaabeg Intelligence and Rebellious Transformation," which won the Native American and Indigenous Studies Association's (NAISA) award for Most Thought-Provoking Article, as well as her 2021 book *As We Have Always Done*, which won NAISA's Best Subsequent Book Award. Simpson does engage with the concept of Indigenous mobility, but this aspect of her work is not taken up to the same extent as those that specifically center a homeland connection. In *As We Have Always Done*, Simpson writes:

> Indigenous peoples and our mobility can certainly be an expression of agency and self-determination within even shattered grounded normativity. Given the reality of settler colonialism, many of us continually reevaluate where we live, whether it is a city or a reserve, in our own territory or not, as a process to figure out how to live with as much dignity as possible. Our answers change as we move through the stages of life. I see this as a theoretical intervention. I see this as us using our mobility as a flight path out of settler colonialism and into Indigeneity. I see mobility imbued with agency as resurgence.[45]

To reiterate, this essay is not a rejection of homeland narratives. Rather, this essay is meant to explore what possibilities are foreclosed upon or what modalities of relationality are undermined when a connection to homeland is held up as a prerequisite for resurgent action.

The rhetoric that emphasizes a homeland connection as a preqrequisite for Indigenous resurgence not only undermines relationality but also the role of mobility and movement in Indigenous knowledge systems. Mobility,[46] critical self-reflection,[47] and dynamism[48] are all relational concepts that inform Indigenous knowledge generation and political action. Intellectual, physical, and emotional movement and dynamism are Indigenous ways of knowing and being. Movement over land generates Indigenous knowledges and activates relationships and responsibilities.[49] The imposition of the reserve system and modern land-claims agreements have created spatial boundaries between Indigenous peoples and lands. Travel and mobility over land are important elements of Indigenous relational paradigms and knowledges that co-constitute who we are and the responsibilities we claim. The role of deliberation, critical self-reflection, and the everydayness of governance also reflects an ethic of movement, dynamism, and mobility. Self-reflection is a form of intellectual and emotional mobility, dynamism, and flexibility. Recovering Indigenous ways of knowing—and collectively deliberating, reflecting on, revising, and implementing these principles—is an important part of decolonial or resurgent work.[50] Mobility and movement are often conceived of as Indigenous peoples following seasonal rounds, but mobility includes Indigenous peoples permanently relocating from one place to another, adopting each other, and joining families and communities together from different lands and nations, not just from within nations and homelands. Indigenous peoples bring their values, knowledges, and modes of relating with them everywhere they go and live.[51] Somehow, this ethic and practice of mobility has become de-emphasized in Indigenous studies and resurgence literature and overshadowed by a more static idealization of homeland connection.

This implied homeland connection requirement for resurgence can be analyzed using the lens of biopower that so many Indigenous scholars, including many Indigenous feminisms and queer theories scholars,[52] employ to interrogate which subjectivities are excluded from what and why. Predominant resurgence discourse seems to privilege, above all else, the experiences of Indigenous peoples (re)connecting to their own ancestral, specific, geographically defined homelands. The central role of homeland is explicated by scholars like Jeff Corntassel (Cherokee Nation), homeland being one of four interlocking features in the peoplehood model he proposes.[53] This privileging of a homeland connection is also implied by whose work and experiences are most popularly held up as exemplars of resurgence writing, and the common use of terminology like "our" or "their" lands as opposed to "the" lands.

While there is a great deal of nuance within the literature on Indigenous resurgence regarding homeland connectedness,[54] privileging the connection to homeland as a necessary aspect of Indigenous subjectivity and resurgence marginalizes Indigenous peoples who are not defined by, and do not feel, a connection to homeland. In an interview between Erin Marie Konsmo (Métis) and Karyn Recollet (Cree), Konsmo writes: "I continue to see the ways that some essentialist resurgence narratives are difficult and make Indigenous resurgence inaccessible."[55] She further argues that some prescriptive approaches to resurgence perpetuate ableism and purity narratives:

> Purity narratives appear in many forms and are often further reinforced by whiteness, misogyny, homo/transphobia, NIMBY and ableism. For any deviations from the normative—white, male, heterosexual, cisgender and able-bodied—are seen as less pure. I want us to consider how these notions are projected further in relation to Indigenous lands and especially as it relates to Indigenous resurgence on the land.[56]

This critique applies to homeland narratives as well in that connection to homeland is implied as a pure and superior type of relationship to land when compared to relationships to other lands and/or communities. The concern is that some Indigenous subjectivities are marginalized by the rhetoric that encourages Indigenous peoples to "go home" to "their own" lands if they have no meaningful connection to their homelands, or simply can't or don't want to go there. I'm thinking particularly of the countless Indigenous women forced to leave their communities as a result of discriminatory provisions of the Indian Act that determine how membership is passed on to children and the irreparable impact this has on their familial ability to foster a physical relationship to specific places. The dogmatic perpetuation of connection to homeland as a requirement for both authentic Indigeneity and resurgent action is a continuation of the structural violence inflicted upon Indigenous women through policies like the Indian Act that marginalize them from their homes. The feelings of loss, desire, and longing that result from this marginalization is felt knowledge that should be considered in our political organizing and dreaming.

Hide-tanning camps are a manifestation of our political dreaming. They are land-based programs designed with specific goals to meet the needs of our communities today. The goal of Indigenous land-based programming is to facilitate opportunities for Indigenous peoples to (re)connect to land, culture, and their communities. In so doing, program designers are attempting to reconnect the mind to the body and humans to nature. Interest in Indigenous land-based programming or land-based learning has increased dramatically over the past ten years, which is demonstrated by the ever-increasing amount of academic literature written about Indigenous land-based programming and learning,[57] as well as the major increase in Indigenous land-based programs, especially in the Northwest Territories where I live.[58] I use the term "land-based programming" rather than "land-based learning" because I'm primarily interested in programs delivered by organizations, collectives, or even Indigenous governments, as opposed to families engaging in their own land-based practices. I'm interested in programming specifically because this seems to be a method for community building and education used more commonly by Indigenous peoples who were or are marginalized from their homelands and the Indigenous communities to which they would have or do have legal rights and/or membership.[59] It's often Indigenous women and Two-Spirit people who end up relocating to other communities, particularly urban areas, and building programs with other similarly marginalized people. The fact that many Indigenous peoples do not have familial access to land-based knowledge and skills is a result of this marginalization, and this is what leads to the development of land-based programs. If the intention of land-based programs is to liberate our minds from the limitations imposed by Western epistemologies, we must interrogate the ways in which colonization contains both our bodies and ways of thinking.

Containment

The colonial imposition of geospatial borders and boundaries has important implications for Indigenous ontologies. I often wonder if the widespread glorification of homeland is influenced by colonial containment, though it is important to note that conceptualizations of homeland vary according to different Indigenous peoples' ways of knowing. This is not meant to critique the work of Indigenous scholars who do feel and value a strong connection to their homelands, and who center it in their work, but to put forth the idea that the universalization of homeland marginalizes some Indigenous peoples in problematic ways and can prohibit the generative potential of our thought systems. The establishment of the reserve system was a way to control and contain Indigenous peoples,[60] and it seems like many people conflate the reserve with homeland, even though the reserve is not always the area with which our ancestors lived. We've been contained in many other ways: physically, emotionally, and ontologically. Starblanket and Stark explain: "This *logic of containment* ensures that just enough Indigenous knowledge or 'culture' in [sic] engaged or incorporated, so long as the settler state and its colonial relations of power are not disturbed. This knowledge of containment operates as an extension of the epistemological and physical violences endemic to settler colonialism."[61] Various scholarship, particularly around land comanagement and land claims, has suggested that the ongoing work to make Indigenous knowledges intelligible and containable by colonizers over time actually does shift the way we think about and relate to the land.[62] Sarah Hunt (Kwakwaka'wakw-Kwagu'ł and Dzawada'enuxw) writes:

> Colonialism in Canada has involved the imposition of western worldviews and the simultaneous suppression of Indigenous worldviews—those heterogenous, place-based ways of knowing through which Indigeneity comes into being. Processes of colonialism in North America involved representational strategies that transformed Indigenous peoples and their lands conceptually and materially, in order to facilitate their displacement and to render them less than human. This ideological imposition has been central to the violent suppression of Indigenous peoples' vitality and sovereignty.[63]

Synthesis is the process of making unintelligible Indigenous knowledge comprehensible to Western thought, or as Hokowhitu puts it: "the violent amalgamation (authentication) of one culture into another, which typically involve[s] encompassing and reconfiguring the incomprehensible into comprehensible forms, the classification of Indigenous forms of knowing into Western ontological catalogs, or simply the denial that many practices even [exist]."[64] Generations of policy designed to contain Indigenous peoples physically were also meant to contain Indigenous peoples ontologically by redefining what we think is real, possible, or legitimate, especially in terms of relationality. These policies were designed to destroy or contain our ways of relating to each other and the land.

Conclusion

The hide-tanning movement is regenerating Indigenous thought and governance systems by centering embodied connection and felt knowledge about joy and violence as the foundation for political action and community building. It is illuminating a resurgent pathway less clearly marked than the dominant homeland narratives. Hide camps have become beacons of light, drawing people in from all directions and nations like fireflies to an intentionally designed transnational Indigenous space that feels good. Within Indigenous thought systems, knowledge is relational, and it is in relationships.[65] The knowledge and relationships that are being generated by the hide-tanning movement transcend colonially imposed ontological and geospatial borders, which is a valuable contribution to Indigenous political movements. Hide-tanning theory values our bodies as sources of the important knowledge that we need in order to mobilize politically. I know this because we reflect on our experiences and emotions during hide camp debriefs, and we use that knowledge to plan for the next camp. Instilling or teaching ethics of kinship by creating opportunities for people to connect to the land is a governance practice that can and does occur through land-based programming like hide-tanning camps. Hide camps are relationally reorienting people back to the land, which is highly political and transformative. Efforts should be taken to frame this work in such a way that does not explicitly or implicitly exclude or marginalize Indigenous subjectivities that do not strongly identify with a connection to homeland. This is important because this exclusion prohibits people from engaging with and contributing to Indigenous-led movements for self-determination. More importantly, implied exclusionary principles like this impose an oppressive level of hierarchy on Indigenous peoples because they dictate what specific, narrowly defined piece of material land Indigenous peoples are supposed to relate or connect to and how. This principle of homeland connection is couched in the rationale of relationality, yet it undermines a broader praxis of relationality, which is a great colonial dissonance within Indigenous studies and resurgent theorizing. This is only one of many insights and interventions that attention to the hide-tanning movement and hide-tanning theory reveals and offers today.

NOTES

1. Nickita Longman, Emily Riddle, Alex Wilson, and Saima Desai, "'Land Back' Is More than the Sum of Its Parts," *Briarpatch*, September 10, 2020, https://briarpatchmagazine.com/articles/view/land-back-is-more-than-the-sum-of-its-parts.
2. Glen Sean Coulthard, *Red Skin, White Masks: Rejecting the Colonial Politics of Recognition* (Minneapolis: University of Minnesota Press, 2014), 13.
3. Rauna Kuokkanen, *Restructuring Relations: Indigenous Self-Determination, Governance, and Gender* (New York: Oxford University Press, 2019).
4. Dian Million, *Therapeutic Nations: Healing in an Age of Indigenous Human Rights* (Tucson: University of Arizona Press, 2013); and Dian Million, "Felt Theory: An Indigenous Feminist Approach to Affect and History," *Wicazo Sa Review* 24, no. 2 (Fall 2009): 53–76.
5. Million, *Therapeutic Nations*, 57.
6. Brendan Hokowhitu, "Haka: Colonized Physicality, Body-Logic, and Embodied Sovereignty," in *Performing Indigeneity: Global Histories and Contemporary Experiences*, ed. Laura R. Graham and H. Glenn Penny (Lincoln: University of Nebraska Press, 2014), 280.
7. Eve Tuck and Marcia McKenzie, *Place in Research: Theory, Methodology, and Methods* (New York: Routledge, 2015), 50.
8. Hokowhitu, "Haka," 280; and Hokowhitu, "Monster: Post Indigenous Studies," in *Critical Indigenous Studies: Engagements in First World Locations*, ed. Aileen Moreton-Robinson (Tucson: University of Arizona Press, 2016), 84.
9. Hokowhitu, "Haka," 296–97.
10. Brendan Hokowhitu, "Monster," 100.
11. Darcy Lindberg, "Miyo Nêhiyâwiwin (Beautiful Creeness): Ceremonial Aesthetics and Nêhiyaw Legal Pedagogy," *The Indigenous Law Journal* 16–17, no. 1 (2018): 51–65.
12. Lindberg, "Miyo Nêhiyâwiwin (Beautiful Creeness)," 60.
13. Gina Starblanket and Heidi Kiiwetinepinesiik Stark, "Towards a Relational Paradigm: Four Points for Consideration; Knowledge, Gender, Land, and Modernity," in *Resurgence and Reconciliation: Indigenous–Settler Relations and Earth Teachings*, ed. Michael Asch, John Borrows, and James Tully (Toronto: University of Toronto Press, 2018), 177–78.
14. Jas Morgan, "Toward an Indigenous Relational Aesthetics: Making Native Love, Still," in *In Good Relation: History, Gender, and Kinship in Indigenous Feminisms*, ed. Sarah Nickel and Amanda Fehr (Winnipeg: University of Manitoba Press, 2020), 195–206.
15. Morgan, "Toward an Indigenous Relational Aesthetics," 195.
16. Leanne Betasamosake Simpson, *As We Have Always Done: Indigenous Freedom through Radical Resistance* (Minneapolis: University of Minnesota Press, 2017), 44.
17. Coulthard, *Red Skin, White Masks*, 13.
18. Simpson, *As We Have Always Done*, 50.
19. Kiera L. Ladner, "Governing Within an Ecological Context: Creating an AlterNative Understanding of Blackfoot Governance," *Studies in Political Economy* 70 (Spring 2003): 125.
20. Simpson, *As We Have Always Done*, 23.
21. Starblanket and Stark, "Towards a Relational Paradigm," 188.
22. Shalene Wuttunee Jobin, *Upholding Indigenous Economic Relationships: Nehiyawak Narratives* (Vancouver: University of British Columbia Press, 2023), 20.
23. Liam Haggarty, "Nehiyawak (Plains Cree) Leadership on the Plain," Our Legacy, n.d., https://digital.scaa.sk.ca/ourlegacy/exhibit_nehiyawak_leadership, quoted in Jobin, *Upholding Indigenous Economic Relationships*, 17.
24. Jobin, *Upholding Indigenous Economic Relationships*, 21.
25. Kuokkanen, *Restructuring Relations*, 2.
26. Kuokkanen, *Restructuring Relations*, 12.
27. Kuokkanen, *Restructuring Relations*, 8.
28. Leroy Little Bear, "Jagged Worldviews Colliding," in *Reclaiming Indigenous Voice and Vision*, ed. Marie Battiste (Vancouver: University of British Columbia Press, 2000), 77–85.

29 Simpson, *As We Have Always Done*, 101; Robyn Bourgeois, "Generations of Genocide: The Historical and Sociological Context of Missing and Murdered Indigenous Women and Girls," in *Keetsahnak / Our Missing and Murdered Indigenous Sisters*, ed. Kim Anderson, Maria Campbell, and Christi Belcourt (Edmonton: University of Alberta, 2018), 65–88; Million, "Felt Theory"; Joanne Barker, "Gender, Sovereignty, and the Discourse of Rights in Native Women's Activism," *Meridians* 7, no. 1 (2006): 127–61; and Joanne Barker, "Gender, Sovereignty, Rights: Native Women's Activism against Social Inequality and Violence in Canada," *American Quarterly* 60, no. 2 (June 2008): 259–66.
30 Million, "Felt Theory," 56.
31 Jobin, *Upholding Indigenous Economic Relationships*, 60.
32 Beverly Jacobs, "Honouring Women," in *Keetsahnak / Our Missing and Murdered Indigenous Sisters*, ed. Kim Anderson, Maria Campbell, and Christi Belcourt (Edmonton: University of Alberta, 2018), 31–32.
33 Bourgeois, "Generations of Genocide," 72.
34 Robert Nichols, *Theft Is Property! Dispossession and Critical Theory* (Durham, N.C.: Duke University Press, 2020), 6, 8.
35 On Indigenous peoples who have relocated out of their homelands, see Renya K. Ramirez, *Native Hubs: Culture, Community, and Belonging in Silicon Valley and Beyond* (Durham, N.C.: Duke University Press, 2007).
36 Emily Riddle, "Mâmawiwikowin: Shared First Nations and Métis Jurisdiction on the Prairies," *Briarpatch*, September 10, 2020, https://briarpatchmagazine.com/articles/view/mamawiwikowin; Sarah Pruys, "Argument Brews over NWT Métis Nation's Plan for New Signs," Cabin Radio, September 5, 2018, https://cabinradio.ca/9142/news/politics/argument-brews-over-nwt-metis-nations-plan-for-new-signs/; and Sarah Pruys, "Kátł'odeeche First Nation Announces Legal Action over Cabins," Cabin Radio, July 16, 2020, https://cabinradio.ca/41384/news/south-slave/katlodeeche-first-nation-announces-legal-action-over-cabins/.
37 Starblanket and Stark, "Towards a Relational Paradigm."
38 Little Bear, "Jagged Worldviews"; Vine Deloria Jr., *God Is Red: A Native View of Religion*, 3rd ed. (Golden, Colo.: Fulcrum Publishing, 2003); and Shawn Wilson, *Research Is Ceremony: Indigenous Research Methods* (Black Point: Fernwood Publishing, 2008).
39 Starblanket and Stark, "Towards a Relational Paradigm," 176.
40 Starblanket and Stark, "Towards a Relational Paradigm," 177.
41 Starblanket and Stark, "Towards a Relational Paradigm," 189.
42 Hokowhitu, "Haka," 291.
43 Hokowhitu, "Monster," 86.
44 Simpson, *As We Have Always Done*, 164; and Leanne Betasamosake Simpson, "Land as Pedagogy: Nishnaabeg Intelligence and Rebellious Transformation," in "Indigenous Land-Based Education," ed. Matthew Wildcat, Stephanie Irlbacher-Fox, Glen Coulthard, and Mandee McDonald, special issue, *Decolonization: Indigeneity, Education & Society* 3, no. 3 (2014): 17.
45 Simpson, *As We Have Always Done*, 197.
46 Starblanket and Stark, "Towards a Relational Paradigm," 192; and Simpson, *As We Have Always Done*, 196.
47 Hokowhitu, "Haka," 293.
48 Jobin, *Upholding Indigenous Economic Relationships*, 54.
49 Little Bear, "Jagged Worldviews"; Starblanket and Stark, "Towards a Relational Paradigm," 191–92; and Leslie Main Johnson, *Trail of Story, Traveller's Path: Reflections on Ethnoecology and Landscape* (Edmonton: Athabasca University Press, 2010).
50 Jobin, *Upholding Indigenous Economic Relationships*, 211.
51 Ramirez, *Native Hubs*; and Evelyn Peters and Chris Andersen, eds., *Indigenous in the City: Contemporary Identities and Cultural Innovation* (Vancouver: University of British Columbia Press, 2013).
52 Qwo-Li Driskill, Chris Finley, Brian Joseph Gilley, and Scott Lauria Morgensen, eds., *Queer Indigenous Studies: Critical Interventions in Theory, Politics, and Literature* (Tucson: University of Arizona Press, 2011); Chris Finley, "Decolonizing the Queer Native Body (and Recovering the Native Bull-Dyke): Bringing 'Sexy Back' and Out of Native Studies' Closet," in Driskill, Finley, Gilley, and Morgensen, *Queer Indigenous Studies*, 31–42; Jodi A. Byrd, *The Transit of Empire: Indigenous Critiques of Colonialism* (Minneapolis: University of Minnesota Press, 2011); and Jennifer Nez Denetdale, "Return to 'The Uprising at Beautiful Mountain in 1913': Marriage and Sexuality in the Making of the Modern Navajo

Nation," in *Critically Sovereign: Indigenous Gender, Sexuality, and Feminist Studies*, ed. Joanne Barker (Durham, N.C.: Duke University Press, 2017), 74.

53 Jeff J. Corntassel, "Who Is Indigenous? 'Peoplehood' and Ethnonationalist Approaches to Rearticulating Indigenous Identity," *Nationalism and Ethnic Politics* 9, no. 1 (2003): 91.

54 Starblanket and Stark, "Towards a Relational Paradigm"; Robert Alexander Innes, *Elder Brother and the Law of the People: Contemporary Kinship and Cowessess First Nation* (Winnipeg: University of Manitoba Press, 2013); and Dallas Hunt, "'The Place Where the Hearts Gather': Against Damage-Centred Narratives of Urban Indigeneity," in *Visions of the Heart: Issues Involving Indigenous Peoples in Canada*, ed. Gina Starblanket and David Long, 5th ed. (Don Mills: Oxford University Press, 2020), 96.

55 Erin Marie Konsmo and Karyn Recollet, "Afterword: Meeting the Land(s) Where They Are At: Conversation between Erin Marie Konsmo (Métis) and Karyn Recollet (Urban Cree)," in *Indigenous and Decolonizing Studies in Education: Mapping the Long View*, ed. Linda Tuhiwai Smith, Eve Tuck, and K. Wayne Yang (New York: Routledge, 2019), 246.

56 Konsmo and Recollet, "Afterword," 239.

57 Megan Bang, Lawrence Curley, Adam Kessel, Ananda Marin, Eli S. Suzukovich III, and George Strack, "Muskrat Theories, Tobacco in the Streets, and Living Chicago as Indigenous Land," *Environmental Education Research* 20, no. 1 (2014): 37–55; John Borrows, "Outsider Education: Indigenous Law and Land-Based Learning," *Windsor Yearbook of Access to Justice* 33, no. 1 (2016): 1–27; and Alexandra Arellano, Joseph Friis, and Stephen A. Stuart, "Pathways to Reconciliation: The Kitcisakik Land-Based Education Initiative," *Leisure/Loisir* 43, no. 3 (2019): 389–417.

58 Jennifer Metisse Redvers, "Land-Based Practice for Indigenous Health and Wellness in Yukon, Nunavut, and the Northwest Territories" (master's thesis, University of Calgary, 2016); NWT on the Land Collaborative, *NWT on the Land Collaborative 2020 Report*, 2020, http://www.nwtontheland.ca/uploads/8/6/5/1/86514372/report_2020_final_web.pdf; NWT on the Land Collaborative, *Evaluative Review of Collaborative Grant Reports*, April 30, 2021, http://www.nwtontheland.ca/uploads/8/6/5/1/86514372/evaluative_review_of_collaborative_grant_reports.pdf; and Meagan Wolhberg and Kyla Kakfwi Scott, eds., "The Pan-territorial On-the-Land Summit," *Northern Public Affairs* 6, no. 1 (2018).

59 Sylvia Maracle, "The Eagle Has Landed: Native Women, Leadership and Community Development," in *Strong Women Stories: Native Vision and Community Survival*, ed. Kim Anderson and Bonita Lawrence (Toronto: Sumach Press, 2003), 70–80.

60 Bruce Erickson, "'Fucking Close to Water': Queering the Production of the Nation," in *Queer Ecologies: Sex, Nature, Politics, Desire*, ed. Catriona Mortimer-Sandilands and Bruce Erickson (Bloomington: Indiana University Press, 2010), 317.

61 Starblanket and Stark, "Towards a Relational Paradigm," 182.

62 Johnson, *Trail of Story, Traveller's Path*; Julie Cruikshank, *Do Glaciers Listen? Local Knowledge, Colonial Encounters, and Social Imagination* (Vancouver: University of British Columbia Press, 2005); and Paul Nadasdy, *Hunters and Bureaucrats: Power, Knowledge, and Aboriginal-State Relations in the Southwest Yukon* (Vancouver: University of British Columbia Press, 2003).

63 Sarah Hunt, "Ontologies of Indigeneity: The Politics of Embodying a Concept," *Cultural Geographies* 21, no. 1 (January 2014): 29.

64 Hokowhitu, "Haka," 280.

65 Wilson, *Research Is Ceremony*, 7.

II

Landscapes of Relationality

Ecology, Restoration, and Indigenous Futures

6

The Munsee Three Sisters Medicinal Farm

A Ground for Cultural Restoration

CHIEF VINCENT MANN AND ANITA BAKSHI

> People from the outside... many really still don't know the story. Many towns have never heard of Ringwood because we were written off, and the story was going to be buried so deep, that no one, a thousand years from now would never have known. [...] We have to start the motion again, have to start rolling all over again, collecting more people, educating more people.
>
> —Wayne Mann[1]

This is a story about a town named Ringwood in a place now known as New Jersey, which was once known by many names, including Lenapehoking. It is a story about lands that have been called home by the Ramapough Lunaape (Lenape) Turtle Clan for many centuries. These lands hold forests and streams, old mining structures, and an important drinking-water reservoir. They also hold deep pockets of contaminated soil. This is a story about how chemical toxicants from a nearby Ford Motor Company plant were buried so deep, just like this story had been.

We tell this story in layers, just as the landscape is composed, working up from the soil to the sky. All these layers connect and feed into each other. We start with "Soil" and describe the contaminated ground that many Native Americans live on or near. In "Seed," we describe the people—their long presence and history in New Jersey and their community today. In "Garden," we focus on what the land provides and on efforts for food sovereignty at the Munsee Three Sisters Medicinal Farm. We end with "Sunlight," where we expand the story out to more connections and relations as we describe our efforts to bring broader public awareness to environmental justice issues in Ringwood and beyond. We explore the significant reciprocities between landform and cultural restoration.

The Ramapough's living tradition has adapted and changed in relation to the ongoing lived experience of settler colonialism and continues to do so today. Culture and land are both alive and dynamic, continually reconstituted in relation to the present.[2]

Let us begin by introducing the storytellers. Vincent Mann is Turtle Clan Chief of the Ramapough Lunaape. He has experienced what we write about in this essay and has taken on the obligation to share his community's story. He is cofounder of the Munsee Three Sisters Medicinal Farm, one of the places we focus on in this essay and an important site for efforts for cultural restoration and food sovereignty. He is working toward long-term goals of cultural restoration and education through many partnerships with universities and land conservancies. As an advocate for cultural and environmental issues, he continues to offer up prayers for humanity and for our natural environment.

Anita Bakshi is a non-Native scholar with training in architecture who has studied contested places and histories. Her parents immigrated to the United States from India, carrying their own stories of the violence of Partition and the loss of home. She has lived and worked in a number of divided cities and societies around the world and was pulled to this work because of the familiarity of the selective narratives and compilations of history and memory that have informed how this history was told. She first worked with Chief Mann on a landscape architecture design studio project, and they have since continued to work together to create representations and visualizations of the Ramapough's history and present environmental justice struggles.

Here we describe the experience of the Ramapough Lunaape Turtle Clan in Ringwood, New Jersey, with environmental degradation, illness, and loss of traditional practices connected to the land. This is the result of the Ford Motor Company's dumping of toxic paint sludge in the mining shafts and forests near their community in the 1960s and 1970s (Figure 6.1). Although partially remediated through the Environmental Protection Agency's (EPA) Superfund program, contaminated material remains on the site to this day despite the significant role the Ramapough continue to play in keeping pressure on the authorities.

We walk through that history before outlining recent efforts led by the Ramapough to reconceptualize land relations and institute cultural-restoration programs geared toward recovering Indigenous environmental knowledge. This connects to what Potawatomi scholar Kyle Powys Whyte terms "collective continuance," which is "a community's capacity to be adaptive in ways sufficient for the livelihoods of its members to flourish into the future."[3] It involves efforts to maintain "the capacity to be adaptive with respect to *relational responsibilities,* or all those relationships and their corresponding responsibilities that facilitate the future flourishing of tribal livelihoods."[4] The farm enacts cultural restoration through the rehabilitation of relationships to the land and ancestral plant species. As the land is reformed to create teaching spaces, medicinal gardens, and a productive landscape, cultural actions and traditions are re-emplaced onto the land.

Like other contributions to this volume, our story centers relationality. It sharpens the focus on relationships with the land across time. Layer by layer, working from the soil that grounds this story, we describe relationships to land that endure, even in the context of pollution, the struggle for recognition of identity, and the ongoing efforts to

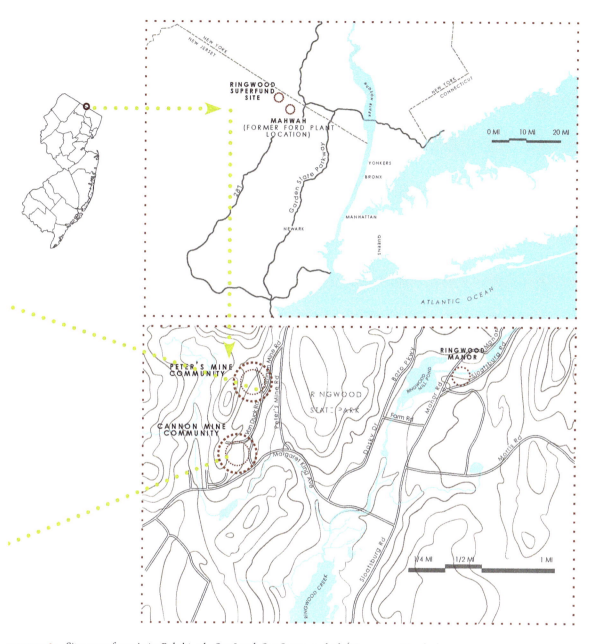

FIGURE 6.1 Site maps, from Anita Bakshi, ed., *Our Land, Our Stories*, 2nd ed. (Vancouver: Hemlock, 2022), 9.

ensure proper remediation. We describe the weight of flawed scholarship on recognition proceedings and the resulting impacts on the ability to maintain land and community relations, describing the difficulties of achieving healthy land and self-determination without recognition. The Munsee Three Sisters Medicinal Farm is a site that allows for the recovering of the epistemology of relationality—enabling the healing of both ecology and community.

This is a story about a particular place and community, but it connects to several larger themes we explore in this essay. It elucidates how relationships to the land are disrupted by environmental pollution. It explains how negative portrayals (both historic and contemporary) of Native American communities make them more likely to have their lands targeted for contamination while leaving them marginalized in the remediation process. It offers just one example of how Indigenous communities are responding with their own programs aimed at restoring connections and Indigenous knowledge and working toward food sovereignty. With this story, we aim to bring all these interconnections to light and describe strategies for creating resources for teaching.

Soil

> That is, continued elder knowledge and many of our people, many of our generations now have lost that. We have not gone back to our elders and asked that information. A lot of our elders were waiting for us to come back and ask for that information. But now, with our people over here, our elders are gone.
> —Michaeline Picaro[5]

Contaminated Ground

The Soil Science Society of America defines soil as the "unconsolidated mineral or organic matter on the surface of the earth that has been subjected to and shows effects of genetic and environmental factors of: climate (including water and temperature effects), and macro- and microorganisms, conditioned by relief, acting on parent material over a period of time."[6] Together, these particles of matter, environmental factors, organisms, and time compose the lands we live on and the territories we claim. Soil is important for this story, since contaminants have infiltrated the ground on which the Ramapough live and may migrate to the lands on which other New Jersey residents dwell.

But before we go into the specifics, we must first share the long background to this story of the American landscape that continues to shape the lived experience of many Native communities. Federal policies were used to turn land into property by the U.S. government through a series of acts geared at the systematic removal and assimilation of Native peoples. These were enacted well into the middle of the twentieth century with acts including the General Allotment Act of 1887, the House Concurrent Resolution 108 (HCR-108) of 1953, and the Indian Relocation Act of 1956. These disrupted relationships to the land and the ability of communities to farm, feed, and fend for themselves on their territories. The Allotment Act resulted in the dramatic loss of Indian land: from 138 million acres in 1887 to only 48 million acres when allotment ended in 1934.[7] One reason among many (including fee simple or fee patent land) for this plunge is that many Native Americans sold their land because they were unable to farm it in the manner proposed by the U.S. government. Cultivation was not possible on some land because of the poor soil quality. No training or equipment was provided, and communities were forced to maintain small parcels of land rather than employ collective strategies.

Even after Native groups adapted and became successful farmers on the lands they had to relocate to, providing for their communities and regaining self-sufficiency, they were not always able to maintain control over their fields and forests. One example of this disruption is the Pick-Sloan Flood Control Act of 1944 for the Missouri River. The Army Corps of Engineers ignored treaties, acquired land through eminent domain, and flooded tribal lands, resulting in the loss of 155,000 acres of Indian farmland and the forced relocation of families. The resultant flooding required one-third of the population from five reservations to relocate and caused the destruction of 75 percent of wildlife and plants and 90 percent of commercial timber production on these reservation lands. "By design, the Pick-Sloan Plan was a destroyer of nations."[8] Even those Native communities lucky enough to have dodged the effects of the policies enumerated above can still face struggles when it comes to accessing clean food and water. This is not a thing of the past but rather continues today.

Wrongful disruptions of food systems can have a great impact on communities where health and well-being are collective. Traci Brynne Voyles has specified that in the case of Native Americans "even the phrase 'environmental racism' can seem to lose all meaning in a tribal context, quite simply because 'racism' has *always* meant environmental violence for Native peoples."[9] An early recorded example is the extermination of tens of millions of bison from 1865 to 1883 by white-hide hunters encouraged by the frontier army.[10] A more recent example is the largest fish kill in history witnessed by the Yurok Nation on the lower Klamath River in California in 2002, when over 34,000 salmon died after water was diverted by farmers and ranchers during a drought year.[11] Disruption has even been executed by universities. The (Ojibwe) Anishinaabeg's ability to harvest *manoomin* (wild rice) has been threatened by the work of researchers at the University of Minnesota, who developed and patented a sterile version of some facsimile of "wild" rice that has contaminated *manoomin* strains and threatened the future of crops in Minnesota.[12]

In recent decades, food sources have been destroyed through pollution. As of 2017, Native American communities lived near approximately 600 of the 1,338 highly contaminated Superfund sites listed across the country. Close to 25 percent of all Superfund sites in the United States are in Indian country, and 16 percent of all Native Americans live within three miles of such sites. Over 600,000 Native Americans live near nuclear test sites, uranium mines, power plants, and dumpsites for toxic waste.[13] This has led to the disruption of traditional economies of fishing, hunting, foraging, and gardening, cutting off access to sources of healthy food.[14]

Just one example can be seen in the experience of the Akwesasne Mohawk who live near two state-mandated Superfund sites in New York. Located at the confluence of several rivers, for generations this community had relied on abundant fish and gardens that could be planted in the rich alluvial soils. Concerns about contamination and precautionary measures like advisories against fishing led residents to stop fishing and abandon their gardens. While such actions helped to prevent further polychlorinated biphenyl (PCB) exposure, people lost sources of good, healthy food and had to become more reliant on commercially available groceries. Fish, a low-fat source of protein and nutrients, was replaced by foods with higher fat and carbohydrate content. Healthy foods had been harvested from the rivers and soil at little to no cost, but healthy options are much more expensive in grocery stores.[15] This exacerbated health problems such as diabetes and cardiovascular disease. The impacts of contamination are compounded for many communities: "Because of subsistence lifestyles, spiritual practices, and other cultural behaviors, Indigenous people often suffer multiple exposures from resource use that result in environmental health impacts disproportionate to those seen in the general population."[16] This ongoing contamination of the land Native American communities rely on severely curtails access to healthy food and leads to poor nutrition.

Wrongful disruptions of food systems can have great impact on communities where health and well-being are collective. According to Kyle Powys Whyte, "*Indigenous* food systems refer to specific *collective capacities* of particular Indigenous peoples to cultivate and tend, produce, distribute, and consume their own foods, recirculate refuse, and acquire trusted foods and ingredients from other populations."[17] For Stuart G. Harris and Barbara L. Harper, "because tribal culture and religion are essentially synonymous with and inseparable from the land, the quality of the sociocultural and ecocultural landscapes is as important as the quality of individual natural resources or ecosystem integrity."[18] As Tlingit scholar Anne Spice points out:

> Toxicity is violence. More specifically, it is settler colonial violence. Toxicity and the invasive infrastructures it spills from separate us from the land by damaging our relations to it. If our lands are toxic, the more we engage in our cultural practices, the more we risk harming our bodies. Toxicity turns our relations against us. It kills us through connection. It eliminates us as Indigenous peoples by making Indigenous practices dangerous. Don't eat the fish, don't drink the water, don't gather the berries. It does the work of settler colonialism by destroying to replace.[19]

For the Akwesasne Task Force on the Environmental Research Advisory Committee, "'The loss of place, relationships and balance can be culturally devastating.'"[20] In response, the Akwesasne Mohawk have instituted a comprehensive cultural-restoration program to bring land, culture, and food back into balance. They set up their own institutional review board—the Akwesasne Environmental Research Advisory Committee—and developed the Akwesasne Task Force on the Environment (ATFE) to take control of research. They have also started a community-gardening program called *Kanenhi:io Ionkwaienthon:hakie* (Mohawk for "We Are Planting Good Seeds") and have instituted a program to teach people how to return to fishing now that remediation of the river has occurred. These programs have led to seed and plant giveaways, the construction of a community greenhouse, fundraising to send members to training sessions and food conferences, and the construction of raised garden beds in individuals' yards throughout the reservation. A pamphlet entitled the *Akwesasne Family Guide to Eating Locally-Caught Fish* offers information about levels of contamination in local waterways and recommendations on how to catch, prepare, and cook fish that are deemed safe to eat.[21] Their experience illustrates the intertwined exchange between land, food, and culture. The Ramapough in Ringwood have faced similar issues on their lands. They have been forced to abandon certain land-based practices as the streams and woods that they have long used have become too contaminated for swimming, drinking, and foraging and their food sources have been compromised by pollution.

The Unsovereign Earth

The Ramapough Lunaape Turtle Clan is at a different stage than the Akwesasne Mohawk in their timeline of contamination and remediation, since much of the paint sludge that has polluted their land for many decades remains in place. The old shafts from the iron mines that once employed many Ramapough were used to dump toxic paint sludge waste from the nearby Ford Motor Company manufacturing plant in the 1960s and 1970s. The Ford Plant in Mahwah, New Jersey, generated hundreds of thousands of cubic yards of waste and millions of gallons of paint sludge. For each car made, five gallons of paint were produced, equating to six thousand gallons of sludge a day.[22] Ringwood Realty, a subsidiary of Ford, took ownership of the mines in 1965 and then hired a contractor to remove waste from the Mahwah plant. Ford records indicate that during these years they disposed of this contaminated material at the Ringwood Mines/Landfill site. Residents recall the sound of large trucks moving down Peters Mine Road in the middle of the night and referred to it as the "midnight landfill." Barrels of sludge and other waste were pushed down the shaft of Peters Mine, tumbling down the seventeen underground levels on a 2,400-foot incline (Figure 6.2).

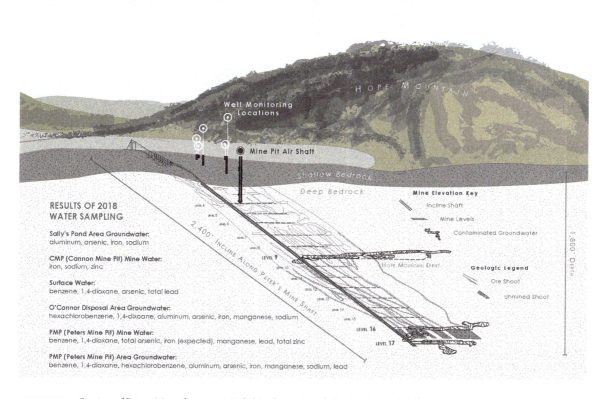

FIGURE 6.2 Section of Peters Mine, from Anita Bakshi, ed., *Our Land, Our Stories*, 2nd ed. (Vancouver: Hemlock, 2022), 157.

FIGURE 6.3 Photograph taken by reporter Jan Barry in early 2005, from Anita Bakshi, ed., *Our Land, Our Stories*, 2nd ed. (Vancouver: Hemlock, 2022), 109. Such documentation convinced editors at *The Record* to take a closer look at the remediation efforts and remaining contamination at Ringwood.

Paint sludge contains carcinogens including lead, arsenic, antimony, PCBs, Bis(2-ethyhexyl) phthalate (DEHP), and acetone. Once they began to feel the impacts of these chemicals in their bodies, expressed as disease and felt through the tragic loss of community members, the Ramapough organized, gathered allies, prepared armloads of paperwork, and advocated to get the dumping sites listed on the EPA's National Priorities List (NPL) as the Ringwood Mines/Landfill Superfund site in 1983. At this point, the EPA made a commitment to remove the contaminants and ensure that the land was once again "protective of human health and the environment."

When the initial site investigation took place in 1984, the five hundred–acre Superfund site contained close to fifty private homes. The EPA identified two liable parties responsible for the contamination: Ford and the Borough of Ringwood. Ford then identified three areas where they had authorized dumping by waste haulers, as well as a potential fourth site. The search for sludge and other waste was limited to these four areas. Ford removed 11,340 tons of sludge during the initial investigation, and the EPA claimed that the source of groundwater, surface water, and sediment contamination had been removed. The site was taken off the NPL in 1994.

Meanwhile, residents continued to find paint sludge deposits (and even entire barrels) in their woods and backyards (Figure 6.3). With the publication of the "Toxic Legacy" series in 2005, reporters at *The Record* in Bergen County, New Jersey, documented and made public evidence of the remaining contaminants that the Ramapough could see in their everyday surroundings. For the first time in the history of the Superfund program, the site was restored to the NPL in 2006. The New Jersey Department of Environmental Protection (NJDEP) began testing residential properties at the site in 2005, and by 2011 this sampling identified elevated levels of lead in the soil on some of the residential properties. The EPA subsequently removed contaminated soil from twenty-three residences from 2011 to 2014. This timeline indicates that people lived for close to forty years in homes built on toxic sludge—forty years of intimate contamination.[23]

Seed

> To me we are the seed. The greatest the seed known is our mother earth. We are her babies. And to me the importance of the seed itself, is that the seed is the gift of life, or the seed can also be the gift of death.
>
> —Wayne Mann[24]

The soil nourishes the seed that grows from it; in our story, the seed is the community. Here we discuss the community's history to reiterate that it is not possible to fully understand the impacts of environmental pollution through scientific data or remediation reports alone. To tell the story of this land, many layers must be considered—similar to sifting through layers of soil—in order to round out a full narrative. It is not just a Superfund site; it is also home, a place of memory and connection. All layers must be examined, including the deep history of this land—not just the history of what happened but also the history of how that history was written and by whom it was written. We must also look at the community living here, at how they have been cast as outcasts by outsiders and the knowledge that they hold and choose to share. This is not just about one story but about making space for different voices to be heard on their own terms. It is not about official recognition; it is about room for contestation and space for all the evidence to be considered.

While the Ramapough Lunaape are a state-recognized tribe, their quest for official recognition has been contentious. Popular legends, as well as academic scholarship, have discounted their Native heritage. They have long been represented in derogatory ways that connect to eugenicist theories about the "dangers" of miscegenation. Journalists and authors have been writing since the 1800s about "wild men," "savages," and "outcasts" living off the land in a "degraded state" (Figure 6.4). They were called the Ramapo Mountain people, or Mountaineers, or Jackson Whites—whatever outsiders decided was the right term—and referred to as "mongrels." These long-standing renderings and legends were followed by a book written about them in 1974 titled *The Ramapo Mountain People* that made the claim that the Ramapough's real ancestors were only Black and Dutch. Over the centuries they have been depicted as a "degenerate" race, and some historians and politicians, as well as the general public, have been influenced to believe that they are not

FIGURE 6.4 Headline from the June 1921 issue of the *New York Tribune* that reads "Wild Men Within Commuting Distance."

really Native American. Such depictions have flattened out complex histories of encounter between Black and Native peoples to fit into neat narratives and squeeze into clearly defined categories of identity.

These perceptions are integral to their environmental justice story. State and local officials approved the dumping of contaminated materials in the Ramapough's neighborhood of Upper Ringwood from 1967 to 1971. Even after the dangers of the contamination became clear, and after the EPA committed to a cleanup of the Superfund site, the sense that this community was expendable and deserving of pollution remained. Reporter Barbara Williams from *The Record* recalls the messages she received about the Ramapough when she was working on the "Toxic Legacy" investigative journalism report about the paint sludge that remained after Ford and the EPA claimed the remediation was complete: "I've been told they deserve everything they get. I can't tell you how many emails I've gotten, or phone calls, from people in the community saying when are you going to tell the real story about the people up there, that they've created their own lives, they've created their own mess."[25]

The first meeting ever between the Ramapough, their attorneys, Ford, the EPA, NJDEP, and the Borough of Ringwood was organized in 2005 by then-mayor Wenke Taule. She recounts that a "Community Advisory Group (CAG) was formed, under the auspices of the EPA, to open communications between the Ramapough and the EPA, which had been non-existent." The Ringwood Council changed in 2008, to a majority that was not as supportive of the Ramapough. According to Taule, "The Ringwood Council stopped the excavation of the O'Connor Landfill, saving Ford $32M, and instead agreed to cap over 100,000 tons of toxic soil in the community. The EPA refused to override this decision. After years of fighting for justice for their community, their local, state and federal government have betrayed the Ramapough once again."[26]

Lacking political capital and facing negative perceptions from many of those in power, the Ramapough were not able to significantly influence how the cleanup proceeded. Denied federal recognition in 1995, they were unable to take control of the remediation process in the same way the Akwesasne Mohawk community has done. As a result, contaminants remain in the ground to this day, and the Ramapough continue to live with a poisoned food web.

In many ways, this part of the story illustrates how colonialism has worked in the Americas. This has involved a constant process of undermining the political and territorial authority of Indigenous communities and the decisions that they are able to make about how their land is used, greatly undermining how they are able to relate to their lands and engage in land-based practices. This happens in many ways, including the pollution that we have outlined above. But it also happens through undermining and calling into doubt identity claims, as well as community and kinship claims. This can be particularly damaging for Indigenous communities since such claims are, for many, at the root of community-governance structures. Thus, relationships to land are eroded from many angles.

Native American History in New Jersey: Beyond the Colonial Archive

New Jersey has three state-recognized tribes: the Nanticoke Lenni-Lenape Tribal Nation, the Powhatan Renape Nation, and the Ramapough Lunaape Nation. The Ramapough today live in three communities, with the Turtle Clan in Ringwood, the Wolf Clan in Mahwah, and the Deer Clan in Hillburn, New York. Their ancestors are from one of the last Native American bands that stayed in New Jersey, against all odds, retreating to the edges of "civilization," as many Indigenous communities did along the Eastern Seaboard. Because land acquisition was central to early colonial settlement in the Americas, settlers first took control over the most desirable lands that had already been cleared by Indigenous peoples. Such land was ideal for extending the plantation system, already established in the Caribbean, to North America.

Many Native American bands left New Jersey as their land was disassembled, leading to dynamic movement over vast territories as bands and tribes were reorganized through resettlement. Some chose to stay in the region, even as they were pushed off more desirable land and into the mountains and swamps. These were places where people were able to escape colonial land systems; they became places where fugitive communities were able to establish new land bases. A study titled "Effects of Land Dispossession and Forced Migration on Indigenous Peoples in North America," published in *Science* in 2021, utilizes a comprehensive dataset and catalogue to determine that "42.1 % of tribes from the historical period have no federally- or state-recognized present-day tribal land base. Of the tribes that still have a land base, their present-day lands are an average of 2.6 % the size of their estimated historical area."[27]

At the time of European contact, early Dutch, Swedish, and English settlers in the lands that became New Jersey encountered a number of different Native American bands with distinct identities and geographical bases. Historians have delineated a linguistic distinction, with the northern groups speaking a Munsee dialect of the Delaware language and southern groups—located in central and southern New Jersey—speaking the Unami dialect. After European contact, these original groups underwent a great number of changes and reorganization of affiliations.[28]

Conflicts and disputes connected to the French and Indian War (1754–1763) and the Treaty of Easton (1758) accelerated the displacement of much of the remaining Native American population from New Jersey. Many Lunaape had moved west, for a time into Pennsylvania: "The story of the westward migration of the Delaware and Munsee is not easy to relate. Forced to abandon a relatively unified homeland in Lenapehoking, they were dispersed and relocated to places as far removed as Texas, Oklahoma, and Wisconsin, and Ontario, Canada."[29] Christian converts moved to south Jersey, to the short-lived Brotherton Reservation (active from 1758 to 1802) near the Pine Barrens. Non-Christian groups were invited to join but chose to live in their own small communities.[30] Life on the reservation was not viable, and most chose to move north to New York and join the Stockbridge community of the Mohican people, eventually settling in Wisconsin as the Stockbridge-Munsee, now a federally recognized group.

The people who came to be known as the Ramapough Lunaape relied upon the protective isolation of the mountains on the border of New Jersey and New York. Manumitted African Americans, or those able to escape slavery, also sought safety in the Ramapo Mountains. According to Gary Nash, "In every part of eastern North America from the 1600s to the 1800s, escaping African slaves sought refuge among Native Americans, relying on a natural affinity between oppressed peoples."[31] While free Black people had enjoyed some measure of independence and economic success, a number of laws began to restrict these freedoms. For example, a 1798 New Jersey law severely limited their right to cross county and state boundaries: "Small wonder that some families chose the relative isolation and freedom of the Ramapos over the increasing discrimination in the more populated lowland areas."[32] Some settled with the Native peoples who remained in northern New Jersey. Over the subsequent generations, these inhabitants of the Ramapo Mountains intermingled, with the unifying community hallmark of cultural adherence to their Native identity.

The question of Ramapough identity involves making sense of the Native peoples who stayed in New Jersey and how they formed community with others moving through the region—which included Native American groups, Africans, and Dutch and English settlers. The complexity of these groups encountering each other—as they were fleeing to escape colonial violence or enslavement, or to find settlement opportunities—has complicated the debate around Ramapough identity. This braided knot of encounter is not well understood through standard American frameworks of identity that tend to focus on pure categories.

Neat and distinct interpretations of identity have been significantly challenged by contemporary scholarship on racial formation that actively refutes earlier essentialist, scientific racialist, and eugenics frameworks.[33] The new scholarship acknowledges the more complex histories of place in the context of Atlantic World studies. To be Native and Black is now understood as not mutually exclusive.[34] *Crossing Waters, Crossing Worlds: The African Diaspora in Indian Country* is an example of one recent volume that describes the complex and intertwined histories of Native and Black communities, Afro-Native intermarriage, and the maintenance of tribal identity in the context of complex interracial histories.[35]

Historians have been writing about such encounters for several decades, such as exemplified by as Nash's 1974 book *Red, White, and Black: The Peoples of Early North America*, now in its seventh edition.[36] In the *American Indian Quarterly*, James Axtell appraised this study as disrupting the "facile characterization of races and cultures into 'primitive' and 'advanced' . . . by a cultural relativism that judges each culture on its own terms. Dynamic whites no longer act upon passive black or red pawns; each group is active in pursuing its own interests."[37] Nash's study helped to inaugurate what is now the thriving field of Atlantic World studies, described here by J. H. Elliott: "The new Atlantic history might be defined as the history, in the broadest sense, of the creation, destruction and re-creation of communities as the result of the movement, across and around the Atlantic basin, of people, commodities, cultural practices, and ideas. It is not the history of the advent—or non-advent—of modernity, a concept that has bedeviled the history of the Americas, but rather of change and continuity in the face of new experiences, new circumstances, new contacts, and new environments."[38]

Through more recent studies on the Black Atlantic and the Red Atlantic, it is now possible to understand various locales in relation to these larger histories of Indigenous, Black, and maroon communities. Colonial archives and repositories of studies tempered in eugenics frameworks can all be better understood in relation to a more rigorous North American studies and a more international framing around racialization, power, and wealth.[39] Many scholars have come to understand that Native American history cannot be approached by limiting sources and evidence to colonial documentation. There is not enough of it, and much that exists is biased. Indeed, the challenge taken up by scholars for the past few decades has been to decolonize methodologies and to engage in more careful readings of colonial documents.[40]

The Ramapough Lunaape Turtle Clan

Native American and Indigenous studies scholars have suggested that we might revisit early American history by expanding beyond the colonial archive to include Indigenous sources of knowledge and recordkeeping.[41] *Place in Research: Theory, Methodology, and Methods* puts forward a strategy of "critical place inquiry" that bridges environmental and Indigenous studies to propose methodologies that engage with place and generate empirical knowledge by centering Indigenous methods.[42] Unfortunately for the Ramapough, their environmental knowledge has not been viewed as legitimate enough to be taken seriously. Their knowledge of land, plants, medicine, and tradition has been discounted over the years and through a number of platforms. Local historians, journalists, and scholars have instead framed them as degenerates who could be easily discounted and dismissed. As we tell our story, we must reference a few other stories that have retained power and dominated the narrative for many decades. Two books in particular have used discussions of race to frame the identity of this community. Those imposed narratives have been given the benefits of authority, while the Ramapough's community knowledge has been discounted.

In 1936, a local journalist-*cum*-historian named John C. Storms, known for taking fanciful liberties with his writing, published a tale in a pamphlet titled *Origins of the Jackson Whites of the Ramapo Mountains* that provided an irresistible nugget of local lore, intrigue, and speculation about the origins of the Ramapough. This salacious tale—full of outlaws and prostitutes and the wanton mixing of races—is worthy of any modern-day tabloid magazine. It features British wenches, enslaved African "prostitutes," a rogue human-trafficking entrepreneur named Jackson, a sunken ship, mercenary soldiers, and a long trek across the wild territory of the new American colonies where farms and fields were pillaged. Storms claims that the people living in the Ramapo Mountains were formed from this ragtag batch of English and West Indian prostitutes, brought to service the needs of soldiers, Hessian mercenaries, "Red Men," "Negroes," and "American Tories."

This tale has exactly the kinds of elements that would have resonated with the bizarre racial imaginations of the age.[43] It was a time of anxieties about whiteness and mixed-race populations in an America that contained distinct racial and legal categories such as quadroon, octaroon, and mulatto (which stayed on the census until 1930). The 1930s, when the pamphlet was published, were the heyday of eugenics in America. Charles Davenport, the leader of the American eugenics movement, had recently formed the Eugenics Record Office (ERO) in nearby Cold Spring Harbor, New York, in 1910.

The Vineland Training School, an institution for the "feeble-minded," a group of much concern to eugenicists, created a study in 1911 titled *The Jackson Whites: A Study in Racial Degeneracy*. The main author was Elizabeth Kite, one of their field workers. This is "the first eugenics study to explicitly consider a mixed-race population, and as a result, [makes] the strongest argument for a biological link between miscegenation and mental defectiveness." The study began in 1909 and involved two years of research that "drew on extensive interviews with neighbors of the Ramapo clan to determine their racial and moral quality. Like the other family studies, the Jackson White study made extensive use of genealogies to trace the inheritance of defective traits."[44] According to Michell Chresfield, this early study set up a framework that linked physical appearance, sexuality, and place to understand "mixed blood" communities. Later studies of Indigenous communities along the Eastern Seaboard would use this same formula.[45]

This broader context of discussions about race and degeneracy in the United States at the time that Storms's tale emerged helps to explain why it lodged into the popular regional imagination. This legend about the Jackson Whites, along with other degrading representations of the community written by newspapermen of the time, embedded into local perceptions and has been hard to shake loose ever since. This unsubstantiated mythology has been repeated, rehearsed, and reheard so many times that it feels like fact. Even to this day, the internet is abuzz with sordid tales about this community; for example, the Weird N.J. website had this to say in 2012: "For many years now there have been stories of a degenerate race of people who live an isolated existence removed from the civilized world in New Jersey's Ramapo Mountains. As far back as the revolutionary war New Jerseyans have heard, and told, tales of a motley group of social outcasts who had taken refuge in the northeastern hills of the state and inbred to the point of mutation." It is still up on their website today.[46]

The Ramapo Mountain People, written by David Steven Cohen and published in 1974 by Rutgers University Press, provides another narrative that would play into this long-standing belief about the difference and otherness of this community. This book draws on some of the information described above, collected by institutions like the Eugenics Record Office and the Vineland Training School, including their 1911 study. No discussion is provided as to the nature of this material and its connection to the eugenics movement. Instead, it is simply presented as a natural and authoritative source of unbiased information. Such studies draw from eugenics theories such as "tri-racial isolates" and "tri-racial blood," frameworks of social-scientific analysis that are now outdated.

The case is made in the book that the community came about as the result of settlement by the mixed-race children of Dutch men and African women in the early 1800s, discounting any possibility of Native heritage. This served to galvanize the community to incorporate as the Ramapough Mountain Indians in 1978, as they began to push back against being defined by others. Cohen's book was long used as an authoritative source on Ramapough identity, so much so that the New Jersey General Assembly found it necessary to go through the book and, point by point, examine and then dismiss the evidence that Cohen presented. To this day, the book is brought up as a definitive source, even by well-credentialed academics, as we have discussed at length elsewhere.

Cohen did his fieldwork for the book in the late 1960s and brought to the work a background in genealogy and folklore. He focused on researching the history of the folk reference to "Jackson Whites," a pejorative term used locally to describe the Ramapough. Much of his research is dedicated to tracing the genealogies of three free Black landowning families up to 1776, when the last records were available. He then connects the history of these three families to the Ramapough by tracing the migration of just one individual (John Van Dunk III) to the Ramapo Mountains, thereby discounting any possibility of Indigenous ancestry. He appears to make the assumption that intermingling or intermarriage would negate any Native heritage, expecting that Native customs, traditions, stories, and intergenerational knowledge would immediately disappear. This certainly is in line with the limited and truncated racial imaginaries of the time about purity and the decay that was supposed to come with miscegenation.

The book contains only a few pages that focus on Native American history prior to the early 1800s.[47] A book published just twelve years later by Herbert C. Kraft titled *The Lenape: Archaeology, History, and Ethnography* contains a robust discussion of Native American history in New Jersey from European contact to the modern era. Kraft in fact discounts Cohen's earlier work, stating: "The origins of these people are very controversial, but it is clear that some are descended from local Munsee-speaking Indians who moved into the isolated Ramapo Mountains seeking a haven from the Dutch and English settlers in the latter half of the seventeenth century. They were joined later by multiracial settlers of varied backgrounds who intermarried with the Indians."[48]

While we have written a more robust critique of *The Ramapo Mountain People* in our 2022 book *Our Land, Our Stories*,[49] here we will just point out that the book has been refuted by other scholars, certified genealogists, and public officials. Still, it remains a convenient source that can be used when it aligns with state or industry interests. For example, the proposed decision about the Ramapough's case for federal recognition was leaked to the gaming industry weeks before the application was presented to the Bureau of Indian Affairs, as they were concerned about possible competition for their casinos after the passage of the 1988 Indian Gaming Regulatory Act.[50] Numerous public officials—including Bruce Babbitt (former secretary of the interior from 1993 to 2001) and William Cary Edwards (former New Jersey general assemblyman and attorney general)—have called foul on the flawed and tainted recognition process for the Ramapough. But the decision still stands.

Studies that draw mainly from colonial sources are viewed by some as more authoritative or scientific. As Devon A. Mihesuah points out, "Many historians and anthropologists . . . argue that Indians cannot accurately recount their past using oral traditions. They refuse to use informants, believing modern Indians' versions of their tribes' histories are 'fantasies.'"[51] Take, for instance, Cohen's casual dismissal of the Ramapough's environmental knowledge: "Many of the same herb cures I collected from the Ramapo Mountain People have also been collected from the Delaware Indians. But this cannot be taken as proof of the alleged Indian ancestry of the Mountain People. Because the Indians knew more about the indigenous plants, both Europeans and Africans in America freely borrowed these Indian herb cures. They were common knowledge in colonial America."[52]

Certainly, the lack of federal recognition has served to weaken or limit sovereignty, and the Ramapough were marginalized in the remediation process and negotiations with Ford. The recent remediation plan decision published by the EPA makes it clear that Ford was able to get away with a cheaper cleanup. After decades of debate, in a Record of Decision document published in October 2020, the EPA decided to cap the site in lieu of a full cleanup.[53] According to Jeff Tittel, director of the New Jersey Sierra Club, "Instead of having a full clean up on this hazardous site, EPA looked the other way. Now they are letting Ford cap the site and save $40 million. EPA cares more about Ford Motor Company saving money than they do about protecting the health of the Ramapough people and their environment."[54] Would this have been possible if the Ramapough were federally recognized? Or even if they were regarded with more respect and granted full humanity?

A Poisoned Food Web

Ramapough elders speak of the subsistence lifestyle they once had, foraging for wild carrot and watercress (which are no longer safe to eat), as well as game they have long hunted in the woods. Families used to harvest a lot of food from their gardens and would raise livestock such as chickens and pigs. One community elder moved out of Ringwood in 1968 but would still visit often. In 1969 or 1970, she remembers her husband bringing home a bunch of watercress gathered in Ringwood. After eating it, they felt unusually itchy and stopped foraging in the woods and along the streams. This was one of the first signs that something was wrong. Nonetheless, some residents continue to use nearby sites for hunting. The pollution of soil and water in Ringwood has led to a poisoned food web. This is a disruption of sources of nutritious food and a disruption of land-based knowledge.

A number of scientific assessments have sought to determine just how dangerous it is to live, gather, and hunt in Ringwood. In 2011, the New Jersey Department of Health and Senior Services (NJDHSS) conducted a public health assessment that concluded that there were completed exposure pathways between contamination and human ingestion/absorption. Lead levels tested in children indicated dangerously high exposure rates. However, those high rates were attributed to incidental ingestion of contaminated soil, sediment, paint sludge, and surface water, not to direct ingestion of animal and plant tissue.[55] Deer, squirrel, rabbit, and turkey were tested for contamination, and while the EPA concluded that even though contaminants present in animal muscle tissue tested higher than the reference tests, they were not considered high enough to harm human health if consumed.

It is important to note that test results vary widely between laboratories. Squirrels from the site were tested by four different agencies: the NJDHSS, NJDEP, EPA, and ATSDR (Agency for Toxic Substances and Disease Registry). NJDEP issued an advisory that consumption of squirrel should be limited due to the high levels of lead present in tissue samples. The EPA rejected the findings by blaming a defective blender used to process tissue samples as the reason for the high levels of lead found in the squirrel.[56] Wild carrot (*Daucus carota*) from three different contamination sites was tested for metals and synthetic organic chemicals by the EPA and NJDEP. Even though tests showed lead levels many times higher than in the control tests, the tests were deemed inconclusive because the amount of lead found in the carrots collected at contamination sites did not correlate to the low levels of lead found in the soil. They claimed the differing amounts cast doubts on the accuracy of the reference area and site data. The organizations cannot say conclusively whether consuming wild carrot will cause harm to human health (Figure 6.5). Despite the inability of these agencies and their associated testing laboratories to draw conclusive results, the health impacts on the Ramapough are clear, as studies have concluded that their "increased exposure opportunities [to the Superfund site] are significantly associated with certain later-life chronic diseases."[57]

It is important to understand that some Ramapough live *in* the Superfund site, not near it. The EPA removed contaminated soil from twenty-three *residential* properties. Residents recall playing with paint sludge as children, making mud pies in the woods, and sledding down "Sludge Hill" (now the SR-6 removal site). Despite the sustained, long-term, extreme proximity to toxic sludge, the Ramapough have had a difficult time making the case that their illnesses are connected to the toxicants. It is up to citizens to prove that health conditions are caused by pollution, and there are many challenges to making this case, since ailments can be attributed to other factors such as diet or lifestyle. Exposure from many decades ago could have affected people's immune systems, as well as other organ systems, while there may be nothing detectable in their blood today. With respect to the mixture that composes paint sludge, expertise is lacking in analyzing effects of chemical synergy and understanding the consequences of chemical reactions. Some cell-culture studies of the synergistic effects of mercury and

FIGURE 6.5 A representation of the effects of paint sludge pollution on the food, from Anita Bakshi, ed., *Our Land, Our Stories*, 2nd ed. (Vancouver: Hemlock, 2022), 126.

2,3,7,8-tetrachlorodibenzo-*p*-dioxin indicate that toxicity can be increased with binary mixtures of chemicals that have also been shown to have existed simultaneously in upper Ringwood at the Superfund site.[58]

It is doubtful that scientific inquiry will ever be able to conclusively trace present-day illnesses in Ringwood directly back to the paint sludge. Many chemical exposures in utero and/or during early infancy and childhood can increase the risk for several adult diseases, including (but not limited to) obesity, asthma, behavioral modifications, and heart disease. But it is difficult to track the relationship between these later-life disease outcomes with their early-life exposure roots. Nonetheless, Dr. Judith Zelikoff, a toxicology professor in the Department of Medicine at New York University Grossman School of Medicine who has been working with the Ramapough since 2013, has stated that the chemical contamination in upper Ringwood likely contributed to, or exacerbated, some of the health issues and/or disorders that were self-reported by the Ramapough and non-Native Americans in Ringwood.[59]

The discussion in this section has attempted to summarize the long histories of colonization, dispersal, reorganization, contamination, and remediation that the Ramapough have experienced as a community that has been subject to derogatory depictions by outsiders for as long as they can remember. Their evidence, either of their Native heritage or of the impacts of pollution on their health and life expectancy, has not been accepted as conclusive proof. The effect of this contaminated ground on their environmental justice story cannot be overstated. As a community, they continue their efforts to rebuild what has been lost, to emplace projects of cultural restoration in this soil, and to seed new futures.

Garden

> We won't know if the Ramapough will continue to survive, but through our actions and our deeds, and creation of the Munsee Three Sisters Medicinal Farm, to strive for food sovereignty for our people, for economic growth for our people, for education culturally and otherwise, those seeds of hope have been planted, and the only thing we can do is keep remembering that every time that we offer up a prayer, that those prayers will always be answered.
>
> —Vincent Mann[60]

The Ramapough today are instituting their own programs geared at restoring Indigenous environmental knowledge through activities such as waterway community paddles, Munsee-language classes, and other elements of a cultural-restoration program. An important site for this undertaking is the recently inaugurated Munsee Three Sisters Medicinal Farm in Sussex County, New Jersey, founded in May 2020 by Chief Vincent Mann and Michaeline Picaro (Figure 6.6). The nine-acre site sits adjacent to a protected forest and wildlife habitat at the Muckshaw Ponds Preserve. The farm is part of a partnership between the Ridge and Valley Conservancy and the Foodshed Alliance, which leases Muckshaw Farm and has launched the Sustainable Agriculture Enterprise Program (SAgE). This program offers long-term, affordable leases to farmers. The Muckshaw Farm property includes 201 acres of interconnected ponds, accessible to the public with hiking trails running through rare and endangered plants. This area contains a hatching ground for turtles on the farm itself that will be protected and enhanced for nesting—a blessing for the Turtle Clan.

FIGURE 6.6 Drawing of Chief Vincent Mann and Michaeline Picaro with Chief Mann's words about the purpose of the Munsee Three Sisters Medicinal Farm, from Anita Bakshi, ed., *Our Land, Our Stories*, 2nd ed. (Vancouver: Hemlock, 2022), 129.

FIGURE 6.7
Lenape blue "pulling corn" seeds. Photograph by Chief Vincent Mann.

Through the SAgE program, the Foodshed Alliance works with farmers, connecting them to resources, as well as providing business-management and marketing training. The Ramapough have also partnered with the Experimental Farm Network, which protects and repatriates seeds to Native peoples. They received Lenape blue "pulling corn" seeds (Figure 6.7) that will be grown to seed on the farm and then distributed to other farmers, thereby expanding the network. They are also growing Munsee tobacco that Chief Mann received as a gift in 2015 at the medicine garden in the town of Ramapo, another Ford dumping site. One plant became 120, which were gifted to others, and several were planted on the Munsee Three Sisters Medicinal Farm, grown for seed and for use in ceremony.

Working with volunteers to quickly establish a productive landscape, Mann and Picaro laid out crop rows and three medicine circle gardens. In the farm's first season, they were able to harvest the Three Sisters—corn, beans, and squash—as well as melons and Munsee tobacco. As Picaro has posted on the farm's website:

> Nurturing the land will allow for the life stored in the seeds to sprout into life and grow, resulting in a symbiotic relationship caring for soil, seeds, and plants producing a bountiful harvest for all. The soil is the great connector of lives, the source and destination of all. It is the healer and restorer and resurrector, by which disease

FIGURE 6.8 Drawing representing Picaro's words about nurturing seeds, from Anita Bakshi, ed., *Our Land, Our Stories*, 2nd ed. (Vancouver: Hemlock, 2022), 131.

FIGURE 6.9
Greenhouses under construction at the farm. Photograph by Chief Vincent Mann.

passes into health, age into youth, death into life. Without proper care for it we can have no community, because without proper care for it we can have no life. It takes a community to raise a farm.[61] (Figure 6.8)

The farm is growing in multiple directions. Two greenhouses for starting seeds and extending the growing season were donated and constructed (Figure 6.9), thousands of bulbs of

The Munsee Three Sisters Medicinal Farm   143

FIGURE 6.10 Chief Vincent Mann and Michaeline Picaro with friends, relations, and volunteers at the farm, wearing Munsee Three Sisters Medicinal Farm T-shirts designed by Picaro. Photograph by Chief Vincent Mann.

garlic were planted, potatoes are in the ground, and many leafy greens have filled the crop rows. The farm is an integral part of the Ramapough's efforts toward food sovereignty. The costs of going to the grocery store are high, and many in Ringwood have lost access to the foods they once foraged due to the contamination. The crops grown here will provide an affordable source of clean and healthy food. Valerie Segrest, the coordinator of the Muckleshoot Indian Tribe's Food Sovereignty Project, has described the importance of such efforts: "At the core of tribal sovereignty is food sovereignty. This is significant because we know that our traditional foods are a pillar of our culture, and that they feed much more than our physical bodies; they feed our spirits. . . . They are living links with our land and our legacy, helping us to remember who we are and where we come from."[62]

The farm is a home for important Native crops, but it is also a site for building connections with other plant and human relations (Figure 6.10). The Ramapough plan to grow produce and medicinal crops that are important to other groups and cultures, as well as to plan outreach to nearby communities such as Newark, so that children can visit the farm and learn about Native American culture as well as sustainable farming practices. They recognize that many other marginalized communities in the state share the same struggles for environmental and food justice and they seek to play a role in enhancing access to healthy food and learning opportunities for growers. The farm will serve as a teaching space and landscape of connection to cultural traditions. In this way, it is a ground for exchange between

FIGURE 6.11
Michaeline Picaro with the corn at the Munsee Three Sisters Medicinal Farm. Photograph by Chief Vincent Mann.

landform and cultural restoration. Kaitlin Reed (Yurok/Hupa/Oneida) has pointed out the importance of such land-based practices, stating: "By healing the land, we heal ourselves." She suggests that "by engaging with community-centered environmental restoration projects, we can restore relationships with each other and with our environments. If we understand genocide as the forcible breaking down of relationships, healing from genocide necessitates the rebuilding and strengthening of relationships Indigenous peoples have had with the natural world since the beginning of time."[63]

The vision the Ramapough hope to achieve over the next decade is to enhance the programming and spaces at the farm and to institute trainings about medicinal plants in order to establish a new generation of knowledge keepers. They will be purchasing seeds, developing farming practices, and designing and building structures on the farm for gathering and teaching (Figure 6.11).

Sunlight

> You guys are the future. It's up to you guys to spread the word to the world. Because the young will listen to the young, and again I can't stress it enough. You guys are the future. Not your moms, not your dads, not your grandparents. You guys are the future for the future.
>
> —Wayne Mann[64]

How do we tell this story? How do we bring it into the light?

Now that we have taken you through the many challenges faced by the Ramapough, we wind this story down with a consideration of how we might address these challenges. We have been thinking carefully about strategies for sharing this story—with all its layers and complexities—in a way that clearly spells out all the evidence and takes a long view of the histories presented here. We have worked collaboratively to find better strategies for bringing together all the layers we described above into relationship with each other so that readers and viewers might understand how they connect to and influence each other.

The storytellers have collaborated before on a writing project—*Our Land, Our Stories: Excavating Subterranean Histories of Ringwood Mines and the Ramapough Lunaape Nation*. We created that book as a resource for teaching a number of important historic and current issues: Native American history in what is now known as New Jersey; the history of how a people's identity was discredited through legends of degeneracy and through scholarship that amplified those popular misperceptions; the health and environmental implications of contaminants that Ford Motor Company dumped in a residential neighborhood; the failure of the EPA to remediate a site it was obliged to ensure was made safe; a tireless campaign to ensure the safety of the entire watershed; and the personal stories of connection and loss of the Ramapough Lunaape Turtle Clan who stayed in the land of their ancestors to keep the memory and names of places alive.

Our Land, Our Stories presents data about the impacts of pollution and narratives of human experience side by side. While environmental studies will often separate the data from the experience, we focus instead on the interconnections. Michif scholar Max Liboiron, who directs the Civic Laboratory for Environmental Action Research, has pointed out that discussions of "Nature" will "focus on only some aspects of relations, such as soil, air, water, animals, and plants, but not on human people, events, memories, spirits, or obligations. Nature describes colonial relations with capital-L Land. Whether Nature is understood as wild and heartless, the helpless victim of industrial assault, or the raw stuff of scientific enquiry, one of Nature's defining characteristics is that it is separate from humans, even if there is a closeness or affinity between them."[65]

FIGURE 6.12 Snapshots and quotes from *The Meaning of the Seed,* from Anita Bakshi, ed., *Our Land, Our Stories,* 2nd ed. (Vancouver: Hemlock, 2022), 133.

Instead, we aim to share the full story—the interconnections between the land (both before and after it was polluted) and the people who are in relationship with that land. A second edition of the book includes visualizations of stories shared by Turtle Clan members; enhanced interactive pages for use by teachers; and new sections about environmental deregulations, Indigenous environmental movements, and the politics of federal recognition for Native American communities. We designed and printed the book ourselves and are selling it as a fundraiser to support initiatives at the Munsee Three Sisters Medicinal Farm. We chose to handle the responsibilities of publication, marketing, and distribution ourselves to gain the ability to recirculate the profits in a way that will directly benefit the community instead of the publishing industry. The materials presented in the book are also available, free of cost, in a digital exhibit we created for Rutgers University Libraries to enable easy access for educators and anyone who wants to learn about these stories.[66]

In addition to the book, we created a documentary film. In September 2020, we gathered at the Munsee Three Sisters Medicinal Farm to film a talking circle of Ramapough

The Munsee Three Sisters Medicinal Farm   147

elders and their relations and partners. The resulting film, *The Meaning of the Seed*, illustrates the relationship to the land and the development of new practices and understandings among younger generations (Figure 6.12). We state in the introduction to the film: "We all inherit soil and roots created by generations and histories. This filmed talking circle shares lessons for survival and growth, for the seeds we can plant, to grow into brighter futures." The film is rooted in the same impulse as the farm, part of the Turtle Clan's larger efforts for cultural restoration. Like the farm, the film is meant to create a space for teaching and learning and is a forum to (first) listen and then share stories by engaging with the discussion prompts provided in our "Watch Party Seed Packet."

The Meaning of the Seed asks viewers to consider the ongoing violence embedded in the settler-colonial landscape we live on and to understand the many stories that live here for the Ramapough. There are painful stories of loss but also stories of survival, resistance, and growth. We aim to show, through multiple perspectives, how land is central to Ramapough struggles and actions—the injustices they have experienced, their land-based traditions, and their efforts to work with the land to move toward cultural restoration and food sovereignty. With this film, we want to encourage viewers to think about their relationship to the land anew and to show that environmental justice work involves many layers and aspects. These include the political and scientific but also the emotional, cultural, and spiritual.

The film tells the story of the soil, the seed, and the garden by shedding light on our histories on this land. It highlights the environmental connections that unite many different populations in ties of responsibility and stewardship. It tells a story about the meaning of the seed, about what the seed means to a people.

Utilizing a variety of formats, our projects incorporate multiple voices and create a multimedia forum for sharing important stories of land and loss, of survival and recovery. This is part of an approach for advocating for environmental justice by elucidating and representing the connections between the environmental, cultural, and political histories of the Ringwood Mines/Landfill Superfund site. The main aim of the project is to clarify contested narratives through clear graphic representations that illustrate the connections between different sets of scientific data, environmental-remediation reports, records of the site's industrial history, and personal narratives of the cultural and spiritual traditions of the Ramapough Lunaape Nation.

Dina Gilio-Whitaker (Colville Confederated Tribes) has emphasized the need for more environmental justice (EJ) scholarship focused on the particular struggles of Native communities:

> Academics in environmental studies, Native studies, and other disciplines educate students on the histories and principles of EJ in different EJ communities, but they face a dearth of literature from which to teach on the topic relative to Indigenous peoples. . . . American Indian activists doing EJ work, however, tend to be quite knowledgable about the issues they are working for and the histories that inform those issues. As a result, they inevitably end up having to educate, with no additional financial compensation, the various groups they interact with, people with whom they often have contentious relationships to begin with.[67]

Her brilliant book *As Long as Grass Grows: The Indigenous Fight for Environmental Justice from Colonization to Standing Rock* provides a broad overview of what environmental justice is for Native peoples. We hope to contribute to this important body of literature through our project by providing resources for educators and community organizations.

As we have described throughout this story, colonial frameworks and epistemologies have comprehensively managed to separate complex relationships into distinct parts. This has operated to divide peoples into specific racial categories and to view environmental science, history, culture, and human experience through separate lenses. Instead, we have told the story to create overlays and afterimages that encourage readers to develop understandings of deeper connections. It is not possible to understand the Superfund site in Ringwood without also engaging with all these other dynamics of history, eugenics racial "science," traditional foodways, and local and national politics. While colonial epistemologies divide and separate, Indigenous epistemologies show relationality, connection, and responsibility.

A seed looks deceptively simple. But it contains within it the embryo, endosperm, and seed coat. Each unassuming little fleck or sphere has within it a root, a stem, and one or more leaves. Wrapped around it is a nutritive tissue that will feed it with starch, oil, and protein when the conditions are right. The seed coat can keep it protected, alive, and potent for years—even decades or centuries. This story grows from a particular place and was birthed in a distinct soil, but it also connects to the landscape that we all share.

> The meaning of the seed ... The seed as it is seen by most is not alive, but to us Lunaapeewak (Munsee People) the seed is alive.
>
> When the time comes that the winds shift and we awake from our long sleep and storytelling time and as our Grandfather warms our Mother Earth we set about talking to our relatives and we begin to place those into the earth in our mother.... [A]nd as we nurture and sing to these seeds they begin to turn into the embryo, a being of the plant family.
>
> Through further nurturing and singing and speaking they begin to get their roots and start their journey growing through their different stages of life. Through all this time we continue to offer our prayers up to Kiishelemokweng (Our Creator) for this sacred gift, the gift of life and sustenance.
>
> And as we journey together with our relative through all its stages of its life we are reminded of our own journeys from when we were just seeds as well.
>
> —Vincent Mann[68]

NOTES

1. Wayne Mann, in *The Meaning of the Seed*, 1:52–2:22, https://www.youtube.com/watch?v=vrmioVAmCA0&t=2071s.
2. Eve Tuck and Marcia McKenzie, *Place in Research: Theory, Methodology, and Methods* (New York: Routledge, 2015), 57. They write that land "is both a notion and an action."
3. Kyle Powys Whyte, "Justice Forward: Tribes, Climate Adaptation and Responsibility," *Climatic Change* 120, no. 3 (October 2013): 518.
4. Whyte, "Justice Forward," 519.
5. Michaeline Picaro, in *The Meaning of the Seed*, 14:43–14:47.
6. Soil Science Society of America, "Soils Overview," https://www.soils.org/files/about-soils/soils-overview.pdf.
7. David Treuer, *The Heartbeat of Wounded Knee: Native America from 1890 to the Present* (New York: Riverhead Books, 2019), 150.
8. Nick Estes, *Our History Is the Future: Standing Rock versus the Dakota Access Pipeline, and the Long Tradition of Indigenous Resistance* (London: Verso, 2019), 152.
9. Traci Brynne Voyles, *Wastelanding: Legacies of Uranium Mining in Navajo Country* (Minneapolis: University of Minnesota Press, 2015), 24.
10. David D. Smits, "The Frontier Army and the Destruction of the Buffalo: 1865–1883," *The Western Historical Quarterly* 25, no. 3 (Autumn 1994): 312–38.
11. Glen Martin "Salmon Kill Linked to Level of Klamath River's Flow—Reduced for Irrigation—Played a Role in Huge Die-Off, U.S. Study Finds," *SF Gate*, November 19, 2003, https://www.sfgate.com/green/article/Salmon-kill-linked-to-level-of-Klamath-River-s-2548262.php.
12. Winona LaDuke, "Wild Rice: Maps, Genes, and Patents," in *Recovering the Sacred: The Power of Naming and Claiming* (Chicago: Haymarket Books, 2015), 167–90.
13. Judith T. Zelikoff, Krina Shah, Gabriella Meltzer, Oyemwenosa Avenbaun [*sic*], Yu Chen, and Fen Wu, "Environmental Health in Ringwood," in *Our Land, Our Stories: Excavating Subterranean Histories of Ringwood Mines and the Ramapough Lunaape Nation*, ed. Anita Bakshi, 2nd ed. (Vancouver: Hemlock, 2022), 111.
14. Elizabeth Hoover, *The River Is in Us: Fighting Toxics in a Mohawk Community* (Minneapolis: University of Minnesota Press, 2017).
15. Hoover, *The River Is in Us*, 215.
16. Hoover, *The River Is in Us*, 12.
17. Kyle Powys Whyte, "Indigenous Food Systems, Environmental Justice, and Settler–Industrial States," in *Global Food, Global Justice: Essays on Eating under Globalization*, ed. Mary C. Rawlinson and Caleb Ward (Newcastle upon Tyne: Cambridge Scholars Publishing, 2015), 147.
18. Stuart G. Harris and Barbara L. Harper, "A Native American Exposure Scenario," *Risk Analysis* 17, no. 6 (1997): 793.
19. Anne Spice, "Processing Settler Toxicities: Part II," *Footnotes*, June 23, 2018, https://footnotesblog.com/2018/06/23/processing-settler-toxicities-part-ii/.
20. Akwesasne Task Force on the Environmental Research Advisory Committee, "Superfund Clean-up at Akwesasne: A Case Study in Environmental Justice," *International Journal of Contemporary Sociology* 34, no. 2 (1997): 283, quoted in Hoover, *The River Is in Us*, 26.
21. Saint Regis Mohawk Tribe, Environment Division, *Akwesasne Family Guide to Eating Locally-Caught Fish*, November 2013, https://www.epa.gov/sites/production/files/2016-09/documents/srmt_fish advisory_webfinal.pdf.
22. Jan Barry, Mary Jo Layton, Alex Nussbaum, Tom Troncone, Lindy Washburn, Barbara Williams, and Thomas E. Franklin, "Ford, the Feds, the Mob: Making a Wasteland," *The Record* (Bergen County, N.J.), October 2, 2005.
23. EPA, "Ringwood Mines/Landfill, Ringwood Borough, NJ: Cleanup Activities," United States Environmental Protection Agency, https://cumulis.epa.gov/supercpad/SiteProfiles/index.cfm?fuseaction=second.cleanup&id=0200663. From 1987 through 2016, over sixty thousand tons of paint sludge and associated soils and 113 drums containing wastes were removed from the Ringwood Mines Superfund site and disposed of off-site. Considering that the EPA estimated seventy thousand tons of material

in the Peters Mine Pit area, more than one hundred thousand tons in the O'Connor Disposal Area (OCDA), and forty thousand tons in the Cannon Mine Pit area, much contaminated material remains in the ground today.

24 W. Mann, in *The Meaning of the Seed*, 13:35–13:53.
25 *Mann v. Ford*, directed by Maro Chermayeff and Micah Fink (HBO, 2010).
26 Wenke Taule, "The Community Advisory Group (CAG) and the Superfund Cleanup," in Bakshi, *Our Land, Our Stories*, 74.
27 Justin Farrell, Paul Berne Burow, Kathryn McConnell, Jude Bayham, Kyle Whyte, and Gal Koss, "Effects of Land Dispossession and Forced Migration on Indigenous Peoples in North America," *Science* 374, no. 6567 (2021), https://www.science.org/doi/10.1126/science.abe4943.
28 Herbert C. Kraft, *The Lenape: Archaeology, History, and Ethnography* (Newark: New Jersey Historical Society, 1986), xv.
29 Kraft, *The Lenape*, 233.
30 Kraft, *The Lenape*, 231–32.
31 Gary B. Nash, "The Hidden History of Mestizo America," *The Journal of American History* 82, no. 3 (December 1995): 947.
32 Ralph Sessions, *Woodsman, Mountaineers, and Bockies: The People of the Ramapos, April 14–August 18, 1985* (New City, N.Y.: The Historical Society of Rockland County, 1985), 12.
33 Thomas C. Leonard, *Illiberal Reformers: Race, Eugenics, and American Economics in the Progressive Era* (Princeton, N.J.: Princeton University Press, 2016).
34 James F. Brooks, ed., *Confounding the Color Line: The Indian-Black Experience in North America* (Lincoln: University of Nebraska Press, 2002); Valena Broussard Dismukes, *The Red-Black Connection: Contemporary Urban African-Native Americans and Their Stories of Dual Identity* (Los Angeles: Grace Enterprises, 2007); Jack D. Forbes, *Africans and Native Americans: The Language of Race and the Evolution of Red-Black Peoples* (Urbana: University of Illinois Press, 1993); and Claudio Saunt, *Black, White, and Indian: Race and the Unmaking of an American Family* (New York: Oxford University Press, 2005).
35 Tiya Miles and Sharon P. Holland, eds., *Crossing Waters, Crossing Worlds: The African Diaspora in Indian Country* (Durham, N.C.: Duke University Press, 2006).
36 Gary B. Nash, *Red, White, and Black: The Peoples of Early North America* (Englewood Cliffs, N.J.: Prentice-Hall, 1974).
37 James Axtell, review of *Red, White, and Black: The Peoples of Early North America*, by Gary B. Nash, *American Indian Quarterly* 3, no. 4 (Winter 1977): 375–76.
38 J. H. Elliott, "Atlantic History: A Circumnavigation," in *The British Atlantic World, 1500–1800*, ed. David Armitage and Michael J. Braddick (Houndmills: Palgrave Macmillan, 2002), 239–40, quoted in Ignacio Gallup-Diaz, "Introduction: Atlantic Perspectives," in *The World of Colonial America: An Atlantic Handbook*, ed. Ignacio Gallup-Diaz (New York: Routledge, 2017), 5.
39 Paul Gilroy, *The Black Atlantic: Modernity and Double Consciousness* (Cambridge, Mass.: Harvard University Press, 1993). See also J. H. Johnston, "Documentary Evidence of the Relations of Negroes and Indians," *The Journal of Negro History* 14, no. 1 (January 1929): 21–43, for an earlier article describing the long history of relationships between Black and Indigenous communities.
40 Linda Tuhiwai Smith, *Decolonizing Methodologies: Research and Indigenous Peoples*, 2nd ed. (London: Zed Books, 2012).
41 Alyssa Mt. Pleasant, Caroline Wigginton, and Kelly Wisecup, "Materials and Methods in Native American and Indigenous Studies: Completing the Turn," *Early American Literature* 53, no. 2 (2018): 409.
42 Tuck and McKenzie, *Place in Research*.
43 See Nash, "The Hidden History of Mestizo America," for a history of perceptions about mixed-race people.
44 Michell Chresfield, "Creoles of the Mountains: Race, Regionalism, and Modernity in Progressive Era Appalachia," *The Journal of the Gilded Age and Progressive Era* 21, no. 1 (2022): 31.
45 Chresfield, "Creoles of the Mountains," 32–33.
46 Mark and Mark, "History and Legends of the Mysterious 'Jackson Whites,'" Weird N.J., September 26, 2012, https://weirdnj.com/stories/fabled-people-and-places/jackson-whites/.
47 David Steven Cohen, *The Ramapo Mountain People* (New Brunswick, N.J.: Rutgers University Press, 1974).

48 Kraft, *The Lenape*, 241.
49 Bakshi, *Our Land, Our Stories*, 50–70.
50 Bruce Babbitt, "Letter to the Secretary of the United States Senate," November 7, 1995.
51 Devon A. Mihesuah, introduction to *Natives and Academics: Researching and Writing about American Indians*, ed. Devon A. Mihesuah (Lincoln: University of Nebraska Press, 1998), 2.
52 Cohen, *Ramapo Mountain People*, 173.
53 EPA, "EPA Finalizes Cleanup Plan to Address Groundwater Contamination at the Ringwood Mines/Landfill Superfund Site in New Jersey," United States Environmental Protection Agency, October 1, 2020, https://www.epa.gov/newsreleases/epa-finalizes-cleanup-plan-address-groundwater-contamination-ringwood-mineslandfill.
54 Jeff Tittel, "EPA Cleanup Plan for Ringwood Is a Sellout to Ramapoughs, Continues Toxic Nightmare," Sierra Club, November 18, 2020, https://www.sierraclub.org/new-jersey/blog/2020/11/epa-cleanup-plan-for-ringwood-sellout-ramapoughs-continues-toxic-nightmare.
55 New Jersey Department of Health and Senior Services, *Health Consultation: Childhood Blood Lead Data in the Population Living near the Ringwood Mines/Landfill Site, July 1999 to December 2010*, 2011, https://www.state.nj.us/health/ceohs/documents/eohap/haz_sites/passaic/ringwood/ringwood_mines_landfill/ringwood_childpb_hc_12_11.pdf.
56 New Jersey Department of Health and Senior Services, *Health Consultation: Evaluation of Metals and Synthetic Organic Chemicals in Biota; Ringwood Mines/Landfill Site, Ringwood Borough, Passaic County, New Jersey: Draft for Public Comment*, 2009, https://www.state.nj.us/health/ceohs/documents/eohap/haz_sites/passaic/ringwood/ringwood_mines_landfill/ringwood_biota_pc_6_09.pdf.
57 Gabriella Meltzer, Oyemwenosa Avenbuan, Fen Wu, Krina Shah, Yu Chen, Vincent Mann, and Judith T. Zelikoff, "The Ramapough Lunaape Nation: Facing Health Impacts Associated with Proximity to a Superfund Site," *Journal of Community Health* 45, no. 6 (2020): 1202.
58 Lakshmanan Jagannathan, Cynthia C. Jose, Vinay Singh Tanwar, Sudin Bhattacharya, and Suresh Cuddapah, "Identification of a Unique Gene Expression Signature in Mercury and 2,3,7,8-tetrachlorodibenzo-*p*-dioxin Co-exposed Cells," *Toxicology Research* 6, no. 3 (2017): 312–23.
59 Bakshi, *Our Land, Our Stories*, 110.
60 Vincent Mann, in *The Meaning of the Seed*, 18:20–19:06.
61 Michaeline Picaro, "The Beginning," Munsee Three Sisters Medicinal Farm, June 13, 2020, https://munseethreesisters.org/photos/hello-world/.
62 Dina Gilio-Whitaker, *As Long as Grass Grows: The Indigenous Fight for Environmental Justice from Colonization to Standing Rock* (Boston: Beacon Press, 2019), 87.
63 Kaitlin Reed, "We Are a Part of the Land and the Land Is Us: Settler Colonialism, Genocide and Healing in California," *Humboldt Journal of Social Relations* 1, no. 42 (2020): 43.
64 W. Mann, in *The Meaning of the Seed*, 34:54–35:14.
65 Max Liboiron, *Pollution Is Colonialism* (Durham, N.C.: Duke University Press, 2021), 48.
66 Anita Bakshi, Anna Forsman, and Kathleen Hammerdahl, "Our Land, Our Stories," Rutgers University Libraries Digital Exhibit, https://blogs.libraries.rutgers.edu/our-land-our-stories/about.
67 Gilio-Whitaker, *As Long as Grass Grows*, x.
68 Chief Vincent Mann, quoted in Bakshi, *Our Land, Our Stories*, 132.

7

Ottawa Governance through Anishinaabe Ecological Restoration

Nmé, Ethnobotany, and Memory

NATASHA MYHAL

Situating Myself

Boozhoo / Aaniin Natasha nindiznikaaz, makwa nindoodem, Baawating Anishinaabe izhinikaade ishkonigon wenjibaayan. As I begin this essay, I humbly greet you in the Anishinaabe language Anishinaabemowin. In Anishinaabemowin, reservation can be interpreted as "leftover land," and the land that I come from is now known as Sault Ste. Marie, located in Michigan's Upper Peninsula. My Anishinaabe family, the Lamberts, made their home in St. Ignace, Michigan. However, I was raised away from my community in the suburbs outside of Cleveland, Ohio. My introduction in Anishinaabemowin shares our worldview and informs our relations to land/water and more-than-humans. I am a beginner speaker of Ojibwemowin,[1] and as a beginner, I am coming to learn Anishinaabe stories as an adult.[2] This is due to the impacts of the boarding schools on my family. This essay represents some of my theorizations that are informed by my 2021–2022 community work with the Little River Band of Ottawa Indians Tribal Natural Resources Department. Moreover, I am Anishinaabe first before anything else and am accountable to all Anishinaabeg, including more-than-humans. For me, stating my positionality first defines who I am as an Anishinaabekwe,[3] as well as who I am as a researcher, and reflects the Anishinaabe ways of knowing that I bring to this essay.

Introduction: Contextualizing Indigenous Conservation, Ethnobotany, and Nmé

Nmé (lake sturgeon) are healers. Marty Holtgren, Stephanie Ogren, and Kyle Whyte describe the role of nmé, saying, "The fish has been able to both heal old wounds and create new, sustainable, [sic] relationships among people, even in a watershed where these relationships have been strained by settler colonialism."⁴ Although the Little River Band of Ottawa (hereafter Little River Ottawa) continue to live with present-day implications of settler colonialism, relationships with nmé are sustained by the Nmé Stewardship Program created by the Little River Ottawa in the early 2000s. This essay accounts for Anishinaabe relations to nmé and how their movements have been altered by colonialism. I position the Nmé Stewardship Program within the Little River Band of Ottawa Indians Tribal Natural Resources Department as part of Anishinaabe ethnobotany, a field typically centered on plants, as also including nmé/fish knowledge supported by Anishinaabe ecological memories.

Ecological memory is a form of knowledge that relies on networks of relations between the land and more-than-human beings. Anishinaabe ecological memory entails a process of carrying, recalling, and recording pertinent ecological knowledge and serves as a form of ethnobotany. The Anishinaabeg's ability to care for a place is informed by generations of knowledge that support an ecological memory or the ability to know a web of relations that shape particular regions or places. In this essay, I will describe the role of nmé in ethnobotany by examining their relationship with plant relatives and how they support ecosystem health. Specifically, I focus on how nmé restoration and repopulation repair other flora and fauna important to the Little River Ottawa, such as *manoomin* (wild rice). I use the framework of Anishinaabe ecological memory as represented through stories that help us understand Anishinaabe ethnobotany and ecological memory. These stories encode ecological knowledge based on deep relations to place and illustrate how Anishinaabe restoration is a practice of care. Anishinaabe memories help one to understand and remember responsibilities to an ever-changing environment. The renewal of Indigenous restoration practices represents *how* tribal nations are embodying resurgence *themselves* and interrupting colonial power.⁵ An analysis of everyday, land-based practices is what Leanne Betasamosake Simpson describes as bringing Indigenous pasts and the present together.⁶ Centering Indigenous ancestors in the past implies the past tense. Anishinaabe ecological restoration brings land-based practices to the here and now and renews our ancestors' practices. This essay will provide an example of such land-based practices that focus on restoring Ottawa more-than-human relations. Instead of focusing on tribal efforts that *mirror* settler-colonial conservation that reflect the rationalities of settler-conservation practices, Ottawa relations are a set of restoration practices that allow tribes to act *now*, tying the individual to the collective through practices that are significant to them.

First, I draw on the Anishinaabe creation story to illustrate the relationship between Anishinaabe peoples and their more-than-human relatives, with a particular focus on relations with nmé and *manoomin*. I then examine how relations with nmé were ruptured through extractive industry and resultant environmental contamination and degradation, in addition to the land dispossession and alienation reproduced through colonial implementations of treaties in the United States. In this section, I describe landmark moments between the Anishinaabe and the United States and examine the implications of the 1836 Treaty of Washington. As I argue, relational ruptures reproduced through extractive industry and treaties affected nmé's roles in environmental governance while also affecting Anishinaabe peoples' ability to care for nmé. Following this, I consider how Ottawa struggles for sovereignty amid conditions of colonial legacies are informed by an Anishinaabe relational framework rather than solely a rights-based framework premised on settler legal orders. I then introduce how the Little River Ottawa conceptualize conservation through their Nmé Stewardship Plan. I frame introductions of settler colonialism through Anishinaabe understandings of Wiindigo. Second, I engage with how the Anishinaabe conceptualize movement within their environments through a brief retelling of the Anishinaabe migration story. I then describe landmark moments between the Anishinaabe and the United States, and I examine the implications of the 1836 Treaty of Washington and the impact of industrialism on nmé fisheries. I describe the connections between Anishinaabe ethnobotany and ecological memory, focusing on how both support a healthy return of nmé. In the final section, I discuss the role of Indigenous governance and how it functions to guide tribal natural resources management and conclude with a discussion of the importance of Indigenous restoration practices. My essay presents a pathway toward the call for Land Back within the historical-political context of colonial land theft/land wrongs by illuminating how Indigenous peoples continually remake life and assert the right to govern and heal their lands in accordance with their own systems of knowledge.[7]

Movement, Migration, and Journeying in Anishinaabe *Aki*

Water and land embody Anishinaabe knowledge. The Anishinaabe are deeply tied to both water and land through their traditional stories that continue to offer teachings for them. As a foundational example, the Anishinaabe creation story details a great flood that covered all of Anishinaabe land, leaving only one small area where many animals took refuge.[8] After many animals dove deep into the waters to attempt to grab a piece of soil/earth to re-create the land, it was only the smallest muskrat who was successful in their attempt to bring back a piece of land to surface from underwater. The piece of earth was then put on the turtle's back, and the earth slowly grew into the island today known as North America. This story illustrates how re-creating a new world for the Anishinaabe relied on relations to both water *and* land. These relations to water and land are reflected in Anishinaabe understandings of territory. Watersheds are where water *meets* land. In this space, multiple more-than-human relatives are brought together. The Big Manistee River traverses through Manistee National Forest and the current boundaries of the Little River Ottawa ancestral reservation. In Anishinaabemowin, the Big Manistee River is called *ministigweyaa*, which roughly translates to "a river with islands at its mouth."[9] This watershed is part of Anishinaabe homelands and serves as a relational place where water and land support animal and plant life. This watershed is also significant because it may have once held the largest nmé for the Anishinaabe.[10]

The Little River Ottawa consider nmé to be one of their oldest clan relatives, who helps guide seasonal rounds and is a protector of other culturally important relatives such as *manoomin*. Therefore, nmé themselves hold stories alive with memory for the Little River Ottawa within this watershed (Figure 7.1).

FIGURE 7.1 Big Manistee River. Photograph by NOAA.

Movement defines the shared relations between nmé, more-than-humans, and the Little River Ottawa. The Ottawa people, as part of the Three Fires Confederacy, have a culturally and historically significant relationship with Nayaano-nibiimaang Gichigamiin (the Great Lakes).[11] The story of the Anishinaabeg's arrival to Nayaano-nibiimaang Gichigamiin is one of slow movement across centuries.[12] The Anishinaabeg were instructed by seven spiritual beings from the ocean to move to where food grew on water because a light-skinned race was going to land on the shore and bring death and destruction to their peoples. Knowing this, they migrated from the east, along the St. Lawrence Seaway, in search of *manoomin* and made several stops along the way. One stop was at Wawiiantanong (the Detroit River), where the distinct groups of the Anishinaabe emerged: the Ottawa, Potawatomi, and Ojibwe.[13]

Stories of Anishinaabe migration reveal important, life-sustaining, reciprocal relations between water, more-than-humans, and the Anishinaabe themselves. The migration story is what Kyle Whyte, Jared Talley, and Julia Gibson describe as an "Anishinaabe tradition of journeying."[14] The Anishinaabe adapted to new environments and thus restructured themselves and their relations to more-than-humans in Nayaano-nibiimaang Gichigamiin.[15] The Ottawa shared closed relations with the Ojibwe and Potawatomi and even held relations with Anishinaabe communities that lived further away, including the Nipissing, Algonquin, and Mississauga across various waterways.[16] The Anishinaabe built relationships as they traveled across the Great Lakes region. Once the Anishinaabe were introduced to *manoomin*, they stayed in the area with their families. It was at this time that they were also introduced to their nmé relative, known as the keepers of *manoomin*.[17] This welcome from nmé, in my eyes, indicates that the abundance of *manoomin* is tied to the health and restoration of nmé. Furthermore, the Anishinaabe are fish people, and nmé as the protector of wild rice means that these food sources are tied to each other. The phrase "food as medicine"[18] is useful here, as the Anishinaabe knew and valued the importance of nmé and *manoomin* sustaining them as they continued to move throughout the Great Lakes region.

Other stories refer to a spirit called Wiindigo, a giant, cannibal monster who brought death and destruction to the Anishinaabe. Wiindigo stories are often used as cautionary tales within Anishinaabe oral traditions[19] and can be a useful device for framing colonization and the exploitation of Anishinaabe natural resources. Wiindigo is often depicted as a cannibalistic monster, and Wiindigo stories reflect *how* colonialism operates through an infrastructural invasion of Indigenous lands and waters that inflicts ecological violence.[20] One Wiindigo story, told by Bezhigobinesikwe Elaine Fleming, describes how colonization and historical trauma travel together, transforming and "ravaging" ecologies and lifeways they encounter.[21] I consider the imbalance Wiindigo created and the response this elicits from the Little River Ottawa and nmé in the context of restoring relations with more-than-humans. In other words, Ottawa approaches to the environment and nmé stewardship practices address the impact of Wiindigo. Wiindigo is a cautionary figure and continues to possess society today through colonization, capitalism, and climate change. Thus, stories of the Ottawa peoples also speak to being in place and relation to one another amid ongoing settler colonialism.

Nmé—the oldest fish species in the Great Lakes—is central to the subsistence and spiritual and cultural practices of many Anishinaabeg peoples, shaping Ottawa understandings of themselves over multiple generations, as nmé used to be abundant on the Grand River in Michigan.[22] Nmé's role as a clan relative or *doodem* means that the Anishinaabe held and continue to hold relations with animals. These relations call on us to rethink approaches to collaboration that emphasize a human-dominated approach in favor of those that emphasize an interspecies collaboration that attends to the ways in which animals tell stories with humans.

Anishinaabe conceptions of ecological relations do not enforce a divide between human and more-than-human beings. A nonhierarchical and nonhuman-centric understanding of ecologic relations shows that nmé experienced their own history of surviving environmental changes, including periods of climate change such as the Pleistocene. Just as the Anishinaabe experienced disturbances from settler colonialism coupled with environmental change, so have nmé. Biologists refer to nmé as "living fossils," as they have remained similar biologically for over 150 million years.[23] Scientists dependent on Western/colonial systems classify and understand plants and animals in accordance with Western/colonial epistemologies of time and geological cycles.[24] This ignores the role of science in Westward expansion and colonialism.[25] The scientific classification of Anishinaabe plant and animal relatives as specimens to be collected and categorized was a fundamental component of colonial administration and control on Anishinaabe territory. This was a violent process that contributed to the rupture of Anishinaabe human and more-than-human relations, and that was felt by nmé and Anishinaabe peoples alike. In contrast, Ottawa epistemologies and practices of ecological restoration emphasize an understanding of how the land/water support the Anishinaabeg's relation with nmé and other nonhuman relatives.

Anishinaabe understandings of themselves and the environment are, in part, shaped by nmé migrations. Nancy Langston writes, "Fish migrations shaped human cultural patterns, clan governance, and seasonal movements in the upper Great Lakes"[26] (Figure 7.2).

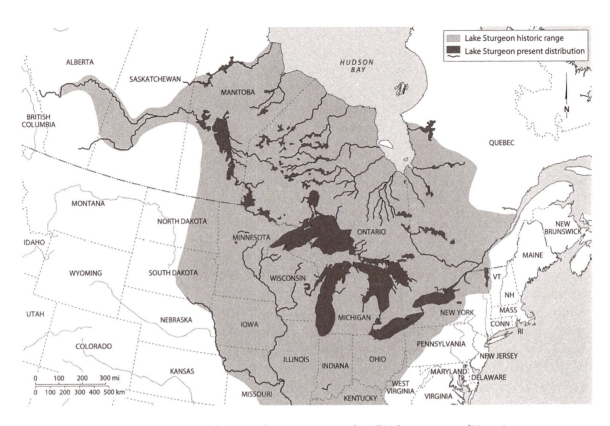

FIGURE 7.2 Nmé's historic and current range. Map by Bill Nelson, courtesy of Nancy Langston.

Nmé guided Anishinaabe seasonality because of their movements from large lakes to small streams to reproduce, leading to the return of nmé. When the Anishinaabe returned for nmé's arrival in their spawning grounds, it meant that they themselves were also protected because of nmé's return. Nmé are known as the "spiritual keeper of the fisheries" who not only provide sustenance but also help tribes make decisions on when and where to fish.[27] Nmé hold knowledge of stressors that impact the land/water. The integration of nmé in the clan system, fundamental to the organization of Ottawa governance, has helped the Little River Ottawa weave together their knowledge systems tied to the land and water. Nmé guide Ottawa relations with one another, more-than-humans, and other tribes. Nmé have also played a role in Ottawa interactions with traders and settlers who would come to disrupt Anishnaabeg and nmé homelands through settlement.

Natural Resources: Locality, Trading, and Settler-Colonial Technologies

Despite the arrival of settlers, the Anishinaabe continued to follow the various waterways and move extensively throughout the Great Lakes region to trade. Through the exchange of goods, the Ottawa maintained relations through alliances.[28] The Ottawa became prominent traders in the Great Lakes fur trade (1650s and 1660s) with the French and eventually other Europeans.[29] The Ottawa were deliberate with where they built their villages in the lower peninsula of Michigan, which supported access to fisheries, their gardens, and riverways.[30] Living close to water enhanced the Ottawa's mobility and close partnerships with other tribes and Europeans for trading. The Ottawa continued to use waterways such as the Grand River to support and sustain their community.[31]

However, the settler push for territorial expansion eventually altered these harvests within Anishinaabe homelands while introducing settlers to nmé. Following the War of 1812, the Michigan Ottawa's villages remained next to rivers, and they continued their cultural practices.[32] Nmé became an important trade item, as Nancy Langston describes: "Dried sturgeon became the most important source of protein they [settlers] could get from the tribes."[33] At first, Europeans appreciated nmé and traded with the Ottawa for them, but eventually cooperation shifted to control and then to exploitation. The European ideology of possession drove settlement and resource exploitation, which pushed the Anishinaabeg away from their fisheries and their land base.

Settler priorities in the Michigan region were motivated by a need to transform the land/water and remove the Ottawa from their lands in order to stake a claim for themselves. As this encroachment on Anishinaabe lands and resources continued, settlers competed in international markets that valued nmé. In the second half of the ninteenth century, traders used nmé for steamship fuel and sold nmé eggs in Europe as "Russian caviar."[34] As this trade became profitable for European Americans, they began creating their own fisheries and took control over the entire nmé harvest.[35] With the start of commercial fishing in the mid-nineteenth century, settler fishers pressured the American and Canadian governments to adopt policies that restricted Anishinaabe fishing rights.[36] Settlers knew that fish like nmé were economically valuable. They created policies to limit the mobility of the Anishinaabe and facilitate the exploitation of nmé. The settler methods that exploited nmé made it harder for the Anishinaabe to maintain relations with nmé.

With the rise of commercial fisheries, nmé became a nuisance and then an economic commodity. The sharp scutes of the sturgeon often tore through fishermen's nets.[37] Despite this annoyance, settlers used sturgeon to power boilers on steamboats. Sturgeon continued to be overharvested, as there was significant demand for sturgeon caviar in Europe. By the 1900s, sturgeon fisheries were severely depleted, and by 1925 most sturgeon fisheries had collapsed.[38] The exploitation of nmé affected their ability to care for *manoomin* and Anishinnabe peoples, meaning that sturgeon could no longer continue their role as keepers of *manoomin* if there were no sturgeon left in the lakes and streams to protect and watch over the wild rice. The overharvest of sturgeon by settlers also indicates that the Anishinaabe could no longer honor the spiritual, cultural, and material relationship they had with them. The loss of sturgeon is tied to the loss of wild rice.

Exploitation of Land through Treaty Agreements

Before the collapse of the sturgeon fisheries, Anishinaabe mobility was limited by government attempts to push the Anishinaabe out of their ancestral homelands. The push for total access to Anishinaabe homelands and resources disrupted their existing ecological relations. However, despite the common colonial goal of displacement, the Ottawa were treated differently depending on which colonial officials (French or British) were in the region. Grand Traverse Band citizen and legal scholar Matthew L. M. Fletcher describes the Ottawa as having a close relationship with the French that allowed them greater control of the Lower Peninsula and the Grand River area.[39] The Anishinaabe continued to hunt, gather, and fish in their homelands. The Ottawa continued to trade throughout the region and moved seasonally to sustain themselves.[40] Every fall, the Ottawa harvested fish from inland rivers and lakes. Nmé was one fish the Ottawa continued to harvest by using forty- to fifty-foot spears in the fall and winter.[41] The seasonality that the Anishinaabe relied on shifted as treaty negotiations began alongside the growth of European fisheries and the expansion of the fur trade.

During the nineteenth century, settler governments negotiated treaties with Anishinaabe tribes in the Great Lakes. Through treaties, the Anishinaabe retained rights to hunt, gather, and fish in the land/water they ceded under immense pressure from the U.S. government. Sturgeon remained an important food source for the Anishinaabe, and it was important to protect the right to fish in their discussions. Extractive technologies (such as dams and steamboats) within Anishinaabe territories sped up logging industries while degrading the health of the environment.

In the 1820s, treaties also became a form of extraction and a means of securing settler desires for development. The 1836 Treaty of Washington was a large land-cession treaty that led to the creation of reservations. This treaty included the Grand River Valley that was of particular interest to settlers, who saw the area as underdeveloped. The desire to develop this area was a driving factor in treaty negotiations. Henry Schoolcraft, an Indian agent, led negotiations with the Anishinaabe starting in 1822. Schoolcraft was aware that the Ottawa would not agree to ceding the Grand River Valley, so he brought the Ojibwe into the land dealings.[42] The land in question was not considered Ojibwe land. However, the Ojibwe had debts from the fur trade, and Schoolcraft used this leverage to force them to attend treaty negotiations.[43] Several other factors coerced the Anishinaabe into signing the treaty by limiting access to tools they relied on, putting Anishinaabeg subsistence rights at risk. As one stark example, President Andrew Jackson cut the Indian Office budget that funded blacksmiths who made fishing hooks, hunting guns, and farming equipment for the Anishinaabe.[44] Settler objectives at this time were to obtain as much land for development as possible, while the Anishinaabe wanted to protect their hunting, gathering, and fishing rights from increased encroachment.

Industrial resource development flourished after the 1836 treaty and altered the environment the Anishinaabe relied on. Increased mining and logging altered free-flowing rivers and deforestation in the late nineteenth and early twentieth centuries.[45] This had detrimental impacts on the waters in which nmé lived. Free-flowing streams were altered from the increased erosion and sedimentation from this practice. Waste from paper mills was put into rivers and dams, blocking nmé and other fish migratory routes. The effects from mining and logging would leave lasting impacts on Michigan's environments. Langston shares that in 1885 "8.6 million pounds of sturgeon were harvested from the Great Lakes. By 1928 the catch totaled only 2,000 pounds."[46] The nmé population fell drastically from these stressors. Later, conservation offices in Wisconsin and Minnesota in the twentieth century would enforce no commercial fishing or catch and release rules.[47] These policies fell short of revitalizing the nmé population in the Great Lakes, and the Anishinaabe suffered the most as nmé /Anishinaabe relationships were harmed as settlers failed to live up to treaty agreements, destroying ecological relations central to Anishinaabe and nmé life.

While nmé carry ecological memory for Anishinaabeg, settlers choose to forget about nmé and the Anishinaabeg's knowledge shared with them about nmé. This act of forgetting, or settler memory,[48] informed and created colonial conditions that the Anishinaabe and other Indigenous peoples continue to navigate today.[49] Settler legal orders have been central to creating these conditions. As early as 1880, the State of Michigan began to restrict Anishinaabe hunting, gathering, and fishing practices that were guaranteed by the 1836 treaty.[50] Similarly, in the 1960s, the State of Michigan began to restrict commercial fishing in favor of more recreational fishing.[51] In the 1970s, several Anishinaabe and Ottawa tribes fought to defend their treaty rights using the federal court system.[52] These rights would eventually be upheld in *United States v. Michigan*, which found that the five signatory tribes to the 1836 treaty, including the Little River Ottawa, have fishing rights in the Great Lakes of Huron, Michigan, and Superior.[53] Anishinaabe tribes and their ability to fish should not be regulated by the state. Thus, the Anishinaabeg's "right" to fish exists beyond Western legal frameworks and, from an Anishinaabeg perspective, relies on ongoing relations with nmé.

Rights versus Relations

Anishinaabe stories describe relational responsibilities that underscore Anishinaabe sovereignty. For example, the story of Nenabozho going fishing honors existing and current relationships with the land/water.[54] In their recounting of the story "Nenabozho Goes Fishing," Heidi Kiiwetinepinesiik Stark and Kekek Jason Stark narrate how an Anishinaabe relational paradigm is better suited for addressing the damage done by the courts.[55] The Nenabozho story describes Nenabozho going ice fishing and remembering relations between plants, animals, and fish that ground Anishinaabe life. Focusing on relationships emphasizes responsibilities toward one another. Stark and Stark incorporate current issues for Anishinaabe communities in their retelling of the Nenabozho story, explaining that Nenabozho was approached by a game warden who cited him for fishing off the reservation, even after Nenabozho reminded the warden of his treaty rights.[56] This story reflects the 1974 Wisconsin Walleye Wars that involved two Ojibwe brothers from the Lac Courte Oreilles Band. They were cited by the Wisconsin Department of Natural Resources office for fishing on their off-reservation ceded territories, a right guaranteed to them through the Treaty of St. Peters (1837) and La Pointe (1842).[57] The story of Nenabozho emphasizes both the use of the courts and fishing on the land to assert Indigenous sovereignty. While legal action can be useful for affirming rights from a Western perspective, from an Anishinaabeg perpective, relationships exist beyond courts, and these relationships guide their responsibilities to more-than-humans. Anishinaabe stories, such as "Nenabozho

Goes Fishing," make space for the Anishinaabe to form their own relationships with the land/water. These relationships inform the inherent sovereignty the Anishinaabe have to exercise the right to hunt, fish, and gather and emphasize the responsibilities we (the Anishinaabe and settlers) have with creation. The Anishinaabe did not ignore settlers but instead created room for them to share an understanding of the relations they follow in the hopes that they would follow a similar approach.[58] This is a perspective that settlers largely misunderstand.

Indigenous political issues today continue to be entangled with the environment. To understand this entanglement, Cherokee scholar Clint Carroll provides a framework that theorizes the resource- and relationship-based approaches of tribal natural resources departments.[59] A resource-based approach emphasizes the economic value of a certain resource, whereas a relationship-based approach views the land as living and essential to maintaining all relationships Indigenous peoples have.[60] This framework illustrates how Indigenous knowledge complicates environmental governance. Carroll's work calls upon Indigenous governments to address concerns of Cherokee traditional knowledge keepers as central to their own initiatives. I build upon Carroll's work by drawing attention to relationships between the Little River Ottawa and the more-than-human world. Specifically, I examine how Ottawa environmental governance is practiced through nmé-restoration practices and contributes to Ottawa sovereignty by responding to the legacies of colonialism through reestablishing and maintaining relationships between Anishinaabe peoples, the land/water, and nmé.

Ottawa Approaches to Conservation

Colonialism has had a dramatic impact on nmé, contributing to their decimation. Today's current population of nmé is less than one percent of the historic population, and they are listed as threatened or endangered by nineteen out of twenty states in their range.[61] All more-than-humans benefit from nmé's existence, including the Anishinaabe, as they have sturgeon clan families that have roles and responsibilities to support the well-being of their communities.[62] The Little River Ottawa were reaffirmed as a federally recognized tribe in 1994 by President Bill Clinton. Soon after this reaffirmation, the Little River Ottawa established government programs, including a natural resources department. One of the first programs developed was the Nmé Stewardship Plan in 2001, which has allowed them to work toward restoring nmé in a culturally responsive way.[63]

The Nmé Stewardship Plan was created by both tribal members and tribal biologists, who were part of the Nmé Cultural Context Task Group, in an effort to return nmé to their home waters. The process of restoring nmé is attuned to life cycles and seasons. In the spring, young nmé are collected from the river and taken care of by tribal biologists until fall. Then, nmé are released back into the same river. This method keeps nmé in their original waters. The method of "home" tribal biologists use correlates with conservation biology's emphasis on maintaining the unique genetic attributes that home waters provide for fish.[64] Nmé knowledge is complex and connects them to their home watershed; through the return of nmé to their home waters, their presence supports continued interactions

FIGURE 7.3 Nmé. Photograph by Natasha Myhal.

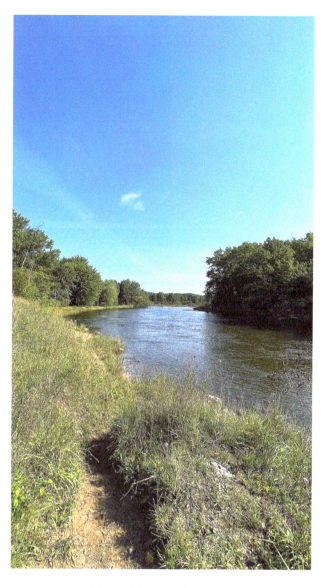

FIGURE 7.4 Big Manistee River watershed. Photograph by Natasha Myhal.

between the Ottawa and other more-than-human relatives. The Nmé Stewardship Plan was initially started to help support and bring back *manoomin* to the ancestral reservation territories.[65] At the time, the Little River Ottawa were trying to reintroduce *manoomin* to their waters but were not having success. The connection of nmé supporting *manoomin* meant that both programs needed to be implemented for both relatives to be restored in a healthy way.

An Anishinaabe approach to environmental restoration is holistic and responds to the changing ecological systems nmé endure. While the aim of the plan is to restore nmé health, the plan also recognizes "the health and improvement of the animals, plants, and people living within the watershed" as part of their holistic approach. This approach centers not only the Anishinaabe relationship with nmé, but other animals and plants that depend on nmé for survival. To achieve this balance, the Anishinaabemowin concept of *mino-bimaadiziwin* is integral, which translates to "living in a good and respectful way."[66] Together, *mino-bimaadiziwin* and the health of the watershed restore balance and maintain relationships between humans, plants, and animals to the land/water.

Anishinaabe memories expressed through ethnobotanical stories and Indigenous conservation, such as the Nmé Stewardship Plan, support the proliferation of more-than-human relationships that, in turn, reverse settler alienation. The Nmé Stewardship Plan, as an active response to Wiindigo, centers Indigenous ways of knowing and relationships with nmé to address the fragmentation of knowledge due to colonization. Ethnobotany involves settler science in conjunction with Indigenous knowledge. Settler science is not dismissed for Indigenous conservation efforts. Instead, the role that settler science has played in Ottawa restoration efforts is a critical contribution. Nmé-Ottawa relationships, coupled with Anishinaabe ethnobotany, show a way of remembering that Anishinaabe peoples can understand and heal from that supports an Anishinaabe understanding of *mino-bimaadiziwin*. Balance also implies movement, and for the Anishinaabe, they have always incorporated mobility into their practices (Figures 7.3 and 7.4).

Anishinaabe Relations to Plants and Animals

Anishinaabe approaches to ethnobotany, such as those demonstrated through the Nmé Stewardship Plan, are examples of culturally responsive approaches to the field. Anishinaabe ethnobotany involves not only the revitalization of plant knowledge but also the revitalization of the Anishinaabe language. Both the language and plant knowledge are vital to supporting living memories that explain how plants and animals work together and thus the ecological knowledge that undergirds restoration programs and environmental governance more broadly. The living memories within these Anishinaabeg stories are passed down from generation to generation, outlining individual and community responsibilities toward the land/water. For the Anishinaabe, plant beings existed before animals and therefore can exist alone.[67] Thus, both humans and animals are reliant on and depend on plants for survival.

The Anishinaabe story of Nanabush, a half-human, half-spirit, details this coexistence. Ojibwe scholar Basil Johnston shares that Nanabush was sent to the Anishinaabe when they were very sick so that they could learn about the healing qualities of plant medicines. Nanabush instructed Odaemin, a boy who died at that time when the Anishinaabe were sick, to watch animals and how they interacted with plants in order to share those observations with the Anishinaabe.[68] Nanabush and Odaemin worked together to learn about the healing qualities of plant medicines, qualities that animal beings also possessed. As Johnston notes, "By watching the animals, Odaemin learned the properties of plants."[69] When Nanabush left Odaemin, an essential teaching Odaemin carried going forward was the ability to learn. This particular Anishinaabe story outlines how the Anishinaabe should interact with all forms of creation and how those relations are transformed over time.

This story of Nanabush incorporates relationality. Shawn Wilson offers a necessary description of this in his book, *Research Is Ceremony: Indigenous Research Methods*, where relationality is described as the "importance of relationships" and "the heart of what it means to be Indigenous."[70] These relations extend to place, the land/water that connect Indigenous peoples to their migration or origin stories. Relationality as a concept also informs Indigenous legal orders. John Borrows describes the concept of resurgent relations, which center Indigenous peoples' relationships to the natural world that inform their legal systems.[71] *Aki* (earth) guides the Ottawa's earliest memories, and those memories are invested in contemporary relationships. I believe that one's memory is an important source of medicinal knowledge. Just as Odaemin learned about the healing qualities of plants to cure sickness, so too are the Little River Ottawa healing their more-than-human relative, nmé, from colonialism. The Little River Ottawa are strengthening relations between themselves and nmé and the relations nmé have with other plants and animals. The Nmé Stewardship Plan's view of healing the entire watershed includes how animals and plants work together to achieve that balance and how humans must pay careful attention to both plants and animals.

The Nmé Stewardship Plan is an excellent example of how nmé teach the Anishinaabe the importance of relationships with more-than-humans around them. Since nmé are known as the keepers of *manoomin*, there is a dependency between animal and plant knowledge. Ottawa ecology is illuminated further in the story of Nanabush. Nanabush instructed the Anishinaabe to pay close attention to each animal's interactions with plants, as sometimes the name for a plant or tree contains the name of the animal who taught them about that plant.[72] Knowledge of nmé is maintained through the names of sacred plants that the Anishinaabe use. Ojibwe ethnobotanist Scott Herron shares that the Anishinaabemowin name for wild ginger is *name pin*, which translates to "sturgeon potato."[73] Red Bear, an interlocutor Herron worked with, shares that wild ginger received its name because "it smells like fish when it is first harvested."[74] The Walpole Island Heritage Centre shared with Herron that *name pin* is sacred in Anishinaabe communities due to it being rare to find and its use as a smudge in ceremonies.[75] One can learn about the healing qualities of plants from paying close attention to how animals use them. Today, nmé provide a new set of relationships with the Little River Ottawa, a set of relationships different from what their ancestors had.

Anishinaabe Ethnobotany as Returning to Oneself

The *biskaabiiyang* methodology credited to Laura Horton translates to "returning to oneself" and encourages Anishinaabe researchers to evaluate how they themselves have internalized colonial practices.[76] Processing the effects of colonialism creates space for a return to Anishinaabe teachings and stories.[77] Wendy Makoons Geniusz describes this practice as creating a "common ground" for Anishinaabe researchers and community members to begin research.[78] Research in partnership with Indigenous communities can bring up a wide array of emotions. Research must start with a reflection on the personal impacts of colonialism to support current programs that address contemporary challenges for Indigenous communities.

The Anishinaabe have philosophies that support the well-being of their communities. The *biskaabiiyang* methodology relies on *gikendaasowin* (knowledge), *inaadiziwin* (Anishinaabe psychology, way of being), and *izhitwaawin* (culture, customs, history). Drawing from these Anishinaabemowin words, they construct an Anishinaabe worldview. This worldview influences the truths that Anishinaabe researchers should follow. The Nmé Stewardship Plan and the *biskaabiiyang* methodology together describe the interrelatedness of animals and plants that influences Anishinaabe ethnobotany. This practice centers Anishinaabeg knowledge of plants and animals over time. The interrelatedness comes from Anishinaabe teachings that surround and encompass more-than-humans, expressed through Ottawa conservation practices today. Anishinaabe teachings continue to hold important values that inform one's relationship to the land/water and support an Anishinaabe ecological memory.

Memory informs the balance needed within watersheds. Nmé support *mino-bimaadiziwin* as they spend the first eight months of their lives in rivers before moving toward the Great Lakes, only returning to rivers when they are old enough to spawn. The movement between water spaces and the Nmé Stewardship Plan represent Anishinaabeg sustainability. As Holtgren, Ogren, and Whyte explain, "[B]y reclaiming the nmé's rightful place within the watershed, balance would be restored to the river's other nonhuman kin."[79] This shift presents a story not only about nmé but also the ecosystems that all more-than-humans rely on in this region. The reintroduction of nmé populations holds promising implications for other more-than-humans that depend on nmé. Ottawa restoration practices create a space for human relationships with animal and plant relatives. The *biskaabiiyang* methodology acknowledges that not all *gikendaasowin* comes from plants and that animals bring Anishinaabe knowledge of their plant relatives.[80] Anishinaabe sustainability focuses on maintaining an ecosystem balance that supports the relations between plants *and* animals who live within this watershed. These relations stem from Anishinaabe stories, memories, and languages, all of which detail how to live in a sustainable way with the land/water.

Even within Indigenous conservation, settler colonialism continues to traverse place and impact human relationships to/with land and more-than-humans. Potawatomi scholar Kyle Whyte describes the Nmé Stewardship Plan and its partnership with settler conservation as "sharing responsibilities" to address accountability towards the land/water, nmé, and each other.[81] Similarly, Geniusz shares that Anishinaabe ethnobotany should take into account Western science's solutions to problems it has caused.[82] Anishinaabe knowledge brings back lost *gikendaasowin* due to settler science. Dams and impacts from historical forestry practices are present within the Big Manistee River watershed, impacting Ottawa memories. Today, Anishinaabe restoration practices "'make memories' on the landscape" that represents a terrain of knowing foundational to Anishinaabe being in the world.[83] Nmé and Ottawa relationships, situated over time, represent a particular memory that is grounded in their ancestral land/water.

Moving Forward with Indigenous Restoration and Governance

Indigenous restored relations with the land and water matter. The ability for Indigenous peoples to reclaim land physically and ideologically is necessary for Indigenous sovereignty. Land Back calls for the material return of land, but this movement goes beyond this by calling for the renewal of Indigenous peoples' spiritual and kinship ties with the land/water. This allows for a reflourishing of Indigenous knowledge and legal traditions that support an entire community and the everyday practices that shape Indigenous forms of governance.

The Nmé Stewardship Plan is one example of how Ottawa peoples address ruptures from colonialism and articulate their own forms of sovereignty that value more-than-human relationships. Tribal natural resources departments are reasserting stewardship by navigating how to live in an ever-changing environment and how to respond to the environmental pressures that Indigenous peoples face today. Restoration practices such as the Nmé Restoration Plan develop strategies based on the holistic view of Ottawa conservation that includes not only nmé but also the water, plants, and other animals that depend on the Manistee watershed for survival. I believe that this program provides a way to understand the shared relations between nmé and other more-than-humans, such as *manoomin*, in a transformational way. The Nmé Stewardship Plan informs Anishinaabe ethnobotany to include the importance of nmé/fish knowledge. In other words, ethnobotany is not only knowledge of plants but of nmé as well. The revival of nmé has the potential to bring back knowledge associated with plant and animal relatives and the many facets of their coexistence.

Ottawa relations with nmé have continued, and nmé have recently reappeared significantly in the public's memory. In April 2021, a U.S. Fish and Wildlife team caught an estimated hundred-year-old female sturgeon in the Detroit River. The sturgeon likely hatched in the 1920s when Detroit became the fourth-largest city in America.[84] The particular significance of this moment means that this nmé endured and survived large fisheries, increased industrialism, and immense environmental change to its habitat. The places where nmé continue to reside hold memories that remind the Anishinaabe of their inherent Indigenous ecological memory that lives on despite ongoing settler colonialism. The way that memory may express itself plays an integral role in shaping Ottawa attitudes about the environment. The hundred-year-old nmé found in the Detroit River evokes a past that is remembered differently by the Anishinaabe and settlers. However different these remembrances may be, Anishinaabe ecological memory is a lived theory of knowledge, informed by stories that continue to contain ways of knowing that allow both Anishinaabe and more-than-humans to thrive.

NOTES

1. Ojibwemowin means "the Anishinaabe language."
2. Any errors in this essay are mine alone.
3. Anishinaabekwe is the Anishinaabe word for "woman."
4. Marty Holtgren, Stephanie Ogren, and Kyle Whyte, "Renewing Relatives: One Tribe's Efforts to Bring Back an Ancient Fish," *Earth Island Journal* 30, no. 3 (Autumn 2015): 56.
5. See Walter D. Mignolo and Catherine E. Walsh, *On Decoloniality: Concepts, Analytics, Praxis* (Durham, N.C.: Duke University Press, 2018).
6. Leanne Betasamosake Simpson, *As We Have Always Done: Indigenous Freedom through Radical Resistance* (Minneapolis: University of Minnesota Press, 2017), 192.
7. Shiri Pasternak and Hayden King, *Executive Summary: Land Back; A Yellowhead Institute Red Paper*, 2019, https://redpaper.yellowheadinstitute.org/wp-content/uploads/2019/10/red-paper-executive-summary-final-1.pdf.
8. There are many versions of the Anishinaabe creation story, and these versions can vary depending on the region. Amanda Robinson, "Turtle Island," The Canadian Encyclopedia, November 6, 2018, https://www.thecanadianencyclopedia.ca/en/article/turtle-island.
9. Kenny Pheasant, email message to author, October 5, 2022.
10. The Anishinaabeg include the Ojibwe, Ottawa, and Potawatomi. Each nation speaks Anishinaabemowin and belongs to the Algonquian language family.
11. "The Great Lakes in Ojibwe," The Decolonial Atlas, December 1, 2014, https://decolonialatlas.wordpress.com/2014/12/01/the-great-lakes-in-ojibwe/.
12. "The Ojibwe People," Minnesota Historical Society, n.d., https://www.mnhs.org/fortsnelling/learn/native-americans/ojibwe-people.
13. "Ojibwe Migration,"ArcGIS StoryMaps, n.d., https://www.arcgis.com/apps/Cascade/index.html?appid=4cca54af01514d1bb48e48c0ae99b942.
14. Kyle Whyte, Jared L. Talley, and Julia D. Gibson, "Indigenous Mobility Traditions, Colonialism, and the Anthropocene," *Mobilities* 14, no. 3 (2019): 322.
15. Whyte, Talley, and Gibson, "Indigenous Mobility Traditions, Colonialism, and the Anthropocene," 322.
16. Michael A. McDonnell, *Masters of Empire: Great Lakes Indians and the Making of America* (New York: Farrar, Straus and Giroux, 2015), 12.
17. Nancy Langston, *Climate Ghosts: Migratory Species in the Anthropocene* (Waltham, Mass.: Brandeis University Press, 2021), 81. See also Patty Loew, *Indian Nations of Wisconsin: Histories of Endurance and Renewal* (Madison: Wisconsin Historical Society Press, 2001).
18. Eric Graber, "Food as Medicine," American Society For Nutrition, February 22, 2022, https://nutrition.org/food-as-medicine/.
19. Steve Pitt, "Windigo," The Canadian Encyclopedia, September 9, 2012, https://www.thecanadianencyclopedia.ca/en/article/windigo.
20. Winona LaDuke and Deborah Cowen, "Beyond Wiindigo Infrastructure," *The South Atlantic Quarterly* 119, no. 2 (2020): 253.
21. LaDuke and Cowen, "Beyond Wiindigo Infrastructure," 252; and Bezhigobinesikwe Elaine Fleming, "Nanaboozhoo and the Wiindigo: An Ojibwe History from Colonization to the Present," *Tribal College: Journal of American Indian Higher Education* 28, no. 3 (Spring 2017), https://tribalcollegejournal.org/nanaboozhoo-wiindigo-ojibwe-history-colonization-present/.
22. James M. McClurken, *Our People, Our Journey: The Little River Band of Ottawa Indians* (East Lansing: Michigan State University Press, 2009), 8; and Kyle Powys Whyte, "Our Ancestors' Dystopia Now: Indigenous Conservation and the Anthropocene," in *The Routledge Companion to the Environmental Humanities*, ed. Ursula K. Heise, Jon Christensen, and Michelle Niemann (London: Routledge, 2017), 210.
23. Langston, *Climate Ghosts*, 76.
24. See Heather Davis and Zoe Todd, "On the Importance of a Date, or Decolonizing the Anthropocene," *ACME: An International Journal for Critical Geographies* 16, no. 4 (2017): 761–80.
25. See Pratik Chakrabarti and Michael Worboys, "Science and Imperialism since 1870," in *The Cambridge History of Science*, vol. 8, *Modern Science in National, Transnational, and Global Context*, ed. Hugh Richard Slotten, Ronald L. Numbers, and David N. Livingstone (Cambridge: Cambridge University Press, 2020), 9–31.

26 Langston, *Climate Ghosts*, 80–81.
27 Langston, *Climate Ghosts*, 82.
28 In Algonquian, the word *Ottawa* means "traders."
29 McClurken, *Our People, Our Journey*, 6–7.
30 McClurken, *Our People, Our Journey*, 7.
31 McClurken, *Our People, Our Journey*, 7.
32 McClurken, *Our People, Our Journey*, 8.
33 Langston, *Climate Ghosts*, 85.
34 Langston, *Climate Ghosts*, 87.
35 Langston, *Climate Ghosts*, 87. See also Tim E. Holzkamm, "Sturgeon Utilization by the Rainy River Ojibwa Bands," *Papers of the Algonquian Conference* 18 (1987): 155–63.
36 Langston, *Climate Ghosts*, 86.
37 See Wayne H. Tody, "Whitefish, Sturgeon, and the Early Michigan Commercial Fishery," in *Michigan Fisheries Centennial Report: 1873–1973* (Lansing: Michigan Department of Natural Resources, 1974), 45–60.
38 Paul Joseph Vecsei, "Life History and Population Dynamics of Lake Sturgeon, *Acipenser fulvescens*, in the Muskegon River, Michigan" (PhD diss., University of Georgia, 2011), 5.
39 Matthew L. M. Fletcher, *The Eagle Returns: The Legal History of the Grand Traverse Band of Ottawa and Chippewa Indians* (East Lansing: Michigan State University Press, 2012), 6; and James M. McClurken, "Ottawa," in *People of the Three Fires: The Ottawa, Potawatomi and Ojibway of Michigan* (Grand Rapids: The Michigan Indian Press Grand Rapids Inter-Tribal Council, 1986), 2.
40 McClurken, *Our People, Our Journey*, 2.
41 Fletcher, *The Eagle Returns*, 11.
42 Fletcher, *The Eagle Returns*, 18.
43 Fletcher, *The Eagle Returns*, 19.
44 Fletcher, *The Eagle Returns*, 20.
45 Langston, *Climate Ghosts*, 88–89.
46 Langston, *Climate Ghosts*, 90.
47 Langston, *Climate Ghosts*, 91.
48 Kevin Bruyneel writes about memory as it informs settlers' acknowledgment and erasure of Indigenous peoples in *Settler Memory: The Disavowal of Indigeneity and the Politics of Race in the United States* (Chapel Hill: University of North Carolina Press, 2021).
49 Whyte, "Our Ancestors' Dystopia Now," 208.
50 Fletcher, *The Eagle Returns*, 115.
51 Fletcher, *The Eagle Returns*, 116.
52 *United States v. Michigan*, 471 F. Supp. 192 (W.D. Mich. 1979).
53 *Michigan's 1836 Treaty Fishery Guide*, Chippewa Ottawa Treaty Fishery Management Authority Public Information & Education Committee, May 1999, 10, https://dspace.nmc.edu/bitstream/handle/11045/24108/1836TreatyFisheryGuide.pdf?sequence=1&isAllowed=y.
54 Nenabozho (Nanabozho or Nanabush) figures heavily in Anishinaabe oral traditions and is often described as a cultural hero, creator, and trickster.
55 Heidi Kiiwetinepinesiik Stark and Kekek Jason Stark, "Nenabozho Goes Fishing: A Sovereignty Story," *Daedalus* 147, no. 2 (Spring 2018): 17–18.
56 Stark and Stark, "Nenabozho Goes Fishing," 18.
57 Stark and Stark, "Nenabozho Goes Fishing," 19. See also Larry Nesper, *The Walleye War: The Struggle for Ojibwe Spearfishing and Treaty Rights* (Lincoln: University of Nebraska Press, 2002).
58 Stark and Stark, "Nenabozho Goes Fishing," 21.
59 Clint Carroll, *Roots of Our Renewal: Ethnobotany and Cherokee Environmental Governance* (Minneapolis: University of Minnesota Press, 2015), 8–9.
60 Carroll, *Roots of Our Renewal*, 8.
61 Holtgren, Ogren, and Whyte, "Renewing Relatives," 55.
62 "Anishinaabe Teachings of the Fish (Giigoonh)," Sault Ste. Marie Tribe of Chippewa Indians, https://www.saulttribe.com/images/Anishinaabe_Teachings_of_the_Fish_Flyer.pdf.
63 Holtgren, Ogren, and Whyte, "Renewing Relatives," 56.

64 Holtgren, Ogren, and Whyte, "Renewing Relatives," 56.
65 Jay Sam (tribal historic preservation officer for the Little River Ottawa), personal communication, July 2022.
66 Holtgren, Ogren, and Whyte, "Renewing Relatives," 56.
67 Basil Johnston, *Ojibway Heritage* (Toronto: McClelland and Stewart, 1976), 33.
68 Johnston, *Ojibway Heritage*, 80–81; and Wendy Makoons Geniusz, *Our Knowledge Is Not Primitive: Decolonizing Botanical Anishinaabe Teachings* (Syracuse, N.Y.: Syracuse University Press, 2009), 67.
69 Johnston, *Ojibway Heritage*, 81.
70 Shawn Wilson, *Research Is Ceremony: Indigenous Research Methods* (Black Point: Fernwood Publishing, 2008), 80.
71 John Borrows, "Earth-Bound: Indigenous Resurgence and Environmental Reconciliation," in *Resurgence and Reconciliation: Indigenous-Settler Relations and Earth Teachings*, ed. Michael Asch, John Borrows, and James Tully (Toronto: University of Toronto Press, 2018), 50.
72 Geniusz, *Our Knowledge Is Not Primitive*, 69.
73 Scott M. Herron, "Ethnobotany of the Anishinaabek Northern Great Lakes Indians" (PhD diss., Southern Illinois University, Carbondale, 2002), 177.
74 Herron, "Ethnobotany of the Anishinaabek Northern Great Lakes Indians," 206.
75 Herron, "Ethnobotany of the Anishinaabek Northern Great Lakes Indians," 177.
76 Geniusz, *Our Knowedge Is Not Primitive*, 9.
77 Geniusz, *Our Knowledge Is Not Primitive*, 7.
78 Geniusz, *Our Knowledge Is Not Primitive*, 9.
79 Holtgren, Ogren, and Whyte, "Renewing Relatives," 56.
80 Geniusz, *Our Knowledge Is Not Primitive*, 69.
81 Whyte, "Our Ancestors' Dystopia Now," 209.
82 Geniusz, *Our Knowledge Is Not Primitive*, 106.
83 Keith Thor Carlson and Naxaxalhts'i (Albert "Sonny" McHalsie), "Stó:lō Memoryscapes as Indigenous Ways of Knowing: Stó:lo History from Stone and Fire," in *The Routledge Handbook of Memory and Place*, ed. Sarah De Nardi, Hilary Orange, Steven High, and Eerika Koskinen-Koivisto (London: Routledge, 2020), 145.
84 Paulina Firozi, "Biologists Reeled in a 240-Pound Fish from the Detroit River that Probably Hatched a Century Ago," Washington Post, May 5, 2021, https://www.washingtonpost.com/science/2021/05/05/240-pound-fish-detroit-river/?fbclid=IwAR3KwC97nVP056tbX4I_nZmIGr2jqUH0kdQaGkLEbdFt3P6c5DAhdf49ctg.

8

Language, Territory, and Law

Mapuzugun as the Basis for Mapuche Spatial Planning and Territorial Reconstruction

MIGUEL MELIN AND MAGDALENA UGARTE

Planning, Mapuche Existence, and Internal Colonialism in Wallmapu

The relationship between the Chilean state and the Mapuche nation is marked by an ongoing history of violence, land dispossession, and internal colonialism that started in the mid-nineteenth century and continues today.[1] The material effects of the state-led military occupation of Wallmapu (Mapuche traditional territory) are illustrated not only by the structural impoverishment of communities but also by the spike in land-use conflicts over Mapuche lands in recent decades.[2] Planning has been instrumental in enabling these processes through strategies of land appropriation and control such as land-use designations, surveying, town building, and place naming, making land available for occupation and extraction while attempting to impose a homogenizing territorial logic grounded in Western spatial principles.[3]

When thinking about planning, our understanding is twofold. On the one hand, we refer to the "formulation, content, and implementation of spatial public policies" such as the ones just described, which have generally become dominant within the framework of modern nation-states.[4] On the other, we understand planning in more expansive terms, as the practices that guide how humans interact with, manage, and sustain our existence within the shared spaces where we live and of which we are a part. The argument we develop in the following pages starts from the premise that dominant, state-led planning discourses and practices have invisibilized the existence of Mapuche spatial-planning systems that predate the Chilean state and have continued despite governmental attempts to disarticulate spatial organization and social relations through the imposition of the reservation system, known as *radicación*.[5] We see this negation of Mapuche spatial-planning traditions as one of the elements at the heart of current land-based conflicts on Mapuche territory.

The complicity of planning with Indigenous land dispossession is part of a larger colonial apparatus that not only sought to remove Mapuche people from their territories but also to disrupt their political, cultural, spiritual, and legal systems through diverse mechanisms operating in tandem. Echoing settler-colonial processes in other contexts, the processes of *radicación* and land usurpation cannot be understood separately from the systematic theft of Mapuche livestock during the military occupation that impoverished the nation and weakened its economic exchange practices.[6] Or from the imposition of legal and governance frameworks that have coercively redefined social relations, ways of resolving internal conflict, and Mapuche political organization.[7] Or from the introduction of schooling and other assimilationist institutions meant to extinguish Mapuche cultural practices and subjectivity through the imposition of the Spanish language, often intertwined with religious practices.[8] As a result, today around 80 percent of Mapuche people in Chile neither speak nor understand their traditional language.[9]

In the face of this ongoing violence, this essay uses the Mapuche language Mapuzugun as an entry point to explore questions of land dispossession and territorial fragmentation, as well as Mapuche existence, resistance, and resurgence. More specifically, we situate Mapuzugun as the basis for territorial presence and spatial planning in what are now Chile and Argentina, engaging with the ways in which the language embodies Mapuche connections to land through toponymy, while also articulating the interconnected relationships between people (*che*), space or land (*mapu*), and life in all its forms (*ixofillmogen*).[10] We also explore how Mapuzugun expresses and mobilizes the normative principles (*az mapu*) guiding such relationships and ways of existing in the Mapuche worldview.[11]

As we elaborate in the following pages, according to Mapuche knowledge the origin of human beings and the different family lineages that make up the nation (*che*) emerges from the *mapu*, hence the notion of Mapuche (people from the land).[12] The Mapuche did not come from elsewhere but literally sprung from their territories.[13] It is thus impossible to conceive Mapuche existence as unfolding detached from the places that make life possible and in a language other than Mapuzugun. Mapuche place-names or toponyms materialize these inherent relationships, connecting people and the spaces they inhabit. Mapuche toponyms do much more than name or describe places. They embody and make possible the coexistence of people and land, turning normative precepts about respectful life relations into particular ways of using and interacting with each space and with each other. Place-names not only designate but also express meanings and delineate the behaviors and activities that can take place to ensure Mapuche existence. We argue that by allowing Mapuche people to communicate with the landscapes they emerge from and belong to, Mapuzugun gives life to Mapuche spatial planning.[14] As a whole, language, territory, and law weave together into a grounded normativity that emerges from Mapuche presence in place.[15]

These deep interconnections have important implications for the spatial disciplines, expanding theoretical discussions about planning and Indigenous peoples in settler-colonial contexts today. Understanding Mapuche spatial planning as an expression of Mapuche law and governance locates Mapuche planning practices in the realm of the political and the normative.[16] It re-signifies practices that are not often seen as planning or that openly confront state planning—including reclaiming Mapuche place-names and de facto land recuperation—as active efforts to enact Mapuche normative principles and reconstruct Wallmapu according to planning tenets emerging from Mapuche knowledge and sovereignty. More specifically, understanding Mapuzugun as the basis for Mapuche spatial planning gives visibility to practices that might not otherwise be seen as territorial resistance. Examined through the lens of grounded normativity, language revitalization, the reclamation of toponyms, connecting to the land in Mapuzugun through ceremony, and the exercise of Mapuche spatial planning can be seen as mutually constitutive practices of resurgence and self-determination in a context of internal colonialism.

Although grounded in the specificity of discussions about spatial planning, language, and law in Wallmapu, our use of the term "resurgence" resonates with the works of Indigenous scholars within and beyond Mapuche territory who explore the myriad ways Indigenous peoples "are trying to center Indigenous practices and thoughts in [their] lives as everyday acts of resistance, and grow those actions and processes into a mass mobilization."[17] From the reactivation of cultural and spiritual spaces and practices, to processes of re-territorialization and land occupation to restore native forest and grow food, to the reinstatement of traditional diets and the exercise of Indigenous customary law, at the center of resurgence efforts is the restoration of the processes and knowledges—including "social, political, spiritual, and legal systems"—that constitute and enable Indigenous life.[18] Our argument positions the reclamation of Mapuche spatial planning and the exercise of Mapuzugun in this light.

In what follows, we first discuss how Mapuche conceptualizations of spatial relations are grounded in the inseparability of people, language, and territory at different scales. The next section outlines the connections between Mapuche law (*az mapu*) and the spatial principles it encapsulates. We also elaborate how Mapuzugun is the vehicle that articulates such precepts and how people become the enactors of Mapuche spatial principles. We then explore the emergence of new Mapuche "territorial identities" in the context of land dispossession and displacement. The next section examines Mapuche toponomy as the materialization of Mapuche existence in Wallmapu and an embodiment of their spatial-planning principles. The essay concludes with a discussion about how, from this perspective, the struggles for language revitalization, land recuperation, and the enactment of Mapuche law are one. More importantly, we argue that the persistence of Mapuzugun throughout Wallmapu and the reclamation of Mapuche toponyms today is a clear expression of the uninterrupted presence of Mapuche people on their territory and a testimony to the resistance and resurgence of Mapuche spatial planning in the face of state violence.

Mapu: Territory as Wholeness

In the Mapuche worldview, the notion of *mapu* refers to and encompasses the territorial, symbolic, and cosmic space in its wholeness. It comprises the earth as such—the surface where human and other forms of life unfold (*nag mapu*)—but also the celestial space that

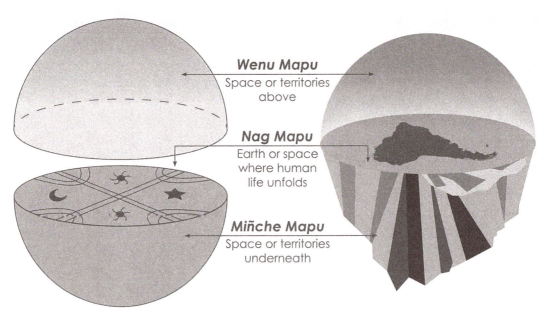

FIGURE 8.1 Dimensions of *mapu*. Illustration by Miguel Melin and Magdalena Ugarte, adapted from https://misistemasolar.com/cosmologia-mapuche/.

stretches over the earth (*wenu mapu*) and the underground world (*miñche mapu*).[19] It is a word in the Mapuzugun language, a language that is itself the voice of such spatial wholeness and that *che* help mediate and mobilize when they speak. In this way, an inherent relationship emerges between language and space every time and in every dimension where Mapuzugun-speaking people interact with the *mapu*, whether they do so in spiritual and ceremonial ways, as a means of subsistence, or with sociocultural purposes.

Acknowledging the multiple dimensions that the spatial notion of *mapu* as wholeness encompasses (Figure 8.1), here we focus on the physical and symbolic space known as *nag mapu*, which refers to the lands and physical territory that make up Mapuche country or Wallmapu. Ancient Mapuche people (*kuyfikecheyem*) planned their territory following the patterns of nature and the diverse forms of life that existed therein (*ixofillmogen*). The planning of their territory was always grounded in full respect for the existence of diverse neighboring nations, particularly the Aymara and Quechua in the northern parts of Mapuche territory. While they developed long-lasting and fraternal trading and border relations, the Mapuche nation was never part of the Tawantisuyo or Abya Yala. Rather, it maintained an independent life based on alliances and confederated forms of territorial organization known as *fütalmapu*, which were based on extended family networks spread throughout Wallmapu, covering large parts of what are now the center and south of Chile and Argentina.

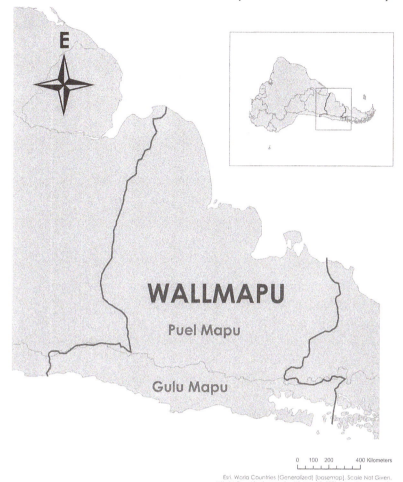

FIGURE 8.2
Map of Wallmapu. Illustration by Miguel Melin and Magdalena Ugarte, adapted from Miguel Melin Pehuen, Pablo Mansilla Quiñones, and Manuela Royo Letelier, *Cartografía cultural del Wallmapu: Elementos para descolonizar el mapa en territorio mapuche* (Santiago: LOM, 2019), 57.

According to the collective memory of Mapuche elders (*kimche* or *fvchakeche*)—who are sources and holders of Mapuche knowledge and language—the symbolic meanings and cultural orientation of Mapuche spatial notions emerge from Mapuzugun. The language structures *nag mapu* (or the immediate geographic space) into four fundamental dimensions called *meli wixan mapu*, which can be equated with the four cardinal directions. Since times of political-territorial independence, Wallmapu has been organized into four vast macro territorial units: *puel mapu* (eastern territories, what is now Argentina), *gulu mapu* (western territories, what is now Chile), *pikun mapu* (northern territories), and *willi mapu* (southern territories). Unlike Eurocentric spatial ideals that place the north as the point of reference, for the Mapuche the east—*puel mapu*—emerges as the guiding

Language, Territory, and Law 175

TABLE 8.1 Toponyms and anthroponyms in Wallmapu

TOPONYM	MEANING	EXAMPLES OF FAMILY LINEAGES EMERGING FROM THAT PLACE
Pagipüllü	Land of pumas	Cayupagi (Cayupan)
		Millapagi (Millapan)
		Mankepagi (Manquepan)
		Wenupagi (Huenupan)
Keupuwe	Place where *keupu* (type of stone) is extracted	Melikeupu (Meliqueo)
		Antükeupu (Antiqueo)
		Kolükeupu (Coliqueo)
		Kayukeupu (Cayuqueo)
Rukañamku	Space / home where the eagle lives	Meliñamku (Melin)
		Kuruñamku (Curin)
		Catriñamku (Catrin)
		Mariñamku (Marin)

Note: Hispanicized Mapuche family names are indicated in parentheses.

point, the direction that guides life, traditions, good living, and the positive energies that all human activities are directed toward in the first place.[20]

The experiences, practices, and narratives of Mapuche elders in the Mapuzugun language conceive the territory as part of their own existence, not as a separate entity. As a founding principle for Mapuche people and culture, the notion of *mapu* extends to encompass life and all forms of existence (*ixofillmogen*), including *che* who spring from the territory and become the spokespeople for the *mapu*. This conceptualization finds ground in the origins of the Mapuche nation as a collective whose roots can actually be found on the land itself and its different elements, which is where their own family names or *küpan* (anthroponymy) come from, along with the names of their places of origin or *tuwün* (toponymy).[21] The physiognomy, features, or presence of flora and fauna in a given territory also become the features and characteristics of a family lineage that are expressed in the family name (Table 8.1). While prior to the *radicación* process, Mapuche names merged the individual and family name into one, the roots of today's Hispanized Mapuche last names still reflect those connections to territory: *ñamku* (eagle), *kura* (stone), *manque* (condor), *pangi* (puma), *nawel* (tiger), *lewfü* (river), *lafken* (sea), and *milla* (gold), among others.[22] Subsequently, on *nag mapu* all forms of Mapuche life unfold, including social and cultural life and Mapuche forms of organization and subsistence, all of which are structured through a language that the Mapuche themselves have called "the language and voice of the *mapu*" or Mapuzugun.

In this way, the coexistence between people and *mapu*—mediated by a set of normative precepts expressed in Mapuche law (*az mapu*), as we elaborate in the next section—gives birth to a way of planning and sharing the territory along with ways of designating each space that are expressed in Mapuche toponyms. These place-names capture the deep meaning of each space, the activities that can unfold on it, the types of vegetation that grow there, its spiritual relation to people, and its location and orientation in relation to the four cardinal points (*meli wixan mapu*), among others. In the context of today's socio-spatial configuration, there are still some elements of continuity of Mapuche knowledge and practices, such as the exercise of *nguillatun* as the main ceremony and the existence of *nguillatuwe* (the place where such ceremony takes place). However, several transformations, changes, and ruptures are evident, both those related to peaceful intercultural contact, exchanges, and border relations in Wallmapu and those resulting from the military occupation and territorial dispossession of the Mapuche led by the Chilean and Argentinian states starting in the nineteenth century.

Az Mapu and Spatial Planning: Grounded Normativity on Mapuche Territory

In recent community-based research, some Mapuche scholars have sought to examine the existence (or absence) of normative principles emerging from Mapuzugun narratives today, both norms related to ethics and values and norms of a procedural and conceptual nature.[23] Building on Mapuche collective memory as expressed in the stories of *fvchakeche*, the notion of *az mapu* has been reclaimed as the glue that consolidates a Mapuche normative system that is alive in oral history and still exercised in some territories.

The notion of *az mapu* has at least two meanings. The first one refers to the characteristics of the landscape in a given territory. For instance, the *az mapu* of the Andes mountain range has to do with the mountains, *Araucaria* trees, and other species that are the defining features of those spaces; it also includes the climate of the Andes. Smaller areas within a given territory also have their own *az mapu* that includes the people who live therein and identify with its geography: flat lands, the presence or absence of native plants, the existence of certain birds and native animals, the color of the soil. It is the convergence of all these elements that gives a particular territory its identity and representativeness—its *az*—making it possible to differentiate one territory from another.[24] The notion of *az mapu* also has another meaning: a set of norms and guidelines that define the relationships between humans and that guide Mapuche people to establish good and respectful relations with the natural and supernatural worlds. These rules are meant to ensure a balanced coexistence with the environment, and, depending on how Mapuche people decide to engage with these different elements, people might either live together in harmony with or be sanctioned by the natural and supernatural worlds because of their transgression.[25]

As Miguel Melin Pehuen, Patricio Coliqueo Collipal, Elsy Curihuinca Neira, and Manuela Royo Letelier argue, these two meanings intertwine to create norms and ways of interacting, and therefore particular ways of doing and relating with each other emerge in everyday life and in ceremonial activities.[26] In Mapuche legal tradition (and echoing Indigenous legal regimes in other settler-colonial contexts), "individuals are patterned into Nature, not outside of Nature; and, with that patterning comes responsibilities. The *logos* of law is in the land. There is a symbiotic relationship between humans and the earth/cosmos, and more specifically, between humans and place."[27] This involves the use of certain words or accents in Mapuzugun that define particular uses and relationships with space and the land.[28] In doing so, all these elements—the physical landscape, all forms of life within, including human life, and the language that makes such designations and communication possible—delineate specific protocols and patterns of behavior, such as how *pürün* (dances) must unfold during a *nguillatun* or the role assigned to certain traditional authorities like *machi* (healers) during ceremonies.

As a whole, *az mapu* refers to the organization of life and its complex relationship with *che*, as well as to how humans organize and interact with space in Wallmapu. In other words, the notion of *az* reveals the ordering of things, of social life, of cultural practices, and of the cycles of *mogen* (life in all its forms). We suggest that Mapuche spatial-planning practices are, therefore, inherently embodied within that normative system, always framed in relation to the physical orientation and cultural representation of the territory facing the east, as described earlier (Figure 8.2). The east is the reference point where Mapuche life and existence as a whole emerge from and toward which they flow. The language is thus the vehicle that articulates such normative precepts, and people become the enactors of Mapuche spatial principles. To the extent that people behave according to the ordering norms expressed in *az mapu*—including social and spatial ordering—they are valued and considered members of the community. Otherwise, they receive the relevant sanctions in order to determine whether they can belong to the collective, even risking being marginalized from their social world as a result of violating Mapuche norms.[29]

Speaking about the experience of Indigenous peoples in what is now known as Canada, Dene scholar Glen Sean Coulthard and Nishnaabeg scholar Leanne Betasamosake Simpson have used the term "grounded normativity" to refer to the "the systems of ethics that are continuously generated by a relationship with a particular place, with land, through the Indigenous processes and knowledges that make up Indigenous life."[30] This notion resonates closely with the inherent connections between Mapuche law and territory we have described in the preceding pages and with the role Mapuzugun plays in enabling Mapuche ways of relating to the *mapu* and to each other. In fact, the idea of grounded normativity highlights how it is precisely the "relationship [of Mapuche people] to the land itself [that] generates the processes, practices, and knowledges that inform [their] political systems."[31]

But *az mapu* does not only encompass a set of normative reflections and practices that have emerged from the historical exercise of Mapuche ancestral sovereignty and cultural control in Wallmapu, "theories and practices that form Indigenous constructions of reality, of life, and of how to ethically relate to the plant and animal nations, our families, the waters, the skyworld, communities, and nations."[32] It also involves the identification of conceptual bases and their practical application in today's political context that is marked both by a coercive relationship with the Chilean state—including the loss of Mapuzugun—and by important spaces of cultural resistance and control resulting from a history of institutionalized dispossession.[33]

From *Fütalmapu* to "Territorial Identities"

As a result of the occupation of Mapuche territory, a new context marked by external influences, increased intercultural interaction, and Mapuche cultural resistance has emerged within the reserves. The survivors of the invasion, spread over a fragmented

Wallmapu that accounts for just 5 percent of their ancestral territory, have been brought into a forced legal form of settlement that due to its rigid nature has forced Mapuche people to re-signify their spaces following *az mapu* norms.³⁴ If in times of political-territorial independence the four vast macro territorial units in Wallmapu—*puel mapu, gulu mapu, pikun mapu,* and *willi mapu*—had consolidated balanced and symmetrical relationships with the Spanish Crown and the early nation-states of Chile and Argentina, under the new scenario different kinds of asymmetrical relationships develop, now marked by domination, dependency, and territorial inequalities.³⁵ These new spaces and relationships have led to the rise of "territorial identities," which are essentially reduced and reconfigured *fütalmapu*. The term is a relatively recent, Hispanicized concept that denotes different segments of the Mapuche nation based on their geographic location, as well as certain cultural particularities shared by people inhabiting those territories. They include the *pewenche* (who live in the Andes mountains near *pewen* trees), the *lafkenche* (located on the Pacific coast), the *wenteche* (inhabiting the central valleys), and the *nagche* (near the Nawelbuta mountain range). The *williche* (located in the south) keep the ancestral denomination associated with their geographic location in the southern parts of Mapuche territory.

The emergence of these new "territorial identities" is an expression of Mapuche cultural resistance and survival, a space of refuge in the face of a new adverse scenario that threatens the subsistence and continuation of Mapuche culture and identity. The *pewenche* "territorial identity" is a case in point, given its rise as a result of the territorial occupation and displacement suffered by the Mapuche in the central valleys that they have historically inhabited. It was their forced relocation to the mountain highlands to escape the military invasions led by Chile and Argentina (euphemistically called Pacification of the Araucanía and Campaign of the Desert, respectively) that led to the consolidation of *pewenche* identity.³⁶ Within these reduced spaces, new kinds of family bonds that are more inward oriented have developed and strengthened over time.

While the term "territorial identities" echoes the notion of *fütalmapu*, we use the concept in quotation marks as a way of stressing that these newer denominations are a consequence of the processes of territorial dispossession and dislocation mentioned earlier and, in our view, do not replace or threaten the cohesiveness of the Mapuche people as a historical, linguistic, cultural, and political community.³⁷ In the words of Sergio Caniuqueo Huircapan, "[T]his is why when the current territorial-identities discourse resorts to concepts like territorial control it does so to denote the need to exercise territoriality, which is [a need] inherent to peoples who have exercised sovereignty at some point, who have had and managed a territory. A territory from which different relations have emerged, ranging from securing food to the . . . creation of social models."³⁸

The military occupation and colonial settlement of Wallmapu not only forcefully displaced Mapuche people from their traditional territories and confined them to reservation lands—oftentimes far away from the places they had historically inhabited—but also triggered a process of forced migration to cities.³⁹ Faced with a limited land base in areas often unsuitable for agriculture, and with their livestock in the hands of the state and newly arrived settlers, Mapuche people found their means of subsistence decimated.⁴⁰

The settler-colonial architecture of the Chilean state in Wallmapu impoverished the Mapuche nation to the point where many had no option but to leave their reservations to find ways of surviving in urban areas.[41]

During the twentieth century, large waves of Mapuche people arrived in large urban centers like Santiago and Concepción as well as in intermediate cities like Temuco, Valdivia, and Osorno. Now inserted in Chile's market economy largely as precarious wage workers, Mapuche people had to confront discrimination and were generally relegated to low-skilled jobs, being forced to become part of the working class living at the fringes of urban spaces.[42] Today, around 80 percent of the total Mapuche population in Chile lives in cities.[43] In recent decades, some urban Mapuche people, particularly in Chile's capital Santiago, have coined the term *warriache* (people of the city) to denote their particular location.[44] Like the "territorial identities" described earlier, the emergence of this label is also the result of the colonial dispossession experienced by the Mapuche and can be seen to a great extent as a political articulation among segments of what Enrique Antileo Baeza has called the Mapuche diaspora.[45]

It becomes clear that the process of Mapuche territorial reconfiguration and re-signification has been subject to both intra- and intercultural forces, and the reach, usage, and vitality of the Mapuche language cannot be understood outside of such processes. The existence of linguistic variants, new cultural practices, and a sometimes rigid self-ascription to one of those emerging territories in certain areas of Wallmapu is a relatively new phenomenon in Mapuche society, one that is to a great extent the result of contact. As Mapuche linguist Elisa Loncon Antileo describes:

> *Wigka* [white] ways of life implied poverty, low quality of life so that Mapuche [people] felt ashamed about themselves. First, their lands were taken away and that is how their home was impoverished. As children grew up they had bad jobs and entered *wigka* life—marginal and precarious. This way of life negatively impacted Mapuche knowledge. Mapuche names were lost, they were called "indians." Their language was lost and in school only Spanish was spoken. Their knowledge was lost, and it was called folklore. That is how Mapuche knowledge started to get lost.... Mapuche youth had no strength, they felt ashamed about their culture, about their language. And Mapuche people hid their own identity.... Mapuche history, Mapuche stories did not make it into the school [system], and that is how Spanish became more important in the city, in the school, in public institutions. Mapuzugun was no longer needed.[46]

From the perspective of native Mapuzugun speakers today, however, the variations in the Mapuche language that have developed in each "territorial identity" do not reveal substantive changes in the deeper meanings, words, or expressions used in different territories. In practice, intelligibility and communication between speakers from different "territorial identities," as well as urban Mapuzugun speakers, have not been affected.[47] As such, the foundation for Mapuche spatial planning remains intact. Not only that, but the processes of language revitalization unfolding both on the reservations and in cities, as we elaborate in the following pages, are forms of resistance and resurgence that are actively paving the way for the reconstruction of Mapuche territory.

Mapuche Toponymy: Naming the Land, Enacting the Law

We have shown how Mapuzugun—as the language of *mapu* and of the people who inhabit it, as the language of space, and therefore as the language of territory and all its elements—is a crosscutting element that articulates how the Mapuche nation organizes itself and its territory. We have also suggested that the notion of *az mapu* is foundational to understanding Mapuche spatial planning, providing normative grounds for land distribution, settlement, and use, and delineating both restrictions and protective principles to safeguard those spaces that have ceremonial or patrimonial significance, or that people hold special spiritual connections to. Here we argue that to the extent that *az mapu* norms have also guided the designation of place-names in Mapuzugun and defined how people should interact with each space, Mapuche toponyms are one of the cornerstones of Mapuche spatial planning. On the one hand, the existence of Mapuzugun place-names to this day is an undeniable confirmation of Mapuche settlement and territorial presence in Wallmapu over the centuries. On the other, toponyms have historically outlined a particular way of living on the territory, including what types of activities and relations could be carried out or not in particular spaces. They embody a grounded normativity "based on deep reciprocity, that [is] inherently informed by an intimate relationship to place."[48]

Although always expressed in Mapuzugun, it is important to distinguish between diverse types of place-names associated with different aspects of Mapuche sociocultural, economic, and spiritual life. Toponyms first emerged as a way to describe and interact with the territory (Table 8.2), so names like Kolüko (red waters) capture the natural features of a particular place, such as the presence or abundance of certain flora and fauna, the color of the soil, or the existence of significant stones. Others designate and authorize subsistence or economic activities, such as those related to the production of certain goods. For instance, Ukuwe denotes the place where it was possible to extract *uku*, a kind of little stone used in pottery making to make ceramics more resistant to high temperatures. Until this day, there are still remnants of the place where this ancestral activity used to occur. Similarly, Wampolwe is the place where *wampos* were crafted. Originally, *wampos* were the coffins where the dead were put to rest as they embarked on their journey to *wenu mapu*, but the term also describes everyday means of transportation like punts, canoes, and even larger vessels. Other toponyms signal landmarks that invite ceremony, honoring, and respect, as is the case for significant natural forces like the Llaima volcano or ceremonial spaces like *nguillatuwe*. Anküwe (*ankü* means deserted, dry, treeless, the notion of being breathless) is a famous and respected ancient hill near the Tolten River. It is a place of special significance that possesses spiritual characteristics. Similarly, a landmark hill called Azankul, near the town of Victoria in the Araucanía Region, is especially significant, since its topography and vantage point allowed the Mapuche people to view the vast horizon of the territory, from the Llaima volcano in the Andes Mountains to the Pacific Ocean.

TABLE 8.2 Toponymy in Wallmapu

PLACE-NAME	MEANING
Anküwe	Dry place / place where things get dry
Hueñivales	Friend / friendly
Kautin	Cut river
Kitrawe	Arable land
Kolüko	Red waters
Kurra Mawiza	Rocky mountain
Llaima	Respected / respectable
Longko Kapurra	Goat head
Lonkimay	Thick / dense head
Malalkawellu	Horse corral
Malleko	Paternal uncle
Pagipüllü	Land of pumas
Piren Wigkul	Snowy mountain
Rukapillan	Home of the spirits
Tolwaka	Cow forehead
Txürwa	Gathering place
Ukuwe	Place to extract *uku* (little stone used for pottery)
Wampolwe	*Wampo* (canoe)-building place

While toponyms emerged from *az mapu* to describe and define particular ways of engaging with and planning the territory, the everyday and ceremonial use of Mapuzugun to communicate with the land and with *gen* (spiritual entities that are the caretakers of a particular space) is what enacts those normative principles, giving life to and nurturing such interrelations. Mapuche people speaking the language are the vehicles of *az mapu*. As such, the loss of the language in the current context of Mapuche subordination has not only disrupted intergenerational knowledge transmission but also the exercise of customary law and the reproduction of Mapuche spatial-planning principles.

In fact, the *fvchakeche* have observed a direct correlation between the loss of language, the weakening of cultural practices, the impossibility to communicate with the territory, and the loss of native flora and fauna. Historically, Mapuche people have engaged with the land in Mapuzugun through prayer asking for the presence of *lawen* (medicine), for the waters to flow, and for rain to nurture the landscape and provide all the elements for subsistence; the land would respond to such requests. Today, large areas in Wallmapu have been devastated by the forestry industry and large-scale exotic tree plantations that have destroyed the native forest and *ixofillmogen*.[49] In spite of this, there are still some pockets of native vegetation in some areas. In places where native forest still exists, like Foliko or Xuf Xuf, the elders have observed how the presence of medicinal plants and the way the lands and waters respond vary from territory to territory, depending on the strength of the presence of Mapuzugun in different areas. In regions where people still speak the language and do ceremony in Mapuzugun, like Xuf Xuf, they can still communicate with the land and receive what they ask through their prayers, like the subsistence of wetlands, the growth of certain medicines, or changes in the weather and the presence of rain when they pray to the *wigkul* (hill). In Foliko, on the other hand, where the language has been totally lost (although there is still some native forest left), people can no longer communicate with the *wigkul*, and medicine has suddenly disappeared.

Over the last four decades, important efforts have emerged to revitalize the language, both within communities living on reservations and in urban areas, deepening the more informal, organic processes of familiar language transmission happening across generations in some places.[50] For instance, member communities of the Mapuche Territorial Alliance—a grassroots organization working for the reconstruction of the Mapuche nation through the restoration of its processes—have organized internally to deepen and restore the use of Mapuzugun by actually conducting their gatherings and ceremonial activities in the language and by encouraging people to speak it at home.[51] In a more formalized fashion, other grassroots organizations like the Federación Mapuche de Estudiantes (FEMAE) have led language-immersion camp programs like the Internado Lingüístico Kimayiñ Tayiñ Mapuzugun. In collaboration with the Academia Nacional del Mapuzugun and the Comunidad de Historia Mapuche, the explicit purpose of this three-week initiative is to teach, practice, and strengthen the Mapuzugun language among Mapuche and non-Indigenous students.[52] At the level of local governance, thanks to local Mapuche mobilization, the municipalities of Galvarino and Padre Las Casas have made Mapuzugun one of their official languages, in addition to Spanish.[53] Besides their symbolic significance, measures of this kind extend the reach of the language and provide Mapuzugun speakers with culturally pertinent services. In large cities like Santiago, grassroots urban Mapuche initiatives like Universidad Libre Mapuche have offered Mapuzugun language classes for children and adults, Mapuche and non-Mapuche alike. Universidad Libre Mapuche is an independent educational project grounded in a critical intercultural approach that seeks to share Mapuche education perspectives on different fronts, including language revitalization, critical Mapuche history, and Indigenous policy analysis.[54] Bilingual radio shows like *Wixage anai* (loosely translated as *Wake Up, Get Up*), which first saw the light in 1993, have also played a crucial role in positioning Mapuzugun in mainstream media and providing a platform for Mapuche content and knowledge, expanding the role played by rural community radio stations historically and today.[55] Some Mapuche poets have taken up the written word to capture Mapuche experiences and use the Mapuzugun language with political as well as expressive purposes.[56] More broadly, the growing presence of urban *rukas* (traditional Mapuche dwellings and gathering spaces) in cities like Santiago is one more expression of Mapuche self-determination; they also serve as cultural hubs where Mapuche language, traditions, and knowledges find place.[57]

We see these acts of resistance and resurgence stretch well beyond attempts to rebuild a language base, strengthen cultural cohesiveness, and ensure intergenerational knowledge reproduction. By restoring the integrity of Mapuche processes, they also lay the foundation for the reconstruction of Mapuche territory.[58]

Reclaiming the Language, Reclaiming the Land: Mapuzugun Revitalization as Territorial Reconstruction

One of the first written records about the Mapuzugun language in what is now known as Chile was authored by Spanish Jesuit missionary Luis de Valdivia. Titled *Arte, y gramatica general de la lengua que corre en todo el Reyno de Chile, con un vocabulario, y confessonario* [*sic*], the book describes the vitality and geographical reach of Mapuzugun, the use of which stretched from the surroundings of Coquimbo in the north to Reloncaví Sound "and beyond" in the south.[59] Other historical sources, such as the writings of Chilean Jesuit abbot Juan Ignacio Molina, also confirm the linguistic richness and communicative capacity of the Mapuche language in relation to the needs and ways of life of its speakers.[60]

Despite vast historical evidence about the strength and continuation of Mapuzugun, this essay started from the acknowledgment of the relations of subordination, domination, and internal colonialism that the Mapuche nation experiences today.[61] As we discussed in the introduction, the cultural instruments that define such relationships have been unilaterally imposed by the dominant Chilean society and are grounded in a Western and monocultural rationality.[62] Examples include the legal system and its regulatory mechanisms, the educational system, and existing spatial-planning systems that are founded on the occupation of Mapuche territory and have forcefully produced behaviors and ways of speaking, thinking, and doing that impact the Mapuche nation as a collective. These mechanisms materialize the coloniality of power underlying Chile's nation building, the "long-standing patterns of power that emerged as a result of colonialism, but that define culture, labor, intersubjective relations, and knowledge production well beyond the strict limits of colonial administrations," targeting Indigenous knowledges, ways of being, and existence.[63]

As Melin, Coliqueo, Curihuinca, and Royo argue, given the current state of subordination and domination of the Mapuche people, *fvchakeche* and *wechekeche* (young leaders) are seeking to reconstruct the notion of *kuyfi*, which can be understood as the idea of ancestral territory that existed prior to the Chilean occupation of Wallmapu.[64] In this context marked by territorial fragmentation and loss of the language, the cultural practices and conceptual enactments that subsist in Wallmapu—as well as among the survivors of the military occupation now living in urban areas who are committed to the revitalization of Mapuzugun—can be seen through the lenses of resistance and resurgence that have emerged from the ancestral territorial unit known as *lofmapu*.[65] This is where the cultural foundation that enables ceremony can be found, allowing Mapuche people to reenact and consolidate Mapuche ways of being, both on their ancestral territory as they have done since time immemorial and in the spaces where they have been forced to migrate and where new forms of existence have unfolded. In the face of state violence, we understand the persistence of Mapuzugun and the reclamation of Mapuche toponyms throughout Wallmapu today as a clear expression of the uninterrupted existence of Mapuche people on their territory and as a testimony to the subsistence of Mapuche spatial planning. They confirm the subsistence, validity, and application of *az mapu* today. As Kahnawake Mohawk scholar Audra Simpson argues, these practices are the "invocation of the prior experience of sovereignty and nationhood, and their labor in the present . . . [as] people [think] and [act] as nationals in a scene of dispossession."[66]

Even more, the struggles for language revitalization, land recuperation, and the exercise of Mapuche law are in fact one. And restoring Mapuzugun—the language and the voice of the *mapu* as wholeness—is crucial to ensure the continuation of Mapuche connections to territory and the reconstruction of the Mapuche nation. For as Leanne Betasamosake Simpson clearly puts it, "Indigenous resurgence, in its most radical form, is nation building, not nation-state building, but nation building, again, in the context of grounded normativity by centring, amplifying, animating, and actualizing the processes of grounded normativity as flight paths or fugitive escapes from the violences of settler colonialism."[67]

Concluding Thoughts

What is the significance of foregrounding the inherent interconnections between Mapuche language, territory, and law for scholars and practitioners in the spatial disciplines? Why is the notion of grounded normativity relevant to discussions about planning in settler-colonial contexts?[68] And more specifically, how does understanding Mapuzugun as the basis for Mapuche spatial planning challenge or expand prevailing discussions about planning and Indigenous peoples today? We would like to conclude these pages by sketching some ways in which the argument we have developed takes planning theory in new directions.

First, as we briefly mentioned in the introduction, understanding Mapuche spatial planning as an expression of *az mapu* and governance openly situates Mapuche planning practices in the realm of the political and the normative.[69] As Ugarte argues, this framing moves away from conceptions that see Indigenous ways of planning just as a distinct form of planning grounded in cultural differences and in doing so discount Mapuche territorial claims and actions that are actually grounded in the exercise of a sovereign presence in place that predates the nation-state. On the contrary, a framing through the lens of grounded normativity helps to reconceptualize practices that might not often be seen as planning or, even more, that might appear to openly confront state planning of/on Mapuche territory, such as disregarding imposed national and internal borders, reclaiming Mapuche place-names, de facto land recuperation, and other forms of direct action in Wallmapu meant to reconstruct Mapuche territory. While often portrayed as transgressions to existing planning and private property regimes, in the case of what are now Chile and Argentina, we see these actions as expressions of *az mapu* and therefore as the exercise of Mapuche spatial planning.[70] These struggles echo Land Back movements that have strengthened in recent years that put forward the "demand to rightfully return colonized land . . . to Indigenous Peoples" in ways that enable the integrity of Indigenous life and sovereignty.[71] Not only do they put into question the legitimacy of state-led planning systems, but most crucially they illuminate how taken-for-granted planning assumptions no longer hold, including ideas about authority, legality/illegality, and ownership.

Closely connected to the idea above, it follows from our discussions that Mapuche spatial planning can be seen as a form of resistance in a context of internal colonialism, both through large-scale land recuperation actions and through everyday practices taking place on the territories. As Simpson suggests, the notion of grounded normativity gives visibility to practices that might not otherwise be seen as territorial resistance, such as the reclamation of toponyms, connecting to the land in Mapuzugun through ceremony, and efforts around language revitalization like the ones we have discussed.[72] The exercise of Mapuche spatial planning today signifies both the continuation and the resurgence of place-based ways of existing in and understanding space that emerge from particular connections to Mapuche territory. Importantly, as the Land Back Editorial Collective clearly puts it, Indigenous peoples are not "asking for just the ground. . . . [They] want the system that is land to be alive so that it can perpetuate itself, and perpetuate [Indigenous peoples] as an extension of itself."[73] In this way, by asserting the inseparability of language, territory, and law, Mapuche spatial planning is not just another form of understanding human-environment relations but a way of ensuring the continuation of a nation. In Simpson's words, "[G]rounded normativity has always fueled Indigenous resistance and continues to happen all the time in Indigenous communities—it is just often misread by others," which leads us to our last point.[74]

From the perspective we have developed here, processes that might not conventionally be seen as falling under the scope of planning, such as language revitalization, are inseparable from discussions about land recuperation, existence in place, and territorial reconstruction. Mapuche language revitalization efforts today could easily be portrayed as cultural survival practices among landless people in the face of settler-colonial dispossession, especially when such efforts take place in urban areas, far away from ancestral Mapuche lands. However, to the extent that Mapuzugun provides the foundation for Mapuche connections to territory and articulates the normative principles of *az mapu*, as we have argued, mobilization efforts to restore the language and the praxis of speaking Mapuzugun are in fact a central planning tool that is paving the ground for the continuation of Mapuche place-based connections to their territories and to each other. State-led planning efforts have actively sought to break down Mapuche life and political orders over the centuries precisely by targeting Indigenous peoples' relationship to land.[75] In the face of this violence, Mapuche spatial-planning practices that are founded on the interconnectedness between language, lands, and law rearticulate a vision for the future. The resurgence of Mapuche language is also the resurgence of Mapuche existence.

NOTES

1. Pablo González Casanova, *Democracy in Mexico*, 2nd ed. (New York: Oxford University Press, 1970).
2. Comisión Económica para América Latina y el Caribe (CEPAL) and Alianza Territorial Mapuche (ATM), *Desigualdades territoriales y exclusión social del pueblo mapuche en Chile: Situación en la comuna de Ercilla desde un enfoque de derechos* (Santiago: Naciones Unidas, 2012); and Víctor Toledo Llancaqueo, "Políticas indígenas y derechos territoriales en América Latina: 1990–2004; ¿Las fronteras indígenas de la globalización?," in *Pueblos indígenas, estado y democracia*, ed. Pablo Dávalos (Buenos Aires: CLACSO, 2005), 67–102.
3. Sergio Boisier Etcheverry, "Territorio, estado y sociedad en Chile: La dialéctica de la descentralización; Entre la geografía y la gobernabilidad" (PhD diss., Universidad de Alcalá, 2007); Magdalena Ugarte, "Antes de la ciudad: Reflexiones sobre la planificación territorial y urbana como instrumento de despojo indígena," in *Urbanización planetaria y la reconstrucción de la ciudad*, ed. Arturo Orellana, Felipe Link, and Juan Noyola (Santiago: RIL, 2016), 465–89; and Marcos Valdés, "Políticas públicas, planificación y pueblos indígenas en Chile," Centro de Documentación Mapuche, December 2001, http://www.mapuche.info/mapuint/Valdes011200.html.
4. Oren Yiftachel, "Planning and Social Control: Exploring the Dark Side," *Journal of Planning Literature* 12, no. 4 (1998): 395.
5. Magdalena Ugarte, Mauro Fontana, and Matthew Caulkins, "Urbanisation and Indigenous Dispossession: Rethinking the Spatio-Legal Imaginary in Chile vis-à-vis the Mapuche Nation," *Settler Colonial Studies* 9, no. 2 (2017): 187–206; and Andrés Estefane, "Estado y ordenamiento territorial en Chile, 1810–2016," in *Historia política de Chile, 1810–2010*, vol. 2, *Estado y sociedad*, ed. Francisca Rengifo (Santiago: Fondo de Cultura Económica, 2017), 87–138.
6. Glen Sean Coulthard, *Red Skin, White Masks: Rejecting the Colonial Politics of Recognition* (Minneapolis: University of Minnesota Press, 2014); Hirini Matunga, "Theorizing Indigenous Planning," in *Reclaiming Indigenous Planning*, ed. Ryan Walker, Ted Jojola, and David Natcher (Montreal: McGill-Queen's University Press, 2013), 3–32; Libby Porter, *Unlearning the Colonial Cultures of Planning* (Farnham: Ashgate, 2010); and Héctor Nahuelpan Moreno, "Formación colonial del Estado y desposesión en Ngulumapu," in *Ta iñ fijke xipa rakizuameluwün: Historia, colonialismo y resistencia desde el país mapuche*, ed. Héctor Nahuelpan Moreno et al. (Temuco: Comunidad de Historia Mapuche, 2013), 119–52.
7. Miguel Melin Pehuen, Patricio Coliqueo Collipal, Elsy Curihuinca Neira, and Manuela Royo Letelier, *AzMapu: Una aproximación al sistema normativo mapuche desde el rakizuam y el derecho propio* (Santiago: published independently, 2016).
8. Elisa Loncon Antileo, "El mapuzugun desde el pensamiento mapuche: Pasado, presente y futuro," *Americanía: Revista de estudios latinoamericanos* (2017): 204–19; José Quidel Lincoleo, "Chumgelu ka chumgechi pu mapuche ñi kuxankagepan ka hotukagepan ñi rakizuam ka ñi püjü zugu mew," in *Awükan ka kuxankan zugu Wajmapu mew: Violencias coloniales en Wajmapu*, ed. Enrique Antileo Baeza, Luis Cárcamo-Huechante, Margarita Calfío Montalva, and Herson Huinca-Piutrin (Temuco: Comunidad de Historia Mapuche, 2015), 21–56; and Juan Porma Oñate, "Violencia colonial en la escuela: El caso de la comunidad José Porma en el siglo XX," in *Awükan ka kuxankan zugu Wajmapu mew: Violencias coloniales en Wajmapu*, ed. Enrique Antileo Baeza, Luis Cárcamo-Huechante, Margarita Calfío Montalva, and Herson Huinca-Piutrin (Temuco: Comunidad de Historia Mapuche, 2015), 189–206.
9. Instituto Nacional de Estadísticas, *Síntesis de resultados: Censo 2017*, June 2018, https://www.censo2017.cl/descargas/home/sintesis-de-resultados-censo2017.pdf.
10. Miguel Melin Pehuen, Pablo Mansilla Quiñones, and Manuela Royo Letelier, *Cartografía cultural del Wallmapu: Elementos para descolonizar el mapa en territorio mapuche* (Santiago: LOM, 2019).
11. We approach this work from our different standpoints but shared commitments. Miguel is a Mapuche researcher, intercultural educator, and Mapuzugun speaker, as well as one of the founders of the Mapuche Territorial Alliance, a grassroots organization that advances cultural and political resurgence. He has led numerous community-based research projects and coauthored publications about Mapuche cultural knowledge, law, and counter-mapping in order to support the territorial demands of his people. Magdalena is a Chilean planning scholar and educator whose research and teaching examine the relationship between planning, law, and settler-colonial dispossession while also striving to put academic work at the service of Indigenous planning agendas. The reflections we present here emerge from years

of joint research work, conversations, and a shared concern for the possibilities of Mapuche planning in the larger project of Mapuche territorial reconstruction given today's context of internal colonialism.

12 Melin, Coliqueo, Curihuinca, and Royo, *AzMapu*, 28.
13 Melin, Mansilla, and Royo, *Cartografía cultural del Wallmapu*.
14 Ted Jojola, "Indigenous Planning—An Emerging Context," *Canadian Journal of Urban Research* 17, no. 1 (2008); and Matunga, "Theorizing Indigenous Planning."
15 Coulthard, *Red Skin, White Masks*.
16 Magdalena Ugarte Urzua, "Normative Worlds Clashing: State Planning, Indigenous Self-Determination, and the Possibilities of Legal Pluralism in Chile" (PhD diss., University of British Columbia, 2019), 164–87.
17 Leanne Betasamosake Simpson, "Indigenous Resurgence and Co-resistance," *Critical Ethnic Studies* 2, no. 2 (Fall 2016): 24. See also Jeff Corntassel, "Toward Sustainable Self-Determination: Rethinking the Contemporary Indigenous-Rights Discourse," *Alternatives* 33, no. 1 (January–March 2008): 105–32; *Ta iñ fijke xipa rakizuameluwün: Historia, colonialismo y resistencia desde el país mapuche*, ed. Héctor Nahuelpan Moreno et al. (Temuco: Comunidad de Historia Mapuche, 2013); Melin, Coliqueo, Curihuinca, and Royo, *AzMapu*; Fernando Pairican, "Sembrando ideología: El *Aukiñ Wallmapu Ngulam* en la transición de Aylwin (1990–1994)," *SudHistoria*, no. 4 (January–July 2012): 12–42; Leanne Betasamosake Simpson, *Dancing on Our Turtle's Back: Stories of Nishnaabeg Re-creation, Resurgence and a New Emergence* (Winnipeg: Arbeiter Ring, 2011); and Toledo Llancaqueo, "Políticas indígenas y derechos territoriales en América Latina."
18 Simpson, "Indigenous Resurgence and Co-resistance," 26.
19 Melin, Mansilla, and Royo, *Cartografía cultural del Wallmapu*, 27.
20 Melin, Mansilla, and Royo, *Cartografía cultural del Wallmapu*, 36–37.
21 Melin, Mansilla, and Royo, *Cartografía cultural del Wallmapu*, 26.
22 Melin, Mansilla, and Royo, *Cartografía cultural del Wallmapu*, 26.
23 Melin, Coliqueo, Curihuinca, and Royo, *AzMapu*.
24 Melin, Coliqueo, Curihuinca, and Royo, *AzMapu*, 20.
25 Melin, Coliqueo, Curihuinca, and Royo, *AzMapu*, 22.
26 Melin, Coliqueo, Curihuinca, and Royo, *AzMapu*, 22.
27 C. F. Black, "On Lives Lived with Law: Land as Healer," *Law, Text, Culture* 20 (2017): 165.
28 Melin, Coliqueo, Curihuinca, and Royo, *AzMapu*, 22.
29 Melin, Coliqueo, Curihuinca, and Royo, *AzMapu*, 22.
30 Simpson, "Indigenous Resurgence and Co-resistance," 22.
31 Glen Coulthard and Leanne Betasamosake Simpson, "Grounded Normativity/Place-Based Solidarity," *American Quarterly* 68, no. 2 (2016): 254.
32 Simpson, "Indigenous Resurgence and Co-resistance," 22.
33 Melin, Coliqueo, Curihuinca, and Royo, *AzMapu*.
34 Government of Chile, *Informe de la Comisión de Verdad Histórica y Nuevo Trato con los pueblos indígenas* (Santiago: Comisionado Presidencial para Asuntos Indígenas, 2008), 387–90.
35 Carlos Contreras Painemal, "Los tratados celebrados por los mapuche con la Corona Española, la República de Chile y la República de Argentina," (PhD diss., Freien Universität Berlin, 2010); and CEPAL and ATM, *Desigualdades territoriales y exclusion*.
36 José Bengoa, *Historia del pueblo mapuche*, 3rd ed. (Santiago: SUR, 1996).
37 José Bengoa and Eduardo Valenzuela, *Economía mapuche: Pobreza y subsistencia en la sociedad mapuche contemporánea* (Santiago: PAS, 1984).
38 Sergio Caniuqueo Huircapan, "Antagonismo territorial, una tensión productiva para pensar el colonialismo chileno," *Revista articulando e construindo saberes* 5 (2020): 13 [translation our own].
39 Enrique Antileo Baeza, "Migración mapuche y continuidad colonial," in *Ta iñ fijke xipa rakizuameluwün: Historia, colonialismo y resistencia desde el país mapuche*, ed. Héctor Nahuelpan Moreno et al. (Temuco: Comunidad de Historia Mapuche, 2013), 193–213; and Álvaro Bello, "Migración, identidad y comunidad mapuche en Chile: Entre utopismos y realidades," *Asuntos indígenas*, nos. 3–4 (2002): 40–47.
40 Bengoa and Valenzuela, *Economía mapuche*.
41 Antileo Baeza, "Migración mapuche y continuidad colonial."
42 Bengoa, *Historia del pueblo mapuche*; and Loncon, "El mapuzugun desde el pensamiento mapuche," 209.

43 Instituto Nacional de Estadísticas, *Síntesis de resultados*.
44 Andrea Aravena, "Los mapuches-warriaches: Procesos migratorios contemporáneos e identidad mapuche urbana," *América indígena* 49, no. 4 (2003): 162–88.
45 Antileo Baeza, "Migración mapuche y continuidad colonial."
46 Loncon, "El mapuzugun desde el pensamiento mapuche," 214–15 [translation our own].
47 Loncon, "El mapuzugun desde el pensamiento mapuche," 215.
48 Coulthard and Simpson, "Grounded Normativity/Place-Based Solidarity," 254.
49 Mauro Fontana, "Cuarenta años de transformaciones socio-espaciales en el territorio nagche de Lumaco" (master's thesis, Pontificia Universidad Católica de Chile, 2008).
50 María Catrileo, "Revitalización de la lengua mapuche en Chile," *Documentos lingüísticos y literarios UACh*, no. 28 (2005); and Loncon, "El mapuzugun desde el pensamiento mapuche."
51 "La reconstrucción como eje de nuestra práctica política," Alianza Territorial Mapuche, n.d., https://www.alianzaterritorialmapuche.com/p/la-reconstruccion-como-eje-de-nuestra.html.
52 "Internado lingüístico 'kimayiñ tayiñ mapuzugun,'" Comunidad de Historia Mapuche, March 2, 2015, https://www.comunidadhistoriamapuche.cl/internado-linguistico-kimayin-tayin-mapuzugun/.
53 Loncon, "El mapuzugun desde el pensamiento mapuche," 216.
54 "Quiénes somos," Universidad Libre Mapuche, n.d., https://ulmapuche.wordpress.com/about/.
55 Luis Cárcamo-Huechante and Elías Paillan Coñoepan, "Taiñ pu amulzugue egvn: Sonidos y voces del Wajmapu en el aire," in *Ta iñ fijke xipa rakizuameluwün: Historia, colonialismo y resistencia desde el país mapuche*, ed. Héctor Nahuelpan Moreno et al. (Temuco: Comunidad de Historia Mapuche, 2013), 341–58.
56 Loncon, "El mapuzugun desde el pensamiento mapuche," 217; and Maribel Mora Curriao, "Poesía mapuche del siglo XX: Escribir desde los márgenes del campo literario," in *Ta iñ fijke xipa rakizuameluwün: Historia, colonialismo y resistencia desde el país mapuche*, ed. Héctor Nahuelpan Moreno et al. (Temuco: Comunidad de Historia Mapuche, 2013), 305–39.
57 Rosario Carmona Yost, *Rukas mapuche en la ciudad: Cartografía patrimonial de la región metropolitana* (Santiago: Universidad Academia de Humanismo Cristiano, 2017).
58 Melin, Coliqueo, Curihuinca, and Royo, *AzMapu*; and Simpson, *Dancing on Our Turtle's Back*.
59 Luis de Valdivia, *Arte, y gramatica general de la lengua que corre en todo el Reyno de Chile, con un vocabulario, y confessonario* [sic] (Sevilla: Thomás López de Haro, 1684).
60 Juan Ignacio Molina, *Compendio de la historia civil del Reyno de Chile*, vol. 2 (Madrid: A. de Sancha, 1795).
61 González Casanova, *Democracy in Mexico*; and Silvia Rivera Cusicanqui, *Ch'ixinakax utxiwa: Una reflexión sobre prácticas y discursos descolonizadores* (Buenos Aires: Tinta Limón, 2010).
62 Melin, Coliqueo, Curihuinca, and Royo, *AzMapu*.
63 Nelson Maldonado-Torres, "On the Coloniality of Being: Contributions to the Development of a Concept," *Cultural Studies* 21, nos. 2–3 (2007): 243. See also Aníbal Quijano, "Colonialidad del poder, eurocentrismo y América Latina," in *La colonialidad del saber: Eurocentrismo y ciencias sociales; Perspectivas latinoamericanas*, ed. Edgardo Lander (Buenos Aires: CLACSO, 2000), 201–46.
64 Melin, Coliqueo, Curihuinca, and Royo, *AzMapu*, 22–23.
65 Simpson, *Dancing on Our Turtle's Back*; and Melin, Coliqueo, Curihuinca, and Royo, *AzMapu*, 68.
66 Audra Simpson, *Mohawk Interruptus: Political Life across the Borders of Settler States* (Durham, N.C.: Duke University Press, 2014), 33.
67 Simpson, "Indigenous Resurgence and Co-resistance," 22.
68 Coulthard, *Red Skin, White Masks*.
69 Ugarte, "Normative Worlds Clashing," 187–88.
70 Melin, Coliqueo, Curihuinca, and Royo, *AzMapu*.
71 Nickita Longman, Emily Riddle, Alex Wilson, and Saima Desai, "'Land Back' Is More Than the Sum of Its Parts," *Briarpatch*, September 10, 2020, https://briarpatchmagazine.com/articles/view/land-back-is-more-than-the-sum-of-its-parts. See also Ella Hartsoe, "Land Back beyond Borders," *Briarpatch*, March 1, 2021, https://briarpatchmagazine.com/articles/view/land-back-beyond-borders; and Julie Tomiak, "Land Back/Cities Back," *Urban Geography* 44, no. 2 (2023): 292–94.
72 Simpson, *Dancing on Our Turtle's Back*.
73 Longman, Riddle, Wilson, and Desai, "'Land Back' Is More Than the Sum of Its Parts."
74 Simpson, "Indigenous Resurgence and Co-resistance," 25.
75 Coulthard and Simpson, "Grounded Normativity/Place-Based Solidarity."

9

Moving with Land

BlackIndigenous Stories of Place

NNENNA ODIM AND PAVITHRA VASUDEVAN*

Introduction: "The Face Starts to Look like a Whole Land"

The children's storybook *Auntie Luce's Talking Paintings* (hereafter referred to as *Talking Paintings*) opens with a girl, Ti Chou, describing a painting in her mother's bedroom in an unnamed location, a place that could be many lands, away from their family home in Ayiti. It is a painting of her face, eyes closed and dreaming. "[I]f you look long enough," she tells us, "it starts to look like a whole land—brown hills melting into yellow valleys melting into red riverbeds, and even the rivers' silver light, running smooth over the rocks."[1] On the facing page (Figure 9.1), Ti Chou's face appears as a mountain outlined in the land. Her neck folds into the curves of hills under a setting sun. The brushstrokes, filling in her brown skin, blend into the "yellow valleys melting into red riverbeds." Her braids trail into flocks of birds, a gentle breeze, then a river's flow. Her closed eyelids direct our attention toward an internal register of how the body feels, senses, and imagines the possibilities in life. The body is a repository for memories of land, sky, and water.

This portrait of Ti Chou, and the fluid colors that disappear the boundaries of body and earth, offers an imaginary of caring for place that we read as the everyday relationality of BlackIndigenous diasporic life. BlackIndigenous people hold knowledges of the lands that they live with and move through, knowledges held by and transmitted through young children. In this story of self-discovery, a young BlackIndigenous girl leaves her parents and cold winters, returning to Ayiti, the land of mountains and her family home, where she reconnects with her roots while spending time with her mother's sister, Auntie Luce.

---

* We are grateful to Dr. Nicole Burrowes for her guidance with scholarship on race and Indigeneity in the Caribbean. University of Texas, Austin, undergraduates Pradhitha Boppana and Trin Viet Ho assisted us with citations and proofreading.

FIGURE 9.1 Ti Chou's face appears as a mountain outlined in the land. Images from *Auntie Luce's Talking Paintings* reproduced with permission from Groundwood Books, Toronto. Text copyright © 2018 by Francie Latour, illustrations copyright © 2018 by Ken Daley. www.groundwoodbooks.com.

From Auntie Luce, Ti Chou learns about everyday life in Ayiti[2] while cooking oatmeal for breakfast and black mushrooms for dinner and while shopping at the market with an aural backdrop of tap-tap buses, the ocean's tides, and boys selling water. In conversations with Auntie Luce about why she paints, Ti Chou learns what being Ayitian means in the aftermath of enslavement, displacement, and revolution.

Auntie Luce's interactions with Ti Chou reveal the body as an archive of place, in which place is not singular but a layering of relations that comprise BlackIndigenous life. Caribbean scholar Alexis Pauline Gumbs describes how the bodily archive becomes a repository of life, at once holding the geopolitical histories that have ruptured relations to place and the sense of belonging that persists in the face of displacement.[3] The body, Tonawanda theorist Mishuana Goeman reminds us, is not the individual, impermeable, and sovereign entity of colonial imagining.[4] Rather, the body operates simultaneously across three relational scales: the individual body in relation with community; the individual in relation with land and more-than-human life; and the community's social body in relation with national bodies of settler states. In collapsing the settler-imposed hierarchy of scales, an Indigenous feminist reading of the body reveals "a wrestling to find a place in which the spatial and temporal are not controlled solely by settler discourse and bodies and lands become conduits of connection rather than impermeable entities."[5]

In this final essay of the collection, we offer a close reading of the children's book *Talking Paintings*, penned by Ayitian writer Francie Latour and illustrated by Dominican-Canadian artist Ken Daley. We read for the possibilities of thinking *with* children as our guides, in considering how knowledges of place are carried and conveyed by BlackIndigenous people across generations. With Francie Latour's storybook as a guiding text, we nuance how BlackIndigenous people of the Caribbean, whose "bodies and lands [are] conduits of connection," hold relations to place across dividing lines of nations, physical geographies, and generations. Given the complex entanglements of identity and place in the enduring afterlife of colonization, particularly in the Caribbean context, BlackIndigeneity as an analytic reminds us that building liberatory futures is necessarily a coalitional project. Alongside and beyond sovereignty, Land Back movements are calls for repairing relations to place(s) and more-than-human kin ruptured by colonial racial capitalism. The embodied storytelling practices that have transmitted BlackIndigenous place-based knowledges offer crucial lessons while battling for territorial integrity and sustaining honored ways of life. In particular, we attend to young children as important actors in BlackIndigenous history. Latour's storytelling animates BlackIndigenous children as archivists in ancestral knowledges that account for, yet move beyond, the violences of colonial racial capitalism.

On this visit to Ayiti, when Ti Chou sits to be painted by Auntie Luce, she learns that history is more than simply bright colors, that the spectrum of colors from light to dark is necessary to speak to the complexity of BlackIndigenous life. Auntie Luce's "talking paintings" become Ti Chou's friends, portraying lesser-known Ayitian heroes like Sanité Bélair and Catherine Flon alongside Ti Chou's elders. From these paintings, Ti Chou seeks and finds her place in a BlackIndigenous lineage of "arrivants" to the Caribbean, who have sustained and rebuilt relations to place and kin through forced and voluntary migrations.[6] Latour's reimagining of the body beyond the individual, and of place beyond the here and now, "ground[s] relationality to the physical ruptures of land beyond possession and dispossession."[7] We invite you to this reading of Ti Chou's journey to Ayiti, bringing into focus the reverberations of revolution, heartache, uncertainty, and, crucially, joy as entangled histories of BlackIndigenous life that, as Auntie Luce describes, are "almost too hard to look at."[8]

In the section that follows, "Context: BlackIndigenous Geographies of the Caribbean," we introduce BlackIndigeneity as an analytic grounded in solidarity and relationality across the entangled and divisive histories of racism and coloniality in the Caribbean. In "Methodology: Reading Beyond the Frame," we explain how we read images as translations of sensorial experience and as reflecting bodily and place-based BlackIndigenous knowledges that exceed the frame of the page. Our analysis of *Talking Paintings* will speak to three key themes that emerge through close reading. In the section "To Paint History Takes Darkness, Brightness, and All the Colors In Between," we discuss how Auntie Luce's paintings articulate an anticolonial geopoetics,[9] an imaginary of BlackIndigenous futurity that emerges from within the interstices of colonial racial domination. In the section "Our Faces Are like Maps," we consider how the geopolitics of African diasporic life reverberate in the body as collective memories of homes now and past. In the section "I Wonder What Stories [My Hands] Will Tell," we engage questions of uncertainty, ancestry, and belonging within lineages as generating possibilities for solidarity against domination.

Context: BlackIndigenous Geographies of the Caribbean

Our use of the term "BlackIndigenous" draws on the work of Amber Starks, Robin Boylorn, and Dominique Hill, who refuse the colonial grammars that force separation or division across plural identities.[10] Boylorn and Hill's work speaks to the enforced separation of gender and race for young Blackgirls, for whom these categories are intertwined in shaping their lived experience. Extending this strategy, we recognize that if BlackIndigenous were written otherwise, the space inserted in written text would serve as a syntactical boundary reinforcing the notion that Blackness and Indigeneity are fundamentally distinct and irreconcilable categories. We use the term "BlackIndigenous" to recognize and counter what Claude Ake describes as the coloniality of knowledge written into the structure and equilibrium of the English language by which the complex and intersecting historical processes of uprisings, enslavement, conquest, and genocide are reduced to discrete identities.[11] In reviewing how Blackness and Indigeneity are constructed as discrete categories, Bennett Brazelton describes Black Indigeneity as "first, the filiation of Black and Native peoples and the enduring history of Black Natives; second, recognizing African indigeneity and the Black diaspora as a spread of indigenous peoples; third, the multiple complications of space and place brought about by the question of indigenization."[12] With BlackIndigenous, we build on conversations happening across Black and Indigenous studies to invite the possibility of shared relational space into the tense vacuums created by the disciplinary siloing of colonial knowledge production. We also seek to redress the erasure of Black life from the purview of Indigenous studies, itself a form of anti-Black violence, even as we grapple with the particular histories of Blackness and Indigeneity in the Caribbean that caution us from conflation or equivalence.

The histories of land, labor, and life in the Caribbean highlight the many entanglements that exist as a result of empire and expansion and the challenges to building relations of solidarity in the aftermath of colonization. The production of racialized difference[13] in the Caribbean was steeped in colonial desires to steal land, establish plantations, and create internal and communal strife. D. Alissa Trotz and Linda Peake, for example, describe how African and Indian women, who faced similar struggles and conditions as plantation workers, came to be racialized very differently in terms of sexuality, domesticity, and capacity for wage labor when enslavement and indentured labor regimes ended and their utility as laborers was no longer a primary consideration.[14] In these ways, as colonial descriptors became fixed as markers of identity and status, they sublimated the shared experience of being colonized, shaping Caribbean freedom struggles along distinctly racialized terms. However, as Nicole Burrowes's work on 1930s Guyana shows, even when Black and Indian workers organized in solidarity to challenge the plantation economy's racial logics, their struggle did not recognize "the colonial logic of erasure that existed and undergirded their labour."[15] Amerindian/Indigenous peoples who were systematically made invisible by the British imperial state—dispossessed from coastal areas to interior lands and excluded from the census and local governance—came to be "positioned as outsiders, non-citizens and nonentities," where Black and Brown peoples were enrolled as subjects.[16]

Caribbean scholars have shown how colonizers framed Black and Brown peoples in the Caribbean as "native" to undermine Indigenous claims to land, a settler-colonial strategy of Indigenous dispossession and disappearance that persists today. For some scholars, this clearly positions Black and Indian peoples in the Caribbean as complicit in ongoing settler colonialism.[17] For other scholars, the entanglements of Indigenous dispossession with the processes of enslavement and indentured labor that brought African and Indian peoples to the Caribbean complicate questions of complicity, even as they recognize the Caribbean as Indigenous space.[18] Melanie J. Newton offers important context for understanding claims to Indigeneity by Caribbean anti-colonial nationalists in the 1960s of African and Indian descent. She suggests that in struggling to reconcile their diasporic status with the prevalent discourses of "third world" decolonization movements, whose claims to sovereignty were based on Nativeness, they "[collapsed] the Caribbean's historical trajectories of diasporization and aboriginality into one another."[19]

We recognize that Caribbean identity formation has multiple and varied trajectories with significant political stakes. How people identify today is, on the one hand, the product of how their ancestors were racialized or invisibilized during colonization and, on the other, a consequence of how identities were (re)claimed in anti-colonial projects for self-determination in response to and in the aftermath of colonization. Communities of mixed African/Indian and Indigenous descent have at times offered radical critiques of state projects while in other instances have served to justify the ongoing coloniality of the state.[20] Blackness, Brownness, and Indigeneity have been variably configured in the Caribbean to justify settler colonialism and its continuation in postcolonial states, highlighting the parasitic infrastructures of white supremacy and colonial racial capitalism that divide communities resisting domination.

Building on Maile Arvin's framework of Indigeneity as an analytic, we suggest that BlackIndigeneity allows us to hold together the contradictory tendencies of how anti-Black racism and coloniality articulate in the Caribbean, at times enrolling Black people in the settler-colonial project and, at other times, ignoring the continuity of their ancestral practices and claims to Indigeneity.[21] In articulating BlackIndigenous as an analytic, we question the reduction and fixity implicit in approaching Blackness and Indigeneity as stationary categories and gesture toward the possibility of solidarity and relationality. We do so in response to Leanne Betasamosake Simpson's call for "place based ethical frameworks" that transcend racial and colonial divisions and reimagine relationships between Black, Indigenous, and other racialized peoples as "constellations" that reorient liberation as a coalitional project of fugitivity and futurity.[22] Echoing and building on Simpson, Michelle Daigle and Margaret Marietta Ramírez describe decolonial geographies as "constellations in formation," which they describe as "the embodied knowledge of Indigenous peoples coming into dialogue and relationship with those of Black and other dispossessed peoples."[23]

In naming BlackIndigeneity, we turn our attention to the complex, and at times uncertain, ways that relationality persists in the everyday life, communal practices, and social-ecological relations of Caribbean peoples of African descent. In doing so, we understand "indigeneity as not just a category determined by racism and colonialism but also by the knowledge and praxis of indigenous peoples," in this case African-descendant Indigenous peoples, for whom practices, rather than birthright, may serve as the basis of coalitional politics.[24] As Arvin recognizes, the claim to Indigeneity can serve to counter or reproduce coloniality and racism. In Puerto Rico, Guyana, the Dominican Republic, and other countries in the Spanish Caribbean, "sometimes people cling to their Indigenous heritage, to the point of sometimes erasing the African."[25] By contrast, in Ayiti, Africanness stands strongly with los Arawakos. Ayiti is a country where beautiful mahogany and ash complexions situate Indigeneity within—rather than in opposition to—Blackness. While some historians contest whether Taíno Arawak people survived colonization, some Ayitians claim Arawakan and African descent in the same breath. We find it significant that the name Ayiti, an Arawak word, was claimed by revolutionaries for the emergent republic to honor the anti-colonial spirit of those who had cared for the lands for lifetimes prior to colonization.[26]

Here, we attend to how ways of life develop in relation to local land- and waterscapes among communities racialized or self-identifying as Black or African, as well as among those communities of mixed ancestry who explicitly claim Indigeneity.[27] Within this analytic, BlackIndigenous describes many African diasporic peoples across the Caribbean who hold "local knowledges" of the land.[28] We draw on this children's storybook, set in the lands of Ayiti, to grapple with how revolutionary Caribbean histories coexist with imperial exploitation and economic suffocation, fueled by fear of BlackIndigenous power. Amid contemporary conversations that detail the challenges of everyday life in the Caribbean, this storybook describes a young child returning to these lands to discover her identity through connections with history, place, and ancestry.

We see BlackIndigeneity as generatively expanding what Simpson calls the "ecology of intimacy," the possibilities of consensual relations that expand "connectivity based on the sanctity of the land."[29] We see three implications to our reading of *Talking Paintings* as a guiding text for BlackIndigeneity. First, BlackIndigenous children are foregrounded as vital participants in storytelling who hold and retell memories, disrupting the uneven power dynamics in who can recall intimate place relations. Within storytelling, we can trace a child's connections across lands and waters, illuminating how the bodies of community, land, more-than-human life, and the social body in relation to (and exceeding) the settler state.[30] Second, we consider how colors and textures offer expressive literacies in BlackIndigenous storytelling that work alongside, but move beyond, the written word. Third, we are alerted to broader political implications where uncertainty generates questions of Black and Indigenous political projects that accept colonial divisions.

Methodology: Reading Beyond the Frame

Our methods of reading beyond the frame for the vibrancy and viscerality of images are influenced by Tina M. Campt's work on Black visuality. In particular, Campt's notion of "still-moving-images" describes images as affective registers.[31] To feel with and through images requires that we engage the "overlapping sensory realms of the visual, the sonic, the haptic, and the affective labor that constellates in, around, and in response to such images."[32] In analyzing *Talking Paintings*, we closely examine each page to read beyond the frame, speculating upon the before and the after of images. We read for details in the illustrations—the brushstrokes and vibrant hues of teal, magenta, and chestnut; in the placement of blank spaces and shadows; in the facial expressions and body postures of characters; and in the foregrounding and backgrounding of images. We analyze images by imagining how Ti Chou's character and, by extension, BlackIndigenous children may receive and understand their ancestry. We reflect on the histories specific to BlackIndigenous life that are registered by the composition of the illustrations and speculate on the significance of particular images considered alongside the words on the page. Focusing on the body as an archive, we consider how gestures and text conveying emotional and sensorial experiences might index ruptures and recoveries that show up as embodied experiences.

In this storybook, moments of embodied learning, rooted in the intimate ecologies of BlackIndigenous life, occur through the person of Ti Chou, a young child who learns about Ayitian history from speaking with her Auntie Luce and observing her body movements while she paints. We join Indigenous scholars like Yankton Dakota writer Zitkala-Sa who narrates children's embodied experiences resisting colonial education, writing in the early twentieth-century context of resisting exploitation in Indian boarding schools.[33] In one short story about beadwork, Zitkala-Sa watches her mother's fingers twist the needle to string tiny beads one by one. Learning how to thread the white sinew and noticing the finger twists, close eye attention, and slow body movements were embodied aspects of learning the ways of her people.[34] Like Zitkala-Sa, Ti Chou watches Auntie Luce closely while sitting to be painted. To understand these moments as aspects of storytelling is to recognize what Tanana Athabascan theorist Dian Million theorizes as felt knowledges, "colonialism as it is *felt* by those whose experience it is."[35] The emotions felt by communities who experience the atrocities of colonizers and the resulting poison of colonialism are, in Million's work, a central aspect of Indigenous epistemologies, those inherited practices that organize and undergird human life and Indigenous relations to place.[36] Felt knowledges come from long-held connections with lands, waters, and beings. Felt knowledges inform actions and theory based on experiences and analysis, lending power to stories "that are otherwise separate to become a focus, a potential for movement"[37] and "significant political action."[38]

Young children closely observe elders, listen to histories, and notice movements as embodied and felt knowledges. In Ti Chou's storybook world, felt knowledges appear in the feeling of crouching on the stairs while overhearing conversations of family members talk about corrupt Ayitian leaders or in watching Auntie Luce take her time deciding colors while painting the dirt path to her studio. Auntie Luce translates sensorial experience by painting the history of Ayiti. Describing this experience through illustrations is an opportunity to communicate the many ways young children might feel connections to land, by reminiscing on color, texture, sensation, and emotions that move beyond the written word as knowledge. We draw connections to young children and the ways Million's felt knowledges nuance the stories of migration and land relationships that young children might tell. Children are fundamental to the intergenerational transmission of Indigenous epistemologies where there is reciprocity in the giving and receiving of stories.[39] In our work, we draw on moments where Ti Chou, interacting with her environment, becomes curious and aware of communications with land, water, wind, history, and futurity. These moments signal for us the development of felt knowledges.

We read Ti Chou's questions to Auntie Luce as instances of sensing what is at stake in hearing and learning the stories of her people and their homeland, an affirmation for young children of their layered knowledges and connections to lives lived before and after their own. As readers and artists, as listeners and storytellers, young children are untrained in colonial epistemic practices that approach textual and visual representations as stagnant objects. In our reading and writing, we engage with the storybook as children do, exploring text and image as moments replete with interpretative possibilities. In doing so, we seek to curate and evoke the multiple embodied and layered registers of BlackIndigenous life. Blackness is not stagnant, nor is Indigeneity. We examine each image kaleidoscopically; a single glance is based on a single angle, offering only one aspect of a prismatic story. With a turn, the colors pick up light or glare or shadow in an instant. Foregrounding the kaleidoscope of BlackIndigenous experiences highlights the hues in resistance while naming the violence of conquest and racialization.

We read for the poetics of BlackIndigeneous life by referencing ways of being that exist beyond the written word and racialized labels. We learn from Indigenous scholars who recall the ways the body expresses knowledge and theory. Simpson situates Nishnaabeg theory in a context of being generated and regenerated through embodied practice, "woven within kinetics, spiritual presence, and emotion," echoing Million's emphasis on the power of story to make one feel and move.[40] We join these theorizations with scholars of Black geographies who engage the body as lyrical poetry, inextricably weaving people and community together in the creating of history.[41] Madiana/Martiniquan writer Édouard Glissant's poetic landscape[42] brings together the written and unwritten geographic expressions of sensing, knowing, theorizing, expressing, and imagining space and place.[43] The felt knowledges transmitted by Auntie Luce and reciprocated by Ti Chou communicate a poetics of possibility, of BlackIndigenous articulations of self, others, and place that emerge from the interstices of ruptured histories with land to create new grounds for relationality.[44]

"To Paint History Takes Darkness, Brightness, and All the Colors In Between"

Auntie Luce's paintings suggest a mode of BlackIndigenous anti-colonial geopoetics, an approach to storytelling the ruptures and excesses of ongoing racial and colonial violence.[45] Midway through the storybook, we see an image of Auntie Luce describing her painting process to Ti Chou. The text reads, "I paint to remember what I've seen and heard and smelled and felt." Auntie Luce's description of painting as a translation of sensorial experience into image may be expanded more generally to intimate a mode of geopoetics that translates the experiences of the individual, collective, and relational body into stories that make meaning of BlackIndigenous life in relation to place.[46]

In the partnership of text by Latour and images by Daley, we read for the multiple temporalities and textures of BlackIndigenous life. Each visual holds a moment in memories where the skin tingles, hot flashes race through the body, and heartbeats quicken as the details in brushstrokes awaken the senses. Campt reimagines visual archives by theorizing the sensorial affect of images beyond the visible and the seen.[47] In her work, images are expanded beyond the moment of their capture, embedding them in the context of what came before and after; photographs and drawings are "still-moving-images," impinging on the audience to invest their own affect and labor in connecting with them. In analyzing the images in *Talking Paintings*, we engage the "overlapping sensory realms of the visual, the sonic, the haptic, and the affective labor that constellates in, around, and in response to such images" to examine how colors may archive BlackIndigenous sensorial relations to place and memory, igniting experiences in the reader. Painting these histories calls on the artist to return to memories, recalling the skin tingles and racing heartbeats of everyday moments, and then to choose the tints and colors that evoke similar sensations. Some pages offer daytime scenes with oranges, yellows, and reds, while others weave blues, grays, and yellows with nighttime skies. We read each choice of color and stroke in reference to BlackIndigenous experiences grounded in memories of particular places and historical moments.

Early in the storybook there is an image of Ti Chou, returning from the airport with Auntie Luce (Figure 9.2). They drive through island streets of familiar scenes with bright market colors of blues, grays, and fuchsias depicting "boys selling water ice by the

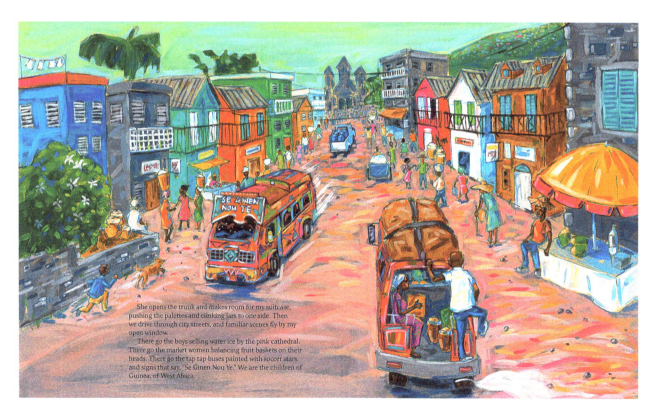

FIGURE 9.2 A scene of island market adventures with tap-tap buses and colorful buildings. Images from *Auntie Luce's Talking Paintings* reproduced with permission from Groundwood Books, Toronto. Text copyright © 2018 by Francie Latour, illustrations copyright © 2018 by Ken Daley. www.groundwoodbooks.com.

Moving with Land 199

pink cathedral" and "market women balancing fruit baskets on their heads."[48] Opening Ti Chou's visit to Ayiti with this scene introduces the reader to the vibrant pinks of cathedral walls and the fuchsias, salmons, and jades of fruit in baskets, a palette particular to the lands and waters of the Caribbean. The choice of colors for each image widens the narrative frame of BlackIndigenous histories and memories beyond heartache, or even resilience, to glimpse joy in community and everyday market scenes. In the market, we see people walking the land, stopping to chat with a neighbor or to visit fruit stalls, pressing the guava fruit for ripeness and talking down the price of cold water. The colors of everyday life in Ayiti can offer reminders of how care shows up in communities resisting the horrors of colonial violence, where market walks are part of familiar routines woven into learning the land. The palette of gem tones evokes the familiarity of the market, reminding us that terror and threat are but moments within an ongoing relationality of communal and ecological life. The accompanying image on the page includes the words "Se Ginen Nou Ye," translated as "We are the children of Guinea of West Africa," which signal diasporic relations; the words "we" and "children" offering lineage and a glimpse into communities reclaiming history together. These early scenes situate us in Ayiti's land histories, beginning with the market where tap-tap buses and walking are the primary modes of transportation and continuing with Ti Chou's journey, as we leave the busy marketplace, winding through roads into the country where homes are built into the hilly topography.

Near the end of the storybook, two facing pages (Figure 9.3) depict what appears to be the same location, visualized with colors of stark contrast—the first dense with hues of dark grays and blues, and the other saturated with bright pinks and oranges. One tells a story of midnight military raids, while the other speaks of sunshine days and of children riding bikes and playing outside. We take a closer look to reflect on the before and after of these images.

On the left-hand page, three soldiers enter. Hints of brown skin peek out from beneath masks, helmets, and gloves. The blues in their uniforms converge to black, and the shape of a rifle is held by the gloved hands of one soldier. The ground is bare, colored blue and navy with no clear or discerning brushstrokes. Another soldier holds a beaming light, one of few splashes of bright paint. One of the soldiers bangs on a closed door. We feel a chill as we notice their uniform blue masks and the four brushstrokes that emanate from the fist banging, hinting at the force used to hit the door. The image speaks to Ayiti's history of military and state violence, the "crooked presidents and bad armies"[49] that Auntie Luce teaches Ti Chou about, who preyed on communities, shattering long-held relationships with crops, education, family, and physical health. We notice the bright yellow of lights shining inside homes as heads duck behind hurriedly closed windows. In the center of the page, a man runs to hide, singular, soft, white brushstrokes hinting at speed. One woman, in the midst of closing her shutters, quickly waves to come inside into safety. Above this scene, the moon dulls in the night sky, hinting at the fear that wafts in the air. The images register as a full sensorial experience. We can imagine dust shuffling into the air as people run for safety; the anguish of breathing softly to remain unheard while soldiers search; the exhaustion after clenching your body for hours; and the desire to eventually find a different life away from the lands you know best. We are moved by how these brushstrokes

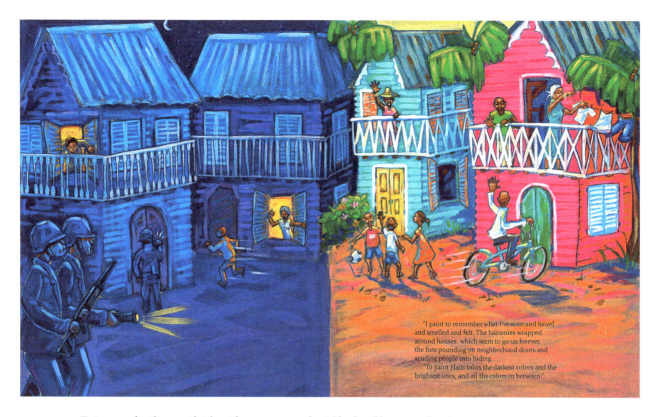

FIGURE 9.3 Twin pages detailing a midnight raid on one page and neighborhood homes on the other. Images from *Auntie Luce's Talking Paintings* reproduced with permission from Groundwood Books, Toronto. Text copyright © 2018 by Francie Latour, illustrations copyright © 2018 by Ken Daley. www.groundwoodbooks.com.

communicate histories of precarity and neglect imposed by corrupt elites in collusion with imperial powers. Each touch of horsehair to canvas speaks to a memory driven by profit-hungry French leaders who imposed sanctions and held illegitimate financial debts over generations of Ayitians. The geopolitical context of upheaval imbues a heaviness to the image. As a painter, what would it mean to recall a specific shade of maroon or oak, but be denied the ability to put color to canvas because of corrupt trading practices that constrict choice?

On the facing page, there is an obvious shift in colors. It is daytime, and the afternoon sun attracts people to ride bikes, hang clothes, and say hello to neighbors. We observe how the sunshine transitions the painting from midnight raids to relief and joy. Our eyes are drawn to a salmon house with an arched emerald door and the thick, diagonal, crisscrossing lines of whites and grays of the balcony railings. Multiple brushstrokes have been used to thicken the rails and distinguish each home, calling us to notice the balconies through the painter's attention to them. We think of how balconies highlight the everydayness of domestic life and a relationship with sunshine and the world outside the home. One woman hangs freshly washed clothes on a line, inviting sunrays to dry the fabrics. Another neighbor waves from the balcony, a prime spot to watch the courtyard of children smiling

Moving with Land 201

while playing soccer, bare legs and T-shirts hinting at the island humidity. We appreciate the illustrator's attention to the colors of more-than-human life, alerting us to the many characters influencing a story. In the previous image, furtive splashes of yellow and orange amid the blues and grays spoke of concealment from impending violence. On this page, the marigold hues speak to the warmth of the sun's rays on palm leaves and the glare on bicycle wheels. Large amber palm trees cascade over two homes of teal, blues, salmons, and fuchsias. The wide-open windows of a teal house with a yellow rectangular entrance door offers us a peek within. From the second-floor balcony, a woman wearing her big, broad sun hat hails a neighbor riding past, white brushstrokes trailing the bike rider, as he too greets passing neighbors. Brushstrokes of straight, vertical, and white lines contour the balcony railings, the tin roofs, and the closed shutters.

How might these pages placed next to one another speak to how disparate memories become held together in relation to a single place? How might the juxtaposition of violence in shadowed nighttime with mundane life in brightly lit daytime speak to the emotional ungrounding young BlackIndigenous children might feel as they overhear parents discussing another military regime's midnight raid back home? In these paired images, we recognize the multiplicity of experiences shaping BlackIndigenous diasporic life in the neocolonial politics that make migration a matter of experience for so many and in the layered memories of home where violence and vibrancy are entangled. We are especially struck by the splashes of yellow in the first image that sit amid the blues and grays of soldier uniforms, closed shutters, and bated breath. The marigold hues speak to enduring life and illuminate why, as Auntie Luce describes, painting Ayiti takes "darkness, brightness, and all the colors in between."[50] Colors offer connections to the breadth of collective memories that remind us that BlackIndigenous relations have survived by being nurtured despite and amid ruptures. Bright marigolds remain because they are quickly hidden from soldiers imposing fear and anguish. Ancestral stories told by candlelight are passed on through generations despite attempts to extinguish the flame.

We read these twinned pages as examples of memories that overlay colonially imposed heartache, forced migration, and military raids with laughter-filled bargaining over fruit stands and loud shouts for one-dollar water. Through gliding brushstrokes, the textures of paint touching canvas, and the mixture of colors, the painter as storyteller articulates a geopoetics of BlackIndigenous life as a labor of caring for place and kin across waters, continents, and generations. The labor required to sustain the possibility of life amid ongoing colonial racial violence is an often unrecognized form of political work that Pavithra Vasudevan and Sara Smith term "domestic geopolitics."[51] Domestic geopolitics speaks to the work of sustaining home and belonging in the context of ruptured relations to place and signals that such labor functions on a different political register than that of (post-/settler-)colonial states vying for imperial attention.

Talking Paintings details the composition of BlackIndigenous life through attention to brushstrokes, colors, and depth of paint pools. The hues in paint recall the senses, the experiences that go unsaid but are felt. The vibrant colors continue those conversations that occur across land and body, mind and soul. Such storytelling practices recall troubled histories where revolutions mark the depth of heartache, ruptures, erasures, and reclamations and, within and beneath these, the silenced, hidden, and uncovered histories of the Arawak people. These are voices of stories "before, before" the onset of colonial rule, by the Spanish, the French, and the "American," but also stories of the "after" or the "before/and still now" that persist as embodied resonances despite colonial subjugation and genocide.[52]

"Our Faces Are like Maps"

In the middle of the book, Auntie Luce reassures Ti Chou that her history is held in the lines and creases of her face, saying, "[O]ur faces are like maps."[53] We consider geopolitical relations across BlackIndigenous diasporic life where the reverberations of political histories are held as knowledges in the body, holding memories of home as the now flows with times past.

At the opening of the page (Figure 9.4), we see a collage of images that we read as a map of BlackIndigenous history. A path of cowrie shells on sand-colored dirt leads to a row of village huts crowned with straw. We see a chiseled face mask with bronze tones and two figures of Benin royalty adorned with gold, tears rolling down their faces. Blended into this image, we see a line of people walking, their ankles and wrists in shackles, overseen by a soldier in uniform, signaling natal alienation, the violent rupturing of relations

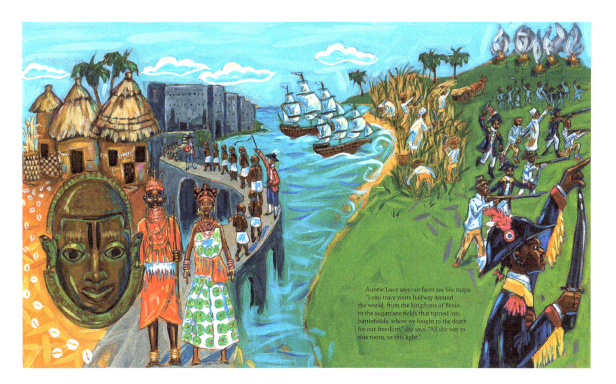

FIGURE 9.4 Collage map of images detailing BlackIndigenous history with royal leaders and revolution. Images from *Auntie Luce's Talking Paintings* reproduced with permission from Groundwood Books, Toronto. Text copyright © 2018 by Francie Latour, illustrations copyright © 2018 by Ken Daley. www.groundwoodbooks.com.

to place and kin that characterized enslavement of African peoples. A ship moves through tumultuous waters, marking the voices, histories, and lives of those lost in the voyages of the transatlantic slave trade. The grammar that justified the Middle Passage, rendering people in terms of property, carried them onto the shores of the "New World," where the lives and bodies of African peoples were consumed by growing cash crops for colonizers. In the next phase of the image, we see sugarcane fields become the battlegrounds of revolution. These are the geopolitical histories that Auntie Luce tells Ti Chou she recognizes in her face, the creases and crinkles marking lines of time, resistance, heartache, and history.

We read the collage as a map of stories, heavier brushstrokes marking the borders between distinct places and historical moments that flow into one another. Each horsehair touch to the canvas layers the multiple histories of BlackIndigenous life into one another—stories of Ayiti, the land of mountains long before the Spanish and the French, before, before, and stories as well of those who, brought forcibly to Ayiti, remade their terms of belonging. The gray of the waves moving the ship flows into the shoreline, becoming the clothes of Africans forced to grow sugarcane. The imprint of a cowrie shell holds the memory of laughter while searching the water for cowrie shells and learning with many other living water creatures. The long strokes of gold illustrating straw speak of the symphony created by nimble fingers and focused attention required to prepare a strong thatched roof.

When Auntie Luce closes her cartography of BlackIndigenous life with the phrase "all the way to this room," she brings us back to her studio.[54] On the next pages, we see Ti Chou in Auntie Luce's studio, marveling at portraits of Ayiti's revolutionary heroes—Jean-Jacques Dessalines, Toussaint Louverture, Sanité Bélair, and Catherine Flon—who refused colonial domination and fought to reimagine their terms of freedom. In the portraits of Ayiti's greater- and lesser-known heroes, Auntie Luce gestures to the global significance of Ayiti as the first successful revolt against enslavement, the island that overthrew empire and became the promise of another future.[55] On the next two pages (Figure 9.5), we see portraits of Ti Chou's grandfather and great-grandmother, reminding Ti Chou that rebellion, more than aspiration, is an inheritance. In the contours of Ti Chou's face, Auntie Luce reads the map of histories, detailing disrupted relations to place and freedom dreams across BlackIndigenous life.

What we see is a map: not a map of territory as defined by the colonial plantation regime, but a cartography of the plots where life is desired, imagined, enacted, and inherited.[56] Auntie Luce's map visualizes the memories of everyday life that populate the margins of Ayiti's *longue durée* of colonial racial violence. In reading these histories in Ti Chou's face, Auntie Luce maps the traditions of struggle, the grasping for and holding on to freedom that is BlackIndigenous life in the present. The colonial imposition of authority onto/into bodies shapes people's lives and relationships to place through repeated dispossession. Against such colonial territorializing of bodies, Auntie Luce traces the contours of Ti Chou's life in expansive generational and geographical terms, connecting her individual person to BlackIndigenous life across vertical and horizontal scales.[57] In doing so, she suggests an alternate set of BlackIndigenous ecological relations that speak to the labor of care

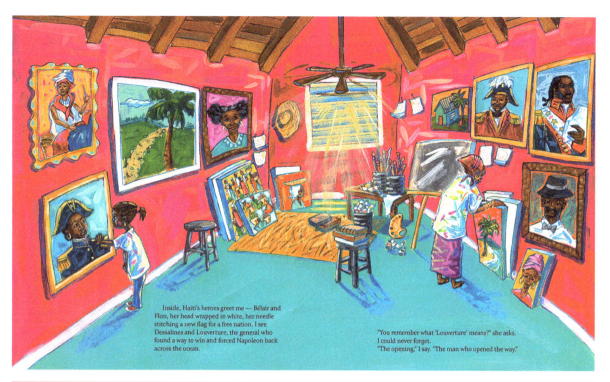

FIGURE 9.5 Portrait of Ti Chou's grandparent hung with revolutionary Ayitian leaders in Auntie Luce's studio space. Images from *Auntie Luce's Talking Paintings* reproduced with permission from Groundwood Books, Toronto. Text copyright © 2018 by Francie Latour, illustrations copyright © 2018 by Ken Daley. www.groundwoodbooks.com.

Moving with Land   205

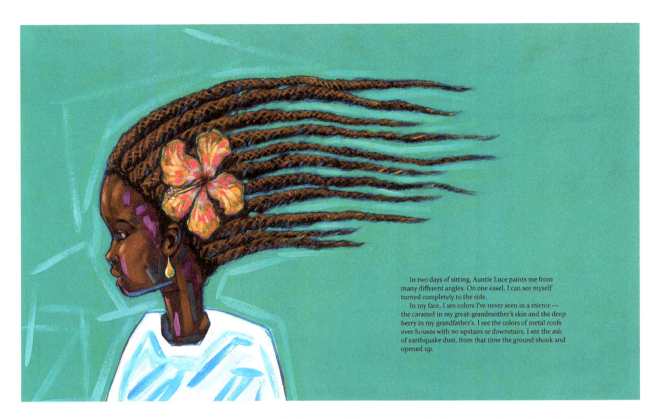

FIGURE 9.6 Portrait of Ti Chou with a hibiscus flower in her long twists. Images from *Auntie Luce's Talking Paintings* reproduced with permission from Groundwood Books, Toronto. Text copyright © 2018 by Francie Latour, illustrations copyright © 2018 by Ken Daley. www.groundwoodbooks.com.

and rebellion, of what it means to take care of the land and learn the land, what it means to fight for land and free it from the entrails of sugar, along with freeing their own bodies from the shackles that bind. There are both histories of dispossession, as the accompanying text indicates ("from the kingdoms of Benin, to the sugarcane fields that turned into battlefields"[58]), and histories of maintaining relations with the earth, of cowrie shells gathered and made into regalia, suggesting aspirations to autonomy and sovereignty. We see, with Auntie Luce, creases in Ti Chou's face and hands, lines that echo the trails dug into the dirt to reground ancestral relations in this place, in this now.

After two days of sitting for Auntie Luce, Ti Chou observes a portrait of herself (Figure 9.6). She is facing sideways, a hibiscus flower pinned to her braids flowing behind her, as though carried by a gentle breeze. She tells us, "In my face, I see colors I've never seen in a mirror—the caramel in my great-grandmother's skin and the deep berry in my grandfather's. I see the colors of metal roofs over houses with no upstairs or downstairs. I see the ash of earthquake dust, from that time the ground shook and opened up."[59] Auntie Luce's portrait of Ti Chou reflects back to her glimpses of the history that she could not see in herself. The rich hues of skin and earth suffuse the canvas of her face, evoking the layers of social and ecological life that are her inheritance. Ti Chou's observation of the deep berry of her grandfather's skin tone and the caramel of her great-grandmother's references the complicated pooling of African, Taíno, and European ancestry that constitutes BlackIndigenous genealogy. In the next breath, she notes "the colors of metal of roofs over houses with no upstairs or downstairs" and "the ash of earthquake dust."[60] Her words recall the precarity of life for many Ayitians today, the simple infrastructures of single-level homes and the earthquakes that threaten them. This is a precarity produced by underdevelopment that makes weapons out of extreme weather events like earthquakes and hurricanes, turning Ayiti's foundations into rubble repeatedly.[61] Auntie Luce's cartography traces the connecting lines of revolution, enslavement, colonization, and unnatural disasters across history, the conditions that suffocate BlackIndigenous life and produce structured precarity; and yet there is the continuation of life, the finding of joy, and the creation of new place-based relations in these circumstances.

"I Wonder What Stories [My Hands] Will Tell"

As a young child, Ti Chou is learning the complicated layers of BlackIndigenous placemaking from Auntie Luce, not only to recognize the deep influence of racial and colonial histories of domination but also to touch the soil of home in refusal of colonial boundaries between water, sky, and land. In this section, we engage questions of belonging, ancestry, and uncertainty within lineages as generating possibilities for solidarity against domination.

Ti Chou's journey home is a story of many soils, some shaped by snow and ice and others by rushing ocean water and island breezes. In the beginning of the book, departing for Ayiti, Ti Chou shares, "It is December, the time of year when I leave the snow and snowman-making behind." She continues, "I step onto an airplane, and when I step off again a wall of heat wraps my body and instantly warms my blood."[62] Ti Chou's narration of seasonal and climatic differences offers an awareness of fluidity in belonging to many homes. We are invited by her words to imagine the snowy lands she leaves behind, the salty oceans she flies over, and the warm lands she descends onto—a typical experience for many BlackIndigenous people whose lives are lived between homes and elsewheres.

Through the reflexivity of Ti Chou, a young BlackIndigenous child, Latour raises questions about the fluidity and uncertainty of lineage, ancestry, and belonging. While sitting to be painted, Ti Chou wonders aloud, "With my slow, broken Kreyòl, would they know I am their daughter?"[63] In Ti Chou's question, we hear the longing to share in Kreyòl, a desire for restoration of relations, a wondering if Ayitian ocean breezes and human breath would welcome her warmly. In her question "would they know I am their daughter?" we hear the pain of wounds inflicted by fists pounding on doors, by parents disappeared and children alienated, by midnight boats forced into stormy waters. Would they know she is their daughter? Their kin? Their skin? Would her slow and broken Kreyòl voice the creases and crevices of a shared and complicated history with land?

Ti Chou's uncertainty raises questions of language as a marker of lineage, signaling other deeper uncertainties. Is the "slow, broken Kreyòl" an attempt to hold the tongue twists, conjugations, *yon melanj* of communications and histories Ti Chou feels and has learned as a BlackIndigenous child? Could "slow" offer an opportunity for the ears to catch the melody of tonal waves that characterize the Kreyòl rhythms, feeling the breeze land on arm hairs and tickle the skin? Is "slow" a chance for eyes to capture the smile creases, forehead wrinkles, and depth of heartache in exiled families' stories of Ayitian revolution? Amid the ruptures in BlackIndigenous land relations imposed by brutal colonial domination and the violence of imposed precarity—as Auntie Luce describes it, "crooked presidents and bad armies"—language becomes a signifier for exclusion, acceptance, or claim. Voiced in her return to Ayiti, Ti Chou's uncertainty reiterates the complexities of BlackIndigenous land relations in the context of multiple forced and voluntary migrations.

How will relations to land and place, the "ecology of intimacy" that constitutes everyday life in Ayiti, show up for this young child when she looks back on this visit home? Will she include the walk down a path of dirt, stones, and grass, "past the chickens and the garden of choublak flowers" that lead to Auntie Luce's painting studio?[64] How will she speak of the chickens that guide her to the studio, the trees that make the chair holding her up, the body ache from sitting, and the histories of revolution that the Ayitian soil holds? Each of these alerts us to the many characters influencing a story and the power young children hold to tell their story. From Auntie Luce, Ti Chou learns the craft of storytelling where memories enliven the mixing shades of acrylic onto canvas. While Auntie Luce chooses which hues of browns, blues, yellows, and pinks to use in painting, Ti Chou listens to learn what it is to paint, what it is to tell the story of the land "woven within kinetics, spiritual presence, and emotion." As she sits, Ti Chou shares that her legs and arms twitch, her jaw locks from trying to sit still. Eventually, the silence and the passage of time help Ti Chou sense the stories laden in the paintings, as she listens for what each brushstroke communicates.

When the painting is done, Ti Chou takes a moment to absorb the stories she's been told while gathering the paintbrushes for a rinse in the sink. The image on this page (Figure 9.7) of the book is of a gush of faucet water, moving closer to the drain, bubbles popping, teals, browns, and pinks swirling together. We see Ti Chou's reflection in the browning water as the colors bleed together, "ash to cocoa to rust, butterscotch to nut, and nut to clay."[65] She looks into her brown eyes sitting atop fluffy cheeks gazing back at her. In this reflection, water drives this *melanj* of vibrant colors into hues of brown. We notice the bright teals poking out in the gushing water, alerting us to the power of water to mirror our self-image, to draw out our similarities, to destroy our homes, and to animate our uncertainties.

Water's fluidity is highlighted in Ti Chou's life as a young BlackIndigenous girl, where finding home becomes elusive amid land ruptures, exiles, and returns. In the water's reflection, we read the ways Ti Chou embodies the complications in BlackIndigenous land relations: water bubbling can signal the ungrounding that emerges from learning ambivalent or difficult histories; water pooling hints at the comfort in feeling connected with family; and water draining gestures toward the uncertainty in how to tell your version of story. In the visualization of Ti Chou's reflection in/with the water, we read an articulation of complex uncertainty in BlackIndigenous land relations, where there is freedom to not know, to not need an answer because possibilities hide in the skin tickles, smile creases, and forehead wrinkles, while reflecting on stories heard. As Ti Chou rinses the hues of

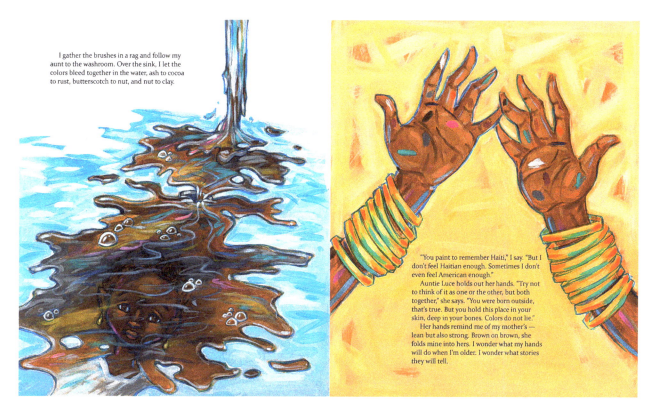

FIGURE 9.7 *Left*: As water drains down the sink, the teals, browns, and pinks flowing together create a reflection of Ti Chou. *Right*: Auntie Luce opens her hands, palms dabbed with paint and forearms adorned in bracelets. Images from *Auntie Luce's Talking Paintings* reproduced with permission from Groundwood Books, Toronto. Text copyright © 2018 by Francie Latour, illustrations copyright © 2018 by Ken Daley. www.groundwoodbooks.com.

brown from the paintbrush and the water rushes to the drain, her reflection in the flows of water hints at how fluidity can show up in ancestral histories and memories of young children with BlackIndigenous land relations.

Through Ti Chou, we consider how BlackIndigenous children of the Caribbean hold relations to futurity and place across dividing lines of temporality, physical geographies, and generations. Still in the studio, Ti Chou says, "I wonder what my hands will do when I'm older. I wonder what stories they will tell."[66] Ti Chou's wonderings recall the traversals of ancestry and futurity that Jacqui Alexander calls "pedagogies of crossing," where stories navigate learning the "multiple operations of power" and histories.[67] Alexander suggests that we engage such pedagogies to learn more about the dialectics of history that are "imperative [to] making the world in which we live intelligible to ourselves and to each other—in other words, teaching ourselves."[68] Ti Chou is writing her own story by learning the stories of family and lands. Ti Chou's words of "when I'm older" recall the aging of memories as young BlackIndigenous children move with land, holding questions and uncertainties about their place in history. In this storybook, children offer curiosities into history as they eavesdrop on adult conversations about the Ayitian revolution, sensing the

Moving with Land 209

residual heartache of rupture. How do these memories age and continue through generations? How will Ti Chou share these memories of cultivating resistance when she is older?

Memories weave histories of ancestors, descendants, and spirits across *many soils*, and layered stories live on through the land. In reflecting on Ti Chou's questions, we wonder how family memories live through blood, body, and soil. We consider how young BlackIndigenous children may share the stories of ruptures in land relations poisoned by capitalist consumption, stories of soils that bleed from exploitation, stories of sands that harden and nourish, and stories of waters that sing of the future. In BlackIndigenous land relationships, futurity lives in the possibilities of soils traveling with story, in the reckoning with complicated connections with lineage, and in the reimagination of belonging in relations to land. In *Talking Paintings*, we listen as the images tell the story of BlackIndigenous land relations where touching home happens in many forms, as we move with land.

Conclusion

Within a BlackIndigenous analytic, solidarity emerges as a complicated opportunity for resisting colonial infrastructures and reclaiming ruptured ancestral relations to place. *Talking Paintings* finds hope in the details of family history, in the heartache of losing connections with land, and in the tentative reclamation of a child seeking her roots. We see three implications for the significance of storytelling here that are more than metaphorical: one, how young children receive and hold ancestral knowledges; two, the significance of ancestral practices of embodied learning for resurgent struggles; and three, the value of what we have called complicated solidarity in extending decolonial constellations of formation to those with tentative or ruptured claims to place.[69]

First, in *Talking Paintings*, the primary voice we hear is Ti Chou's, a young girl with familial ties to Ayiti. Listening to her perspective, we hear ancestral voices from land,[70] water, sky, and kin that flow through descendants. We listen as she questions her reflection, walks the dirt roads, learns the fight in revolution, and senses the tingles of storytelling. Ti Chou highlights how uncertainty opens up possibilities for knowing. Young BlackIndigenous children offer testimonies of ancestral land relations infused with uncertainty, and they ask us to listen. In *Talking Paintings*, we join Ti Chou on this journey.

Second, we focus on the body as an archive that registers many communications of story. *Talking Paintings* offers visuals that connect with sensations on the skin, in how the eyes capture twists and turns of the body, how the rhythms and sounds awaken memories of historical trauma and resilience. In *Talking Paintings*, colors animate the retelling, calling the reader to remember "place based ethical frameworks" in the form of the children's storybook.

Lastly, we engage complicated solidarity, as the layered land relations in BlackIndigenous life are, pulling from Alexander and Chandra Talpade Mohanty, "location specific but not necessarily location bound."[71] In one image of the book (Figure 9.8), we see Ti Chou's family, their bodies wrapped in winter clothes, their mahogany faces holding an intense stare as Ti Chou's aircraft lifts off. Beyond the airport window lies a city's

FIGURE 9.8 An airport scene of Ti Chou's family, their bodies wrapped in winter clothes, their mahogany faces holding an intense stare as Ti Chou's aircraft lifts off; on the left side, Ti Chou steps onto the tarmac in Ayiti. Images from *Auntie Luce's Talking Paintings* reproduced with permission from Groundwood Books, Toronto. Text copyright © 2018 by Francie Latour, illustrations copyright © 2018 by Ken Daley. www.groundwoodbooks.com.

downtown skyline with billowing mounds of snow. We wonder about the heartache of moving away from revolutionary soil, warm sunshine, and family gatherings in search of reliable income and accessible housing and in response to muted fears of climate catastrophe. We feel these contours in complicated solidarity, where families make sacrifices even as they desire and sustain connections with ancestral lands. The curving brushstrokes tell the stories of multiple ancestors of Ayitian soil, those who were brought there, those whose bodies become the soil, those who join the waves, those who live in exile, and those who refuse to leave. In these intersections of solidarity, communities resist and negotiate colonial logics that commodify labor, erase Indigeneity, and maim Blackness.

The lessons we draw from Ti Chou's reflections speak to the broader significance of the Caribbean for anti-colonial politics. The Caribbean has been central to hemispheric histories of revolution, enslavement, indenture, dispossession, and genocide. The specific and differential ways in which Blackness and Indigeneity have been articulated and entangled in the Caribbean present a challenge for any reductive forms of sovereignty articulated through identity or ancestral claims to territory. More importantly, the Caribbean has long been a wellspring for anti-colonial thought and practice. If we understand storytelling's central role in remembering and envisioning alternatives to colonial racial capitalism, Caribbean stories are vital to building a world otherwise.[72]

Talking Paintings asks us to listen closely for those quiet lessons that are carried as embodied knowledges, for those gestures recall lessons from water, sky, and land. As Land Back and decolonizing movements reverberate, BlackIndigeneity as an analytic reminds us that to repair our relations—to place, to more-than-human kin, and to one another—is to wrestle, as Ti Chou does, with layered and tentative claims to place and ancestry. BlackIndigenous storytelling reimagines connection, not through fixity but through fluid routes of migration, through the knowledges that travel with diasporas and the soils that travel with stories. Stories such as these, of BlackIndigenous folks of Caribbean descent, offer young children, their families, the educators who teach them, and the scholars who work with them an opportunity to advance a notion of complicated solidarity while naming our altered relations with water and land.

NOTES

1 Francie Latour, *Auntie Luce's Talking Paintings* (Toronto: Groundwood Books, 2018).
2 See David Geggus, "The Naming of Haiti," *New West Indian Guide/Nieuwe West-Indische Gids* 71, nos. 1–2 (1997): 43–68.
3 Alexis Pauline Gumbs, *Spill: Scenes of Black Feminist Fugitivity* (Durham, N.C.: Duke University Press, 2016).
4 Mishuana R. Goeman, "Ongoing Storms and Struggles: Gendered Violence and Resource Exploitation," in *Critically Sovereign: Indigenous Gender, Sexuality, and Feminist Studies*, ed. Joanne Barker (Durham, N.C.: Duke University Press, 2017), 101.
5 Goeman, "Ongoing Storms and Struggles," 101.
6 Jodi A. Byrd, "Weather with You: Settler Colonialism, Antiblackness, and the Grounded Relationalities of Resistance," *Critical Ethnic Studies* 5, nos. 1–2 (2019): 207–14.
7 Byrd, "Weather with You," 211.
8 Latour, *Auntie Luce's Talking Paintings*.
9 Angela Last, "We Are the World? Anthropocene Cultural Production between Geopoetics and Geopolitics," *Theory, Culture & Society* 34, nos. 2–3 (March–May 2017): 147–68.
10 Robin M. Boylorn, "Blackgirl Blogs, Auto/ethnography, and Crunk Feminism," *Liminalities: A Journal of Performance Studies* 9, no. 2 (April 2013): 73–82; and Dominique C. Hill, "Blackgirl, One Word: Necessary Transgressions in the Name of Imagining Black Girlhood," *Cultural Studies, Critical Methodologies* 19, no. 4 (August 2019): 275–83.
11 Claude Ake, *Social Science as Imperialism: The Theory of Political Development* (Ibadan: University of Ibadan Press, 1979). See also the work of Ama Ata Aidoo, *After the Ceremonies: New and Selected Poems* (Lincoln: University of Nebraska Press, 2017).
12 Bennett Brazelton, "On the Erasure of Black Indigeneity," *Review of Education, Pedagogy, and Cultural Studies* 43, no. 5 (2021): 391.
13 See the work of Ruth Wilson Gilmore, "Fatal Couplings of Power and Difference: Notes on Racism and Geography," *The Professional Geographer* 54, no. 1 (2002): 15–24.
14 D. Alissa Trotz and Linda Peake, "Work, Family, and Organising: An Overview of the Emergence of the Economic, Social and Political Roles of Women in British Guiana," *Social and Economic Studies* 49, no. 4 (2000): 189–222.
15 Nicole Burrowes, "Sugar Strikes: Confronting Plantation Legacies in British Guiana," in *Legacies of Slavery and Indentured Labour*, vol. 7, ed. Maurits Hassankhan and Farzana Gounder (New Delhi: Manohar Press, forthcoming), 8.
16 Burrowes, "Sugar Strikes," 4.
17 Shona N. Jackson, *Creole Indigeneity: Between Myth and Nation in the Caribbean* (Minneapolis: University of Minnesota Press, 2012).
18 Melanie J. Newton, "Returns to a Native Land: Indigeneity and Decolonization in the Anglophone Caribbean," *Small Axe* 17, no. 2 (July 2013): 108–22; and Burrowes, "Sugar Strikes."
19 Newton, "Returns to a Native Land," 120.
20 Sarah England, "Mixed and Multiracial in Trinidad and Honduras: Rethinking Mixed-Race Identities in Latin America and the Caribbean," *Ethnic and Racial Studies* 33, no. 2 (February 2010): 195–213.
21 Maile Arvin, "Analytics of Indigeneity," in *Native Studies Keywords*, ed. Stephanie Nohelani Teves, Andrea Smith, and Michelle H. Raheja (Tucson: University of Arizona Press, 2015), 119–29.
22 Leanne Betasamosake Simpson, *As We Have Always Done: Indigenous Freedom through Radical Resistance* (Minneapolis: University of Minnesota Press, 2017), 228–29.
23 Michelle Daigle and Margaret Marietta Ramírez, "Decolonial Geographies," in *Keywords in Radical Geography: Antipode at 50*, ed. the *Antipode* Editorial Collective (Hoboken, N.J.: Wiley-Blackwell, 2019), 79.
24 Arvin, "Analytics of Indigeneity," 121.
25 Burrowes, "Sugar Strikes," 2.
26 Brazelton, "On the Erasure of Black Indigeneity," 382.
27 Corinne L. Hofman, Jorge Ulloa Hung, Eduardo Herrera Malatesta, Joseph Sony Jean, Till Sonnemann, and Menno Hoogland, "Indigenous Caribbean Perspectives: Archaeologies and Legacies of the First Colonised Region in the New World," *Antiquity* 92, no. 361 (2018): 200–216.

28 Bagele Chilisa, *Indigenous Research Methodologies*, 2nd ed. (Los Angeles: SAGE, 2019).
29 Simpson, *As We Have Always Done*, 8.
30 On the intergenerationality of violence and healing, see Goeman, "Ongoing Storms and Struggles," 106–8.
31 Tina M. Campt, "The Visual Frequency of Black Life: Love, Labor, and the Practice of Refusal," *Social Text* 37, no. 3 (2019): 31.
32 Campt, "The Visual Frequency of Black Life," 27.
33 Dexter Fisher, "Zitkala Sa: The Evolution of a Writer," *American Indian Quarterly* 5, no. 3 (August 1979): 229–38. See also Sharlene Mollett, "Hemispheric, Relational, and Intersectional Political Ecologies of Race: Centring Land-Body Entanglements in the Americas," *Antipode* 53 no. 3 (2021): 810–30.
34 Fisher, "Zitkala Sa," 234.
35 Dian Million, "Felt Theory: An Indigenous Feminist Approach to Affect and History," *Wicazo Sa Review* 24, no. 2 (Fall 2009): 58.
36 Million, "Felt Theory," 56.
37 Dian Million, "There Is a River in Me: Theory from Life," in *Theorizing Native Studies*, ed. Audra Simpson and Andrea Smith (Durham, N.C.: Duke University Press, 2014), 32.
38 Million, "Felt Theory," 58.
39 See Fikile Nxumalo and kihana miraya ross, "Envisioning Black Space in Environmental Education for Young Children," *Race Ethnicity and Education* 22, no. 4 (2019): 502–24.
40 Simpson, *As We Have Always Done*, 151; and Dian Million, "Felt Theory."
41 Katherine McKittrick, *Demonic Grounds: Black Women and the Cartographies of Struggle* (Minneapolis: University of Minnesota Press, 2006).
42 Édouard Glissant, *Poetics of Relation*, trans. Betsy Wing (Ann Arbor: University of Michigan Press, 1997).
43 McKittrick, *Demonic Grounds*.
44 Million, "Felt Theory," and Byrd, "Weather with You."
45 Last, "We Are the World?," 151.
46 Goeman, "Ongoing Storms and Struggles," 101.
47 Campt, "The Visual Frequency of Black Life."
48 Latour, *Auntie Luce's Talking Paintings*.
49 Latour, *Auntie Luce's Talking Paintings*.
50 Latour, *Auntie Luce's Talking Paintings*.
51 Pavithra Vasudevan and Sara Smith, "The Domestic Geopolitics of Racial Capitalism," *Environment and Planning C: Politics and Space* 38, nos. 7–8 (2020): 1160–79.
52 Latour, *Auntie Luce's Talking Paintings*.
53 Latour, *Auntie Luce's Talking Paintings*.
54 Latour, *Auntie Luce's Talking Paintings*.
55 Gerald Horne, *Confronting Black Jacobins: The United States, the Haitian Revolution, and the Origins of the Dominican Republic* (New York: Monthly Review Press, 2015).
56 Sylvia Wynter, "On How We Mistook the Map for the Territory, and Reimprisoned Ourselves in Our Unbearable Wrongness of Being, of Desêtre: Black Studies Toward the Human Project," in *A Companion to African-American Studies*, ed. Lewis R. Gordon and Jane Anna Gordon (Malden, Mass.: Blackwell, 2006), 107–18; and Katherine McKittrick, "Plantation Futures," *Small Axe* 17, no. 3 (November 2013): 1–15.
57 Goeman, "Ongoing Storms and Struggles."
58 Latour, *Auntie Luce's Talking Paintings*.
59 Latour, *Auntie Luce's Talking Paintings*.
60 Latour, *Auntie Luce's Talking Paintings*.
61 Neil Smith, "There's No Such Thing as a Natural Disaster," *Items: Insights from the Social Sciences*, June 11, 2006, https://items.ssrc.org/understanding-katrina/theres-no-such-thing-as-a-natural-disaster/.
62 Latour, *Auntie Luce's Talking Paintings*.
63 Latour, *Auntie Luce's Talking Paintings*.
64 Latour, *Auntie Luce's Talking Paintings*.
65 Latour, *Auntie Luce's Talking Paintings*.
66 Latour, *Auntie Luce's Talking Paintings*.

67 M. Jacqui Alexander, *Pedagogies of Crossing: Meditations on Feminism, Sexual Politics, Memory, and the Sacred* (Durham, N.C.: Duke University Press, 2005), 6.
68 Alexander, *Pedagogies of Crossing*, 6.
69 Daigle and Ramírez, "Decolonial Geographies," 79.
70 Dian Million, "'We Are the Land and the Land Is Us': Indigenous Land, Lives, and Embodied Ecologies in the Twenty-First Century," in *Racial Ecologies,* ed. Leilani Nishime and Kim D. Hester Williams (Seattle: University of Washington Press, 2018), 19–33.
71 M. Jacqui Alexander and Chandra Talpade Mohanty, "Cartographies of Knowledge and Power: Transnational Feminism as Radical Praxis," in *Critical Transnational Feminist Praxis*, ed. Amanda Lock Swarr and Richa Nagar (Albany, N.Y.: SUNY Press, 2010), 27.
72 Pavithra Vasudevan, Margaret Marietta Ramírez, Yolanda González Mendoza, and Michelle Daigle, "Storytelling Earth and Body," *Annals of the American Association of Geographers* (2022), DOI: 10.1080/24694452.2022.2139658.

CONTRIBUTORS

OLIVIA ARIGHO-STILES is a lecturer in Latin American Studies at the University of Essex and a research associate on the Rethinking Values of the Anthropocene project at the University of Bristol. She was previously a postdoctoral fellow in the Indigenous Ecologies and Environmental Crisis research cluster at University College London. Her PhD in sociology was awarded by the University of Essex in 2022. It examined the history of ecological thought within highland Indigenous movements in Bolivia between 1920 and 1990. She holds a BA in History from the University of Oxford and an MA in Latin American Studies from University College London.

ANITA BAKSHI teaches in the Department of Landscape Architecture at Rutgers University. Following several years in architectural practice, she received her PhD in the history and theory of architecture from Cambridge University with the Conflict in Cities research program. Her research focuses on contested landscapes and histories, environmental justice, and the relationship between architecture and sociology. She edited the book *Our Land, Our Stories: Excavating Subterranean Histories of Ringwood Mines and the Ramapough Lunaape Nation* (2022), in partnership with the Ramapough Lunaape Turtle Clan. She is the author of *Topographies of Memories: A New Poetics of Commemoration* (2017) and coauthor of *Collaborations in Architecture and Sociology* (2024, with Zaire Dinzey-Flores).

MICHELLE DAIGLE is Mushkegowuk (Cree), a member of Constance Lake First Nation in Treaty 9, and of French ancestry. She is an assistant professor in the Centre for Indigenous Studies and the Department of Geography and Planning at the University of Toronto. Her research examines colonial capitalist dispossession and violence on Indigenous lands and bodies, as well as Indigenous practices of resurgence and freedom. Her current research focuses on the renewal of Indigenous relations of care that emerge through Mushkegowuk waterways and how those generate decolonial possibilities within conditions of extractive violence. Her writing has been published in *Antipode, Environment and Planning D, Political Geography,* and *Decolonization: Indigeneity, Education & Society.*

HEATHER DORRIES is an assistant professor jointly appointed to the Department of Geography and Planning and the Centre for Indigenous Studies at the University of Toronto. Her research focuses on the relationship between urban planning and settler colonialism and examines how Indigenous intellectual traditions—including Indigenous environmental knowledge, legal orders, and cultural production—can serve as the foundation for justice-oriented approaches to planning. She is currently revising her book manuscript, *Planning the End of the World: Indigenist Planning Theory and the Art of Refusal*, which demonstrates how Indigenous knowledge systems can inform resurgent forms of planning and urbanism. She is a coeditor of *Settler City Limits: Indigenous Resurgence and Colonial Violence in the Urban Prairie West* (2019). She is of Anishinaabe and settler ancestry and a member of Sagkeeng First Nation in Treaty 1.

CHIEF VINCENT MANN is the Turtle Clan Chief of the Ramapough Lenape Nation. He is a trustee of the Highlands Coalition and a former member of the Ringwood Mines Superfund site Citizen Advisory Group (CAG). He is currently working on co-creating the United Lunaapeewak with the long-term goals of cultural restoration and education for the broader public. He is a cofounder of the Munsee Three Sisters Medicinal Farm, an initiative to restore food sovereignty for the clan and to create local jobs. He has established many partnerships to address the health concerns of his community and to bring greater awareness to environmental justice and land issues. These include work with the Division of Environmental Medicine at NYU Langone Health on a community-health survey; a collaboration with the Clement A. Price Institute on Ethnicity, Culture, and the Modern Experience at Rutgers University–Newark on an "Archive of the Lenape Dispossession"; and the publication of *Our Land, Our Stories: Excavating Subterranean Histories of Ringwood Mines and the Ramapough Lunaape Nation* (2022) with Rutgers University's Department of Landscape Architecture.

RUTH H. MATAMOROS MERCADO is a Miskitu Indigenous lawyer and assistant professor in the Department of Geography and Environment at the University of North Carolina, Chapel Hill. She completed a PhD and a MA in Latin American Studies at the University of Texas, Austin, and holds a law degree from the Universidad Nacional Autónoma de Nicaragua, León. Her research interests center on Indigenous land relations in Nicaragua and Honduras, examining the social, political, economic, and cultural dimensions of land dispossession. Utilizing an Indigenous research framework and methodological approach, she delves into areas including decolonial Indigenous and feminist geographies and Traditional Ecological Knowledge (TEK). Her doctoral research delves into the perspectives of the Miskitu people, exploring their intricate relationship with land and territory across different historical, economic, social, and political contexts. In 2014, she was part of the interdisciplinary team that proposed that Nicaragua be constituted as a plurinational state in the constitutional reforms implemented that year by the Asamblea Nacional de Nicaragua.

MANDEE MCDONALD is a Maskîkow PhD candidate in the Faculty of Native Studies at the University of Alberta and the Hide Camp Director at Dene Nahjo in Sǫ̀mbak'è, Denendeh (Yellowknife, *Northwest Territories*, Canada). Her research focuses on Indigenous land-based learning, program evaluation, Indigenous resurgence, and governance. She is a moose and caribou hide tanner and has been organizing hide-tanning programming since 2013. Her writing has been published in *Decolonization: Indigeneity, Education & Society*, *Northern Public Affairs*, and *Visions of the Heart: Issues Involving Indigenous Peoples in Canada* (2020).

MIGUEL MELIN is a research associate with the Institute of Indigenous and Intercultural Studies at the Universidad de La Frontera, Chile. He is a member of and spokesperson for the Ralipitra Lof on Mapuche territory, as well as one of the founders of the Mapuche Territorial Alliance, a grassroots organization that promotes Mapuche cultural and political resurgence. He is a speaker of Mapuzugun (Mapuche language) and a bilingual intercultural teacher. He has led several community-based research projects with Mapuche communities and coauthored several publications about Mapuche cultural knowledge, including Mapuche law, Mapuche land-use planning, and ancestral forms of Mapuche mapping, in order to support the territorial demands of his people.

JAMES MILLER is an assistant professor in comparative Indigenous studies with a joint appointment in the Departments of Canadian-American Studies and Salish Sea Studies and the College of the Environment at Western Washington University. A Kanaka Maoli scholar, architect, and urbanist, he runs the 'Ike Honua design lab, centering Indigenous knowledge in building resilient communities through architectural and planning frameworks. Under the lens of climate change adaptation, his research investigates the role of Indigenous design knowledge in the creation of culturally supportive environments. Currently, he is investigating the transboundary placemaking of Indigenous communities from the Marshall Islands and the intersection of Oceanic Indigenous knowledge in building community resilience. His scholarship provides a space for Indigenous knowledge systems tied to the production of the built environment to be recognized within fields dominated by Western-centric worldviews. He holds a PhD in sustainable architecture from the University of Oregon with specializations in cultural sustainability and Indigenous design knowledge.

NATASHA MYHAL is Ojibwe, a citizen of the Sault Ste. Marie tribe of Chippewa Indians, and Ukrainian-American. She is an assistant professor of Indigenous Environmental Studies in the School of Environment and Natural Resources at The Ohio State University. She received her doctorate in Critical Ethnic Studies from the University of Colorado, Boulder, with a graduate certificate in Native American and Indigenous Studies. Her research examines Indigenous restoration programs in the Great Lakes, specifically working with the Little River Band of Ottawa Indians Tribal Natural Resource Department's Lake Sturgeon Restoration Program to create a climate change management plan. Employing scholarship and methods from the field of Indigenous Studies, Natasha's work centers Indigenous environmental justice across the historic and ongoing inequalities of settler colonial resource management and extraction.

NNENNA ODIM (she/her) is Igbo from Biafra and Arawakan. She is also the associate director of participatory action research at Beloved Community. Her time listening to young children as a Kindergarten teacher, supporting regional leaders, implementing state/city policy, designing academic research plans with communities in migration, and laughing with family are testimonies to the ways our communities tell stories. Her work and research focuses on how the voices and expertise of communities come alive in storytelling. Drawing on the intersections across Black geographies, Indigenous and place-based studies, and early childhood education, she has published articles about storytelling in communities, futuristic visions in early childhood, resisting anti-Black violence, and inequity in early childhood studies.

MAGDALENA UGARTE is an assistant professor in the School of Urban and Regional Planning at Toronto Metropolitan University, where she teaches courses in social and community planning, planning theory, and public policy. Her research critically examines the relationship between planning, settler colonialism, and other forms of institutionalized dispossession, as well as how communities historically excluded from planning plan for themselves. For the past decade, she has worked with Mapuche partners in Chile on participatory action research projects that engage with questions of Indigenous planning and Indigenous law.

PAVITHRA VASUDEVAN (she/they) is an assistant professor of African and African Diaspora Studies and Women's, Gender, and Sexuality Studies at the University of Texas, Austin. Vasudevan was a recipient of the 2022–2023 American Council of Learned Societies Fellowship for her first book project, *A Toxic Alchemy: Race and Waste in Industrial Capitalism*, an ethnography of aluminum smelting in the Southern United States. As a critical and feminist geographer, their work examines structural oppression through the embodied experiences, everyday lives, and political practices of communities threatened by hazardous environments. Vasudevan approaches scholarship as storytelling, using film, performance, poetry, and creative writing to write stories in service to building a better world. https://pavithravasudevan.com

SOFIA ZARAGOCIN is an assistant professor in the international relations department of Universidad San Francisco de Quito, with research interests in decolonial feminist geography and processes of racialization of space. She has written on geographies of settler colonialism along Latin American borderlands and decolonial feminist geography, as well as on mapping gender-based violence in Ecuador. She is part of the Critical Geography Collective of Ecuador, an autonomous interdisciplinary group that seeks territorial resistance through a wide range of socio-spatial geographical methodologies. She is also a cofounder of the Reexistencias Cimarrunas collective, which works on structural racisms from a hemispheric approach.

INDEX

Abya Yala, 6–8, 15n13, 27, 28, 30, 32, 33, 174; defining, 24
Academia Nacional del Mapuzugun, 183
Aelon Kein Ad, 83, 91–94, 95–96
agrarian reform, in Bolivia, 48
Agrarian Reform Law, 48
AGROPODER, 55, 59n94
ahupua'a, 99–100
Aikau, Hōkūlani K., 90
Ake, Claude, 194
Akwesasne Environmental Research Advisory Committee, 128
Akwesasne Mohawks, 127–28, 133
Akwesasne Task Force on the Environment (ATFE), 128
Albó, Xavier, 40, 45
Alianza para el Progreso de Miskitus y Sumus (ALPROMISU), 74
Aloha 'Āina, 85
ALPROMISU. *See* Alianza para el Progreso de Miskitus y Sumus
Altamirano-Jiménez, Isabel, 3
Amaru, Tupaj, 45
American Indian Movement (AIM), 4
Anishinaabe, 12–13; creation stories, 15n13, 153–58; ecological memory of, 154; ecological relations conceived by, 157; ethnobotany of, 165–66; governance of, 167; mobility of, 155–58, 159–61; natural resources and, 158–59; plant and animal relations, 164–65; treaty agreements with, 159–61
Anishinaabekwe, 153, 168n3
Anküwe, 181–82
Antileo, Elisa Loncon, 180
anti-racism, 21–22, 27, 32
Apaza Calle, Iván, 45
Arkansas, Rimajol communities in, 83, 91, 95, 96–97
Arvin, Maile, 10–11
As Long as Grass Grows (Gilio-Whitaker), 149

As We Have Always Done (Simpson), 113
Auntie Luce's Talking Paintings, 191, 196–97; brushstrokes in, 201–3; collage in, 203–4; color in, 198–203; embodied learning in, 197; memory in, 210; portraits in, 205, 206; visual analysis of, 196–98; water in, 208–9
Autonomous Regions (Nicaragua), 64, 65, 77n2
Autonomy Law, 75
Axtell, James, 135
ayllus, 45, 48, 53–54
Aymara, 6, 39, 44–45, 51, 174
az mapu, 172, 173, 176–78, 179, 181–82, 184, 185, 186

Babbitt, Bruce, 138
Baeza, Enrique Antileo, 180
Bairros, Luiza, 28
Bakahnu Yuska, 70, 71
Bakshi, Anita, 12, 124, 125
Barker, Adam, 29–30
Barker, Mary, 100
Barrientos, René, 48
Barry, Jan, 130
Bélair, Sanité, 204
Berman-Arévalo, Eloisa, 22
Big Manistee River, 155–56, 163, 166
Bikini Atoll, 93
biopower, 112
biskaabiiyang, 165–66
Black feminism, 28–29
Black Hills, 3–4
BlackIndigeneity, 191–92; cartography of, 203–4; complex ancestries of, 207; geographies of Caribbean, 194–96; migration and, 202; poetics of, 198; solidarity and, 210–11; visual analysis of, 198; water and, 208–9
Blackness, Indigeneity and, 10, 11, 23, 198, 211
Black Panthers, 5–6

Bledsoe, Adam, 22
Boletín Chitakolla, 52
Bolivia, 11, 13, 39, 40, 41, 44, 46–47; agrarian reform in, 48; food dependency in, 53; *katarista* movement in, 39–55; politics of Indigeneity in, 41–42; race relations in, 47
Bonfil, Guillermo, 68
Borrows, John, 165
Boylorn, Robin, 194
Brazelton, Bennett, 194
Brazil, 13, 32, 39–40
Briarpatch, 106
Brotherton Reservation, 134
Brown, April, 96
buen vivir (good living), 26, 39, 62, 71
Bunza, Matt, 98
bwebwenato (storytelling as oral history), 97

Cabnal, Lorena, 7–8; on *cuerpo-territorio*, 29
Cáceres, Berta, 13–14
de la Cadena, Marisol, 44–45
Cahua, Madelaine, 23
campesino movement, 40, 42, 44, 47, 48, 51–52, 55
Campt, Tina M., 196, 199
Canada, 1; experience of Indigenous peoples in, 178; Land Back movement in, 45
capitalism: epistemic dimensions of, 44; racialized, 27, 193
Carettas, Martina Angela, 8, 30
Caribbean: anti-colonial politics in, 211–12; dispossession strategies in, 194–95; Indigeneity, 194–95
Carneiro, Sueli, 28
Carroll, Clint, 3, 11, 162
Case, Emalani, 83, 85, 90

221

Center for the Coordination and Promotion of the Peasantry (MINK'A; Bolivia), 50–51
Centro por la Justicia y el Derecho Internacional, 62
CEPAL. *See* Comisión Económica para América Latina y el Caribe
Chila, Macabeo, 49, 54
Chile, 180; Mapuche people in, 171–186
Chresfield, Michell, 136
Cirilo, Alvaro, 75–76
Clement, Tiem, 97
Coba, Lisset, 30
Cohen, David Steven, 137
"collective continuance," 68, 124
collectives, in Latin America, 27–28
Collipal, Patricio Coliqueo, 177
colonialism, 2, 106, 157; anti-colonial politics in Caribbean, 211–12; containment and, 115–17; forms of, 24–25; land naming under, 23; mercantile, 66; RMI and United States, 103n47; Wallmapu and, 171–73. *See also* settler colonialism
colonos (settlers), 61–62, 66
Comisión Económica para América Latina y el Caribe (CEPAL), 187
Compact of Free Association (COFA), 89, 97, 103n41
Confederación Sindical Única de Trabajadores Campesinos de Bolivia (CSUTCB), 40, 42
Connelly, Sean, 100, 103n40
Copa Cayo, Isidoro, 53
Coquimbo, 184
co-resistance, 31–33
Corntassel, Jeff, 2, 114
Coulthard, Glen Sean, 5, 83, 178
Council of Popular and Indigenous Organizations of Honduras (COPINH), 14
Cox, Avelino, 76
critical geography, 23, 29, 30–31
Critical Geography Collective of Ecuador, 25, 27
critical race theory, 27
Crossing Waters, Crossing Worlds (Miles and Holland, eds.), 135
CSUTCB. *See* Confederación Sindical Única de Trabajadores Campesinos de Bolivia
cuerpo-territorio, 7–8, 11, 21–22, 28–29, 32, 33; as decolonial feminist method, 30; defining, 30; the hemispheric and, 31; and anti-racism, 32

Dakota Access Pipeline (DAPL), 40
Daley, Ken, 198
Davenport, Charles, 136
Davis, Angela, 28
decolonization, 2, 6; feminist, 28–31; the hemispheric and, 22–28; in Latin America, 42–43
Delap-Uliga-Djarrit, 93
Denendeh (Canada), 105
Detours (Aikau and Gonzalez), 90
diaspora, 84–85; deep time and, 90–91
Diaz, Vicente, 71, 82, 84, 86, 100
dispossession, 63, 88–89, 204–6; in Caribbean, 194–95; of Mapuche land, 172, 178–80, 186, 187n11 migration and, 133; resisting, 13; via treaties, 154–55; violence and, 7, 9–10
Dixon, Amalia, 75
Downs, Teodoro, 75

Ecuador, 3–4, 16n17, 21, 27–28, 32; Indigenous Congress in, 41; neoliberalism in, 25–27
education: assimilationist, 72–73, 75–76, 197; Marshallese Education Initiative (MEI), 96
Edwards, William Cary, 138
Elliott, J. H., 135
Engels-Schwarzpaul, Anna-Christina, 82
Enlightenment rationality, Indigenous epistemologies challenging, 107
Entenssoro, Victor Paz, 48
Environmental Protection Agency (EPA), 124, 130, 132–33, 138, 150n23
environmental racism, 27
EPA. *See* Environmental Protection Agency
Escazú Agreement, 75
Escobar, Arturo, 90
Estes, Nick, 5
Experimental Farm Network, 142

Federación Mapuche de Estudiantes (FEMAE), 183
femicide, 25
feminism: Black, 28; decolonization and, 28–31; the hemispheric and, 22–23; hide camps and, 110
hide tanning and, 106
fish, 127–28
Fleming, Elaine, 157
Fletcher, Matthew L. M., 160
Flon, Catherine, 204
Flores, Clara, 54
Flores, Victor, 52
Floyd, George, 32

Foodshed Alliance, 141, 142
Forbes, Jack D., 22, 23, 33
forced migration, 91, 94–95, 104n54, 179, 202
Ford Motor Company, 123, 129, 130
Flores Santos, Jenaro, 49
Foucault, Michel, 112
The Fourth World (Coulthard), 5
Frente Sandinista de Liberación Nacional (FSLN), 78n46
Fundamental Education Project, 67, 71, 72
fütalmapu, 174, 178–81
fvchakeche (Mapuche elders), 175, 182, 184

García, María Elena, 5, 6
García Meza, Luis, 49
General Allotment Act of 1887, 126
Geniusz, Wendy Makoons, 165–66
gikendaasowin, 166
Gilio-Whitaker, Dina, 148–49
Glissant, Édouard, 198
Global North, 9, 21, 23, 25
Goeman, Mishuana, 22, 32, 192; on decolonization, 29
Gonzalez, Lélia, 24, 28
Gonzalez, Vernadette Vicuña, 90
Gotkowitz, Laura, 41
Gouldhawke, Mike, 4–5
governance: of Anishinaabe, 167; hide tanning and, 108–11; Ladner on, 109; Nmé Stewardship Plan and, 167; relationality and, 108–9
Grande Ronde, 97
Grand Traverse Band, 160
Great Lakes, 158–59, 160–61
grounded normativity, 12, 83, 85–86, 88, 94, 100, 108–9, 113; defining, 178; on Mapuche territory, 172–73, 177–78, 181, 185–86
gulu mapu, 175, 179
Gumbs, Alexis Pauline, 192

Haesbaert, Rogerio, 29
Halbwach, Maurice, 45
Harney, Stefano, 31
Harper, Barbara L., 128
Harris, Stuart G., 128
Hauʻofa, Epeli, 83
HCR-108. *See* House Concurrent Resolution 108
the hemispheric: *cuerpo-territorio* and, 31; decolonization and, 22–28; defining, 22–23; feminism and, 22–23; limitations of, 24–25; in placemaking, 31–33

Herron, Scott, 165
hide camps, 107–8, 109, 115; as feminist practice, 110
hide tanning, 105, 116–17; feminist analysis, 106; governance and, 108–11
Hilden, Martin, 99
Hill, Dominique, 194
Hokowhitu, Brendan, 107, 112
Holmes, Cindy, 29
homeland narratives, 111–15
Homes, Wright, 90, 100
Honduras, 11, 14, 66
Honolulu, 87, 89–90, 92, 100
hooks, bell, 108
Hoʻoulu ʻĀina, 99–100
House Concurrent Resolution 108 (HCR-108), 126
Huircapan, Sergio Caniuqueo, 179
Hunt, Sarah, 29, 116
Hurtado, Javier, 45, 48

ILO Convention 169, 75
inaadiziwin, 166
Indian Act, 110, 114–15
Indian Gaming Regulatory Act, 138
Indianismo, 46–47
Indian Relocation Act, 126
indígena contribuyente, 42
indígena originario, 42
Indigeneity, 3, 9, 27, 81, 85, 106, 112, 113, 116; BlackIndigeneity, 193, 194–96, 212; Blackness and, 10, 11, 23, 198, 211; defining, 41–42
Indigenous epistemologies, 9–10; art-making in, 108; Enlightenment rationality challenged by, 107
Indigenous land/body relationalities, 6–8
Indigenous peoples, defining, 42–43
Indigenous Peoples' Day, 4
Indigenous political movements, in Latin America, 39–40
Indigenous women, 6
Indigenous worldviews, land and, 2–3
Instituto de Fomento Nacional (INFONAC), 71, 73
interculturality, 26
Internado Lingüístico Kimayiñ Tayiñ Mapuzugun, 183
ixofillmogen, 172, 174, 176, 182
izhitwaawin, 166

The Jackson Whites, 131, 136, 137
Jacobs, Beverly, 110–11
Jichha, 45

Jobin, Shalene, 109
Judah, Kianna Angelo, 98

Kaʻili, Tēvita O., 83, 86, 94
Kanaka ʻŌiwi, 89, 101
Kanaka Maoli (Native Hawaiian), 83, 85, 89–90, 96, 99–100, 103n40, 104n55,
Kapālama, 89
Katari, Tupaj, 11, 40, 45, 49
katarismo, 40, 42; environmental politics and, 51–55; historiography of, 45–47; origins of, 47–51
Kauanui, J. Kēhaulani, 83, 85
Keju, Dial, 92
Kelley, Robin, 76
King, Tiffany Lethabo, 8–9, 22
Klauna Laka, 12, 62–63, 64, 72–73; defining, 68–69; history of, 69–70; land and, 74–77; loss of, 75–76; reciprocity of, 76; self-determination through, 68–71
Kolüko, 181–82
Konsmo, Erin Marie, 114
Kraft, Herbert C., 137–38
Kuna people, Panama, 24
Kuokkanen, Rauna, 109
kuyfikecheyem, 174

Ladner, Kiera, 109
LANDBACK campaign, 4
Land Back Editorial Collective, 186
Land Back movement, 2–3, 10, 13, 15n7, 82, 84–8, 100, 106, 155, 167, 185, 193, 212; hemispheric approach to, 21–32; history of, 3–6, 7
land ownership, 42, 66, 111; collective, 69–70; Miskitu and, 69–70
land relationships, Marshallese, 93–94
land rights, 76; relationality and, 161
Langston, Nancy, 157–58, 159, 160–61
language revitalization, 186
La Paz, Bolivia, 41, 47, 48, 49
Latin America, 9–10, 22; collectives in, 27–28; *cuerpo-territorio* methodologies in, 21–32; decolonization in, 42–43; Indigenous political movements in, 39–40
Latour, Francie, 193, 198
Latwan Laka Kum, 70–71
Law 28 (Nicaragua), 64, 74
Law 445 (Aicaragua), 69, 74, 77n2
The Lenape (Kraft), 137–38
Letelier, Manuela Royo, 177
Ley de Exvinculación (Bolivia), 47
Lima, Constantino, 6

Little River Ottawa, 155–56, 158
Living in the New Houses (Le Corbusier), 88–89
Liwa Mairin, 64
Llica, Marka, 54
Lobo, Susan, 100
lofmapu, 184
Louverture, Toussaint, 204
Lucero, José Antonio, 4, 6

Macusaya Cruz, Carlos, 45–46
Maher, Mónica, 30
Mahina, Hūfanga ʻOkusitino, 86
Maihsa Wilkan Daknika, 70–71
Mandamin, Josephine, 67
Manistee National Forest, 155
Mann, Vincent, 12, 124, 141, 149
Mann, Wayne, 123, 131, 146
manoomin, 127, 154, 156, 163, 165, 167
Manuel, George, 5
mapu, 173–78
Mapuche, 171; diaspora, 180; dispossession of land of, 172, 178–80, 186, 187n11; grounded normativity on territory of, 177–78; spatial planning of, 172–73; territorial identities, 173; toponyms, 176, 181–83
Mapuzugun, 172, 173, 180, 181; revitalization, 184–86
Marek, Serge, 89
Marshallese, 84–85; land relationships of, 93–94; networks in United States, 81–82, 95
Marshallese Education Initiative (MEI), 96
Marshall Islands, 91–94
Martineau, Jarett, 31
Maskigow iskwew, 105, 106
McDade, Tony, 32
McGregor, Deborah, 67
McNeish, John, 44
The Meaning of Seed, 147, 148
meli wixan mapu, 175, 177
memory: Anishinaabe ecological, 154–55, 161, 166–67; BlackIndigenous collective memory in *Auntie Luce's Talking Paintings*, 210; "long memory" vs. "short memory" as defining features of *katarismo*, 45; Mapuche collective memory, 177; Miskitu, 64
mestizaje, 22, 26, 72
"methodological nationalism," 10, 22
migration: Anishinaabe, 155–58, 165; BlackIndigeneity and, 202, 212; dispossession and, 133; forced, 91, 94–95, 104n54, 133, 134, 179; Rimajol

INDEX 223

community and, 96, 97; rural to urban centers, 48, 90;
Mihesuah, Devon A., 138
Military-Peasant Pact (Bolivia), 48–49, 51
Million, Dian, 3, 106, 110, 197
MINK'A (Center for the Coordination and Promotion of the Peasantry), 50–51
mino-bimaadiziwin, 164, 166
Miskitu, 61–63, 72, 77n1; British Empire and, 65–66; houses of, 70; land ownership and, 69–70
MITKA. *See* Movimiento Indio Tupaj Katari
Moana, 83–84, 86, 90, 92–95
mobility, 81; of Anishinaabe, 155–58, 159–61; homeland narratives and, 111–15; as self-determination, 113
Molina, Juan Ignacio, 184
Mollett, Sharlene, 3, 22, 29
mo'oku'auhau, 86–87, 99, 100
Morales, Evo, 39, 45
Morgan, Jas, 108
Moskitia, 11–12, 61–62, 65, 66–68, 74, 77n1
Moten, Fred, 31
Movimiento al Socialismo (MAS), 45
Movimiento Indio Tupaj Katari (MITKA), 40, 53
Movimiento Revolucionario Tupaj Katari (MRTK), 40, 49, 53
Movimiento Revolucionario Tupaj Katari de Liberación (MRTKL), 49
Muckshaw Ponds Preserve, 141
El Mundo Zurdo, 23
Munsee Three Sisters Medicinal Farm, 12, 123–25, 141, 145, 147
Museo Nacional de Etnografía y Folklore (MUSEF), 42

NAFTA. *See* North American Free Trade Agreement
nag mapu, 173–75, 176
NAISA. *See* Native American and Indigenous Studies Association
Nanabush, 164–65, 169n54
NARP. *See* Native Alliance for Red Power
Nascimento, Beatriz, 28
Nash, Gary, 134, 135
National Association of Peasant Teachers, 50
Native Alliance for Red Power (NARP), 4–6
Native American and Indigenous Studies Association (NAISA), 113
Native depth, 81–82, 83, 86, 87, 100, 102n4

Native-to-Native-to-Settler relations, 82, 91, 99–100
natural resources, Anishinaabe and, 158–59
Nay, Eric, 88
NDN Collective, 3–4
Nêhiyawak people, 109
Neira, Elsa Curihuinca, 177
"Nenabozho Goes Fishing," 161
neoliberalism, in Ecuador, 25–26
New Jersey Department of Environmental Protection (NJDEP), 131, 133
New Jersey Department of Health and Senior Services (NJDHSS), 139
Newton, Melanie J., 195
nguillatun, 177, 178
nguillatuwe, 177, 181
Nicaragua, 11–12, 61–63, 74–75, 76, 77n1, 77n2, 78n45; assimilationist education in, 72–73; Indigenous land rights in, 64, 68–69, 71, 76; land appropriation in, 73–74; Miskitu people in, 65–67
nmé (sturgeon), 12, 153–56, 157–58, 159, 160–61
Nmé Cultural Context Task Group, 162
Nmé Restoration Plan, 167
Nmé Stewardship Plan, 162, 164–65, 167
nonhuman entities, 44–45
North American Free Trade Agreement (NAFTA), 5
Northwest Territories, 115

Ochoa, Karina, 25
O'Connor Disposal Area (OCDA), 151
Odaemin, 164–65
Ofensiva Roja de Ayllus Tupakataristas (ORAT), 52, 53
Ojibwe, 156, 160, 168n10
"Oprimidos pero no vencidos" (Rivera), 45
Oregon, 83, 84, 95, 96, 97–99
Origins of the Jackson Whites of the Ramapo Mountains (Storms), 136
Our Land, Our Stories, 138, 146
"Our Sea of Islands" (Hau'ofa), 83

Pachamama, 52
Pacific Islanders, 81
Padre Las Casas, 183
Pagipüllü, 176
Panama, 24
Pana-Pana, 70
pana pana lui laka, 69
Peake, Linda, 194

Peasant Students Association of Bolivia, 50
Pehuen, Miguel Melin, 177
Peralto, Leon No'eau, 85
pewenche, 179
Picaro, Michaeline, 126, 141, 142–43, 145
Pickerill, Jenny, 29–30
pikun mapu, 175, 179
pimâcihowin, 109
placemaking, 21, 22–23; BlackIndigenous, 207; decolonial and anti-racist, 21–33; of Indigenous communities of the Oceanic diaspora, 81, 82–84, 86, 89, 90, 101; the hemispheric in, 31–33; in Land Back movement, 82; Rimajol, 90–91, 96–100
pongueaje, 47
Portugal Mollinedo, Pedro, 45, 46
Powhatan Renape Nation, 133
Prahaku, 64
Pruwan Bikaia, 70
pueblos indígenas, 42
pueblos originarios, 42
puel mapu, 175, 179
pujyus, 54

Quijano, Aníbal, 10, 42–43, 88

racialized capitalism, 22, 26, 27, 33, 193
racialized geographies, 30–31
radicación, 171, 172, 176
The Ramapo Mountain Pepole (Cohen), 137–38
Ramapough Lunaape (Lenape) Turtle Clan, 12, 123, 124, 129, 131–38; identity of, 134–35
Ramírez, Margaret, 23, 31
Ramirez, Renya, 89, 100–101
Rappaport, Joanne, 44
reciprocity, 85–86, 91; BlackIndigenous, 197; of Indigenous communities of the Oceanic diaspora, 97; of *Klauna Laka*, 62, 63, 68–71, 76; of people and their physical environment, 44, 52–54, 67, 70
Recollet, Karyn, 114
Red, White, and Black (Nash), 135
Red Power, 5, 6
Red Women Rising, 4
Reed, Kaitlin, 145
Reexistencias Cimarrunas Collective, 21, 25, 26, 28, 33; anti-racism of, 27; webinars of, 31–32
Refiti, Albert, 81–82, 86
Reinaga, Fausto, 41

relationality, 124–25, 165; governance and, 108–9; land rights and, 161; as methodology, 8–11; placemaking and, 82–83; in resurgence theory, 112
Republic of Marshallesee Islands (RMI), 91, 93, 95; United States colonialism and, 103n47. *See also* Aelon Kein Ad
Research is Ceremony (Wilson, S.), 165
resource nationalism, 40, 47, 55
Rimajol (Marshallese) communities, 81–82, 83, 93, 94–95; In Honolulu, 90, 99–100; in Oregon, 97–99; place-making among, 86–88, 90–91, 94; in Springdale, Arkansas, 96–97
Ringwood, New Jersey 123, 128–29, 132–33, 138–39; Ramapough Lunaape Turtle Clan in, 124–26, 128
Rivera Cusicanqui, Silvia, 45, 51
RMI. *See* Republic of Marshallesee Islands
Roel, Virgiliio, 52
routed normativity, 83, 85–88, 89, 90–91, 97–98, 100–1
Rukañamku, 176
Runa Feminista, 25
Ruru, Jacinta, 2–3

Schwartz, Jessica, 96
Segrest, Valerie, 144
self-determination, 7, 22, 23, 109–10, 113, 195, 106; *cuerpo-territorio* and, 32; through *Klauna Laka*, 62, 68–71, 76; Mapuche, 173, 183
settler colonialism, 1, 9–10, 24, 26, 82, 83, 84, 85–86, 87–90, 113, 116, 185, 195
settlers. *See colonos*
Simpson, Audra, 184
Simpson, Leanne Betasamosake, 29, 31, 83, 112, 113, 154, 178, 185; on resurgence, 108–9
Smith, Sara, 202
soil, contamination of, 126–29, 139, 140
Soil Science Society of America, 126
Speed, Shannon, 10
Spice, Anne, 128
Springdale, Arkansas, 96–97
Starblanket, Gina, 108, 112, 115
Stark, Heidi Kiiwetinepinesiik, 108, 112, 115, 161
Stark, Kekek Jason, 161
Stobart, Henry, 44
Storms, John C., 136
sturgeon. *See* nmé
Superfund sites, 127, 131, 139–40

Sustainable Agriculture Enterprise Program (SAgE), 141, 142
Swinta, 64

Taika nani Daknika, 70–71
Taller de Historia Oral Andina (THOA), 51
Tapia, Luciano, 55
Tauli-Corpuz, Victoria, 13
Tawi-Tawi, 70
Tayac, Gabrielle A., 15n11
TEK. *See* traditional ecological knowledge
"territorial identities," Mapuche, 178–81
Three Fires Confederacy, 156
Three Sisters (corn, beans, squash), 142–43. *See also* Munsee Three Sisters Medicinal Farm
Tiahuanaco Manifesto (1973), 50
Tilsen, Nick, 4
Tittel, Jeff, 138
Tongan, 94
de la Torre, Oscar, 39–40
toxicity, 12, 128, 140
traditional ecological knowledge (TEK) theory, 63; disruption of, 67–68; Whyte on, 67
translocation, 27
transplanting, as "relational construct," 81, 85, 96
Treaty of Easton (1758), 134
Treaty of St. Peters (1837), 161
Treaty of Washington (1836), 154–55, 160
Trotz, D. Alissa, 194
Tuck, Eve, 9
Túpac Katari Peasant Center, 50
Turtle Island, 4, 15n13, 33, 89, 96

Ugarte, Magdalena, 13
Unidad Democrática Popular (UDP), 49
United Nations Declaration on the Rights of Indigenous Peoples, 6, 75
United Nations Trust Territory of the Pacific, 97
United Nations Working Group on Indigenous Populations, 6
United States; colonialism and RMI, 103n47; Marshallese networks in, 81–82, 95
United States v. Michigan, 161
Universidad Libre Mapuche, 183
Unta Dawanka, 63–64
urbanization, and settler planning, 88–90

de Valdivia, Luis, 184
Valencia, Sayak, 25
Vallejo, Ivette, 30
Vā Moana, 12, 81–82, 83, 86, 93, 101
Veracini, Lorenzo, 88
Villarroel, José Teijero, 44
violence, dispossession and, 7–9, 10
Violence on the Land, Violence on Our Bodies, 7
Viveros, Mara, 25, 28
Voyles, Traci Brynne, 127

Wallmapu, 174, 175, 178, 179–80, 184, 185; internal colonialism in, 171–73; toponymy, 176–77, 182
Walpole Island Heritage Centre, 165
Wampolwe, 181–82
wampos, 181
warriache, 180
Wasla, 64
Watts, Vanessa, 6
Webster, William, 69
wechekeche, 184
Whyte, Kyle, 67, 124, 128, 156, 166
wigkul, 183
Wiindigo, 157, 164
Williams, Barbara, 132
willi mapu, 175, 179
Wilson, Fidel, 72
Wilson, Shawn, 165
Wisconsin Walleye Wars (1974), 161
Wixage anai, 183
Women's Earth Alliance, 7
World Council of Indigenous Peoples (WCIP), 6

Xuf Xuf, 182–83

Yampara, Simón, 53–54
Yang, Wayne, 9
Yapti Tasba Masraka (YATAMA), 74
Yazzie, Melanie, 8
Yurok Nation, 127
Yuwi-Yuwi, 70

Zacarias, Naboth, 72–73
Zelaya, José Santos, 64
Zelaya Department, 64
Zelikoff, Judith, 140
Zitkala-Sa, 197
Zuazo, Hernán Siles, 41

DUMBARTON OAKS COLLOQUIUM ON THE HISTORY OF LANDSCAPE ARCHITECTURE

Published by Dumbarton Oaks, Trustees for Harvard University, Washington, D.C.

The Dumbarton Oaks Colloquium on the History of Landscape Architecture series volumes are based on papers presented at scholarly meetings sponsored by the Garden and Landscape Studies program at Dumbarton Oaks. These meetings provide a forum for the presentation of advanced research on garden history, landscape architecture, and urban landscape; they support a deepened understanding of landscape as a field of knowledge and as a practice carried out by landscape architects, landscape artists, and gardeners.

Further information on Garden and Landscape Studies publications can be found at www.doaks.org/publications.

1. *The Italian Garden*, edited by David R. Coffin
2. *The Picturesque Garden and Its Influence Outside the British Isles*, edited by Nikolaus Pevsner
3. *The French Formal Garden*, edited by Elisabeth B. MacDougall and F. Hamilton Hazlehurst
4. *The Islamic Garden*, edited by Elisabeth B. MacDougall and Richard Ettinghausen
5. *Fons sapientiae: Renaissance Garden Fountains*, edited by Elisabeth B. MacDougall
6. *John Claudius Loudon and the Early Nineteenth Century in Great Britain*, edited by Elisabeth B. MacDougall
7. *Ancient Roman Gardens*, edited by Elisabeth B. MacDougall and Wilhelmina F. Jashemski
8. *Beatrix Jones Farrand (1872–1959): Fifty Years of American Landscape Architecture*, edited by Diane Kostial McGuire and Lois Fern
9. *Medieval Gardens*, edited by Elisabeth B. MacDougall
10. *Ancient Roman Villa Gardens*, edited by Elisabeth B. MacDougall
11. *Prophet with Honor: The Career of Andrew Jackson Downing, 1815–1852*, edited by George B. Tatum and Elisabeth B. MacDougall
12. *The Dutch Garden in the Seventeenth Century*, edited by John Dixon Hunt
13. *Garden History: Issues, Approaches, Methods*, edited by John Dixon Hunt
14. *The Vernacular Garden*, edited by John Dixon Hunt and Joachim Wolschke-Bulmahn
15. *Regional Garden Design in the United States*, edited by Therese O'Malley and Marc Treib
16. *Mughal Gardens: Sources, Places, Representations, and Prospects*, edited by James L. Wescoat Jr. and Joachim Wolschke-Bulmahn
17. *John Evelyn's "Elysium Britannicum" and European Gardening*, edited by Therese O'Malley and Joachim Wolschke-Bulmahn
18. *Nature and Ideology: Natural Garden Design in the Twentieth Century*, edited by Joachim Wolschke-Bulmahn

19 *Places of Commemoration: Search for Identity and Landscape Design*, edited by Joachim Wolschke-Bulhmann

20 *Theme Park Landscapes: Antecedents and Variations*, edited by Terence Young and Robert Riley

21 *Perspectives on Garden Histories*, edited by Michel Conan

22 *Environmentalism in Landscape Architecture*, edited by Michel Conan

23 *Bourgeois and Aristocratic Cultural Encounters in Garden Art, 1550–1850*, edited by Michel Conan

24 *Landscape Design and the Experience of Motion*, edited by Michel Conan

25 *Baroque Garden Cultures: Emulation, Sublimation, Subversion*, edited by Michel Conan

26 *Sacred Gardens and Landscapes: Ritual and Agency*, edited by Michel Conan

27 *Performance and Appropriation: Profane Rituals in Gardens and Landscapes*, edited by Michel Conan

28 *Botanical Progress, Horticultural Innovations, and Cultural Changes*, edited by Michel Conan and W. John Kress

29 *Contemporary Garden Aesthetics, Creations and Interpretations*, edited by Michel Conan

30 *Gardens and Imagination: Cultural History and Agency*, edited by Michel Conan

31 *Middle East Garden Traditions: Unity and Diversity; Questions, Methods, and Resources in a Multicultural Perspective*, edited by Michel Conan

32 *Clio in the Italian Garden: Twenty-First-Century Studies in Historical Methods and Theoretical Perspectives*, edited by Mirka Beneš and Michael G. Lee

33 *Interlacing Words and Things: Bridging the Nature-Culture Opposition in Gardens and Landscape*, edited by Stephen Bann

34 *Designing Wildlife Habitats*, edited by John Beardsley

35 *Technology and the Garden*, edited by Michael G. Lee and Kenneth I. Helphand

36 *Food and the City: Histories of Culture and Cultivation*, edited by Dorothée Imbert

37 *Cultural Landscape Heritage in Sub-Saharan Africa*, edited by John Beardsley

38 *Sound and Scent in the Garden*, edited by D. Fairchild Ruggles

39 *River Cities, City Rivers*, edited by Thaïsa Way

40 *Landscape and the Academy*, edited by John Beardsley and Daniel Bluestone

41 *Landscapes of Preindustrial Urbanism*, edited by Georges Farhat

42 *Military Landscapes*, edited by Anatole Tchikine and John Dean Davis

43 *Landscapes for Sport: Histories of Physical Exercise, Sport, and Health*, edited by Sonja Dümpelmann

44 *Segregation and Resistance in the Landscapes of the Americas*, edited by Eric Avila and Thaïsa Way

45 *Land Back: Relational Landscapes of Indigenous Resistance across the Americas*, edited by Heather Dorries and Michelle Daigle